Morten Rand-Hendriksen

Sams **Teach Yourself**

Microsoft®

Expression
Web 2

in **24**
Hours

SAMS   800 East 96th Street, Indianapolis, Indiana, 46240 USA

Sams Teach Yourself Microsoft® Expression Web 2 in 24 Hours

Copyright © 2009 by Pearson Education, Inc.

ISBN-13: 978-0-672-33029-2
ISBN-10: 0-672-33029-6

Library of Congress Cataloging-in-Publication Data:

Rand-Hendriksen, Morten.
  Sams teach yourself Microsoft Expression Web 2 in 24 hours / Morten Rand-Hendriksen.
     p. cm.
  ISBN 978-0-672-33029-2
  1. Web sites–Authoring programs. 2. Microsoft Expression Web. I. Title. II. Title: Teach yourself Microsoft Expression Web 2 in 24 hours.
III. Title: Microsoft Expression Web 2 in 24 hours.
  TK5105.8883.R36 2008
  006.7'8–dc22

                         2008034613

Printed in the United States of America

First Printing September 2008

Trademarks

Warning and Disclaimer

Bulk Sales

Sams Publishing offers excellent discounts on this book when ordered in quantity for bulk purchases or special sales. For more information, please contact

U.S. Corporate and Government Sales
1-800-382-3419
corpsales@pearsontechgroup.com

For sales outside of the U.S., please contact

International Sales
international@pearsoned.com

Associate Publisher
Greg Wiegand

Acquisitions Editor
Loretta Yates

Development Editors
Todd Brakke
Anne Goebel

Managing Editor
Patrick Kanouse

Project Editor
Mandie Frank

Copy Editor
Mike Henry

Indexer
Tim Wright

Proofreader
Arle Writing and Editing

Technical Editor
Greg Kettell

Publishing Coordinator
Cindy Teeters

Designer
Gary Adair

Compositor
Mark Shirar

Table of Contents

Sams Teach Yourself Microsoft® Expression Web 2 in 24 Hours

About the Author

Morten Rand-Hendriksen is the owner and creative director of Pink & Yellow Media, a design company that provides digital media creations for small businesses and television. Through the years he has had many different titles: photographer, studio musician, composer, politician, writer, jeweler, philosopher, artist, and university senate member. But it is in the role of a designer he feels truly at home (at least for the moment).

Morten started designing websites back in 1997, but it wasn't until he moved to Canada in 2002 that he really started to focus on web design as a possible career (surprisingly there were few job listings for Norwegian philosophy majors in Vancouver at the time). Over the years he has worked with many different technologies, but after being introduced to Expression Web 2 he has shifted the focus of the web part of his business almost exclusively to the art of CSS and blog design.

Sams Teach Yourself Microsoft Expression Web 2 in 24 Hours is his first published book. You can also find his tutorials and other design-related musings on his blog at http://blog.pinkandyellow.com and in many different forums and newsgroups throughout the Web.

If you have any questions relating to the book, you can contact Morten by writing to book@pinkandyellow.com.

Dedication

I dedicate this book to my parents, Marianne and Svend, who taught me that with hard work and determination nothing is impossible; Jan Tobiassen for being a friend when no one else was; The House of Lords (and Ladies)—save a seat for me—and Angela, my love, without whom I would float away like a broken kite without a tether.

Acknowledgments

There are times when I sit down and wonder: How on earth did I end up here? Closing in on the end of the journey that has produced this book I find myself looking back on a year filed with coincidences and random events that together have culminated in this moment. If anyone had told me last summer I would be sitting in my couch writing acknowledgements for a Sams Publishing book, I would have laughed out loud. Yet here I am!

There are a great many people whose involvement, however minute, has had a significant part in the saga that led to this book being published. Here they are, as they say in the movies, in order of appearance.

It was a fluke that I got introduced to Expression Web at all. When I was invited to attend an event for the Microsoft Expression Suite at the Canvas Lounge in Vancouver, I almost didn't go. Yet this event would become a defining moment for my life as well as the starting point from which this book would eventually emerge. At the event I was introduced to Paul LaBerge and Qixing Zheng from Microsoft Canada, both of whom would take an interest in my work with Expression Web and offered help and support as I started digging ever deeper into the functionalities of this new application. Through Paul and Qixing I came in direct contact with the Expression Web development team and, in particular, Anna Ullrich who would provide invaluable help both with the application itself and with this book. Her comments and input on the original table of contents were instrumental in forming the book you are now leafing through.

During the fall of 2007, Microsoft did a case study on my company, Pink & Yellow Media, and a project I had created using Expression Studio applications exclusively. This study involved, among others, fellow Scandinavian Håkan Söderbom who rode his motorbike all the way from Seattle to Vancouver for an interview. I would meet Håkan again at Mix08 in Las Vegas where I also ran into Tyler Simpson from the Expression Web team who provided much needed insight into the technical aspects of the application.

Through all of these people my name somehow made it to Steven Guttman, the Production Unit Manager for Expression Web, who one day in March sent me an email saying that Pearson was looking for an author for its new *Sams Teach Yourself Microsoft Expression Web 2 in 24 Hours* book. Hours later I was in touch with Loretta Yates who would put her trust in me as a first-time author and provided much needed help and support as the book took shape. In many ways this book is as much Loretta's work as it is mine.

As the ball got rolling I got introduced to many of the people involved in making my convoluted and often incorrect ESL English (I am Norwegian, after all) into publishable material. These include my development editors Todd Brakke and Anne Goebel who make sure everything makes sense, tech editor Greg Kettell who makes sure what I say is correct and that everything works, copy editor Mike Henry who ungarbles and untangles my somewhat archaic language and horrendous syntactic and typographical transgressions, and project editor Mandie Frank who keeps me in line.

There are countless others involved in both the pre- and post-publishing process I have not mentioned, and they should all be gravely offended for not being named by name. Without their contributions this book would never have made the journey from my mind to the hands of the readers and they should be acknowledged for their invaluable work.

Finally I'd like to thank my friend Alexandra Oosterom and my brother Ole who have diligently read through each and every chapter of my unfinished manuscript and provided valuable input on my many inconsistencies and typographical errors.

We Want to Hear from You!

As the reader of this book, *you* are our most important critic and commentator. We value your opinion and want to know what we're doing right, what we could do better, what areas you'd like to see us publish in, and any other words of wisdom you're willing to pass our way.

You can email or write me directly to let me know what you did or didn't like about this book—as well as what we can do to make our books stronger.

Please note that I cannot help you with technical problems related to the topic of this book, and that due to the high volume of mail I receive, I might not be able to reply to every message.

When you write, please be sure to include this book's title and author as well as your name and phone or email address. I will carefully review your comments and share them with the author and editors who worked on the book.

E-mail: consumer@samspublishing.com

Mail: Greg Wiegand
          Associate Publisher
          Sams Publishing
          800 East 96th Street
          Indianapolis, IN 46240 USA

Reader Services

Visit our website and register this book at www.informit.com/title/9780672330292 for convenient access to any updates, downloads, or errata that might be available for this book.

Introduction

About This Book

Because you have opened this book and started reading the introduction, I am assuming that you are interested in learning how to create websites using Microsoft's new and exciting web development application, Expression Web 2. If so, I congratulate you: By choosing this application as your platform, you are already well on your way to creating functional and well-designed sites based on web standards. In other words, unlike me, you are putting the proverbial horse before the cart and starting at the beginning rather than learning things the hard way.

Expression Web 2 is the second version (duh!) of a web design and development platform that sees Microsoft take a whole new approach to the concept of web standards. As a result, you now have an application that produces standards based websites right out of the box without requiring any tweaking or custom coding on your end. In fact, using Expression Web 2, you can create advanced standards-based websites with lots of fancy interactive features without ever writing a line of code. And with that the threshold for learning, understanding, and creating websites that look and behave the same across all browsers and platforms is lowered to a level anyone can manage.

When I started writing this book, I spent a lot of time thinking about you, the reader; more specifically how to ensure that after reading this book, you would walk away with not only an understanding of the application but also how to use it to get from an idea to a finalized product. The result of my ponderings was a website called MyKipple.com that showcases many of the basic and more advanced functions available in Expression Web 2. By following the tutorials in this book, you will build the MyKipple.com website from scratch and in the process learn how all the different elements come together and how to get the most out of the application. When you have finished the last hour and the site is complete, you will have both the tools and know-how to build your own websites using HTML (Hypertext Markup Language), CSS (Cascading Style Sheets), and the many other functions that Expression Web 2 offers. You will also have a basic understanding of how the application deals with more advanced coding languages such as ASP.NET and PHP, and you'll even learn how to publish a simple Silverlight application.

Accompanying this book is a small web site that contains information about the book itself along with the lesson files for each hour and in time a Wiki or a forum for you the reader to get further information and showcase your work. The web site is located at http://expression.pinkandyellow.com.

Who Is This Book For?

I always ask people why they do what they do because it says volumes about the end result. Therefore it is only fair that I ask myself the same question and provide you with the answer. So, Morten, why did you write this book?

When I started building websites in the 1990s, I really had no clue what I was doing other than a vision of what I wanted to create. And when I looked around for help in the form of books or tutorials, I couldn't find anything that spoke to me. What was available was either too technical or too pointless. No matter where I looked, I could only find basic algorithms on how to perform simple tasks, never detailed explanations of how to get from point A to point B. As a result, I ended up teaching myself how to do things. Needless to say I learned the true meaning of the term "taking the long way around."

So, when I signed up to write this book, I had one main goal in mind: To write the book I was looking for and really needed when I started out—a book that took me all the way from a basic sketch on a napkin to a fully working website and taught me how to use the application at the same time.

As a result, this book is written with the novice designer in mind. No, let me rephrase that: As a result, this book is written in a way that a novice designer will understand and learn from. I make this distinction because even if you are a seasoned designer or developer, I am certain you will find lots of useful information inside these covers.

Being introduced to Expression Web 2 has had an enormous impact on my business because it reduced what used to take hours or days to only minutes. In particular I am talking about the application's excellent CSS features. More than just a design and development application, Expression Web 2 is a tool that helps you learn, understand, dissect, and modify style sheets with unprecedented speed and accuracy. Getting a firm grasp on these tools and understanding how to use them in real-world scenarios will almost certainly make your work with CSS more efficient and productive, regardless of whether this is the first time you've encountered the term *style sheets* or you are a seasoned professional with years of experience.

So, without further ado, I wish you a pleasant journey and hope you come out on the other side with the skills, understanding, and confidence to take on the wild and exciting world of web design.

Lykke til!

Morten Rand-Hendriksen, July 14, 2008

HOUR 1

Get to Know Microsoft Expression Web 2

What You'll Learn in This Hour:

▶ What Expression Web 2 is and what you can use it for

▶ How to navigate and customize the workspace layout

▶ How to open and close toolbars and task panes

▶ How to reset the workspace to the default settings

Opening this book, you probably want to jump right in and start creating websites. But before you start it's a good idea to take the time and familiarize yourself with the program. Whether you are a first-time user or a seasoned web designer, Expression Web 2 has something new to offer. And because you'll be spending a lot of time with the program, learning it before you start working on projects will probably save you both time and frustration. If you are too impatient, you can always jump ahead to Hour 3, "A Website Is Really Just Text—Build One in 5 Minutes," and come back here later. But as my father always told me, "If you want to bottle an elephant, you better read the manual first." Getting to know your tools before using them makes your life easier in the long run.

Introducing Expression Web 2

Expression Web 2 is a complete web publishing suite bundled into one program. It's an HTML editor, a WYSIWYG editor, an authoring tool, a code debugger, a *CSS (Cascading Style Sheets)* generator, and a file management tool all wrapped up in one convenient package—a one-stop shop for putting content on the Web. Whether you are a designer with no previous code experience, a developer with no previous design experience, or somewhere between the two, Expression Web 2 can help you work faster and more effectively.

Did you
Know?

Jargon and acronyms litter the language of web design and development. Rather than providing just a direct translation, I explain each term or acronym the first time it appears in the text.

By the
Way

WYSIWYG: What You See Is What You Get. An acronym used for visual web-editing applications where the user can view and edit the page as it appears in a browser rather than simply viewing and editing code.

As you will quickly see when working with web design, this name is a bit misleading: The fact that a web page looks a certain way in a WYSIWYG editor doesn't necessarily mean it will look the same when viewed through an actual web browser. There are also different kinds of content that cannot be displayed in WYSIWYG editors such as Silverlight applications and dynamic web content. You will be introduced to these components and learn how to deal with this problem later on in the book.

In spite of this the WYSIWYG editor is a powerful tool that gives you a fairly accurate picture of what your design will look like on the web.

Expression Web 2 is a new link in a long chain of web-authoring tools. What makes it unique is that it gives the user the ability to create 100% standards-based sites even without knowing what the term *standards-based* means. Expression Web 2 is in many ways a shortcut that opens the world of standards-based code, previously accessible to only the web developer elite, to anyone using it. And because creating standards-based sites is (or should be) the ultimate goal of any web designer, Expression Web 2 gives you a huge advantage. Of course that doesn't mean your sites will be perfect, but you will spend far less time picking at finicky code and solving browser incompatibilities.

By the
Way

The terms *standards-based* and *web standards* refer to the formal standards and technical specifications set out by the *W3C (World Wide Web Consortium)* to describe how the World Wide Web works. If you follow these standards, your web page *should* look the same in all web browsers. (I emphasize *should* because not all web browsers follow these standards.) By creating standards-based websites, you avoid many of the problems associated with browser incompatibilities and build clean and functional websites accessible to people with disabilities and anyone on slower connections or older computers. The terms refer to a website's coding, not what it looks like. So, don't worry: A standards-based website does not have to be boring or ordinary, just built properly. If you want more information on web standards, a good place to start is the W3C website: www.w3.org.

With Expression Web 2 you can create new pages and sites from scratch or from templates; view, edit, and alter existing pages and sites; and build new server-based applications with *ASP .NET (Active Server Pages .NET)* and *PHP (PHP: Hypertext*

Preprocessor—its name is recursive). In short, Expression Web 2 is a complete package for creating and publishing websites whether on a local computer, a network, or the Web.

Getting and Installing Expression Web 2

Expression Web 2 was launched in May 1st, 2008 and is available through most software retailers or through the Microsoft Expression website (http://www.microsoft.com/expression). Consider purchasing the software as a download from Microsoft rather than through a retailer. Not only is it much quicker than going to a store or ordering from an online retailer, but you save the planet from all the unnecessary waste created in the production and shipping of the product.

If you are new to the field and unsure of whether you want to use this program, you can download from the same site a fully functional trial version that gives you 30 days to make up your mind.

Interestingly you can make your 30-day trial into a 60-day trial if you plan your installation right. It turns out that even though it says "30-day trial period" the trial version of Expression Web 2 expires on the last day of the first month after you installed it. This means that if you install the trial on November 1st it won't expire until December 31st!

Expression Web 2 is designed for the Microsoft Windows platform and works on both Microsoft Windows XP Service Pack 2 and Windows Vista. It also runs on a Mac running Windows XP or Windows Vista via Bootcamp or in virtualization software such as VMWare Fusion or Parallels.

Installing the software, whether it's from a download or from a DVD, is straightforward. If you purchased the software from a vendor, your activation key is inside the box. If you purchased the software from the Microsoft Expression website, you received your activation code during the purchase. If you are using a trial version, you can get a trial activation code by following the link provided during installation.

Did you Know?

If you have any problems with the installation or the program doesn't work after you install it, troubleshooting tips, FAQs, and forums on the Microsoft Expression website can walk you through the process and get you up and running.

Getting Acquainted with the Workspace

When you open Expression Web 2 for the first time, it presents several views, task panes and toolbars containing tools and information (see Figure 1.1). In the middle,

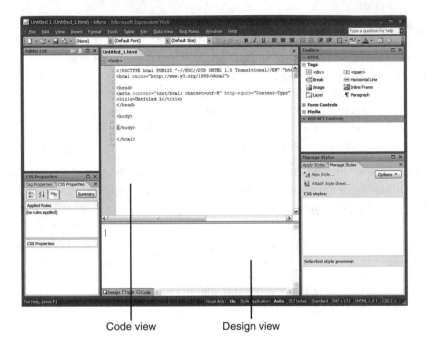

Code view   Design view

the Code view and the Design view show you the current page. Together these panes and toolbars give you a complete picture of the project you are working on and multiple ways of working with and editing that project.

The Program Bar

The address and name of the current file you are working with are at the top of the workspace. Right now it says Untitled 1 (untitled1.html). When you open the program for the first time, it displays this default empty web page. Later on you will learn how to decide what the program displays when it opens.

The Menu Bar

The menu bar is directly under the address bar. This bar is familiar to anyone who has used a computer program. The menu bar is the program's control center from which you can access any tool, feature, or functionality. Clicking a menu item reveals that item's drop-down menu (see Figure 1.2). Sliding your mouse left and right dis-

FIGURE 1.2
Example of a
drop-down menu
from the menu
bar.

plays the drop-down menus for each menu item. Some drop-down menu items have an arrow icon to their right. Hovering your mouse pointer over the arrow reveals additional submenus. We will cover each of these options in later hours. To collapse the menus, simply click anywhere outside the drop-down menu.

Try it Yourself ▼

Use the Menu Bar to Close and Open Design View and Code View

If you have never used a web design application like Expression Web 2 before the window with all its menus and task panes and views might seem a bit intimidating. However, when you understand how to use and manipulate them you will see that they are there for one reason only: To help you get your job done faster and more efficiently.

At the center of the page is the View pane. By default it is split in half horizontally with the Code view on the top and the Design view on the bottom. These views will be explained in detail later but for now let's see how you can change them to see only what you want (see Figure 1.3).

1. Click View and hover the mouse pointer over the Page item.

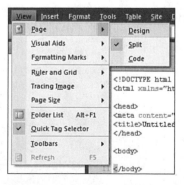

FIGURE 1.3
The View menu
with the Page
submenu open.

2. Click Design in the submenu that opens to the right.

3. Notice that the middle of the workspace now shows only Design view.

4. Repeat step 1 and click Code in the submenu. You now see only Code view.

5. Repeat step 1 and click Split. Notice that doing so restores the workspace to what it was when you started.

Common and Other Toolbars

The Common toolbar is under the menu bar (see Figure 1.4). This toolbar contains the most commonly used functions in the program, such as New, Open, Save, Font, Alignment, and so on. In addition to being an excellent tool for quick access to frequently used functions, the Common toolbar also displays information about your current selections. This toolbar is highly customizable, so fill it with whatever tools you find most helpful.

FIGURE 1.4
The Common toolbar holds the most commonly used tools for easy access.

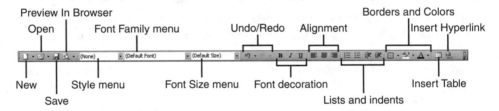

In addition to the Common toolbar are numerous other toolbars that serve different functions (see Figure 1.5). You can activate these toolbars by clicking View on the Main menu and selecting Toolbars. When you open a new toolbar, it floats on top of the workspace. You can grab the toolbar and dock it to the top, left, right, or bottom walls of the workspace or position it somewhere else on your desktop for easy access.

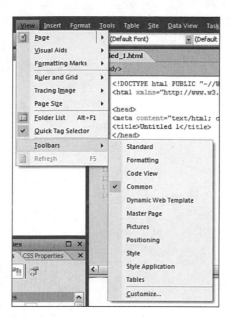

FIGURE 1.5
The different toolbars are accessible from the Toolbars submenu under View.

When you hover your mouse over a button or function throughout the program, a small ScreenTip appears explaining what the button or function does and, in some cases, giving you the shortcut for that action. Learning shortcuts not only speeds up your work but prevents muscle and joint problems caused by excessive mouse use.

Did you Know?

Try it Yourself

Add and Remove Contents in the Common Toolbar

Even though the Toolbars are equipped with many important and helpful functions they can only fit so much content. Because Expression Web 2 comes equipped with far more functions than could fit on any one toolbar and not every designer or developer thinks the same functions are important to have immediately available you can add and delete these functions from the toolbars to customize and personalize your workspace.

1. Click the Toolbar Options button on the far right of the Common toolbar.

2. Hover over the Add or Remove Buttons item and then the Common item that appears to the left as in Figure 1.6.

FIGURE 1.6
From the Common toolbar menu you can select what icons should be visible on the toolbar.

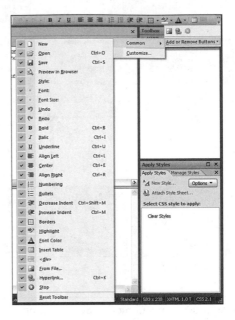

3. Click to deselect the Font item. Notice how the Font area disappears from the view.

4. Click to select or deselect other items to see how the toolbar changes accordingly.

5. Click Reset Toolbar on the bottom to restore the Common toolbar to its original state.

Code, Design, and Split View

As its name suggests, Code view displays the code or "back end" of the file you are working on (see Figure 1.7). All web pages are in reality just code documents and

FIGURE 1.7
Design View, Split View, and Code View buttons as they appear on the bottom of the workspace.

Code view gives you a behind-the-scenes look at the inner workings of your page. Code view has many features to help you in your work, from color coding and line numbering to IntelliSense and snippets. You use this view not only to inspect the code Expression Web 2 created for you but also to make alterations and add your own code. If you are working with a strict code file (.css, .php, .js, and so on) this is the only view available.

When you open a page in your web browser you are really looking at the browser's interpretation of the code in the file. Web pages are written in a markup code language that, when interpreted, turns into what you see in your browser. What you don't see is that many of these pages actually consist of several different files, many of which only contain programming code. These are what I refer to as "strict code files" and they are an important part of functional web design. By placing code in a strict code file you can use this one file as the code source for multiple pages and thus make sweeping changes to all the related files by editing just one. In this book you will learn how to use one such strict code file known as a Style Sheet to control the look and feel of multiple pages at the same time.

Did you Know?

Design view is the WYSIWYG editor (see Figure 1.8). This view emulates a web browser and (at least in theory) displays your files as they will appear in a web browser.

FIGURE 1.8
Folder list task pane.

This is probably where you will do most of your work. In Design view, you can visually edit HTML and other markup files by dragging and dropping content, editing text, and moving borders in much the same way you would work in word processing software such as Microsoft Word. It also features visual aids to help you see how the page functions. Design view provides a much less intimidating approach to web design and people starting out in the subject often prefer it to Code view.

Split view gives you the best of both worlds: Code view on top and Design view on the bottom (see Figure 1.9). In Split view, you can see in real time how changes in

one view effects the other. For a beginner, working in Split view can greatly enhance the learning process whether you come from a coding background or a design background.

As you work on your pages you will need to switch back and forth between the different views frequently. To make this as easy as possible the View pane comes equipped with three buttons to toggle the different views on and off as seen in Figure 1.7.

Left and Right Task Panes

On the left and right sides of the code workspace are four task panes, described in the following sections. These panes contain tools, information, and content you can use in the design process.

Folder List (top left)

The Folder List pane shows the folder and file tree in the project or site you are working within (see Figure 1.8).

Tag Properties and CSS Properties (bottom left)

This pane contains two tabbed subpanes. The Tag Properties (see Figure 1.9) and CSS Properties (see Figure 1.10) panes display the current tag or CSS properties of the selected object. Clicking different parts of the code in Code view shows how the tag properties change depending on the code you click. We will cover both panes in more detail in later hours.

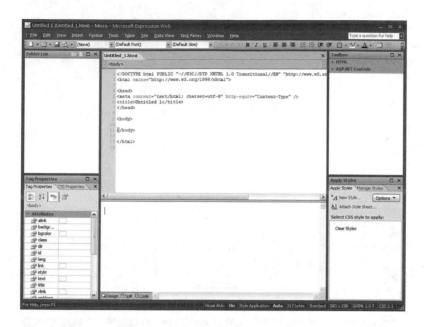

FIGURE 1.10
CSS Properties
task pane.

Toolbox (top right)

The Toolbox pane contains code segments and tags frequently used while editing in Code view (see Figure 1.11). These make up two main sections, HTML and ASP .NET

FIGURE 1.11
Toolbox task
pane.

Controls, and each section has multiple categories. By clicking the + and – icons, you can explode and collapse the categories to see what they contain.

Apply Styles and Manage Styles (bottom right)

This pane contains two tabbed subpanes. The Apply Styles pane displays the CSS styles available to the current page and enables you to apply styles to objects in Design view (see Figure 1.12). The Manage Styles pane has similar functionality with the addition of a preview area where you can see what each style does to your content (see Figure 1.13). Both panes give you the ability to either apply styles or create new styles.

FIGURE 1.12
Apply Styles task pane.

FIGURE 1.13
Manage Styles task pane.

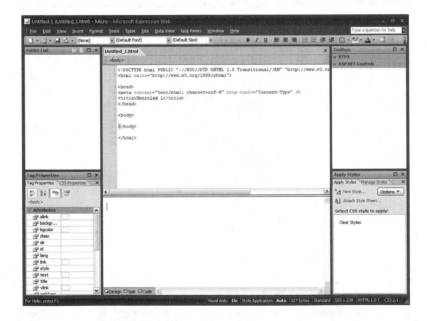

All the task panes are intelligent—they learn from how you use the program. If you use a particular item often, it moves higher on the list to make it more accessible. A rarely used item moves down on the list. The panes also help you by turning currently unavailable functions gray so that you don't waste time trying to do something impossible.

Status Bar

The status bar is at the bottom of the workspace (see Figure 1.14). It provides information about the program itself as well as general information such as file size and overall settings (what code format you are using and so on) of the page you are working on. In addition the status bar has tools that warn you if there is invalid or incompatible code in your page. Unlike the task panes, you cannot move the status bar. If you want to close it you need to click Tools, Application Options and uncheck Show Status Bar under General.

FIGURE 1.14
The Status bar appears on the bottom of the workspace and gives you constant and current information about the file you are working on.

Changing and Customizing the Workspace

Depending on what you are doing, you might want to have a certain task pane or menu more prominently featured or you might want to open a new task pane with more functions. To accommodate this, the workspace is completely customizable: You can grab any horizontal and vertical border within the workspace to make a pane smaller or larger. You can also grab toolbars and task panes and move them around both by repositioning them within the workspace and by undocking and floating them on top of or outside the window (see Figure 1.15). This technique is particularly useful if you are using a dual monitor setup because you can dedicate the main window to Code view and Design view and leave all the tools on the other screen.

As you saw earlier, each task pane can contain several subpanes. Each subpane becomes accessible through tabs. Expression Web 2 groups related subpanes together for convenience, but you are free to move them around in any way you like.

The Task Panes menu on the menu bar controls the task panes (see Figure 1.16). From here you can select what task panes are active (marked by a yellow check mark). If you click one not currently featured in the workspace, the program adds it to the relevant task pane. You can remove a task pane from view by clicking the small X in its upper-right corner.

As you perform different tasks while working on a page or website your needs will change in terms of what tools and information should be prominently displayed and

FIGURE 1.15
The Tag Properties task pane floating above the workspace.

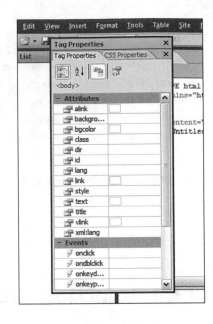

FIGURE 1.16
You can turn all available task panes on and off from the Task Panes menu.

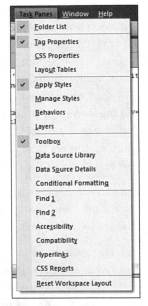

what can be hidden. For this reason Expression Web 2 gives you complete control over what task panes are available and where they are positioned at any time.

1. Hover your mouse pointer over the vertical line that separates the Code and Design views from the right task panes.

2. Click and drag the separator to the left to create more space for the task panes (see Figure 1.20).

3. Do the same with the horizontal line separating the top and bottom task panes to allow more space for the bottom pane.

4. Hover your mouse pointer over the horizontal line that separates Code view and Design view.

5. Click and drag the separator upward to create more space for Design view.

6. Click and hold on the empty gray area at the right side of the menu bar. The pointer changes to a four way arrow. Alternatively you can use the gripper icon at the left side of the bar to do the same.

7. Drag the menu bar down until it is on top of the main content and let go. Notice that it changes shape and appears to float on top of the content (see Figure 1.17).

8. Click and hold the empty gray area of the menu bar again and drag it to the far left of the workspace. It docks to the left wall like a magnet.

9. Click and hold the empty gray area of the Common toolbar, drag it to the far right wall of the workspace, and let it dock there.

10. Click and hold the Apply Styles task pane and drag it around inside the workspace. Notice how it suggests different docking positions depending on which area you hover over (see Figure 1.18).

11. Drag the Apply Styles task pane to the edge of the workspace so that it floats on top before letting go. If you have a dual monitor setup, drag the task pane to the other monitor so that it doesn't cover the main window (see Figure 1.19).

12. Click the Task Panes button on the menu bar (now on the left side of your workspace) and select Behaviors. Notice that even with the Apply Styles pane undocked, the Behaviors tab appears within it.

13. Click and hold the Behaviors tab in the floating pane and drag it away from the pane until it floats on its own (see Figure 1.20).

14. Return the menu bar to its original position by dragging it to dock at the top of the workspace.

15. Return the Common toolbar to its original position below the menu bar in the same way.

16. Click the Task Panes button on the menu bar and select Reset Workspace Layout to restore its original configuration.

FIGURE 1.17
The menu bar
floating on top of
the workspace.

FIGURE 1.17
The menu bar
floating on top of
the workspace.

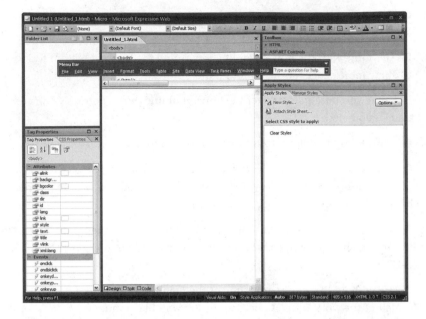

FIGURE 1.18
Suggested posi-
tion for the Apply
Styles task
pane.

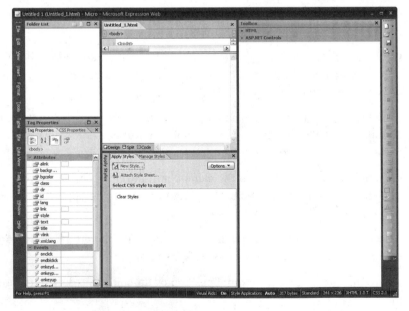

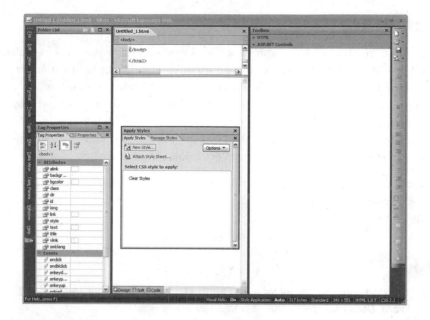

FIGURE 1.19
The Apply Styles pane floating over the workspace.

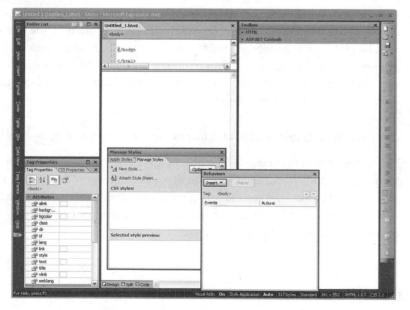

FIGURE 1.20
Behaviors pane floating on its own in the final reorganized workspace.

Summary

In this hour, you learned how Expression Web 2 works and how you can customize it to suit your needs. To some readers, this information might seem rudimentary or even redundant. But as you progress through the next 23 hours, you will see that having a solid understanding of the program makes a world of difference when you encounter new challenges. By knowing the basics, your understanding of the more advanced issues will be much easier. And because you'll be spending a lot of time with this program, it's worth your time to get to know it properly first.

For convenience, this book uses the default workspace and task pane layout. But now that you know how to customize them, feel free to organize their layout any way you see fit.

Q&A

Q. *The Common toolbar looks a lot like the Formatting toolbar in Microsoft Word. Does that mean that it works the same way?*

A. Both yes and no. The Common toolbar has many of the same functions as Microsoft Word's Formatting toolbar, but when you click a button on the Common toolbar, a change happens through the addition or modification of a snippet in the code or hypertext rather than in the text. (The program refers to these code snippets as *styles*.) So yes, they look similar, but no, what happens when you push a button is different.

Q. *Can I accidentally lose a pane or a toolbar and not be able to open it again?*

A. No. All the panes are accessible from the Task Panes button on the menu bar. If you close a pane by accident, you can always open it again from there. Furthermore you can always reset the original layout of the task panes by clicking Task Panes and Reset Workspace Layout. All the toolbars are accessible by clicking View and selecting Toolbars.

Workshop

The Workshop has quiz questions and exercises to help you put to use what you just learned. If you get stuck, the answers to the quiz questions are in the next section. But try to answer the questions first. Otherwise you'll only be cheating yourself.

Quiz

1. *What is the proper way of creating a web page?*

   A. Using only Code view
   B. Using only Design view
   C. Using Split view

2. *How many task panes can you have open at one time?*

   A. 8
   B. 14
   C. As many as you like

Answers

1. D. None of the above. (Sorry, it was a trick question.) There is no right or wrong when it comes to how you create a web page. Some people create spectacular sites using only Notepad, whereas others create just as spectacular sites without ever seeing a line of code. To get the most out of this book, use Split view as much as possible. That way you get to see what happens in Code view when you make changes in Design view and vice versa. But, in the end, what works best is up to the individual user.

2. C. In theory you could fill your entire screen with task panes and toolbars, but if you did it would be hard to get any work done. With that said, however, you are free to set up your workspace any way you please.

Beginning at the End: A Walkthrough of the Finished Project

What You'll Learn in This Hour:

▶ How to import and work with a completed web site in Expression Web 2.

▶ How to preview a site in your browser.

▶ How this book is laid out.

▶ How to use the different tools in Expression Web 2 to explore a web site and learn how it works.

Introduction

When I start to read a book like this I always want to see the end result of all the lessons before I start so that I know what I'm getting myself into. So, rather than making you go through all the tutorials to see what you can build in just a few hours with Expression Web 2, I've decided to start at the very end by showing you the site you will build through these lessons and use it to showcase some of the many features available in this application.

Because websites consist of many different files linked together, it is important to keep everything organized. But to do this, you first need to understand what the different elements are and how they work and relate to each other. By looking at a completed website and using the tools available in Expression Web 2 you will get a firmer grip on how it all comes together.

The methods you learn in this hour will be useful to you down the road as well. In fact, when you finish Hour 24, "Publishing Your Website," I urge you to come back to this hour for a second look. Because you'll come back with a better understanding of how the website works, you'll have a whole new perspective on the different lessons in this hour.

Working With a Completed Website

To be able to work efficiently in Expression Web 2 (or any web design application for that matter), it is important to understand how the application handles files and file relationships. By working with a completed website, you can experiment and learn how Expression Web 2 works with you to keep everything functioning properly as you edit and reorganize the different elements. That way you get an early start developing techniques and understanding that usually comes only much later in the learning process.

The Import Site Wizard is a helpful tool that saves you a lot of time when you need to work on a website built in a different application or by a different designer. Therefore you will probably use it quite frequently.

▼ **Try It Yourself**

Importing a Completed Website

A website is actually just a folder with a group of files linked together. What makes it a *website* is that the files within that folder can be viewed using a web browser. You will get a more thorough explanation of this idea later in this book. By creating a new website in Expression Web 2, you are telling the application that the main (root) folder is the bottom line or foundation and that everything in it relates back to this folder. When you publish your website, the root folder is replaced by the domain name.

To get started, you are going to use the Import Site Wizard to import the finished project into the application as a new website. You can use it to import sites from your local computer or network as well as from external web servers or even directly from the websites themselves.

1. Go to the book website at http://expression.pinkandyellow.com and download the lesson files for this hour to a central location on your computer.

2. Open Expression Web 2.

3. Go to File, Import and select Import Site Wizard. This opens the Import Site Wizard dialog as in Figure 2.1.

3. Select the File System option and use the Browse button to navigate to the location where you placed the lesson files for this hour. Select the folder called MyKipple Final. With the address set, click Next.

4. On the next page (see Figure 2.2), you are asked to define where the local copy of the site should be created. You need to select a folder different from the one the files are in right now. It is always a good idea to keep all your website proj-

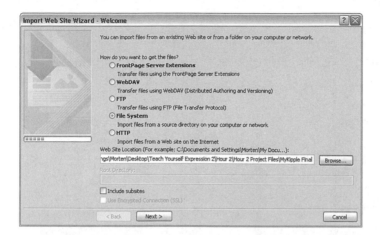

FIGURE 2.1
The Import Site Wizard dialog lets you import an existing site from a multitude of different sources both on your computer and on the Web.

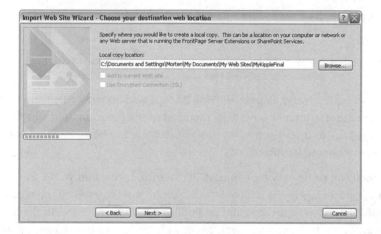

FIGURE 2.2
The second page of the Import Site Wizard lets you define where you want the new website project placed on your computer.

ects in one location on your computer so that they are easy to find. Many people use the My Web Sites folder under [My] Documents for this. Browse to the location you want the new website to be created in, create a new folder called MyKippleFinal, and select it. Click on Next.

5. The final page of the Import Site Wizard tells you that the website has been set up and that you can now start importing files. Click Finish.

Now that you have defined a location for the new website, you need to actually import the files from the original location. Expression Web 2 doesn't do this automatically because in many cases you don't want to import the entire site, just selected files or folders. When the Import Site Wizard closes, you are presented with the Web Site view as shown in Figure 2.3. This view shows you the local website on the left and the remote website on the right. From here you can move files and folders between the local and remote locations either one

FIGURE 2.3
The Web Site
view shows you
the files and
folders of the
local website on
the left and the
remote website
on the right.

by one or in groups. Expression Web 2 keeps tabs on what files have been moved and what files have been modified in the program, and whenever you come back to this view it tells you what files need to be updated on either the local or remote location.

6. When you come out of the Import Site Wizard, Expression Web 2 marks all the files and folders in the remote location for import (marked by the blue arrows pointing left in Figure 2.3) and set Publish All Changed Pages in the lower-right corner to Remote to Local. To copy all the files into your new website, click the Publish Web Site button.

You have successfully imported the new website when you can see that the local and remote websites are identical in terms of files and folders and that the Folder View task pane shows all the files and folders as well, as shown in Figure 2.4.

By the Way

Don't Be Confused by the Names "Local" and "Remote"

As you saw in the preceding lesson, Expression Web 2 separates the website you are working with from the one you are publishing to by naming them *local website* and *remote website*, respectively. But these names can easily be confusing. In the example, you just saw it can be argued that *both* websites are local.

Expression Web 2 considers the website you open in the application as the local website and the one you are publishing the files you have worked on to as the re-

FIGURE 2.4
When the site is successfully imported, you should see the same files reflected in the remote and local sites as well as the Folder View task pane.

mote website, regardless of the actual location of either. This can lead to some very interesting and confusing results: If you want to, you can set up a website so that the files you are working on are on a web server (technically a *remote* location) and publish these files to a hard drive on your computer (technically a *local* location). In that case, the web server would be considered the *local* website and placed on the left whereas the folder on your hard drive would be considered the *remote* website and placed on the right.

If you are ever confused about which location is defined as remote or local you can always check the address bars next to the local and remote website names in the Web Site view (see Figure 2.3).

Previewing the Site in Your Browser

Now that you have set up the MyKipple website in Expression Web 2, look at how the site works in real life. One of the most important habits you need to establish when working with web design is to constantly test what you are doing in one (or preferably several) browsers to see that everything is working as it should. For this reason, you have the ability to preview a page in your browser from anywhere inside the application.

To see the new site as it would appear for any visitor once it is on the Web, go to the Folder View task pane, right-click on the `default.html` file, and select Preview in Browser from the context menu (see Figure 2.5).

This opens the `default.html` page of the MyKipple website in your browser. The `default.html` page is the home page of the website, and from here you can navigate through all the different pages that have been created.

FIGURE 2.5
You can preview any page in your website by selecting Preview in Browser from the right-click menu.

The website itself serves as a good introduction to the different sections of this book. The following sections describe the different functionalities and when you will learn them.

Setting Up a Website and Building Pages

All websites consist of a group of web pages. These pages can contain anything from text to images to interactive elements like Flash movies or Silverlight applications. In Hours 3, "A Web Site Is Really Just Text—Build One in 5 Minutes," and 4, "Building the Home Page—A Look Behind the Curtain," you will learn how to set up a new site and build simple pages.

Hyperlinks

In the MyKipple website, you will see that several segments of text are highlighted in orange. These are hyperlinks that point the browser to different pages either within the website or in external websites. You will learn how to create and manage hyperlinks in Hour 5, "Get Connected—Building Hyperlinks for Navigation and Further Exploration."

Images

If you hover over the Home button on the menu on top of the screen and select My Desk from the drop-down menu, you are taken to a new page with a large image of my desk on the top. Images are an important part of web design and can serve both as content (such as the desk image), as functional elements such as buttons, or even as design elements. You will learn how to insert and manage images in Hours 6, "Get Visual, Part 1: Adding Images to Your Page," and 7, "Get Visual Part 2—Advanced Image Editing, Thumbnails, and Hotspots."

Tables

Go to the Home button again and click on My Wallet in the drop-down menu. This takes you to the My Wallet page, which features a standard HTML table. In the past tables were heavily used as design elements to structure the contents of web pages. But this was never an ideal situation and it caused a lot of problems for designers as well as the people visiting their sites. As a result, designers are moving away from using tables as design elements and now use them only for their intended purpose: to display tabular data. Because the focus of this book is to learn how to design standards-based websites with Expression Web 2, you will learn how to use tables to display tabular data only. Tables are covered in Hour 9, "Get Boxed In Part 1: Using Tables for Content."

Styling the Content

Go back to the home page by clicking the Home button and you will see that the text in the page has many different looks (see Figure 2.6). The heading is big, uppercase, and black; the paragraph text is smaller, gray, and justified. There are subheadings that look different from the main heading, links, a section of text in a box with a different font, and so on. If you were working in a word processing application, you would have applied these different looks or *styles* to each of the sections. But in standards-based web design, you create an external set of styles that define how the different sections look and behave. These styles are created with a code language called Cascading Style Sheets (CSS) and Expression Web 2 is an excellent tool for both learning and working with this language. In Hour 10, "Bringing Style to the Substance with Cascading Style Sheets," you will learn how to create and manage these CSS styles to give your content more identity.

Page Layout

As you just learned, designers used to use tables to create page layouts, but this practice is on the way out. In its place designers are now turning to CSS as their primary

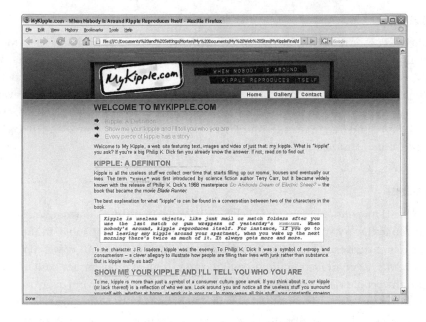

layout tool. In addition to being able to change the look and feel of text and other content, CSS can build containers or *boxes* that wrap the content. Using this technique, you can group different elements together and create styles and substyles to define how these different elements should look and behave. With the proper use of CSS you can create visually stunning and easily approachable web layouts that appear the same across all browsers and platforms. Hours 11, "Boxed In Part 2: Knee Deep in CSS," through 14, "Building the Framework," show you how to create, modify, and apply styles using the built in CSS functionalities of Expression Web 2 as well as by editing code directly. In these hours, you will learn how to use CSS to create advanced layouts for your sites and how external style sheets can control the look and feel of multiple pages from one central location.

Buttons

Buttons are a subgenre of the common hyperlink where the hyperlink is attached to a visual element such as an image or a text box. Because there are many different types of buttons, there are many different ways of making them and each serves its own purpose. In Hour 15, "Buttons, Buttons, Buttons," you will learn how to create several different types of buttons and also when to use these.

Behaviors

To add increased functionality to your pages, you can include small programs in your pages that perform simple actions when they are triggered by the visitor. Expression Web 2 has a series of these common actions known as *behaviors* built in for easy application. You can see one such behavior if you go back to the My Desk page, click on the Kenny Squeeze Toy hyperlink further down on the page, and click the image of the Kenny squeeze toy on the new page. As seen in Figure 2.7, this particular behavior opens a new small window that shows a larger version of the image. In Hour 16, "Using Behaviors," you will learn about the different behaviors available in Expression Web 2 and how to use them to create interactive experiences for your visitors.

Frames and Layers

Back in the Home page, if you hover over the hyperlink named Do Androids Dream of Electric Sheep?, you'll notice that a small window appears inside the page showing

FIGURE 2.7
In Hour 16, you will learn how to use behaviors to create effects such as this pop-up window that opens when you click on the smaller image on the main page.

an Amazon.com page. This is called an *inline frame* or *iFrame* and it is a technique that cuts a hole in your current page and places content from a different page inside it. In this example, the iFrame is placed inside a layer so that it hovers over the rest of the page rather than appearing alongside it. In Hour 17, "Frames and Layers," you will learn how to use frames and layers to place interactive and external content inside or on top of your regular content to make external preview windows and other advanced effects. You will also learn how to make a frames-based web page and how these differ from regular web pages.

The Drop-Down Menu

Aside from the content itself, I would argue that the navigation is the most important feature of any website. There are many ways of creating functional navigation and some are better than others. One of the most intuitive and visually exciting navigational tools you can put on your website is the drop-down menu (see Figure 2.8). As with everything else, there are several different ways you can make such a drop-down menu and each has advantages and drawbacks. In Hour 18, "Building a Functional Menu," you will learn how to create two different types of drop-down menus: the Layers-based menu and the Pure CSS menu. Both of these are highly functional and both are used heavily throughout the Web. The final MyKipple site you are looking at now uses the Pure CSS drop-down menu.

FIGURE 2.8
A drop-down menu adds functionality as well as style and interactivity to your website. You will learn how to make two different drop-down menus in Hour 18.

Contact Forms

The Internet allows for a two-way conversation between the website owner and the visitor. To facilitate this type of communication, there is a large group of tools known as *forms* built into the main code language of the Internet, HTML. Using forms you can create anything from a simple email form to advanced forum, blog, and even e-commerce functionalities. Under Contact on the main menu are two options: FPSE (FrontPage Server Extensions) form and PHP form. These are two different email forms created using two different technologies, each designed to run on a different type of server. In Hour 20, "Get Interactive with Forms," you will learn how to build and configure web forms and built-in functionality in Expression Web 2 to create a contact form based on FrontPage Server Extensions. However this form will work only if your web server has FrontPage Server Extensions installed. As an alternative, you will learn how to build an identical email form using a different code language called PHP in Hour 22, "Beyond the Basics: PHP in Expression Web 2."

The Email Forms Don't Work!

If you try to use the email forms, you will immediately notice that they don't actually work. This is not because there is something wrong with the forms or you have done anything wrong on your end. Both the FPSE and the PHP forms use *server-side scripts* to generate emails. And as the name suggests, server-side scripts need to run on a server to work. When you preview your pages in your browser from Expression Web 2 you are not using a web server, but just looking at your local files.

In Hours 20 and 22 you will be introduced to an application known as Expression Development Server and learn how to use it to preview the functionality of the email forms. If you want to see a fully working version of the email forms right now, go to www.mykipple.com.

Flash and Silverlight Galleries

Under Galleries you will find two options: Flash and Silverlight. In Hour 21, "Working with Flash and Silverlight," you will learn how to include Flash movies and Silverlight applications into your pages. Both these types of content are created using dedicated applications and you can only use Expression Web 2 to insert them into your pages and configure their data files. In that hour, you will get a glimpse into the world of both Flash and Silverlight and even build a Silverlight application from scratch to get a basic understanding of how these technologies work and interact with your website. You will also learn how to insert Flash-based videos from sites such as YouTube into your site.

The Silverlight Gallery Doesn't Work!

As with the email forms, the Silverlight gallery doesn't work when you preview it in your browser. This is because Silverlight is a server-side script language and requires a web server to run. You will learn how to trick the browser to preview your Silverlight application anyway in Hour 21, but until then if you want to see a fully working version of the Silverlight gallery right now, go to www.mykipple.com.

Watch Out!

Exploring the Website in Expression Web 2

Back in Expression Web 2, you can use the different features to explore the website and understand how it works. The application comes equipped with a set of tools to help you get a quick overview of the different elements the site is made up of as well as how everything is put together to work.

On the bottom of the Web Site view you have four buttons: Folders, Remote Web Site, Reports, and Hyperlinks. These are four different ways of viewing your website:

▶ Folders gives you a regular browser view of the files and folders in your website. In other words, it works the same way as the Folder List task pane.

▶ Remote Web Site gives you a view of the local and remote websites side by side and lets you transfer files between the two locations either one at a time or in groups. This is where you actually publish your site to the Web (publishing your site is covered in Hour 24).

▶ Reports gives you a rundown of all the assets in your website and the status of each of these assets. From there you can see for example how many hyperlinks are in the site (and how many of them are broken), how many images it contains, and how many files are *unlinked*—meaning they can't be accessed by the visitor.

▶ Hyperlinks creates a visual map that looks a lot like a mind-map, showing your files and how they relate to each other through hyperlinks. This tool makes it easy to understand how the site is organized.

Click on the Reports button to see the stats of the new website you imported. Expression Web 2 produces a list of all the different assets grouped in specific categories as in Figure 2.9.

Two of the most important items on this list are Slow Pages and Broken Links. The Slow Pages report gives you a list of all the pages estimated to take more than 30 seconds to load on a 56kbps connection. This report is important if you expect a lot of visitors with slower connections and shows you whether any of your pages is unnecessarily large or heavy to load. You can change the default connection speed the report tests for by going to Tools, Application Options and selecting the Reports View tab.

When you click on Broken Hyperlinks the Hyperlinks report will open displaying all the broken and unverified hyperlinks. By default all external links are considered unverified until they are verified by the application. When you open the Broken or Un-

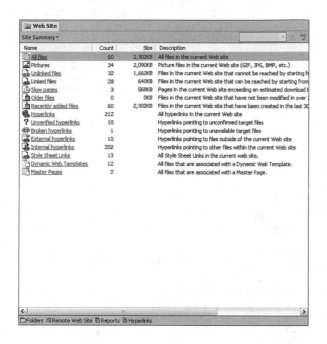

FIGURE 2.9
Reports gives you a complete overview of all the assets in your website and how they relate to each other.

verified report, Expression Web 2 asks whether you want it to verify the external links for you (see Figure 2.10). The application goes to each of the hyperlink locations to

FIGURE 2.10
Expression Web 2 can help you verify that all your hyperlinks point to real pages or assets.

ensure that they are valid. If so, the hyperlink is checked off as valid. If not, it is checked off as broken.

Try It Yourself

Fix a Broken Hyperlink

After running the report, there should be one broken hyperlink pointing to a file called bagOpennies.jpg. You can fix broken hyperlinks right from the report without even opening the page itself.

1. Right-click on the broken hyperlink and select Edit Hyperlink. This opens the Edit Hyperlink dialog (see Figure 2.11).

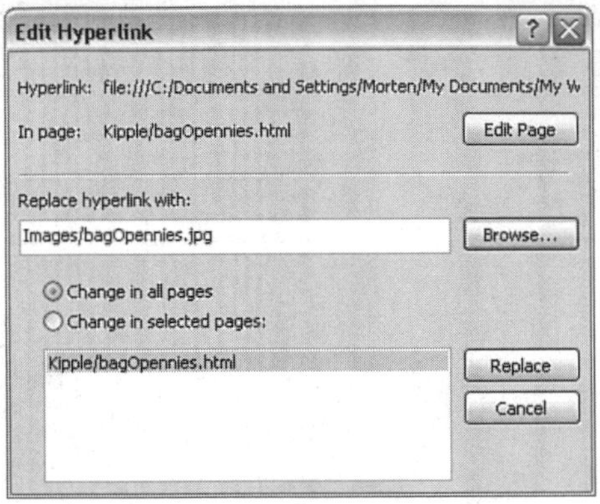

FIGURE 2.11
You can fix broken hyperlinks from the Reports view without ever opening the pages themselves.

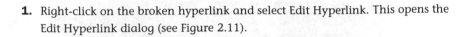

2. From here use the Browse button to find the correct file. It is under the Images folder and is called bagOpennies.jpg.

3. Click the Replace button and the hyperlink is automatically updated in all the pages where it is featured.

Keeping Your Pages Functional

As you learned earlier, a website consists of a group of files and folders that are linked together. That means for the individual pages of the site to work, all the links between them have to be correct and up to date. One of the many important features of Expression Web 2 is that it keeps tabs on your files for you, making the necessary changes throughout all your files when something is changed.

As long as you make the changes to your pages, files, and folders inside Expression Web 2, the application makes all the necessary changes to the related files to make everything run smoothly. So, if you want to move a file or folder into or out of another folder, always use either the Folder List task pane or the Folder view and the links to your files and folders will be updated automatically. A short example puts this into context.

Right now the root folder (main folder) of the website contains two files: `kippleStyles.css` and `layout.css`. These two files (known as *style sheets*) contain all the CSS or styling code for all the pages of the site, and as a result every page has a link to them. To make the style sheets easier to find, you want to put them in their own folder called Styles.

1. Switch to Folders view and click on the folder icon in the upper-right corner to create a new folder. Give it the name Styles.

2. Drag and drop the `kippleStyles.css` and `layout.css` files into the new Styles folder.

3. A dialog briefly appears telling you that the files are being renamed. This means that all the links that point to these two files from all the pages are being updated to reflect the change in location. When the dialog disappears, preview the `default.html` page in your browser again to make sure nothing changed.

When you preview the pages in your browser it appears as if nothing has changed, but in fact the links to the external style sheets have been changed in every single page. If Expression Web 2 hadn't changed all the links to the two files you moved, all the pages would have appeared as regular text without the backgrounds and different styles. By using this drag-and-drop technique, you can move any and all files inside your site and be certain that Expression Web 2 updates the links that point to them so that everything keeps working as it is supposed to.

Never Move Your Files Outside of Expression Web 2

Watch Out!

A common mistake of new web designers is moving files or folders using the regular browser window in their operating system rather than inside Expression Web 2. If you move a file or folder that way, the hyperlinks that tell the browser where these files are when the pages are displayed will not be updated, and as a result you end up with a page that doesn't work properly. If you want to move a file from one folder to another, you should *always* use the Folder List task pane or Folders view to ensure that all your hyperlinks are updated accordingly.

Summary

Expression Web 2 is a powerful web design and management tool that lets you easily build and publish advanced websites based on web standards. In this hour, you explored the final product you will end up with after following all the tutorials in this book and used it to learn how Expression Web 2 works to help you manage your website.

The ability to import an existing website gives you a quick and easy way of picking up an old project or taking over an existing project from someone else. In this hour, you learned how to import an existing website and move the necessary files from a remote location to your websites folder. You also learned how to use the Reports view to manage the files and folders in your website and track any problems or errors that are present. Expression Web 2 is set up in such a way that you can find and fix problems such as broken hyperlinks without actually having to open the pages and make changes there. This ability is a huge timesaver and gives you intimate control of the site even without knowing or understanding exactly how it works.

Finally you learned how to use the Folder List and Folders view to rearrange the files within your website without breaking the many links between them by letting Expression Web 2 handle all the details for you.

What you saw in this hour is just the beginning. In the coming hours, you will learn how to build the MyKipple website from scratch and through that learn how to get the most out of Expression Web 2.

Q&A

Q. *When I preview the MyKipple site in Internet Explorer, a bar appears on top of the page saying that to protect my security it has blocked the page from running scripts and ActiveX controls that would access my computer. Does this mean I have a virus or that there is something dangerous in the MyKipple website project?*

A. Internet Explorer is a little overprotective when it comes to previewing local websites. By that I mean if the same pages were loaded from the Web, you wouldn't be getting that message. You can safely click on the bar and select Allow Blocked Content. There is nothing in the MyKipple website project that would harm your computer in any way.

Q. *The contact pages/Silverlight gallery doesn't work at all! There's something wrong with these files.*

A. The contact forms and Silverlight gallery all work by utilizing server-side scripts. When you preview these pages directly from Expression Web 2, the scripts cannot run. If you want to test these pages properly in your browser from the local location, you can do so by triggering Expression Development Server. For more information on this check Hour 21 for the Silverlight gallery, Hour 20 for the FrontPage Server Extensions form, and Hour 22 for the PHP form.

Workshop

The Workshop has exercises to help you put to use what you have just learned.

Exercise

Open the Hyperlinks view by clicking the button on the very bottom of the view and select any of the pages in the Folder View task pane to see how it relates to other pages and files. You will see that all the pages that link *to* the page are placed on the left and all the pages the selected page links to are placed on the right. You can click on any of the other icons in the view to see how these files relate to further files as well.

HOUR 3

A Website Is Really Just Text—Build One in 5 Minutes

What You'll Learn in This Hour:

▶ How to create a new website

▶ How to create a new page

▶ How to create and edit simple text content using Design view

▶ How to test your first web page in multiple browsers

Introduction

Now that you have seen what this program can do, it's your turn to make your own project. You start at the very beginning with a blank site and one Hypertext Markup Language (*HTML*) page, and work your way from there to the fully functional site you saw in Hour 2, "Beginning at the End: A Walk-Through of the Finished Project."

Creating a New Website

As you saw in Hour 2, a website is a grouping of related files and folders under one main folder. In fact, a website such as www.pinkandyellow.com is little more than a folder on a server you can access through the Internet. By creating a new website in Expression Web 2, you are telling the program "This folder is where I will put all the text, images, and other files I want to share with everyone in world when they visit the website. Please keep track of them for me." In response, Expression Web 2 keeps tabs on what you do and makes constant changes to your files to keep the website working properly. It does so by creating a set of hidden metadata files that describe the site and its contents. That way the information about how your site functions is stored even if you delete the program from your computer or hand over the project to another Expression Web 2 user.

The first thing to do when you start a new project is to create a new website. You can do this from the File menu or from the drop-down menu attached to the New icon on the Common toolbar. This opens a dialog called New, which displays the different options available to you (see Figure 3.1).

FIGURE 3.1
The New dialog gives you the ability to create new web sites from scratch or from templates.

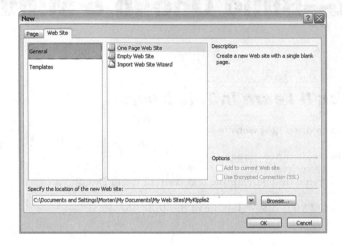

From here you have the option of making a general website or one from a template. Under General are three more options: One Page Web Site, Empty Web Site, and Import Web Site Wizard. The One Page Web Site option creates a website with a home page file called `default.html`. The Empty Web Site option creates a website with no files. The Import Web Site Wizard lets you import an already existing site from a local folder, a network folder, or the Web.

By the Way

Don't take titles such as One Page Web Site and Empty Web Site too literally. People often think of computer programs as very rigid and inflexible and start to worry when they see definite descriptions like these. When I showed this program to a design novice, he asked me what to do when he wanted to create a site with more than one page. It might seem silly to most people, but his confusion was completely understandable in much the same way that my old high school teacher could never understand that the computer casing was not the hard drive. It's all a matter of perspective. In reality, programs are (at least for the most part) very flexible and titles such as these are merely general descriptions. Using a One Page Web Site template in Expression Web 2 just means that you start with a folder with one file. In fact, strictly speaking, a one-page website isn't a website at all—it's just a single web page. Likewise an "Empty Web Site" is a website folder that starts with no files in it with the expectation that more files will be added later.

At the bottom of the dialog is the suggested address for your new website. The address varies depending on your computer's operating system and setup. To avoid confusion, you should always create a new folder with the same name as your project and use it as your website folder. You can use the Browse button to select any folder on your hard drive, on a local network, or on an external server, such as your website or root folder, but keeping your files on your hard drive is usually the best solution.

It's a good idea to have a central location where you keep all your websites. Expression Web 2 will suggest you use the My Web Sites folder located under [My] Documents, but you can use any folder you want. This book uses the My Web Sites folder as the central location for all projects.

Try it Yourself ▼

Create a New One-Page Website

Creating a new website should always be the first step when starting a new project. In this task, you create a new website with one HTML page.

1. Click File and hover over New to expose the submenu, and then click Web Site.

2. In the New dialog, select General and One Page Web Site.

3. Click the Browse button next to the address bar on the bottom of the dialog and navigate to the My Web Sites folder under [My] Documents. Click the Create New Folder button in the upper-right corner of the dialog and name the new folder MyKipple.

4. Click the MyKipple folder to highlight it and click Open. (The Site Name bar will be empty. That's normal.) Click OK to open the new site shown in Figure 3.2.

Did you Know?

When you start Expression Web 2 again after closing it, by default it opens on the last project you were working on. This function is great if you are working on only one project, but can be an annoyance if you have several projects going at once. If you want the program to open on a default blank page instead, you can change the settings under Tools, Application Settings.

▲

The site shown here is the blank canvas you will be working with from hereon out. As you make changes to the files in the website, Expression Web 2 keeps tabs on what you do and makes the necessary modifications in your files to keep everything working properly (see Figure 3.2).

FIGURE 3.2
MyKipple site as
it appears after
creation.

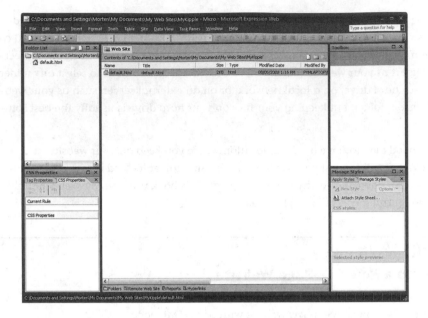

FIGURE 3.2
MyKipple site as
it appears after
creation.

Creating Your First Web Page

Now that you have created a website, the Web Site view appears in place of the Split view you saw earlier. You explored the different functions of this pane in Hour 2. For now let's focus on creating your first web page.

As you can see, your new website contains one file called `default.html`. In the web world, two filenames signify a home page: `default` and `index`. A *home page* is the page the browser looks for if the visitor does not specify a particular filename in the address bar.

`default.html` is an HTML file that contains all the code a web browser needs to display the web page.

> HTML is the most prevalent markup or publishing language for creating websites. A *markup language* is a set of code snippets that define for a browser how it should lay out and format text. Used correctly, HTML is a powerful tool to organize and display large amounts of content in a simple and accessible way. For further information on HTML, visit http://en.wikipedia.org/wiki/HTML.

If you double-click the filename, the file opens up in Split view (see Figure 3.3). As you can see, although it contains some code, it has no content. If you were to open the file in a browser at this point, all you would get is a white page. So, before going any further, you need to add some content.

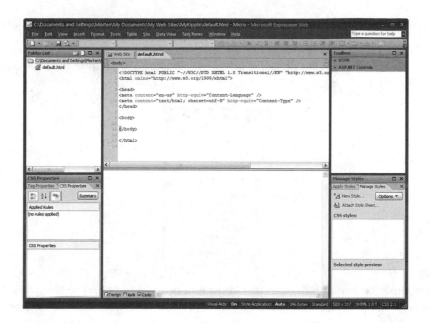

FIGURE 3.3
Even though there are several lines of code in Code View, default.html is empty in Design View because there is no content yet.

To see how easy it is to create a simple web page, switch to Design view so that all you see is the blank page. By setting Expression Web 2 to Design view, it works in much the same way as a word processing application. This is great when you want to edit content quickly. Click anywhere inside Design view and start typing text. The text appears in a dotted box with a "p" hovering over it. This box is a visual aid called Block Selection and it gives a visual representation of what content a particular style applies to (in this instance "p" or "paragraph"). You can turn Block Selection and all other visual aids on and off from the Visual Aids menu under the View menu (see Figure 3.4).

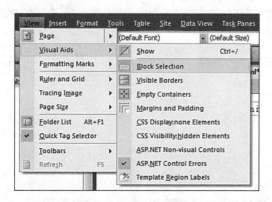

FIGURE 3.4
The Visual Aids menu lets you turn on and off visual aids as you work.

If you click somewhere else on the page, the Block Selection box disappears and you see the text as it appears in a browser. By moving the cursor to the end of this line, you can continue your current paragraph. If you press Enter, the cursor shifts down approximately two lines and Expression Web 2 creates a new Block Selection box.

On the first line, enter your page title and select Heading 1 <h1> from the Style drop-down menu (see Figure 3.5).

FIGURE 3.5
The Style drop-down menu.

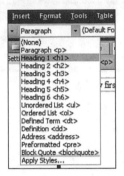

In response, the heading changes to a larger font and is now bold. The Block Selection also changes to h1, telling you that the h1 style is now applied to the content inside. When you press Enter, the program assumes that you want to start a new paragraph and a new "p" box appears under your heading. Enter some more text—enough to fill at least three full lines. If you can't come up with anything to write, simply copy some text out of this book or any other written material lying around.

Create a new paragraph by pressing Enter and typing a subheading. Use the Style drop-down menu to set the style to Heading 2 <h2>. Directly underneath, type one more paragraph, this time using the *I* (italic) and **B** (bold) buttons to *emphasize* and **strongly emphasize** parts of the text.

You need two more elements: A bullet (or unordered) list and a numbered (or ordered) list. As in a word processor, press Enter to create a new line and click the Numbered List button (see Figure 3.6).

FIGURE 3.6
The Numbered List and Bulleted List buttons work in much the same way as they would in a word processor application.

A number appears on the left, the Block Selection box shifts to the right, and its tag changes to "li" (list item). Type a series of list items separating them by pressing Enter. To end the list, simply press Enter to create a new list item and then either click the Numbered List button again to deactivate it or simply press the Back key on your keyboard. Doing so changes the new list item to a paragraph.

Creating a bulleted list is done in the same way: Click the Bulleted List button and create a series of list items.

Finally, click the Save button or press Ctrl+S to save the file and pat yourself on the back: You have created your first web page (see Figure 3.7).

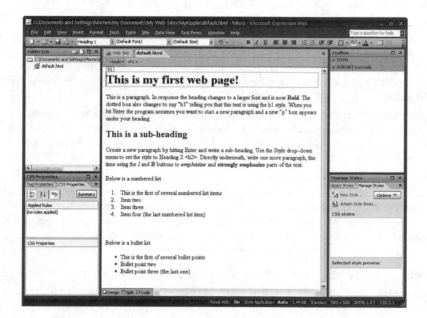

FIGURE 3.7
The result as it appears in Design View in Expression Web 2.

Testing Your Web Page in Multiple Browsers

When you are designing for the Web, it's important to continually test your pages in multiple web browsers to ensure that they work and appear the way you intended. A web browser is nothing more than a program that renders or interprets the code in your page and displays it accordingly. But like human interpreters, there can be large discrepancies among browsers when it comes to interpretation. The WYSIWYG editor in Expression Web 2's Design view is a custom browser built to comply with all web standards. In contrast, not all browsers are as particular about standards and, as a result, your page can look different depending on which browser you use.

Four Browsers You Should Have on Your Computer

A web designer should always have the end user in mind. But you don't know what browser or even what kind of computer the visitor will use when viewing your websites. Making an educated guess is the best you can do.

The majority of the computers connected to the Internet run some version of Microsoft Windows, and most of these computers have Internet Explorer as their default browser. So, Internet Explorer should be at the top of the list. Because Expression Web 2 works only on Windows-based computers, you probably already have Internet Explorer installed by default. If not, you can get it free from Microsoft by visiting http://www.microsoft.com/ie.

In the last few years, Mozilla's Firefox browser has gained enormous popularity and is the biggest competitor to Internet Explorer. Firefox is also a far more "reasonable" browser when it comes to code interpretation because it follows web standards pretty closely. For these reasons, you should also have Firefox installed. You can get it free from Mozilla by visiting http://www.firefox.com.

Most Mac (Apple) users use the default Mac OS browser called Safari. Apple released a Windows version of this browser last year. To ensure that Mac users get the same experience as Windows users, you should also test everything in Safari. You can get it free from Apple by visiting http://www.apple.com/safari/.

Finally there is the Opera browser. Although it doesn't have a large market share, Opera is a popular alternative to the mainstream browsers. It works on many cell phones and other portable devices. Opera is strict when it comes to web standards and can be an excellent tool for uncovering bad code that other browsers glance over. You can get it free by visiting http://www.opera.com.

To help with the testing process, Expression Web 2 can be set up to preview your page in all the different browsers installed on your computer, and in multiple different window sizes. Select File, Preview in Browser to control all this. From here, you can pick which browser and window size to test the page in or you can test it in multiple browsers at the same time.

Alternatively you can press F12 and test the page in only the last browser you selected from the list (Internet Explorer by default). Doing so is fine for now. By pressing F12, the browser opens and you see the local instance of your page just as you would if it was stored somewhere on the Web. As you can see from Figure 3.8, the page looks the same as it did in Expression Web 2. Because you are using only the standard styles h1, h2, p, and li, the text fills the entire width of the window. If you grab the edge of the window and resize it, the text reorganizes itself to fit the smaller or larger space.

FIGURE 3.8
The result as it appears in Internet Explorer 7.

When Browsers Go Bad: Internet Explorer

If you've worked with web design before or you've surfed the web using different browsers you've no doubt run into the infamous Internet Explorer problem where pages that look fine in Internet Explorer are "broken" in other browsers or vice versa. Internet Explorer 6 and 7 have a tendency of displaying pages, and especially those using CSS, very differently from other browsers. This problem is often misconstrued as a problem with the other browsers but in reality it is the result of Internet Explorer interpreting web standards in a non-standard way (no pun intended). This has lead to, amongst other things, the rise of Firefox as an alternative, "I Hate Internet Explorer" groups and a phenomenon known as "IE Hacks" where designers and developers have been forced to come up with special code hacks to circumvent these problems so that their sites will appear identical across all browsers. Fortunately, the Internet Explorer development team has finally realized that this issue causes a lot of grief for designers, developers and even the internet surfing public and with the release of Internet Explorer 8 they seem to have resolved many of these issues and gotten "in line" with the other browsers.

Watch Out!

Summary

In this hour, you learned to create a one-page website from scratch and discovered how to edit an HTML file to make your first web page. You saw that editing simple text content in Design view is no different form editing text in a word processor. You also learned how to test your page in multiple browsers and why, in this case, quantity improves quality.

From here until the end of the book, you will work with this project to make the final site you saw in Hour 2. Starting from scratch is a great way of learning how to do things properly the first time around. In Hour 4, "Building the Home Page— A Look Behind the Curtain," you will expand on the first page by introducing more text content and standard style elements. You will see what goes on in the code and learn a bit about the HTML code language.

Q&A

Q. *When I created a new site, Expression Web 2 opened an entirely new window of the program. Is this normal?*

A. Yes. When you create a new site or open an old one from within Expression Web 2, it opens in a new window. This can get confusing if you don't pay attention, so always keep an eye on the taskbar to see how many sites you have open. A good tip is to close all Expression Web 2 windows (sites) you are not currently working on. That way when you start the program again, it opens on your current project, not on one hidden underneath your main window when you closed it.

Q. *What is the difference between a website and a web page?*

A. Simply put, a website is a group of web pages. A website is a dedicated space on the Web and contains a number of web pages that relate to each other. In practical terms, the combined content at http://www.pinkandyellow.com is a website, whereas a single page under the same domain, like http://pinkandyellow.com/photography/index.htm, is a web page.

Q. *Can I build a website without knowing anything about HTML and other code?*

A. Yes you can. But as you will see in the following hours, understanding the inner workings of a web page can save you a lot of time and energy as well as help you create better sites faster. That doesn't mean you have to become a code guru. You can get a lot done with a rudimentary understanding of HTML.

Workshop

The Workshop has quiz questions and exercises to help you put to use what you just learned. If you get stuck, the answers to the quiz questions are in the next section. But try to answer them first. Otherwise you'll only be cheating yourself.

Quiz

1. *How do you preview a web page in a browser?*

2. *Why is it important to test a page in multiple browsers?*

Answers

1. There are many ways of previewing a web page in a browser. The easiest one is to simply press F12; doing so opens the current page in the default browser. You can also open the page in a browser with a specific window size by selecting File, Preview in Browser and clicking the size you want to use. Finally you can preview the page in multiple browsers simultaneously by clicking Preview in Multiple Browsers on the same menu.

2. No browser is created equally. As a result your web pages might look different depending on the configuration of the visitor's computer. To put it into perspective, Internet Explorer versions 6, 7, and 8 handle web pages in entirely different ways, so although a page looks great in Internet Explorer 8, it might be unreadable in Internet Explorer 6. The best way around this problem is to create standards-based websites, but even then you might run into browser incompatibilities. Continually testing your pages helps you catch problems early and figure out ways to fix them.

HOUR 4

Building the Home Page— A Look Behind the Curtain

What You'll Learn in This Hour:

▶ How to read and edit basic HTML code in Code view

▶ How to import text from Microsoft Word and other documents

▶ How to clean up imported code using Code and Design views

▶ How to use Find and Replace to edit many instances of code at the same time

Introduction

In Hour 3, "A Website Is Really Just Text—Build One in 5 Minutes," you built a basic web page using functions similar to those in a word processing program. But that is just half the story: In web design, what happens behind the curtain is what really matters. It's time to learn some basic HTML and see how the code affects the content. To do this, you build the basic structure of the home page of the My Kipple site.

Opening and Editing an Existing File Using Code View

If you haven't already done so, open the `default.html` file you worked on in Hour 3. The MyKippe site should open automatically when you open Expression Web 2. If not, you can find it by selecting Open Site from the File menu or from the drop-down menu of the Open icon on the Common toolbar (see Figure 4.1).

The Open Sites dialog lists all the sites created in Expression Web 2 (see Figure 4.2). When you create or define a website in Expression Web 2, the program automatically generates a shortcut to facilitate easy access to this list. If you can't find the project on this list, you can navigate to it as you normally would. If you followed the directions in Hour 3, the project is in the My Web Sites folder under My Documents.

FIGURE 4.1
The drop-down menu under the Open icon on the Common toolbar gives you quick access to open files and sites without having to go to the Main menu

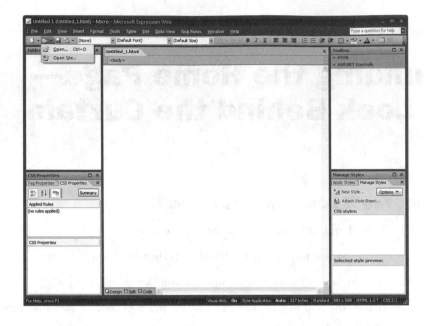

FIGURE 4.2
The Open Site dialog displays all the websites you have created in Expression Web 2. Here seen with the My Kipple project.

The Open Sites dialog isn't restricted to local sites. You can also use it to open and manage external websites both through HTML (Hypertext Markup Language) and FTP (File Transfer Protocol) as long as you have the necessary access codes. In fact you can use Expression Web 2 to make changes to live websites in real time.

Before going any further, let's look at what is happening in the page's code. Select Split view using the button at the bottom of the pane to reveal both Code view and

Design view. Click anywhere on the heading and then click the h1 tag on the Block Selection box. This highlights the content affected by the h1 style in both Design view and Code view (see Figure 4.3). In Design view, you see a box with a gray striped-out

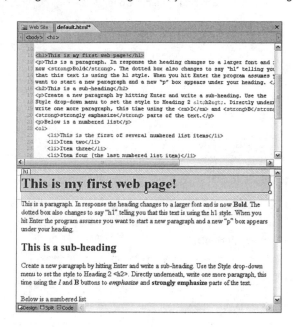

FIGURE 4.3
When clicking on an object in either Code or Design view that object is highlighted in both for easy reference.

area above and below. The gray areas are the default margins for the h1 style. In Code view, you see the text buffered or wrapped on both sides by code tags. These tags tell the browser to display the text in the h1 style.

HTML is a basic code language that can be summarized in one simple rule: Everything is wrapped between a beginning and an end tag. All beginning tags consist of a less-than bracket <, the tag name and/or function, and a greater-than bracket >. End tags look much the same, but with the addition of a forward slash / before the content. In this example, <h1> tags wrap the heading like this:

```
<h1>This is my first web page!</h1>
```

You now have two ways of changing the style of your content. You can use the style drop-down menu as you learned in Hour 3 or you can go into Code view and change the style manually. Try changing the <h1> and </h1> tags to <p> and </p>, and see what happens in Design view.

To use Design view to see changes you made in Code view, you have to click inside the Design view area. This is because as you change the code in Code view, you are temporarily breaking the code. Rather than trying to display broken code, Expression Web 2 waits for you to tell it when you finish editing before it refreshes the WYSIWYG (What You See Is What You Get) editor.

Notice that when you change the beginning tag, Expression Web 2 highlights the end tag in yellow and red to tell you that your code is broken (see Figure 4.4). Likewise the

Error highlighted in Code View

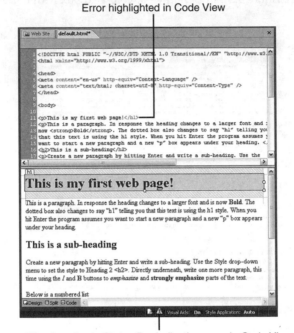

Warning sign in Status Bar indicating error in Code View

status bar on the bottom of the workspace puts up two warning signs: The first one tells you that it detects an HTML incompatibility; the second one tells you that it detects a code error.

By studying the code, you see that all the different styles you applied in Hour 3 are actually the same type of tags:

▶ Heading 1 <h1>

▶ Heading 2 <h2>

▶ Paragraph <p>

▶ Italicized (emphasized) <em>

- ▶ Bold (strongly emphasized) `<strong>`
- ▶ Bullet (unordered) list `<ul>`
- ▶ Numbered (ordered) list `<ol>`
- ▶ List item for both lists `<li>`

The `</body>` tag, which wraps all the content, tells the browser that this is the content to display. The `<head>` tag contains all the meta information that is available to the browser but that the browser does not displayed within the page. Meta information includes the page title displayed at the top of the window, info about the designer, and so on. Finally the `<html>` tag, which tells the browser that the following content is written in the HTML language, wraps both the `<head>` and `<body>` sections. Scroll to the bottom of the Code view and you can see the `</body>` and `</html>` tags that close the page.

Importing Styled Text from a Document

What is a website if not a source of information? You need some real content to work with. Right now the `default.html` file contains whatever text you inserted during Hour 3. The next step is to introduce some real content. In most cases, you will either be provided with or write your own content in some form of word processing software. Your first instinct is probably to cut and paste this content straight into your page. The problem is that word processors attach a large amount of invisible styling code to their documents—code that becomes very difficult to work with after import into an HTML file. To get rid of most of this superfluous code, Expression Web 2 can import this content and translate basic layout and styling for you. It's not a perfect solution, but it's far better than cutting and pasting.

In the set of files you downloaded from the book site is a Microsoft Word document called `MyKippleHome.doc` (see Figure 4.5). Open this document in Microsoft Word and you see a standard document with headings, subheadings, and some text.

The next step is to move all this content over to the `default.html` file and translate the styling to standards-based code. To import the content, you use the File command.

FIGURE 4.5
MyKippleHome
.doc as it appears in Microsoft Word.

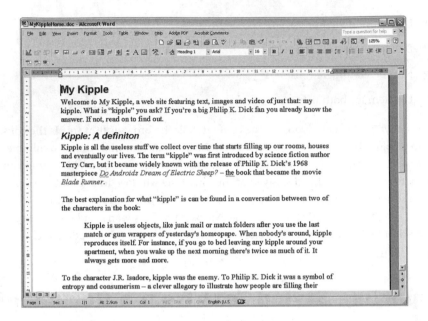

▼

Try it Yourself

Add the Insert File Command to the Common Toolbar

Expression Web 2 is loaded with functions, many of which are not part of the standard toolbars. The Insert File command is one such function. But because you'll use it often in real life, add an Insert File command button to your toolbar.

1. Select Add or Remove Buttons and Customize under the Toolbar options as explained in Hour 1, "Get to Know Microsoft Expression Web 2." Alternatively, select Tools, Customize from the menu bar.

2. With the Commands tab selected, click Insert under Categories.

3. Scroll to the bottom of the Commands menu and find the File option with a paperclip icon next to it (see Figure 4.6).

4. Click the File option and drag it to the far right side of the Common toolbar. Release the mouse button and the paperclip appears on the toolbar next to the Font Color button (see Figure 4.7). Close the Customize dialog.

Before inserting new text, delete all the old content from the default.html file. In Design view, highlight all the content and press the Delete button on your keyboard. You should now have a blank page in Design view and the basic framework of an HTML file in Code view.

▼

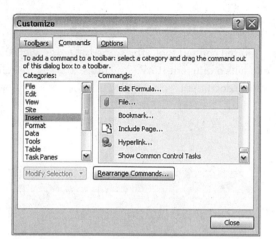

FIGURE 4.6
From the Cus-
tomize dialog
you can add new
functionality like
the Insert File
command to
your toolbars.

FIGURE 4.7
When you add
new functions to
the toolbars they
will appear in the
first open space
to the right.

To import the content of the MyKippleHome.doc file into your project, click the Insert
File button you just added to the Common toolbar. This opens a standard Select File
dialog. Browse to the location where you saved the MyKippleHome.doc file. By default, the Insert File command looks for HTML files. But if you click the Files of Type
drop-down menu, you see the program supports a long list of file types including Rich
Text Format (.rtf), many different versions of Microsoft Word documents (.doc), Microsoft Excel worksheets (.xls), WordPerfect documents (.wpd), and many more. Simply clicking All Files (*.*) shows you all the available files. Select the
MyKippleHome.doc file and click Open.

Depending on the version of Microsoft Word installed on your computer, a warning
saying **Microsoft Expression Web 2 needs a converter to display this file correctly. This feature is not currently installed. Would you like to install it now?**
might appear the first time you use the Insert File command. If you click Yes, Expression Web 2 asks you to insert the Microsoft Office CD and install some new
components. If you don't have the Office CD handy, simply click No. Because of a
quirk in the program, the function still works the way it should but you see the same
warning every time you use the function until you install the necessary components.

Cleaning Up Imported Text

Although the new imported content looks the same in Design view as it did in Microsoft Word, the code tells a different story (see Figure 4.8). By highlighting the heading at the top of the document, you see that the code is no longer as clean as it was earlier:

```
<font FACE="Arial" SIZE="5"><b>
<p>My Kipple</p>
</b></font>
```

FIGURE 4.8
Although the new content looks right in Design View, the content imported from the word document is littered with "bad" code that is not standards based.

You can see that rather than setting the heading to the h1 heading style, the font type and font size are set with two commands: FACE and SIZE. Although this way of styling content works, it is both cumbersome and messy and creates a lot of extra work for anyone who wants to change the content later. For instance, if you have several headings like this throughout your document, you have to insert all that style code every time you add a new heading. As you will see when you start adding more advanced styling to your document, this way of defining the look of your text is also limiting. Furthermore the font element is deprecated meaning it is no longer supported by the W3C and should be avoided if at all possible.

You need to get rid of all this extra code and to clean up the new document. To do this, you can make use of both Design view and Code view. First attach the proper styles to the content. As you can see when you click the heading, Expression Web 2 defines it as a paragraph with some extra styling attached. To fix this, simply set the style to Heading 1 <h1> by using the Style menu as you did before. Use the same technique to set the three subheadings to h2. HTML has a dedicated tag, blockquote, for indented or highlighted paragraphs. Select the indented paragraph and use the Style menu to restyle the paragraph with Block Quote.

Now that all the sections have the proper tags, you can start deleting all the unnecessary code. In Code view, take away all the code before and after the heading tags. Afterward each heading should look like this:

```
<h1>My Kipple</h1>
```

Next you need to get rid of all the extra code attached to the indented section. Because the Block Quote style automatically indents the paragraph, all the other tags are now unnecessary. Right now you have this:

```
<dir>
    <dir>
        <span LANG="EN-CA">
         <blockquote>Kipple is useless objects, like junk mail or match folders
after you use the last match or gum wrappers of yesterday&#39;s homeopape. When
nobdy&#39;s around, kipple reproduces itself. For instance, if you go to bed
leaving
any kipple around your apartment, when you wake up the next morning there&#39;s
twice as much of it. It always gets more and more.</blockquote>
        </span>
    </dir>
</dir>
```

With the superfluous <dir> and <span> tags deleted the section should now read

```
<blockquote>Kipple is useless objects, like junk mail or match folders after you
use the last match or gum wrappers of yesterday&#39;s homeopape. When
nobody&#39;s around, kipple reproduces itself. For instance, if you go
to bed leaving any kipple around your apartment, when you wake up
the next morning there&#39;s twice as much of it. It always gets more
and more.</blockquote>
```

Finally, change the italicized and bolded words to emphasized and strongly emphasized. You can either do this manually by replacing each individual tag in Code view or in Design view by highlighting each section and clicking its respective emphasis button twice—once to get rid of the old code and once to insert the new code. This document has only a few emphasized and strongly emphasized sections, so it's easy to make the changes manually. But because you often have to work with larger documents with many such instances, Expression Web 2 has a dedicated function to do all this work for you.

▼   **Try it Yourself**

Use Find and Replace to Change Multiple Tags at Once

Find and Replace is a great tool to find content and make multiple changes to a document with only a few mouse clicks.

1. Open the Find dialog by clicking Edit, Find on the menu bar or by using the shortcut Ctrl+F. Click the HTML Tags tab.

2. In the Find Tag area, enter **i** or select it from the drop-down menu. Under Replace Action, select Change Tag from the drop-down menu. Doing so opens a third option called To. Enter **em** or select it from the drop-down menu (see Figure 4.9).

FIGURE 4.9
The HTML Tags tab under the Find and Replace dialog can be used to make document-wide changes to specific tags.

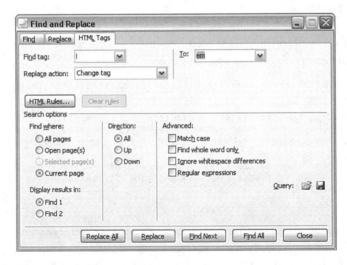

3. Click either Replace All if you are confident you want to replace all the tags, or click Find Next and then Replace for each instance. When you do so, the program replaces both the beginning and end tags throughout the document.

You have now successfully imported and converted the contents of a Word document to standards-based code (see Figure 4.10). The final step is to save the page on top of your old one (Ctrl+S) and test it in multiple browsers to ensure that it looks the way it's supposed to.

▼

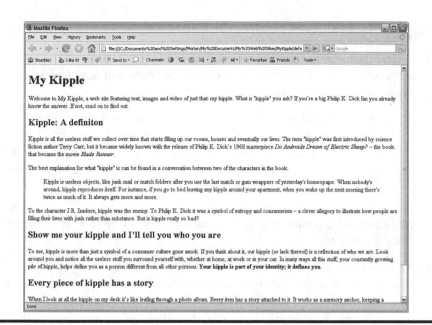

FIGURE 4.10
The new
`default.html`
file as it appears
in Firefox.

Summary

In this hour you took a trip behind the scenes and learned a bit about how an HTML page works. You saw that the code boils down to wrapping the content in a beginning and an end tag and that changing these tags can be done from Code view and Design view and also by using Find and Replace. You also learned how to import text content from external files and clean up the code so that it works properly. In Hour 5, "Get Connected—Building Hyperlinks for Navigation and Further Exploration," you'll create a second page and add hyperlinks to your pages to make them interactive.

Q&A

Q. *When I imported the content from the Word document, there was all this extra code attached to the heading to make it larger and bold. How come simply adding the* <h1> *tags has the same effect?*

A. All browsers interpret predefined styles in HTML in much the same way. All these styles are available from the Styles drop-down menu. If you don't specifically define these styles in your document, they display according to their default parameters. In later lessons, you will learn to change the default styles to your specification and to make new styles.

Q. *Why can't I simply cut and paste the content from a Word document straight into my web page?*

A. A word processor, such as Microsoft Word, inserts a large amount of hidden style code in documents. When you copy and paste text from these programs, all of that code quite literally tags along. One example of this is simple line breaks. When you press the Enter key in a word processor, you are actually inserting two line break codes rather than one. So, when you copy and paste the content to Expression Web 2, an extra line of empty space appears between each paragraph and you have to delete them manually. There are many ways of getting around this problem. One is to copy the content into a pure text editor such as Notepad first and copy it from there into Expression Web 2. But this approach can cause a lot of confusion and extra work because it strips away all the style information and gives you only plain text. There is nothing technically wrong with cutting and pasting content from word processors to Expression Web 2, but it creates a lot of extra work.

Workshop

The Workshop has quiz questions and exercises to help you put to use what you just learned. If you get stuck, the answers to the quiz questions are in the next section. But try to answer them first. Otherwise you'll only be cheating yourself.

Quiz

1. *Why should you use the Import File feature when importing content from an external file?*

2. *In Code view, how do you tell the browser to treat one line of text differently from another?*

Answers

1. Other applications such as word processors apply styling such as font type and size to each individual object. When you cut-and-paste this content into your web page all this styling content comes along with it causing the markup to become cluttered with unnecessary code. The Import File feature strips away most of this extra code and makes it easier for you to format the content properly for the web.

2. To separate and group content HTML uses *tags*. Any content placed between a beginning and an end tag is considered by the browser to be styled by this tag and its attributes and is displayed accordingly. When you apply a particular style to content in Design view you are really wrapping this content in specific tags.

Exercise

Find a Word document you already have on your computer or write a new one. Make sure it has several headings and subheadings along with bold and italicized content and a few lists. With the default.html file open in Expression Web 2, choose Save As under File and select a new name like myTest.html and save it. Delete all the content in your new file and import the content from the Word document. Clean up the code so that it has only styles you can find in the Styles drop-down menu, and all bold and italicized content is strong and emphasized instead. Save the file and test it in your browser to verify that it works properly.

HOUR 5

Get Connected—Building Hyperlinks for Navigation and Further Exploration

What You'll Learn in This Hour:

▶ How to import a new page and link to it

▶ How to create links between pages in your website

▶ How to create links to other websites

▶ How to create links that open in new windows

▶ How to create bookmark links within your page

Introduction

Hyperlinks are an integral part of any website. Hyperlinks (also known simply as *links*) work as both navigational tools within your website and pathways to further resources in your network or on the World Wide Web. They can also perform actions such as opening an e-mail program and sending commands.

The hyperlink in its basic form is nothing more than a colored and underlined segment of text with an address attached. When you click the text, the browser goes to that new address. But hyperlinks don't have to be only text. You can attach them to images, behaviors, and even empty areas within a web page. By knowing the capabilities and limitations of hyperlinks, you can build intuitive, functional, and visually compelling navigational tools and menus to make it easy for visitors to navigate and interact with your site.

For the most part, you use hyperlinks to navigate within your website or link to other websites. But you can also use hyperlinks to give visitors access to other types of files such as documents, compressed archives, and other files. Although a web browser is limited in the file types it can display, it can be set up to interact with other programs on your computer to handle these file types. One such file type encountered often on the Web is Adobe PDF (*Portable Document Format*). If you click a PDF file, your browser asks whether you want to save the file or if you have Adobe Reader or a similar PDF-capable program on your computer. Then the browser automatically calls for the program to open and display the file. The same goes for documents, spreadsheets, and numerous other types of files.

The two most commonly used links are internal links that point to other pages within a website and external links that point to other websites. To start this hour, you make an internal link. But before you can do that, you need to have a new page to link to.

Importing a New Page

Before you can create any hyperlinks you need two pages to link together. Right now, though, your website has only one page. We could create another one, but this is also an opportunity to show you how to import an existing web page into your site.

▼ **Try it Yourself**

Import a New Page to Your Current Project

The lesson files contain a file called myDesk.html. Follow these steps to import that file into your project:

1. From the menu bar, select File, Import, File (see Figure 5.1).

FIGURE 5.1
Importing a new page can be done from the File option under Import in the File menu.

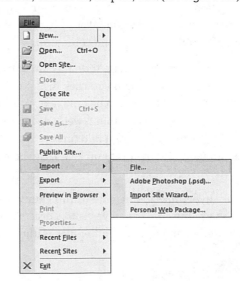

▼

2. In the Import dialog, click Add File and browse to the location where you stored the downloaded lesson files on your computer.

3. Click Hour 5 and select the `myDesk.html` file. Click Open. `myDesk.html` is now visible in the Import dialog (see Figure 5.2).

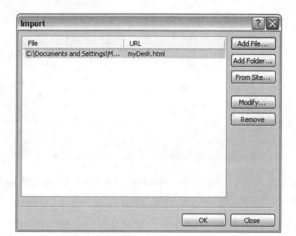

FIGURE 5.2
`myDesk.html` file selected in the Import dialog.

4. Click OK and the `myDesk.html` file shows up in the Folder List task pane.

Creating an Internal Hyperlink

Now you have two files in the My Kipple website project: `default.html` and `myDesk.html`. The next step is to link the two pages to each other with hyperlinks. Open `default.html` by double-clicking the filename and selecting Design view from the buttons at the bottom of the View pane. The first hyperlink you are going to make is an inline link—a segment of text that links to a further explanation of the topic.

Refer to Hour 3, "A Website Is Really Just Text—Build One in 5 Minutes" to see how the default.html page was created. To see how it was modified to its current condition, refer to Hour 4, "Building the Home Page—A Look Behind the Curtain."

Go To!

Inline links are prevalent throughout the Web and are just as useful as menu links because they mainly point directly to highly relevant information or further reading. For example, whereas a menu link might be quite generic and titled something such as "Norwegian Mythological Creatures" or "Scandinavian Christmas Traditions," an inline link would be titled "The Norwegian Nisse" with a link to a page exclusively about this mythical creature.

Did you Know?

Scroll to the bottom of the page and find the last paragraph. On the first line, high-light the words *all the kipple on my desk*. These six words will be the link to the new myDesk.html page. Right-click the highlighted text and select Hyperlink from the menu that appears. Doing so opens the Insert Hyperlink dialog (see Figure 5.3).

FIGURE 5.3
The Insert Hyper-link dialog.

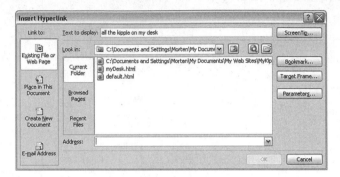

From this dialog, you have complete control of your hyperlinks. On the left you have four options that set where you are linking to:

▶ Existing File or Web Page—Lets you link to a file within your current site or enter a URL to an external web page.

▶ Place in This Document—Lets you link to bookmarks within the document. A *bookmark* is a destination within a document that can be targeted by a link. Longer documents such as FAQ (Frequently Asked Questions) lists and registries use bookmarks heavily.

▶ Create a New Document—Lets you link to a new page you have not created yet. You define a name for the new file and have the option to edit it right away or simply link to the blank page now and edit it later. This is useful if you are building a menu but haven't created the target pages. The reason for this op-tion is obvious: You can't link to something that doesn't exist!

▶ E-mail Address—Creates the code necessary for the browser to open the default email program on the computer and insert a recipient address and even a de-fault subject line if you so choose.

URL means *uniform resource locator*. A URL is the address that takes you to a web page, a file, or a specific server location. The URL to my website is http://www.pinkandyellow.com and the URL to my blog is http://blog.pinkandyellow.com.

In this case you are linking to an existing file, so pick the first option. The Text to Display field shows the text you highlighted earlier. This text will become the link and be visible on the page. If you change the text here, the text in the page changes as well. Directly underneath is a standard browser where you can find and select the file you want to link to. As you can see, the main window lists both `default.html` and `myDesk.html`.

> Expression Web 2 assumes that you are intending to link to other files within your website, so these files are the first option you get. You can navigate away from this folder and link to other files, but any file you link to should always be either inside your website folder (or one of its subfolders) or a file that is already on the Web. Never link to a local file that is not in your website folder unless your website is only for use on your computer—the link will not work anywhere else.

Select `myDesk.html`. Its address shows up in the Address bar. The last step is to add a ScreenTip to the link. This is not necessary, but is required if you want your site to be standards compliant. A *ScreenTip* is a short line of text that pops up next to the mouse pointer when you hover over a link. It gives the user more information about the link. To add a ScreenTip, click the ScreenTip button in the upper-right corner of the Insert Hyperlink dialog. In the Set Hyperlink ScreenTip dialog that opens, type **Learn more about the kipple on my desk** and click OK (see Figure 5.4). Click OK in the Insert Hyperlink dialog to finish the hyperlink.

FIGURE 5.4
The Set Hyperlink ScreenTip dialog.

The text you highlighted before is now blue and underlined, indicating to the visitor that it is a link. Save the file and test it in your browser (see Figure 5.5).

If you hover over the link, a small box with the ScreenTip appears. And if you click it, the browser navigates to the linked file `myDesk.html`. But there's a small problem: After you get to `myDesk.html`, you have no way to get back unless you use the navigation buttons in the browser. You need to create a Home link in the `myDesk.html` file to link back to `default.html`.

FIGURE 5.5
`default.html`
with the new link
and its Screen-
Tip as it appears
in Firefox.

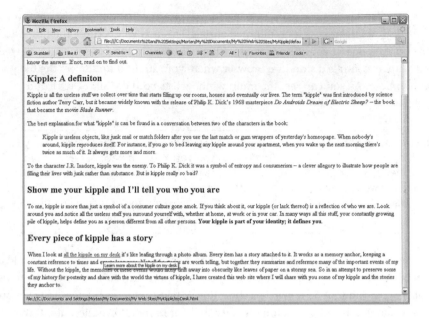

▼   **Try it Yourself**

Create a Home Link in `myDesk.html`

It's important to give the visitor an easy way to get back to the main page of any
website. The easiest way to do this is to create a Home link.

1. Open `myDesk.html` in Design view by double clicking it in the Folder List task pane.

2. With the cursor at the beginning of the first line of the heading, press Enter
   once to shift the heading down one line. Use the Style menu to change the style
   of the new line to Paragraph.

3. Type the word **Home** and highlight it. Then right-click the highlighted word and
   select Hyperlink from the menu that appears.

4. In the Insert Hyperlink dialog, select the `default.html` file and use the Set Hyperlink ScreenTip dialog to give it the ScreenTip text *Go back to My Kipple.*

5. Click OK. Save and test the file in your browser, making sure the ScreenTip
   works and that it links back to `default.html`.

▲

Hyperlink Syntax: Absolute, Relative and Root-relative

As you are creating hyperlinks in Expression Web 2 you will notice that the syntax of the
actual link address changes depending on what you are linking to. There are actually three
different ways of writing a hyperlink address, all of which are used for different purposes.

Absolute hyperlinks are complete addresses that contain all the elements of a URL. They always start with "http://" followed by the domain name (for example "www. pinkandyellow.com") and the destination page if necessary. They are used when linking to pages outside of the current site that have a different domain name.

Relative hyperlinks are addresses that are relative to the current domain or location. They only contain the name of the target page prefixed with any necessary folder moves (for example "default.html"). The browser sees that this is a relative hyperlink and applies the domain and folder location of the current page to the beginning of the link to complete it. If you use relative hyperlinks and you want to navigate from a page stored in one folder to a page stored in a different folder you add the folder prefixes to the hyperlink. For instance a relative link from a page in Folder 1 to a page in Folder 2 would be "../Folder 2/page.html" where the "../" tells the browser you want to go out of the current folder and into a new one. When you create hyperlinks between pages in Expression Web 2 they are always inserted as relative links so that the application can easily update them if you choose to move files around. However if you move the files outside of Expression Web 2, the hyperlinks will be broken.

Root-relative hyperlinks are a subset of relative hyperlinks where all the links are assumed to start from the root folder (domain name) of the site. They differ from the relative hyperlinks in that the address is prefixed by a forward slash (for example "/default.html"). The browser only applies the domain to the beginning of this link. Root-relative hyperlinks are used in place of relative ones in large sites where there is a chance the files will be moved around without using an application like Expression Web 2 to update them. Because they refer to the root of the site rather than the current location of the page they are placed in they will work regardless of where the file is placed as long as they remain under the right domain.

Creating External Links and New Windows

Now that you have created some internal links, it's time to link your website to other external websites. You do this in much the same way that you created your internal links, but instead of selecting a file from your computer, you go to the link's destination and find its URL to insert.

In the second paragraph of the home page (`default.html`) is a reference to the book *Do Androids Dream of Electric Sheep?*. Some of the readers of this website might want to buy this book. Why not give them a link to the book's page on Amazon.com? To do this, you first need the address. In your browser, go to www.amazon.com and search for *Do Androids Dream of Electric Sheep?*. Click one of the search results to get to the book's main page. You want the long string of text in the address bar. Highlight the entire address and copy it by using Ctrl+C (the universal copy shortcut), or right-click the address and select Copy (see Figure 5.6).

FIGURE 5.6
Copying the
Amazon.com
URL for the book
can be done by
right-clicking and
selecting Copy
from the context
menu.

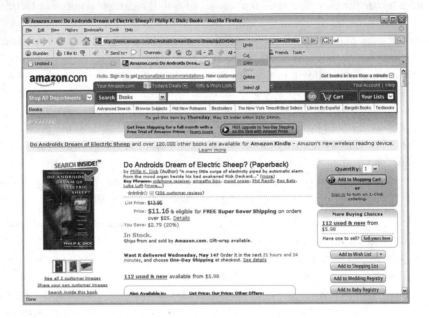

Back in Expression Web 2, highlight the book title in the second paragraph, right-click it, and select Hyperlink as you did before. In the Insert Hyperlink window, select Existing File or Web Page and paste the Amazon.com URL into the Address field by clicking in the text box and pressing either Ctrl+V (universal paste shortcut) or right-clicking and selecting Paste (see Figure 5.7).

FIGURE 5.7
Pasting the Ama-
zon.com URL for
the book by right-
clicking and se-
lecting Paste
from the menu.

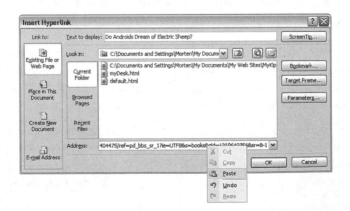

Using the Browsed Pages Option To Obtain Hyperlinks

If you don't want to copy and paste the URL from the browser there is an alternative built into Expression Web 2: The application is connected to the Internet Explorer browser history which means you can get the URL from right inside the program itself. To use this option go to the desired target location in Internet Explorer before creating the hyperlink. Once inside the Insert Hyperlink dialog click the Browsed Pages option (seen in figure 5.8) in the main window to get the browsing history. From here you can select any of the pages you have visited with Internet Explorer recently and the URL to that page will automatically be inserted for you.

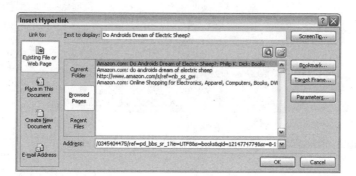

FIGURE 5.8
The Browsed Pages option gives you access to the recent browser history from Internet Explorer.

Open the ScreenTip dialog and type **Do Androids Dream of Electric Sheep? is available from Amazon.com.** Click OK twice and save the new file. Test it in your browser.

But here is a new problem: After the visitor clicks the link, she goes to Amazon.com. How does she get back to your site? Unlike the myDesk.html file, you can't insert a home link in the Amazon.com page. How do you keep your visitor on your site and still let her visit other sites? You edit your site so that external links open in a new window.

Try it Yourself ▼

Set a Link to Open In a New Window

Sometimes you want your links to open in a new window either to keep the visitor on your site or to display relevant information without forcing the visitor to navigate away from the page she is currently on.

1. Right-click the Do Androids Dream of Electric Sheep? link you just created and select Hyperlink Properties (see Figure 5.9).

▼

2. In the Edit Hyperlink dialog, click the Target Frame button on the right.

3. In the Target Frame dialog, select New Window under Common Targets. This tells the browser to open a new window.

4. Double-click OK, save the file, and test it in your browser.

Now when you click the link to the book, the page opens in a new window or tab in your browser. This is a basic way to make links open in new windows.

In Hour 16, "Using Behaviors," you will learn how to use behaviors to make more advanced new windows and pop-up windows.

Creating Links Within Documents Using Bookmarks

Another type of link you can create is a *bookmark*, a hyperlink that points to a specific position in the current page. Designers most often use this type of link to help people navigate larger documents by providing a menu that leads to different sections. Bookmarks are also effective for linking directly to footnotes. Before you make bookmark links, you have to insert the bookmarks in your document. In `default.html`, highlight the first subheading (Kipple: A Definition). Select Insert, Bookmark from the menu bar, or click Ctrl+G. This opens the Bookmark dialog. From here you can set the bookmark's name. The name becomes the address of the bookmark and is included in the hyperlink. For that reason, underscores replace all spaces (see Figure 5.10).

FIGURE 5.10
The Bookmark dialog.

You can change the bookmark name to whatever you want, but it's a good idea to keep it consistent and meaningful, especially if your document has many bookmarks.

When you click OK, you see that the title now has a dotted underline. This is a visual indicator that the text has a bookmark attached. Follow the same process and attach bookmarks to the two other subheadings.

Now all you have to do is make a menu with links to the bookmarks. This menu should go directly under the main heading. Make a new paragraph under the main heading by clicking the beginning of the first paragraph and pressing Enter. In the new first paragraph, create an unordered (bulleted) list. Each list item should be identical to the subheadings, like this:

► Kipple: A Definition

► Show me your kipple and I'll tell you who you are

► Every piece of kipple has a story

Highlight the first bullet point and right-click to open the Hyperlink dialog. By selecting Link to Place in This Document from the left side menu, you open a list of the three bookmarks you created. Select the one that matches your title (see Figure 5.11).

FIGURE 5.11
The Bookmark option under the Insert Hyperlink dialog lets you link to a location within the same page.

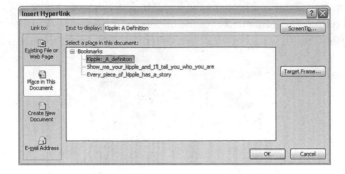

As before, attach a ScreenTip such as Jump to Kipple: A Definition to keep your page standards compliant. Finally click OK and save.

Do the same with the two other menu items. When you are done, save and test in your browser. You'll see that when you click the links, the browser jumps to the bookmarked section. Because the document is relatively short, it might not look like anything is happening when you click a link. But if you reduce the width of your window to about half the size of your screen and then click the links, you should see the page jump. Note that because a bookmark link is no different from any other link, the navigation buttons in your browser work on it as well.

Creating an Email Hyperlink

The final option in the Hyperlink dialog is the E-mail Address link. With this option, you can create a link that opens the visitor's preferred email program and sets the To address and Subject lines. This is the easiest way to provide contact information to your visitors because they don't have to copy and paste or type out the email address themselves.

To create an email hyperlink, you first need some text to work as a link. On the very bottom of the home page, add a new paragraph and type **If you want further information about my kipple, send me an e-mail.** Highlight the *send me an e-mail* portion of the text and open the Insert Hyperlink dialog. Select E-mail Address from the left side menu to open the email options. In the E-mail Address line, enter the email address you want the message to go to. When you start writing, the program automatically inserts a line of code, **mailto:**, directly in front of your address. This code tells the browser that this is not a regular link but an email link. In the Subject line, type the default subject line that you want emails generated from the website to have (see Figure 5.12). The Recently Used E-mail Addresses option displays

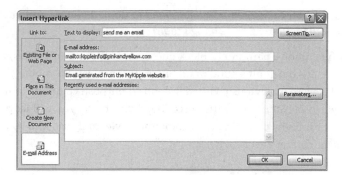

FIGURE 5.12
The E-mail
Address option
under the Insert
Hyperlink dialog
lets you insert a
receiving e-mail
address as well
as a default sub-
ject line.

the most recent email addresses you linked to within Expression Web. Remember to set a ScreenTip for your email link and click OK.

When you test the page in your browser and click the new link, your computer opens your default email program and starts an email with the address and subject line you chose.

Summary

Hyperlinks are what set the World Wide Web apart from other informational sources. By enabling the user to quickly navigate through large amounts of content and instantly move from one source to another, hyperlinks revolutionized the way we find and use information. In this hour, you learned how to create hyperlinks within your own site, to the outside world, and even within one document. Hyperlinks are core components of any website and create navigation as well as links to the rest of the Web. You also learned how to create links that open in new windows. In Hour 16, you will learn how to expand on this technique using Expression Web's built in behaviors.

Q&A

Q. **When I copied and pasted the subheading into my unordered list, the text kept the dotted underline. Is this a problem?**

A. If you copy and paste content such as text in Design view, all the associated attributes come with it. In this case, you copied not only the text itself but also the bookmark. To get rid of the bookmark, highlight the text, right-click, and select Bookmark Properties. Simply click Clear and Expression Web removes the bookmark.

Q. *Why are all my links blue and underlined? I don't like blue and I don't like the underline either. Can I change them?*

A. As with headings, paragraph, block quote, and other default styles, the link or \<a\> style has a default setting in all browsers. That default is blue and underlined. Likewise a previously visited link has a purplish color. In Hour 10: Bringing Style to the Substance with Cascading Style Sheets, you will learn how to style your links by changing their color, font style, and size, and by adding underline and other effects.

Q. *What is the difference between a menu and a link?*

A. A menu is just a series of links styled to look like something else. On a website, any item that takes you somewhere else when you click it is just a link created in the same way you created links in this hour. The reason they look different is that they have heavy styling and use graphics instead of just text.

Workshop

The Workshop has quiz questions and exercises to help you put to use what you just learned. If you get stuck, the answers to the quiz questions are in the next section. But try to answer them first. Otherwise you'll only be cheating yourself.

Quiz

1. *What kind of content can a hyperlink be applied to?*

2. *What are the three different types of hyperlinks and when are they used?*

3. *How does a bookmark differ from a "regular" hyperlink?*

Answers

1. Hyperlinks can be applied to any and all content in a page although it is advisable to restrict them to smaller items like short text segments or images.

2. The three types of hyperlinks are absolute, relative and root-relative. Absolute links are used to link to pages that are not inside your current site. Relative links are used to link to pages that are within your site. Root-relative links are used to link to pages that are within your site when there is a chance the pages will be moved around without using Expression Web 2.

3. Bookmarks are used to make the browser navigate to a certain location within the current page so instead of loading a new page it jumps down or up in the current page to a different location.

Exercise

Throughout the `default.html` page are several items that you can link to sites with further information. For instance, you could link the name Philip K. Dick to the Wikipedia.org page about the author and the name Blade Runner to the imdb.com page about the movie. Use the Web to find further information on these items and make links that point to these sources. Make sure you attach a ScreenTip to each link and that each one opens in a new window.

Get Visual, Part 1: Adding Images to Your Page

What You'll Learn in This Hour:

▶ What the main image file types are and when to use them

▶ How to import an image into Expression Web

▶ How to insert an image into a page

▶ How to change the placement and appearance of an image in a page

Introduction

Because the World Wide Web is a visual medium, making your website visually pleasing is important. The easiest way to do this is by adding images to the text. But images can be so much more than just eye candy. As hinted at in Hour 5, "Get Connected—Building Hyperlinks for Navigation and Further Exploration," an image can also be used as a link or even as a navigational tool. If you dissect websites, you will find images used as borders, backgrounds, buttons, underlines, and even text. The possibilities are endless.

In the past heavy use of images in web sites was frowned upon mostly because people were on slow dial-up connections and the images made the pages heavy and slow to load. But now that broadband internet is becoming more and more prevalent throughout the world web designers rely heavily on image elements to make their sites look better.

The bottom line is this: Used correctly, images can be a great tool to enhance the look and feel of your website.

Images on the Web: Three File Types for Three Uses

At first glance, it looks like all images on the Web have the same format. But in reality they are different. Web designers choose different file formats, with different attributes, depending on how they plan to use an image. That choice in turn affects how a page looks and works.

There are three main image formats currently supported by most browsers. They are GIF (Graphics Interchange Format), JPEG or JPG (Joint Photographic Experts Group), and PNG (Portable Network Graphics). Each format has advantages and limitations:

▶ The GIF format produces the smallest files for quick downloads. Unfortunately, the image quality of a GIF file is quite poor. When introduced, the GIF format was the only transparent alternative available. It gave designers the option to create graphics that could display on top of other graphics or without an unsightly box around them. But this transparency is coarse and effective only with images that have clean lines. In addition, the GIF format can display only up to 256 colors, severely limiting the kinds of images that designers can use it for. For these reasons, the GIF format is best suited for computer-generated content and line drawings. Today's designers use the GIF format mostly to display small icons and buttons (see Figure 6.1).

FIGURE 6.1
A GIF image with transparency on a white background and a transparent background. The file size is 3.82KB.

▶ JPEG or JPG is the most common image format on the Web. Its success stems from its high compression rate and low image noise. JPEG has become the standard format for images not only on the Web but also in digital cameras and other devices. JPEG is a compression format that uses advanced algorithms to recalculate the image data and remove content that is not easily noticed by the human eye. Among the many different things a JPEG compressor does is even the colors, duplicate similar looking areas and compress the actual image code to make it shorter. At high quality settings JPEG compression can be excellent but if you set the compression too high the image can end up looking a bit like a paint-by-numbers painting. The JPEG is "solid" and cannot be made transparent.

FIGURE 6.2
A JPEG image with minimum compression to the left and maximum compression to the right. At minimum compression, the file size is 21KB; at maximum compression, it is 14.2KB.

▶ PNG is the newest of the formats. What sets the PNG format apart is that it has an alpha layer that tells the browser what portions of the image are transparent. As a result, you can superimpose PNGs on top of other images with full transparency. Unlike the GIF format, PNG transparencies are clean but this ability comes at a price: PNGs are much larger files than the two other formats. Even so, the ability to create advanced transparencies makes the format ideal for logos and other superimposed and hovering graphics in websites. Some older browsers do not support PNG transparencies.

FIGURE 6.3
A PNG image with transparency on a white background and a transparent background. Note that unlike the GIF format, the transparency in the PNG is clean. The file size is 7.1KB.

Importing and Inserting an Image

Images are the most common nontext elements featured in web pages. And because images are so heavily used, there are many different ways to handle them depending on how the designer plans to use them.

The easiest use is simply inserting an image into a page. To do that, you need to import the image file into your project. But before you do, it's a good idea to start thinking about how your site is organized. Look at the Folder List task pane, and you see that your site currently consists of two pages: `default.html` and `myDesk.html`. Now you are adding image files to your site, which means they appear alongside your two HTML files. If you were adding just two or three images, this wouldn't be a problem. But as you saw in Hour 2, "Beginning at the End: A Walk-Through of the Finshed Project," the final site has a large number of images and files. So, before things get too complicated, it's a good idea to start organizing everything in folders. In other words, you need to make a folder for your images.

▼ **Try it Yourself**

Create a New Folder and Import a New Image

Folders serve as effective tools for keeping your site organized. Websites have a tendency to fill up with files fast, and it's important to think about file organization early. The Folder List task pane gives you easy access to all the files and folders in your site, and you can use it to create new files and folders as well as organize them.

1. In the Folder List task pane, click the New Folder icon or right-click and select New, Folder (see Figure 6.4).

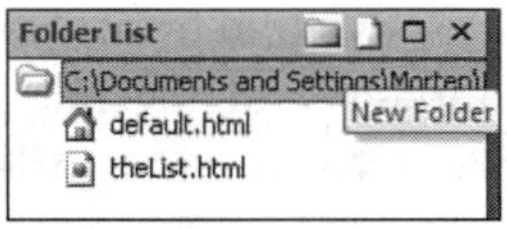

FIGURE 6.4
One of several ways to create a new folder is to use the New Folder button in the Folder List task pane.

Folder List
C:\Documents and Settings\Morten\...
default.html   New Folder
theList.html

2. Name the new folder Images and double-click it.

3. Select File, Import, Import File as you did in Hour 5. In the Import dialog, click Add File and browse to the location where you stored the downloaded lesson files on your computer.

4. Click Hour 6 and select the file called `desk.jpg`. Click Open and then click OK. Expression Web copies the file and stores it in the Images folder. You can see it in the Folder List task pane by clicking on the + icon next to the Images folder (see Figure 6.5).

Watch Out!

Expression Web is quite finicky when it comes to image files. If you add images into your website without importing them through Expression Web, they might not work properly in Design view and you see a small square with a red X instead of the image. This doesn't mean that there is anything wrong with the image; in fact, if you preview the page in a browser, you will see that the image is there. The problem has to do with how Expression Web handles files internally. The best (and only) way of avoiding this problem is to make a habit of importing all image files properly through the Import File dialog.

▼

FIGURE 6.5
The imported image file as it appears under the Images folder in the Folder List task pane once the + icon has been clicked. If you click the - icon the folder is closed and the + icon reappears.

Now that Expression Web has imported the image into your project, it's time to insert it into a page. You can do this in Design view by dragging and dropping the image into the text. To start, open the myDesk.html file. In the Folder List task pane, click and hold the desk.jpg file and drag it to Design view. You will see a grey dotted marker jump around inside the text indicating where image insertion point. Place the image at the beginning of the first paragraph under the heading and let go. Doing so opens the Accessibility Properties dialog (see Figure 6.6).

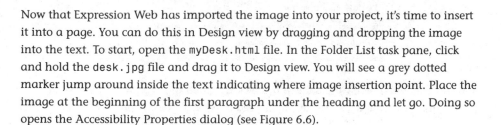

FIGURE 6.6
The Accessibility Properties dialog lets you customize the information attached to the image for those who can't view the image itself.

The Accessibility Properties dialog gives you the option to attach alternative text and a longer description to your images. Some visitors cannot see the images in your page because they are using a text-only browser, a portable device, or a text-to-speech browser. The alternative text displays in place of the image for these users and helps to explain what the image shows. The alternative text should be a description of what the image is. In this case, enter My very messy desk in the Alternate Text text box, and click OK. Expression Web 2 inserts the image in the text at the beginning of the first paragraph (see Figure 6.7).

FIGURE 6.7
The inserted image as it appears in Design view.

Save the file and preview the page in a browser. Something is a bit off—the image breaks the text and leaves a large empty area to the right (see Figure 6.8).

FIGURE 6.8
The page with the inserted image as it appears in Firefox.

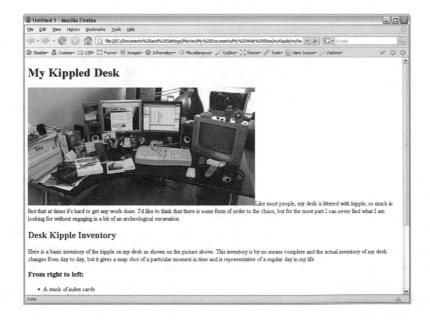

This big void appears because by default web browsers consider images to be "inline" elements meaning they appear along side the other elements on the line just like a letter or word. To fix this problem you need to tell the browser that the image should not be considered part of the text but rather an object the text should wrap around. This can be done using the Picture Properties.

Using Picture Properties to Change the Appearance of an Image

After an image is part of a web page, there are properties and functions available to tell the browser how to display the image and how the image should relate to the surrounding content. In addition to simple HTML properties, Expression Web gives you access to a plethora of image-editing options normally found only in imaging software such as Photoshop and Expression Design. You can access some of these options by right-clicking the image and selecting Picture Properties from the context menu. Doing so opens the Picture Properties dialog (see Figure 6.9).

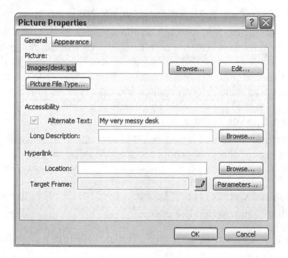

FIGURE 6.9
The General tab of the Picture Properties dialog.

The General Tab

On the General tab, the Picture field tells you what file you are currently working with. You can change the file by using the Browse button or by typing a new filename in the Picture text box.

Directly underneath the Picture text box is the Picture File Type button. If you click this button, a new dialog opens (see Figure 6.10). From here you can convert the file you are working with to any other main image format with a few mouse clicks. If you change the file type in this dialog, Expression Web automatically replaces the image on your page. When you save the page, a dialog asks you where you want to store the new image file.

FIGURE 6.10
The Picture File
Type dialog lets
you change the
file type of your
images.

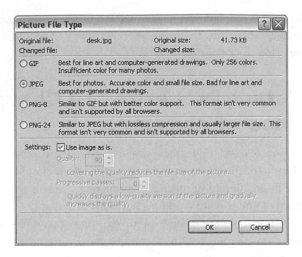

Expression Web 2 Is Not An Image Editor!

Even though you are presented with the option of using Expression Web 2 to change the file formats for images it is not something I would suggest you do. Expression Web 2 is not an image editing program and the options you are given are both restrictive and potentially destructive. By changing the file formats of your images you could inadvertently reduce the quality of your images to the point where they are unusable. For example by changing a transparent PNG to a low resolution JPEG image you could easily end up with an image you can't use at all.

As much as possible, try to use a dedicated image editor to make changes to your images and import the final product into Expression Web 2.

The next section of the General tab is Accessibility. This displays the same options that appeared when you inserted the image.

The final section is Hyperlink. Here you can make the entire image into a hyperlink pointing to a different page, a different site, or a file.

The Appearance Tab

The Appearance tab contains all the code controls for the image (see Figure 6.11). This is where you instruct the browser how to handle the image in relation to other content. The functions under the Appearance tab are styles that Expression Web applies to the image. In later hours, you will learn how to create styles that apply to all images in a site so that you don't have to set them for each individual image.

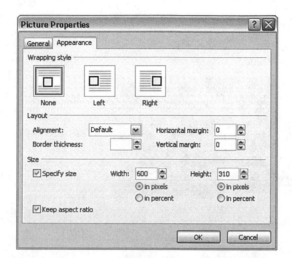

FIGURE 6.11
The Appearance tab of the Picture Properties dialog controls the image in relation to the other content on the page.

▶ The **Wrapping Style** options define how the surrounding text wraps around the image. The three buttons are good illustrations of what the different options mean. None (the default) tells the browser to handle the image as if it were part of the text. This means that the image lines up with the rest of the text like a very large letter and pushes the remaining text to the right to make room. Left means that the image lines up against the left side of the window and the text displays on its right. Right works the same way as the Left option, except the image is now on the right with the text on the left.

▶ Alignment settings apply only if the wrapping style is set to None. In the **Layout** section, the Alignment option gives you control over where the image lies in relation to the remaining text on the line. For example, if you set the alignment to Top, the top of the image aligns with the top of the text line. If you set the alignment to Middle, the middle of the image aligns with the middle of the text line (see Figure 6.12). And if you set the alignment to Bottom, the bottom of the image aligns with the bottom of the text line. Expression Web gives you eight different positions in addition to Default.

FIGURE 6.12
The Alignment attribute is set to Middle, centering the line of text vertically in relation to the image.

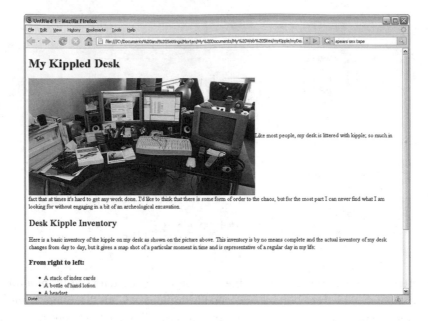

The Layout section also contains the Border Thickness setting (which defines a border or outline for application to the image) and the Horizontal Margin and Vertical Margin settings (which create empty space on the four sides of the image).

▶ The final section of the Appearance tab is **Size**, where you can manually set the size of the image either in pixels or in a percentage of the original size. You can also toggle the Keep Aspect Ratio option on and off. As a rule of thumb, always keep the image size the same as the original file and never change the aspect ratio. If you change the image size, you leave it up to the browser to resize the image and its quality drops dramatically as a result. Changing the aspect ratio distorts the image by making it either too squished or too stretched out. In Hour 7, "Get Visual Part 2—Advanced Image Editing, Thumbnails, and Hotspots," you will learn how to use one of Expression Web's built-in functions to create a thumbnail (small version of your image) that links to the larger version, thereby avoiding the need to resize your images manually.

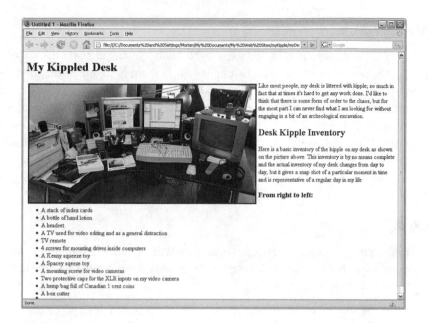

FIGURE 6.13
The page as it appears in Firefox after you style the image.

Try it Yourself ▼

Change the Properties of the Image

By default, an image inserted into a page appears directly next to the line of text where the designer placed it and the image breaks the text. To make the page more appealing, it is necessary to separate the image from the text and give it some breathing room.

1. Right-click the image and select Picture Properties. Select the Appearance tab.

2. Click Left in the Wrapping Style section to align the image to the left and wrap the text to the right.

3. Set the border thickness to three pixels using the up and down buttons or by typing **3** in the box.

4. Set the horizontal and vertical margins to five pixels by using the up and down buttons, or by typing **5** in the boxes, and click OK. Save the file and preview the page in your browser.

The image now appears to the left with the text wrapped to the right. The image has a three-pixel black border, and there is a five-pixel space between the image and the surrounding text. ▲

Summary

Images are an important part of any website. Not only do they increase the visual appeal of the site, but they can also help make the content more interesting and informative. In this hour, you learned that three main image formats are in use on the Web and that each has advantages and disadvantages. You also learned how to import images into your project and organize them in folders. At the end of the hour, you learned how to insert an image into a page using Design view and how to manipulate that image with the functions available in the Picture Properties dialog. You now have the basic building blocks to create a page with text and images.

Q&A

Q. *When I imported an image into Expression Web, it didn't end up in the Images folder but was stored alongside the files in the main folder. Why did this happen and how can I fix it?*

A. If the file you imported was stored in the main (or root) folder, you didn't select the subfolder before you started the import process. To avoid this problem, before you start the importing process, always double-click the folder you want to import files to. If a file ends up in the wrong folder, simply go to the Folder View task pane and drag the file into the right folder. Expression Web automatically updates all the files that link to the file and ensures that they still point to the right place.

Q. *When I inserted an image into my page I accidentally grabbed one of the image's sides and changed its size. Now it looks all weird and stretched. How do I fix it?*

A. If you make a mistake and notice it right away, the easiest way to fix the problem is by selecting Edit, Undo on the menu bar or using the shortcut Ctrl+Z. You can also reset the image to its original size and dimension by opening Picture Properties and unchecking the Specify Size box. Doing so returns the image to its original size.

Q. *When I dragged and dropped an image into a page, it ended up in the wrong place. What do I do now?*

A. The image you placed can be moved anywhere on the page simply by grabbing it with the mouse and dragging it to a different location. Because an image acts like part of the text, you can place it anywhere within the text in the same way you move around words and paragraphs. When you grab an image and move the cursor outside its border and into the text, a small fuzzy gray cursor indicates where the image will land.

Workshop

The Workshop has quiz questions and exercises to help you put to use what you just learned. If you get stuck, the answers to the quiz questions are in the next section. But try to answer the questions first. Otherwise you'll only be cheating yourself.

Quiz

1. *Why is it important to always provide alternative text when inserting an image into a web page?*

2. *What are the differences among GIF files, JPEG files, and PNG files? When would you use each format?*

Answers

1. The alternative text displays whenever the image is not loaded because the connection is too slow, the image is not available, or the visitor is using a text-only or text-to-speech browser. The alternative text is both a courtesy to these users and a necessary substitute if your images do not load.

2. A GIF is a small file size, low-resolution image that can display coarse transparencies. GIFs mainly display smaller icons and simple line graphics. JPEG is the predominant image file format used to save photos. Digital cameras and most other devices save images in this format. The JPEG format has good compression and relatively small file size. PNG is an image file format that has image quality the same as or better than the JPEG format, with the added bonus of clean transparencies. Unfortunately this comes at the price of a larger image file. Some older browsers do not support PNG transparencies.

Exercise

Insert a second copy of the desk.jpg image into the myDesk.html page anywhere you want. Give it alternative text of your choice. Use the Picture Properties dialog to position the image on the right side of the screen, to give the image a thin border, and to provide more margin space than you gave the other image.

Get Visual, Part 2: Advanced Image Editing, Thumbnails, and Hotspots

---

What You'll Learn in This Hour:

▶ How to use the Pictures toolbar to insert and edit images

▶ How to create thumbnails using the Auto Thumbnail function

▶ How to create and edit hotspots

Introduction

Now that you know how to import and insert an image, it's time to look at the new image-editing tools featured in Expression Web 2. The program goes beyond the norm and gives you several quick and easy tools to make changes to your image files—changes that would normally require an image editor. One such feature is the ability to make thumbnails with a few mouse clicks. In this hour, you will learn how to use these tools to make changes to image files you have already inserted into your page.

In addition to being visual elements, images in a web page can be functional elements if you turn them into links and buttons. You can even designate separate areas within an image to interact with the user either by highlighting when the user hovers over them or by linking to other images or pages. You do this by creating hotspots in your image.

Exploring the Pictures Toolbar

In Hour 6, "Get Visual Part 1—Adding Images to Your Page," you learned how to insert an image into a page and how to use the Picture Properties dialog to change the way the image relates to the other content on the page. But what if you want to change the appearance of the image itself? Maybe after you inserted it into the page you noticed that it was too light or needed cropping. Normally this requires you to open the image file in an image editor such as Photoshop or Expression Design, make the necessary changes, reimport the image into Expression Web 2, and finally replace the image on your page with a new one. Well, those days are over. Expression Web 2 has a built-in set of tools to help you do simple image editing without leaving the program. The Pictures toolbar conveniently contains these tools (see Figure 7.1).

FIGURE 7.1
The Pictures toolbar gives you instant access to all the image editing features in Expression Web 2.

As you learned in Hour 1, "Get to Know Microsoft Expression Web 2," all you have to do to open the Pictures toolbar is select View, Toolbars on the menu bar and click Pictures. The Pictures toolbar opens as a hovering toolbar that you can move around the work area. Normally it's easier if you dock your toolbars to the top or sides of the window, but in this case, leaving the toolbar floating makes the next steps easier.

If you haven't already done so, open the myDesk.html file. To activate the functions of the Pictures toolbar, click the image you inserted in Hour 6, "Get Visual Part 1—Adding Images to Your Page." Expression Web 2 always tells you which functions are available by graying out those that are unavailable. Place your cursor anywhere else inside the page and notice that the icons in the toolbar gray out and become unavailable.

The Buttons of the Pictures Toolbar and What They Do

With the image selected, hover over each button to view its ScreenTip and see what function the icon represents.

 Insert Picture

> Insert Picture from File is the only button that remains active no matter where you are in the document. Clicking this button lets you insert a new image in the current cursor location or replace the selected image with a different image.

 Auto Thumbnail

> When you click Auto Thumbnail, Expression Web 2 creates a small version of the selected image and inserts it on the page in place of the larger one. The smaller image (the thumbnail) is fitted with a hyperlink that points to the larger image.

 Bring Forward

Bring Backward

> The Bring Forward and Bring Backward buttons tell the browser to change the stacking order of your content. A good analogy is to think of the page as a deck of cards; when you click the Bring Forward or Bring Backward button, you move the current card up or down in the stack. You use these functions when

you start placing content on top of other content—for example, text on top of an image.

▶ The orientation buttons change the orientation of the image. They are Rotate Left 90° (counter-clockwise), Rotate Right 90° (clockwise), Flip Horizontal, and Flip Vertical . These buttons are useful if you import an image from a digital camera whose orientation is incorrect—for example, a photo taken with the camera in a vertical orientation but the image in a horizontal orientation.

 Rotate Left 90°

 Rotate Right 90°

 Flip Horizontal

 Flip Vertical

▶ The More Contrast and Less Contrast buttons bring the contrast levels of the image up or down. If you add more contrast to an image, the bright colors become brighter and the dark colors become darker. If you reduce the contrast, the image becomes more even. The More Brightness and Less Brightness buttons bring the overall brightness level up and down. If you bring up the brightness level, you usually also have to bring up the contrast level to prevent the image's colors from fading.

 More Contrast

 Less Contrast

 More Brightness

 Less Brightness

▶ The Crop button lets you cut out an area of the image and discard the rest, much as if you used a ruler and a knife to cut out part of a photo. The Set Transparent Color button lets you set a specific color to be transparent. This function works only with GIF images. If you apply the function to a non-GIF image, Expression Web 2 converts the image to the GIF format and reduces its color depth. Expression Web 2 warns you about this before performing any changes. The Color button changes the image by giving it a grayscale or washed-out look. Bevel puts a beveled border on your image to make it look as if it's standing up from the page. Designers often use this function when creating buttons from images. The Resample Image button becomes available only if you change the dimensions of the image in Design view or through the Picture Properties dialog. When you click this button, the image permanently changes to the new dimensions rather than simply resizing in the browser.

 Crop

 Transparent Color

 Color

 Bevel

 Resample Image

▶ The next set of tools let you insert and modify hotspots in the image. Select lets you select the whole image or the respective hotspots within it. The Rectangular Hotspot, Circular Hotspot, and Polygonal Hotspot tools set the hotspots within an image. The Highlight Hotspots button replaces the image with an imagemap in which the hotspots are black and the rest of the image is white. This tool is a visual aid to help you find the hotspots and makes no actual changes to the image.

 Select

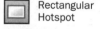 Rectangular Hotspot

 Circular Hotspot

 Polygonal Hotspot

 Highlight Hotspots

 Restore

▶ The most important button on the Pictures toolbar is the Restore button. It restores the image to its original state and undoes all the changes you made to the image since you last saved the page. Be aware that if you save the page you are working in, Expression Web 2 saves the new edited version of the

All the editing functions on the Pictures toolbar (orientation, contrast, brightness, crop, color, and so on) are destructive image-editing tools. *Destructive* means the function permanently changes the file it affects and you cannot reverse the change. For that reason it is paramount that you always keep backup copies of your original image files in case you make changes you are not satisfied with. Likewise, if you use the same image several times throughout your site and you make a change to one of these instances of the image using the Pictures toolbar, the change affects all other instances of that image. If you intend to make a change to an image you are using in multiple locations, you must first make a copy of the image and then apply the change to only the copy.

Using the Pictures Toolbar to Add and Change an Image

Now that you know what the different tools on the Pictures toolbar do, it's time to put them to use. In the project files for this hour is the file KennyOriginal.jpg. This is a picture straight from my digital camera. As you learned in Hour 6, the first step when dealing with an image file is to import it into Expression Web 2 by selecting File, Import File in the menu bar. Make sure the new image is stored in the Images folder in the Folder View task pane. If it isn't there, simply drag and drop the file into the Images folder.

After you import the image, there are three different methods of inserting it into the page. In Hour 6, you used the drag-and-drop option. You can also insert an image by putting the cursor where you want to place the image, opening the Insert, Picture submenu on the menu bar, and selecting From File (see Figure 7.2). Finally, you can use the Insert Picture button on the Pictures toolbar. The last two methods are the same function. Both approaches open a standard browser window from which you select the file you want to insert.

In Design view, place the cursor at the beginning of the second paragraph directly under the Desk Kipple Inventory heading. Use one of the two options described earlier to open the Insert Picture dialog. Navigate to the Images folder and select the KennyOriginal.jpg file you just imported.

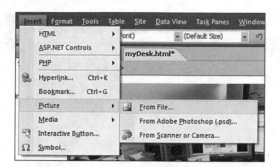

FIGURE 7.2
You can use the Insert Picture from File option on the menu bar to insert an image at the current cursor location.

Expression Web 2 is finicky when it comes to importing image files properly. It is also a bit forgetful when it comes to which files it imported into the program. From time to time, you might notice that recently imported images don't show up in the Insert Picture dialog. To solve this problem, refresh the dialog by right-clicking in the browser window and selecting Refresh.

The same thing goes for the Folder List task pane: Even after images have been imported properly they don't always appear in the file list. To refresh the Folder List task pane click inside it and press the F5 key.

Did you Know?

When you click OK, the Accessibility Properties dialog opens, as it did when you inserted the desk.jpg image in Hour 6. Enter the alternative text **Kenny squeeze toy** and click OK. At this point, you might think you made a mistake because the Design View pane fills with an image that is mostly white with some black in it, much like Figure 7.3.

What you are seeing is the corner of a large image. This is a common problem: The image is not an appropriate size for the Web and therefore it doesn't fit on a web page. In fact, the image you just inserted is more than three times as tall as a regular computer screen. If you click the image and look in the Tag Properties task pane on the bottom left, you can see that the image is 3072 pixels high and 2048 pixels wide. A good rule of thumb is that an image in a web page should never be more than 400 pixels high and 600 pixels wide. So, before you do anything else, you need to drastically reduce the size. To do so, right-click the image, open the Picture Properties dialog, and select the Appearance tab. In the Size section, enable the Keep Aspect Ratio check box and change the Width setting to 400 pixels (see Figure 7.4). The height changes accordingly.

At the same time, change the Wrapping Style setting to Left so that the text moves to the right of the image rather than underneath it. When you click OK, Expression Web

FIGURE 7.3
The page as it
appears in De-
sign view after
you insert the
**KennyOrigina
l.jpg** image.

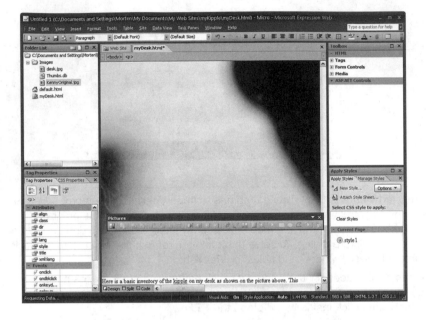

FIGURE 7.3
The page as it
appears in De-
sign view after
you insert the
**KennyOrigina
l.jpg** image.

FIGURE 7.4
You can change
the image to an
exact size from
Picture Proper-
ties.

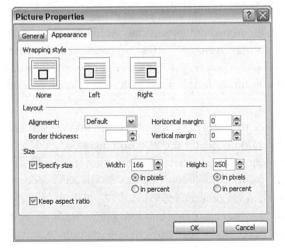

2 reduces the image to a workable size. Now you can alter the image to make it work better within the page. First off, Kenny is facing the wrong way. To turn him to face the text, click the image to select it and then click the Flip Horizontal button on the Pictures toolbar.

The framing of the photo isn't very good and it could use some cropping. With the image still selected, click the Crop button on the Pictures toolbar. This produces a dashed rectangle that indicates the crop area within the image (see Figure 7.5).

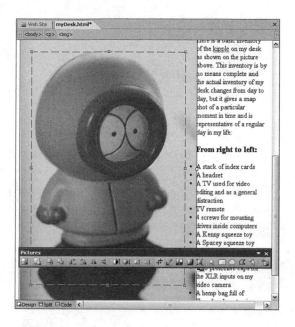

FIGURE 7.5
The crop area in-
side the image
is indicated by a
dotted line with
handles.

Using your mouse, you can either draw a new crop area within the image by clicking and dragging the mouse to create a new rectangle, or simply resize the existing rectangle by grabbing the handles (marked by small squares) in the corners or at the middle of all four sides. Resize the rectangle so that you leave an equal amount of space on all sides of Kenny. When you are satisfied with your crop area, press Enter and Expression Web 2 crops the image.

The photo is a little dark. To lighten the image, select it and click the More Brightness button three or four times. This brings up the brightness of the image slightly.

If you are not satisfied with your alterations, this is the time to start over. If you want to undo any of your changes or just want some practice, click the Restore button to return the image to its original state. If you click the Restore button by mistake, simply go to the Edit menu and select Undo Edit Picture, or press Ctrl+Z on your keyboard.

There is one final step left. You might remember from earlier in the hour that the Resample button becomes active only if you change the size of the image. You might also remember from Hour 6 that you should never make the browser resize your images for you. When you resized the KennyOriginal.jpg image earlier in this hour, you asked the browser to squish the large image down to make it fit certain dimensions. Now you want to resample the image so that the picture in the image file is of the correct dimensions. You can do this in two ways: Either click the Resample button on the Pictures toolbar, or select Resample Picture to Match Size from the Picture Actions drop-down menu found under the small icon attached to the image (see Figure 7.6).

FIGURE 7.6
You can resample the image from the Picture Actions dropdown menu found under the inserted image.

This function overwrites the old image file and replaces it with the reoriented, cropped, and resized image as it appears in Design view. To make the changes permanent (a.k.a. The Point of No Return), simply save the page. Expression Web 2 opens the Save Embedded Files dialog and asks you whether, where, and how you want to save the changed image file (see Figure 7.7). When you are sure the image looks the way you want it to look, click OK and the new image replaces the original one.

FIGURE 7.7
The Save Embedded Files dialog appears every time you have made changes to other external files while modifying the file you are currently saving.

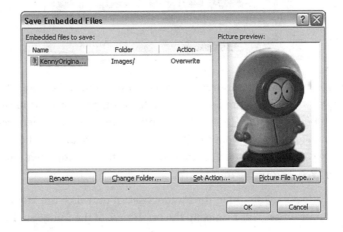

▼ Try it Yourself

Create a Thumbnail Using Auto Thumbnail

Because most web pages contain a lot of content and not all visitors are on high-speed connections, using smaller versions of images (commonly referred to as *thumbnails*) that link to the larger version of the image is common. Using thumbnails helps the page load faster because the browser doesn't have to download large image files. In addition, thumbnails can help designers because they can link to large images rather than inserting them in the page.

In the myDesk.html file, it's obvious that even though you reduced the image to a Web-friendly size, it's still much too big. What you want is a small thumbnail of the

KennyOriginal.jpg image that links to the bigger version. In Expression Web 2, you can do this with a single click of your mouse: With the KennyOriginal.jpg image selected, click the Auto Thumbnail button on the Pictures toolbar or use the Ctrl+T shortcut.

This creates a 100-pixels-wide thumbnail with a blue outline that, when clicked, opens the original full size image in the same window. To finalize this process, it is necessary to save the page. When you save the page, the Save Embedded Files dialog you saw in Figure 7.8 opens and asks you to save a new file called

Hotspot

FIGURE 7.8
Creating a rectangular hotspot around the Kenny figure on top of the TV.

KennyOriginal_small.jpg. This is the smaller thumbnail file that Expression Web 2 created and inserted in your page. By default Expression Web 2 saves the thumbnail in the currently open folder, but you can pick a different folder by clicking the Change Folder button in the dialog. Finally click OK and preview the page in your browser.

If you don't want the thumbnail to have a blue border or you want it to be a different size, you can modify the Auto Thumbnail default settings from the Page Editor Options dialog. To do this, open the Page Editor Options dialog from the Tools button on the menu bar and select the Auto Thumbnail tab. From here you can define the size of the thumbnail by setting the width, height, shortest side, or longest side to a specific pixel length, changing the thickness of the border around the image (0 for no border), and even give the thumbnail a beveled edge.

Note that changes to the Auto Thumbnail settings apply only to new thumbnails and not ones that already exist.

Creating Hotspots

A *hotspot* is a defined area or region within an image that has a hyperlink attached to it. There is no limit to how many hotspots with different hyperlinks you can set in a given image. Hotspots are a great tool if you want to provide further information about a certain element within an image or use an image as a navigational tool.

> Just so there is no confusion: What Expression Web 2 calls a hotspot is more commonly called an *imagemap*.

▼ Try it Yourself

Create a Hotspot and Link It to a File

In Expression Web 2, you can create and edit hotspots from the Pictures toolbar using the hotspot buttons:

1. In the myDesk.html file, click the desk.jpg image to activate the Pictures toolbar. Click the Rectangular Hotspot button, and click and drag the image to draw a rectangle around the Kenny figure on top of the TV (see Figure 7.8). This opens the Insert Hyperlink dialog.

2. In the Insert Hyperlink dialog, find and select the KennyOriginal.jpg file in the Images folder. Set the ScreenTip to **Detail of Kenny squeeze toy** and set the target frame to New Window. Click OK.

▲

Save the page and preview it in your browser. Note that although the desk.jpg image looks unchanged, if you hover your mouse over the Kenny figure on top of the TV, the mouse pointer changes to a hand indicating a hyperlink and a ScreenTip appears. If you click the hotspot, a new window opens showing the KennyOriginal.jpg file.

To edit the hyperlink or ScreenTip attached to the hotspot, simply right-click the hotspot in Design view and select Picture Hotspot Properties. If you want to resize the hotspot, you can do so by clicking it, grabbing the resizing handles, and moving them. You can also reposition the hotspot by clicking and dragging it to a different location within the image.

Hotspots can also be circular or even polygonal. To create a circular hotspot, click the Circular Hotspot button and draw the circle on the image in the same way you created the rectangle earlier. To create a polygonal hotspot, click the Polygonal Hotspot button and use the mouse to define each corner of the hotspot until you outline the desired area. To finalize a polygonal hotspot, you have to set the last corner point on top of the first one. Doing so opens the Insert Hyperlink dialog.

Because it can be hard to see exactly where all your hotspots are located, the Pictures toolbar features a Highlight Hotspots function. Clicking the Highlight Hotspots button replaces the image with an imagemap in which the hotspots have black outlines and the remaining image is gray. If you select one of the hotspots, it turns solid black (see Figure 7.9).

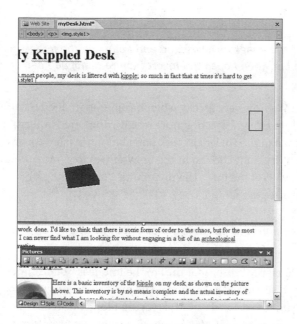

FIGURE 7.9
The `desk.jpg` image with the Highlight Hotspots function turned on.

This tool is only a visual aid and does not affect the image in any way. To close the imagemap and see the original image, simply click the Highlight Hotspots button again or click anywhere outside the image.

Summary

The ability to make quick alterations to images without having to leave the program is a feature that puts Expression Web 2 above the fold. Not to mention that it can be a real time saver as long as you think things through and make backups of your image files before changing them. In this hour, you learned how to use the powerful tools in the Pictures toolbar to edit the appearance of images in your page. You saw that the Reset button on the toolbar gives you the ability to experiment with different effects without ruining your files, and that scaling down large photos to make them fit in your page is a relatively simple task.

You also learned how to use the Auto Thumbnail function to make linked thumbnails of your images with one click. Finally you learned how to set and edit hotspots within an image to create a more interactive and immersive experience for your visitors.

This hour concludes Part I of this book. You now have all the tools necessary to create and edit the content of your website. In Part II, you will learn how to style the content to make it more visually pleasing and easier to read.

Q&A

Q. *I imported the image as instructed and I can see the image in the Folder List task pane but when I open the Insert Picture dialogue I can't find it anywhere.*

A. Expression Web 2 is very finicky when it comes to image files and for some reason it tends to either forget or ignore recently imported images. If you can see the image file in the Folder List task pane but it doesn't appear when you browse for it try right-clicking in the browser window and selecting Refresh. This works 95% of the time. The remaining 5% is usually caused by the image file being corrupt.

Q. *I placed the image in the page but all I get in Design view is a box with a red x in it.*

A. There could be two reasons for this: a) the image is not a supported image file or is not in a supported color mode. The most common cause for this problem is that the image is stored as CMYK (Cyan, Magenta, Yellow, Kelvin) instead of RGB (Red, Green, Blue). CMYK is the color mode for professional printing and does not translate to screen graphics. To correct this you need to open the image in an image editor and change the color mode. b) Expression Web 2 didn't import the image properly. To test if this is the problem preview the page in your browser. If the image appears in your browser it means Expression Web 2 screwed up while importing the image and you'll need to re-import it.

Workshop

The Workshop has quiz questions and exercises to help you put to use what you just learned. If you get stuck, the answers to the quiz questions are in the next section. But try to answer the questions first. Otherwise you'll only be cheating yourself.

Quiz

1. *There are three different methods of inserting an image into your page. Name them and explain how they are used.*

2. *Why should you always use the Resample Picture function when resizing an image on a page?*

3. *How many hotspots can you insert into an image?*

Answers

1. To insert an image into a page, you can drag and drop it directly from the Folder View task pane, use the Insert Picture from File function found under Insert on the menu bar, or use the Insert Picture button on the Pictures toolbar.

2. If you insert a large image on a page and resize it using the Picture Properties dialog, you force the browser to resize the image for you. That means that the browser downloads far more image information than it displays. As a rule of thumb you should always reduce the amount of information downloaded by the browser to an absolute minimum. That means resampling all your images so that the actual image dimensions match the displayed image dimensions.

3. In theory there is no limit to how many hotspots an image can contain. In reality the number of hotspots is limited to the number you can fit within the borders of the image. There is not much sense in inserting so many hotspots that the user can't find them or discern one from another.

Exercise

Use the Polygonal Hotspot tool to create a hotspot around the left screen on the desk and create a hyperlink to the the Pink & Yellow Media Blog located at http://blog.pinkandyellow.com. Give the hotspot a descriptive ScreenTip and set the hyperlink to open in a new window.

HOUR 8

Cracking the Code— Working in Code View

What You'll Learn in This Hour:

- ▶ How to use Code view as a learning tool

- ▶ How to dissect code in Split view

- ▶ How to use IntelliSense to write quick and error-free code

- ▶ What specialized tools are available to you in Code view and how to use them

Introduction

Until now you have worked almost exclusively in Design view using the WYSIWYG (What You See Is What You Get) editor without paying much attention to what goes on behind the scenes. This isn't really a problem because the code Expression Web creates is clean and tidy enough that you don't need to worry too much about it. But if you want to get a full understanding of how websites work and move beyond the basics, understanding at least the fundamentals of coding becomes vital. To this end, Expression Web is a great learning tool because it generates standards-based code out of the box.

You might consider Code view the exclusive domain of web developers and code experts, but the tools Expression Web provides make it easy even for a novice to work in Code view. Not only is it helpful to understand the code end of your site when something doesn't work properly, but you might also want to add custom elements into your site that require access to the back end.

Using Code View as a Learning Tool

More than just a design and development tool, Expression Web is an excellent learning tool for designers and developers of all levels. It's a poorly kept secret that web designers and developers learn from what other people create. By using Design view and Code view, you can do the same no matter what level you are at. Web pages are a bit unusual in that once they are published the code, or blueprint if you will, is available for all to see. That means if you find something you like on a website, you can look at the code to see what is going on and learn from it. In Expression Web, you can even open websites from the Internet without downloading them first. All you have to do is click Open from the File menu and insert the URL to the site you want to take a closer look at. When it is open in Split view, you have full access to all the code and other elements that make up the page and you can see how everything fits together. Just remember that you should never copy code from someone else's page and pass it off as your own. If you use someone else's code, be sure to credit them for it.

In the last four hours, you built a website with two pages containing a variety of content. Now you will use Code view to answer that burning question: How do the pages really work? For a novice, opening a page in Code view can be quite intimidating. Fortunately there is the option of using Split view, so you can see the code and the WYSIWYG editor at the same time.

Code view has a dedicated toolbar you can open from the Toolbar menu under View on the menu bar. For easy access, dock the Code View toolbar under the Common toolbar on top of your workspace. If the Pictures toolbar is still open from the last hour, close it.

To get started, open the `default.html` file in Split view. In Hour 4, "Building the Home Page—A Look Behind the Curtain," you learned that if you click an item in the WYSIWYG editor while in Split view, Expression Web highlights the relevant section of code in Code view. You already know how basic styles such as headings and paragraphs appear in Code view, so let's concentrate on the new elements in the page.

Dissecting Hyperlinks in Code View

In Hour 5, "Get Connected—Building Hyperlinks for Navigation and Further Exploration," you added several hyperlinks to the page. Now you can use Code view to see how they work. Click the hyperlink with the words *all the kipple on my desk* that you created in the last hour. This highlights the same text in Code view. By clicking the highlighted text in Code view and pressing the Select Tag button on the Code View toolbar, all the code within this particular tag highlights (see Figure 8.1). In this case, that is the hyperlink or <a> tag:

```
<a href="myDesk.html" title="Learn more about the kipple on my desk">
all the kipple on my desk</a>
```

The highlighted code shows the basic elements of a hyperlink:

▶ The <a> and </a> tags wrap the content of the hyperlink.

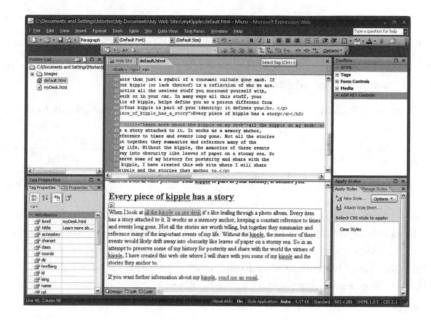

FIGURE 8.1
Using the Select Tag button on the Code View toolbar to highlight the code within the selected tag.

▶ The brackets of the first wrapper contain all the attributes relating to this specific link, separated by spaces. For example, `<a attributeOne="attribute value" attributeTwo="attribute value" attributeThree="attribute value">`.

▶ The destination address is set using the `href` attribute.

▶ The ScreenTip is set using the `title` attribute.

▶ The visible hyperlink text is contained between the `<a>` and `</a>` tags.

If you look at the code for the link to the book on Amazon.com you created earlier in the page, you see that an added attribute, named `target`, is set to `_blank`:

```
<a href="http://www.amazon.com/Do-Androids-Dream-Electric-Sheep/(...)"
target="_blank" title="Do Androids Dream of Electric Sheep? is available
from Amazon.com">Do Androids Dream of Electric Sheep?</a>
```

This tells the browser that the target of the link (that is, what window it should open in) is a new empty window. If no target is set, the link opens in the current window. You can also force the target to be the current window by setting it to `_self`.

At the bottom of the page you inserted a hyperlink to open the default email program on the computer:

```
<a href="mailto:kippleinfo@pinkandyellow.com?subject=Email generated from
the MyKipple website"
title="Send all your questions about this site here">send me an email</a>
```

The `href` attribute in this hyperlink contains a code rather than an address. This code has two sections:

▶ `mailto:` tells the browser that the following is a recipient email address for insertion into the default email program.

▶ `?subject=` tells the browser that the following text is the subject line to insert into the email.

Go To!

> You can learn more about bookmarks in Hour 5, "Get Connected—Building Hyperlinks for Navigation and Further Exploration."

You also created several bookmarks within `default.html`. They are the headings with the dotted underlines in Design view. If you click one of these headings and look at them in Code view, you see that the `<a>` tag wraps them, too. But unlike the hyperlinks, they don't have an `href` attribute. Instead they have a `name` attribute that matches the bookmark name you set in the Bookmark Properties dialog:

```
<h2><a name="Kipple:_A_definition">Kipple: A definition</a></h2>
```

Inspecting the code for the menu items you created at the top of the page, you can see that the `name` attribute preceded by a # works as the hyperlink address to the bookmarks within the document:

```
<a href="#Kipple:_A_definiton" title="Jump to Kipple: A definition">
Kipple: A Definition</a>
```

Hyperlink code can wrap around most elements, not just text. (You can't put a hyperlink around an `<object>` tag, for example.) In the `myDesk.html` file, you created hyperlinks attached to images. To see an example of this, open `myDesk.html` in Split view and click the Kenny figure thumbnail you created using Auto Thumbnail. By highlighting the relevant code using the Select Tag function in Code view, you can see that the only difference between this hyperlink and the earlier examples is that an image has replaced the content between the `<a>` and `</a>` tags:

```
<a href="Images/KennyOriginal.jpg"><img alt="Kenny squeeze toy" class="style2"
height="147" src="Images/KennyOriginal_small.jpg"
style="float: left" width="100" /></a>
```

Images in Code View

In Hour 3, "A Website Is Really Just Text—Build One in 5 Minutes," you learned that all web pages are text documents full of code. But how does that work when it comes to images? When you inserted images into the page, you didn't convert them into code first. And when you click them and inspect them in Code view, all you get is what looks like a hyperlink. So, how do images appear in web pages?

The answer is simple: Images in web pages belong to a group of elements known as replaced elements. A *replaced element* is a segment of code that has no content in itself but instead points to external content that the browser displays in its place. So, when you insert an image into your web page in Design view, you are inserting a small piece of code that tells the browser to find a specific image file, insert it in place of the code, and apply a set of attributes to it.

Select the Kenny figure thumbnail in Design view and look at the section of code highlighted in Code view:

```
<img alt="Kenny squeeze toy" class="style2" height="147"
src="Images/KennyOriginal_small.jpg" style="float: left" width="100" />
```

Unlike the tags you saw earlier, the `<img>` tag doesn't have a corresponding `</img>` tag but rather ends with `/>`, telling the browser that it is closed. This makes sense because as you saw earlier, any text content between a beginning and an end tag is visible in the browser, but there is no such content in the case of an image. Within the tag you find all the information you inserted using the Picture Properties dialog: the `alt` attribute defines the alternative text, the `height` and `width` attributes define the height and width, and the `src` attribute defines the location of the external image file. The remaining attributes, `class` and `style`, are styling elements that Hour 12, "Styling with Code: Fully Immersed in CSS," explains in detail.

When the page opens in a browser, the browser reads the information in the image tag and performs the necessary replacements like this: In this place, insert the `KennyOriginal_small.jpg` image, located under the Images folder, with the alternative text `Kenny squeeze toy`, a height of 147 pixels, and a width of 100 pixels. The image belongs to style class `style2` and should float to the left with the adjoining text flowing around it to the right.

Other replaced elements include, among other things, Silverlight applications, Adobe Flash movies (`.swf` files), both covered in Hour 21, "Working with Flash and Silverlight," and inline frames (iFrames), covered in Hour 17, "Frames and Layers."

Unordered and Ordered Lists in Code View

Working with lists in Design view can get complicated, especially if you have lists within lists. Fortunately lists have a very organized code structure and this makes Code view ideal for advanced list editing.

As you learned in Hour 4, there are two types of lists. Unordered lists, signified by the `<ul>` tag, are what we usually refer to as *bullet lists*. When the browser finds a `<ul>` tag, it assumes that each list item should have a bullet in front of it unless otherwise specified. Ordered lists signified by the `<ol>` tag are what we usually refer to as *numbered lists*. When the browser finds an <ol> tag, it assumes that each list item should have a consecutively higher number in front of it than the last one.

The HTML list structure, regardless of whether it is an unordered or an ordered list, is quite simple. It starts with a <ul> or <ol> tag telling the browser what kind of list it is and then wraps each list item between <li> and </li> tags. The end of the list is indicated by the closing </ul> or </ol> tag. The structure looks like this:

```
<ul>
    <li>First List Item</li>
    <li>Second List Item</li>
    <li>Third List Item</li>
</ul>
```

To change this list from an unordered list to an ordered list, all you have to do is change the <ul> and </ul> tags to <ol> and </ol>.

You can build lists within lists just as easily. The following is an unordered list with three list items where the second one is an ordered list with three subitems:

```
<ul>
        <li>First List Item</li>
        <li><ol>
                <li>First Sub List Item</li>
                <li>Second Sub List Item</li>
                 <li>Third Sub List Item</li>
        </ul></li>
<li>Third List Item</li>
</ul>
```

Go To!

> The items in ordered and unordered lists are usually prefixed by either a number or a bullet but in many cases these elements don't work well with your design. In Hour 13, "Get Visual, Part 3: Images as Design Elements With CSS," you will learn how to turn the numbers and bullets on and off or swap them for image files using CSS.

Tools in Code View

As with Design view, Expression Web has an arsenal of tools available to help you work faster and more effectively in Code view. These tools can be found on the Code View toolbar, in the Toolbox task pane, and inside Code view itself. But first, let's talk about a tool that can help you write code: IntelliSense.

Introducing IntelliSense—Your New Best Friend

IntelliSense is an incredibly useful tool that helps you write proper code faster. The best way to understand exactly what it does is to see it in action. In this example, you insert a new image in Code view with the help of IntelliSense:

1. In Code view, find the subheading Desk Kipple Inventory wrapped by <h2> brackets. Place the cursor at the end of the line and press Enter to create a new line.

2. On the new line, type a less-than bracket: <. A drop-down menu appears below the bracket—this is IntelliSense presenting you with all the available code snippets that start with a less-than bracket. You are inserting an image, so you want the img tag. To find this, enter an **i** and IntelliSense brings up all the available tags that start with **<i** (see Figure 8.2). Use the arrow keys to skip down to <img and press Enter to insert the <img tag.

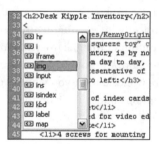

3. Next you need a source for your image. Press the spacebar and IntelliSense pops up with new options. This time it gives you only available attributes for the img tag. As you learned earlier, the image location is set with the src attribute, so type **s** to narrow the search. IntelliSense takes you straight to **src** and all you have to do is press the Enter key.

4. Because the src attribute requires a URL (uniform resource locator), IntelliSense inserts the necessary code and asks you for the location of the image. Click the Pick URL button shown in Figure 8.3 and navigate to the desired file.

5. Before you close the tag, remember to add the alternative text using the alt attribute. This is done by following the same steps as in the preceding steps, but starting with the letter *a*. If you want to, you can add more attributes to your image using IntelliSense.

6. To close the img tag, simply type **/>**. The final code looks like this: **<img src="Images/KennyOriginal_small.jpg" alt="Another thumbnail" />.**

> If you click outside the active text or press Backspace by accident, IntelliSense closes. To open it again, click the List Members button on the Code View toolbar or use the Ctrl+L shortcut.

IntelliSense helps you write a number of different code languages including HTML, CSS, PHP, JavaScript, ASP.NET and even Visual Basic. More importantly, it keeps tabs on your code to prevent you from making errors. For instance, if you insert a beginning tag, IntelliSense automatically inserts a matching end tag. The same goes for braces and quotes. The code output of IntelliSense will match the code settings for the current document. The status bar at the bottom of the work area tells you what code language and version you are working in. If you want to change the IntelliSense settings, open the Page Editor Options under Tools on the menu bar and select the IntelliSense tab.

> You will be introduced to CSS in Hour 10, "Bringing Style to the Substance with Cascading Style Sheets," PHP in Hour 22, "Beyond The Basics Part I: PHP," and ASP.NET in Hour 23, "Beyond The Basics, Part 2: ASP.NET."

The Code View Toolbar

The Code View toolbar has a set of useful tools that can help you write code or understand what is going on inside your code. You have already used a couple of them, but here is a complete description:

List Members

Parameter Info

Complete Word

Code Snippets

▶ The List Members button tells IntelliSense to provide a shortcut menu for the word or segment your cursor is on. The Parameter Info button opens a list of the valid script parameters for the same segment (this applies only to script languages such as JavaScript, ASP.NET, and PHP). The Complete Word button completes the word you are typing based on an educated (and surprisingly accurate) guess.

▶ The List Code Snippets button opens a list of shortcuts to your custom code snippets. Code Snippets is a smart feature in Code view that lets you store frequently used segments of code for easy retrieval through this menu. You can also access the menu by pressing Ctrl+Enter while in Code view. You can add, modify, and delete whatever code snippets you want in the Code Snippets menu by double-clicking the Customize List option and selecting Add.

▶ The Follow Hyperlink button lets you navigate to the destination of the selected hyperlink within Expression Web. The Previous Code Hyperlink and Next Code Hyperlink buttons work in much the same way as the Back and Forward buttons in a browser, taking you back and forth through hyperlinks you have already visited with the Follow Hyperlink button.

 Follow Hyperlink

 Previous Code Hyperlink

 Next Code Hyperlink

▶ The Function Lookup box directs you to the function you select from the drop-down list of the available functions (such as JavaScript or PHP) in your document.

 Function Lookup

---

This box only works if your document contains functions (small programs) that are present in the code. You will create and use functions in Hour 16, "Using Behaviors."

Go To!

▶ Expression Web lets you insert temporary bookmarks that you can use to quickly navigate between segments of your code. The bookmarks appear as small blue boxes on the far left side of the pane next to the line numbers (see Figure 8.4). The Toggle Bookmark button inserts a bookmark at the current line of code. The Next Bookmark and Previous Bookmark buttons navigate between the set bookmarks. The Clear Bookmarks button removes all bookmarks from the document.

 Toggle Bookmark

 Next Bookmark

 Previous Bookmark

 Clear Bookmark

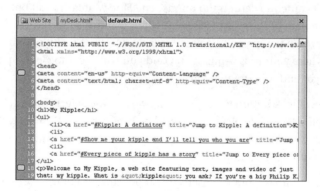

FIGURE 8.4
A Code view bookmark is a small blue box beside the line numbers.

The temporary bookmarks in Code View are solely a visual aid to help in the coding process. They have no actual function in the document itself. These bookmarks should not to be confused with HTML bookmarks which were covered in Hour 5, "Get Connected—Building Hyperlinks for Navigation and Further Exploration."

FIGURE 8.5
The Toolbox task pane.

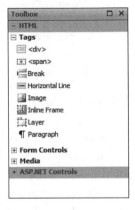

Select
Tag

Find
Matching
Tag

Select
Block

Find
Matching
Brace

Insert
Start Tag

Insert
End Tag

Inseert
Comment

▶ Based on the current location of the cursor, the Select Tag button selects and highlights the active tags and the content within them. This tool is helpful to see what content a certain tag affects. The Find Matching Tag button finds the beginning tag of the selected content when you first press it and the respective end tag when you press it again. This is an excellent tool if you are confused about where your tags begin or end and you can use it to clean up code if beginning or end tags are missing.

▶ The Select Block button works the same way as the Select Tag button except it finds and selects code blocks bracketed by braces rather than tags. The Find Matching Brace button works the same way as the Find Matching Tag button except it also looks for braces rather than tags.

▶ The Insert Start Tag button inserts an empty start tag at the current location. The Insert End Tag button inserts an empty end tag at the current location. You must manually enter the names for these tags.

▶ The Insert Comment button inserts the beginning and end tags for nonfunctional code comments. A *code comment* is text that is visible only in the code itself and has no function other than as a descriptive tool for the developer or anyone else looking at the code. Designers commonly use comments to keep track of changes or explain how or why certain parts of code work.

Common HTML Tags in the Toolbox

In addition to the Code View toolbar, IntelliSense, and Code Snippets, Expression Web also provides a fourth source of commonly used code through the Toolbox task pane (see Figure 8.5). Under HTML, you will find commonly used tags, form controls, and media insertion tools. To use any of these, simply place your cursor where you want to insert the code in Code view and double-click the desired element. You can also drag and drop the elements directly into the code from the task pane. If your Toolbox task pane is closed, you can access the same commonly used code elements along with all other available elements under Insert on the menu bar.

Summary

Understanding the code that makes up a web page can greatly enhance your ability to create professional-looking and functional sites for yourself and your clients. Expression Web's Code view is an excellent tool not only to write flawless and standards-compliant code but also to understand and learn how this code works. With its arsenal of tools, such as IntelliSense, the program keeps tabs on what you are doing and makes sure your code remains valid by inserting all the necessary little extra pieces. It's like having an assistant that looks over your shoulder and makes subtle changes and additions as you work.

In this hour, you learned how to use Code view and Split view to get a better understanding of how the code works. You got an introduction to the many tools for use in Code view, such as the Code View toolbar, IntelliSense, and the Toolbox task pane. You learned how to use those tools and their functions to make quick and error-free changes and additions to your page.

You used Split view to learn a great deal about HTML *semantics;* that is, how the HTML language is put together. Using the Code view tools, you inspected and altered hyperlinks as well as images and by doing so you learned how these code elements work to produce the desired output.

In the coming hours, you will use both Code view and Design view to continue building the MyKipple website. That way you will learn not only how the code works but why it's better to handle some tasks in the back end rather than in the front end.

Q&A

Q. *Why doesn't the* `<img>` *tag close with a separate* `</img>` *tag like the other tags I have used?*

A. Unlike the other tags you have learned about, the `<img>` tag does not affect any visible text but works instead as a replaced element. Any text contained between two tags is visible in the browser. The way you closed the `<img>` tag by simply ending it with `/>` is a shorthand version of the tag code. Ending the tag by closing the beginning tag and following it directly with an end tag produces the same results: `<img src="Images/KennyOriginal_small.jpg" alt="Another thumbnail"></img>`.

Q. *When I insert new code into Code view, other segments of code turn yellow. Why is that?*

A. While you are inserting new code in Code view, you often temporarily break the code. When this happens, Expression Web immediately highlights the incorrect code in yellow to tell you something is wrong. You'll note that when you break the code, only small segments of code actually highlight. Usually these are beginning or end tags. This is because Expression Web tracks the source of the error rather than highlighting the affected area. This makes it easier to clear out any mistakes quickly. On a side note, this function is excellent for debugging websites other developers and designers have created because any errors pop out immediately upon opening them in Code view and can be easily remedied.

Q. *There are all these strange code snippets in my text in Code view, such as* " *and* '. *What do they mean?*

A. If you look closely at the code, you will see that it is full of symbols you would often use in text—symbols such as quotation marks, ampersands, apostrophes, and so forth. These symbols are functional code elements and if they appear as themselves in the code, the browser interprets them as code rather than text elements. To avoid this, all special characters displayed in the text are assigned *HTML entities*; that is, alternative snippets of code that tell the browser which symbol to insert. The most common entities are " for quotation mark, & for ampersand, ' for apostrophe, © for the copyright symbol, and   for a nonbreaking space (used in the same way you would normally press the spacebar if you want to insert an empty paragraph or an empty space). If you don't know the HTML entry for a particular symbol, the easiest way to find it is to simply type in the symbol in Design view and see what it produces in Code view. You can find complete lists of all available HTML entries by searching for *HTML entries* on the W3C (World Wide Web Consortium) website at www.w3.org.

Workshop

The Workshop has quiz questions and exercises to help you put to use what you just learned. If you get stuck, the answers to the quiz questions are in the next section. But try to answer them first. Otherwise you'll only be cheating yourself.

Quiz

1. *How do you find out what tag is affecting a particular portion of the content of your page?*

2. *In this hour you were introduced to two tools that will help you write code. What are they and how do you use them?*

Answers

1. To find the relevant tags for your content, place the cursor anywhere within the content in question in Code view and click the Select Tag button on the Code View toolbar. Doing so highlights the current tags and all content within them.

2. There were two code-writing tools introduced in this hour: IntelliSense and the Toolbox task pane. IntelliSense will help you write proper code by constantly suggesting the closest matching code snippets when you write them and giving you screen tips about what elements this code needs to include to work properly. The Toolbox task pane provides you with drag-and-drop HTML elements for easy insertion into your document.

Exercise

With the help of IntelliSense, use only Code view (not Split view) to insert the KennyOriginal_small.jpg file in the default.html page. Locate the reference to the movie *Blade Runner* in the same page and use Code view to link the text to the IMDB.com entry for the movie. Remember that the active visual link text must be *between* the <a> and the </a> tags. If you are uncertain about the syntax, look at the code for the other links on the page.

Get Boxed In, Part 1: Using Tables for Content

What You'll Learn in This Hour:

- ▶ How to create a table from scratch
- ▶ How to change the appearance of a table
- ▶ How to use the Tables toolbar to work with tables
- ▶ How to use Table and Cell Properties to change the appearance of tables
- ▶ How to use AutoFormat to quickly change the appearance of your tables.

Introduction

So far you have learned about simple text elements such as the headings, paragraphs, and block quotes, as well as lists and links. But these let you display your content in only a linear manner. What do you do if you want to introduce more structured content into your web page or control the position or relation between certain content? In many cases, the answer is tables. Just like in a word processing application, Hypertext Markup Language (HTML) tables can display content in a well organized and structured way. And they work in much the same way as the other text elements, too.

Tables are composed of cells organized in rows (horizontal lines) and columns (vertical lines) just like a spreadsheet. Each element inside the table can be styled to achieve the desired look and feel. You can control the color, size, and appearance of the borders, cells, rows, and columns. Thus, when used correctly, tables can greatly enhance the experience for the visitor by making your content more visually appealing and meaningful.

Five-Minute History of Tables in Web Pages

When HTML originated in the 1980s, it was as a simple standardized markup language for use by physicists to share research data and results on the Web in an easy and manageable way. Much of their data was contained in tables, so tables became an important addition to HTML. But as designers, developers, and the public started to see the potential in HTML and the World Wide Web, the content made available quickly moved beyond simple text documents with a few images and some tables to more advanced designs with background graphics, menus, and advanced interactivity. As the demands of the new users expanded, so did the capabilities of the markup language. As a result, what began as a simple way of communicating text content grew into a hugely complicated code set with heavy focus on the visual aspects of presentation rather than on the content itself.

One of the big elements of this development was the use of tables as a layout tool. If you have ever tried to make content look nice in a word processing application, you know you can use tables to make backgrounds, separate text, and insert other eye candy. This quickly became the standard for web design at the cost of legibility: Nonessential information, such as layout and design code, cluttered the simple HTML markup.

To solve this problem, a new language, called Cascading Style Sheets (CSS), developed. The idea behind CSS was to separate the HTML code from all the styling and layout code and return it to its intended use as a markup language. As CSS became more prevalent, the standard-setting body of the Internet weeded out or deprecated the styling elements that had made their way into HTML.

The idea behind standards-based code, which is what you are making by using Expression Web 2, is to return HTML to its intended use as a markup language and separate it from the styling. In other words, tables are to display tabular data and nothing else. So for example rather than making a menu consisting of a series of table cells with graphic buttons inside you would make a menu using an unordered list styled using CSS.

Go To!

> You will learn how to make specialized menus, such as an unordered list using CSS, in Hour 18, "Making a Functional Menu."

There is an ongoing battle within the design and development community over the use of tables as design elements. I stand firmly on the side of standards-based code and CSS, and only briefly touch on how to use tables as a layout tool. That's not to say doing so is wrong—you are free to design using tables if you choose. But you will not learn how to do so here. With that said, it's time to make tables!

Creating a Table from Scratch

The most use of tables is to display some form of statistical data in which each item has several variables. Good examples of tables are address lists with name, address, phone number, and email address as variables; archives of your books or CDs; or purely statistical data such as temperature variances and financial data. In truth, a table can display any type of information that needs some form of structure.

In this lesson, you create a table based on the contents of your wallet or purse (whichever you prefer). If you don't want to sift through your own belongings, you can find mine in the lesson files. The following steps show you how to create a table in the Design view:

Try it Yourself ▼

Create a Table in Design View

1. Create a new file called myWallet.html, open it in Design view, and give it the heading **The Kipple in My Wallet.**

2. Place the cursor on the next line on the page and click the Insert Table button on the Common toolbar. This opens a drop-down panel consisting of empty boxes (see Figure 9.1). By sliding your mouse over the boxes, you can highlight the number of rows and columns you want. Notice how the box expands if you drag your mouse beyond the five-by-four table initially displayed. The only limit to how many cells you can create is the size of your screen. In this example, you want four rows and three columns. To insert the table, highlight four rows and three columns and click the mouse.

▲

You now have a four-by-three table in your page. By default HTML tables are invisible, meaning they have no color and no borders. They simply separate the content within them, as indicated by the dotted lines.

You can control how tables appear in your page by using the functions found under Tables on the menu bar or by right-clicking the menu and accessing the options from there. But the easiest way to edit your tables is by using the Tables toolbar found under View, Toolbars. If you haven't already done so, close the Code View toolbar from Hour 8, "Cracking the Code—Working in Code View," and dock the Tables toolbar underneath the Common toolbar as in Figure 9.2.

FIGURE 9.1
The Insert Table button on the Common toolbar can be used to easily create tables with different row and column configurations.

Drop down panel

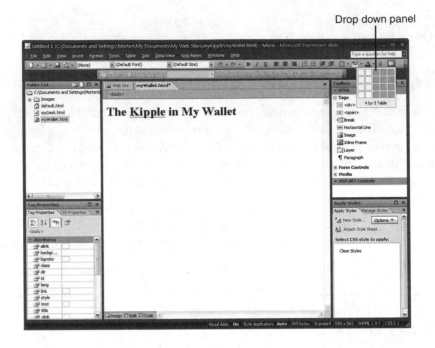

FIGURE 9.2
The Tables toolbar contains most of the tools you need to edit your table.

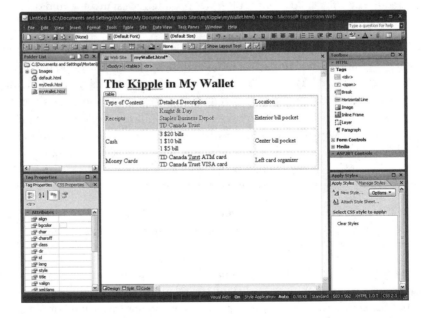

Before going any further, the table needs some content. The three columns represent the three values Type of Content, Detailed Description, and Location. To insert these titles into the first row, select the upper-left corner cell by clicking inside it and start typing. As you write, the cells expand to the right. This is because the cell width and height in a default table is set to auto so that it conforms to whatever content you insert. To move to the next cell, press the Tab key on your keyboard, click the next cell with the mouse, or use the arrow keys. Fill in the next two headlines.

If you want, you can list the belongings of your own wallet or purse or you can simply replace the file you just made with the one from this hour's lesson files.

Changing the Appearance of a Table

When you create a table from scratch, it is set to default. That means all the text in the cells aligns to the left and centers in the vertical space and that all the text looks the same. With the tools built into Expression Web, you can easily change these settings to change the look of your tables.

Creating Table Headings

The first row of your table contains the headings that explains the content below. As such it should stand out. To change the heading row, you first need to select all the cells in the row. You can do this in two ways: either click and hold inside the first cell and drag your mouse over the two others. When the mouse pointer is out of the first cell, it changes to a plus sign indicating that you are selecting more than one cell. You can use this technique to select groups of cells from rows, columns, or both. Alternatively, you can right-click any of the cells in the row and click Select, Row (see Figure 9.3).

With the row selected, you can change the style to Heading 3 to make the headings stand out. You can also change the background color of the cells by clicking the Fill Color button on the Tables toolbar and selecting a new color.

Changing the Vertical Alignment of Cell Content

By default all the content in a table centers vertically in the cells. This looks strange when some cells have one line of text and others have several. To change the vertical alignment of the cells, select the remaining cells using the click-and-hold technique and click the Align Top button on the Tables toolbar. You can choose to align text to the top, center, or bottom of the cells.

 Top

 Center

 Bottom

FIGURE 9.3
You can select a row by right-clicking a cell and choosing Select, Row.

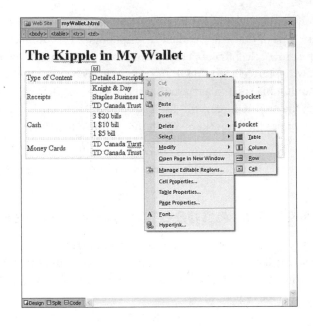

Adding Rows and Columns to the Table

Row Below

Row Above

Column Right

Column Left

When you create a table, you often find that you need to add more rows or columns. If you want to add one or two, the quickest way is to use the Tables toolbar. To add a new row below the last row of your table, select any of the bottom cells and click the Row Below button on the Tables toolbar. You can also add a row above the selected row by clicking the Row Above button. To add a column, you click either the Column Right or Column Left button.

If you want to add several rows or columns, select the cell you want to create new rows or columns next to and choose Table, Insert, Rows and Columns from the menu bar, or right-click and select Insert, Rows and Columns from the context menu. This opens the Insert Rows or Columns dialog where you can set how many rows or columns you want, and whether to insert them above, below, to the left, or to the right of your selection (see Figure 9.4).

FIGURE 9.4
The Insert Rows or Columns dialog lets you insert multiple rows or columns in your table.

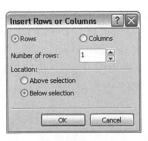

Merging and Splitting Cells

Sometimes it is necessary to merge cells to display certain types of content within the table. Let's say you want to insert a subheading in the table to go underneath the heading and across the whole table. If you simply insert a new row underneath the heading, you still have three columns to work with when you need only one. To insert a subheading in your table, first insert a new row underneath the heading using the Insert Below button. Note that the styling (color) of the heading row is automatically copied down to the new row. After inserting the new row, select all the cells in that row and click the Merge Cells button on the Tables toolbar. Doing so merges the three cells into one. Now you can insert a subheading that goes across the whole table.

 Merge Cells

Likewise, you can split a cell into several new rows or columns using the Split Cell button. After you select a cell and click the button, Expression Web asks how many rows or columns you want to create within that cell.

 Split Cell

You can also merge and split cells by highlighting them, right-clicking and selecting Modify and Merge Cells or Split Cells from the pop-up menu.

 Did you Know?

Deleting Cells, Rows, and Columns from the Table

Now that you know how to add rows and columns to a table, you need to know how to remove them. To delete a cell, right-click the cell and select Delete, Cell from the context menu or click the Delete Cells button on the Tables toolbar. Both actions delete the cell in question and the remaining cells shift to the left to accommodate the deletion. Deleting a cell leaves an empty space filled with the background color.

To delete a row or column, right-click inside a cell on the row or column you want to delete and select Delete, Row or Column or select all the cells in the row or column you want to delete and click the Delete Cells button on the Tables toolbar. Expression Web deletes the row or column and the remaining rows or columns realign themselves to fill the void.

If you delete a cell, row, or column, you also delete all the content within it.

 Watch Out!

To delete an entire table, you can right-click anywhere inside the table and select Delete Table—Expression Web deletes the table.

Changing Row and Column Sizes

When you first entered text into the cells in your table, you noticed that the width of the columns changed accordingly. The same thing happened with the height of the rows when you entered several lines of text in one of the cells. This is because both row height and column width are set to AutoFit by default. In most cases, you want to manually control the height and width of your rows and columns to achieve a certain look. You can do this in several ways:

 Rows Evenly

 Columns Evenly

 AutoFit to Contents

The first method uses the Distribute Rows Evenly, Distribute Columns Evenly, and AutoFit to Contents buttons on the Tables toolbar to make changes to the whole table. To use these buttons, simply place your cursor anywhere inside the table and click the button. The program gives the rows or columns an even distribution based on their content and gives them a fixed height or width.

The second method is a more direct approach by which you manually set the width and height of each row or column by grabbing the margins of the table cells by clicking and holding them with the mouse and pulling them up, down, left, or right. When you let go, the width and height are permanent just like in the first method, but they are now set to your specifications rather than evenly distributed.

The second method also resizes the entire table. By default the table width setting is 100% so that the table fills whatever area it is in (no area is yet defined, so the table fills the entire width of the screen), but you can change it by grabbing the sides of the table and resizing it.

The table's content defines the minimum size of a table and its cells. In other words, a cell cannot be smaller than the size of what is inside it. For example, a cell with three lines of text can not be the height of a cell with two lines of text. Even if you set the height in pixels to be smaller, the cell remains tall enough to fit its contents. And because rows are the height of the largest cell, the content of the largest cell, not the pixel value, which decides how tall each row will be. The same goes for the table as a whole. You cannot make the table smaller than the size of its contents no matter how hard you try. This is one reason why tables are not ideal as layout tools.

Using Table Properties to Change the Appearance of Your Table

If you want to make changes to the size or appearance of the entire table, you need to open Table Properties by right-clicking anywhere inside the table and selecting Table Properties or selecting Table, Table Properties on the menu bar. From here you can change all the main aspects of your table (see Figure 9.5).

The Size setting lets you define how many rows and columns the table should have. The Layout setting sets the alignment and float of the entire table in relation to the page, the width and height of the table in pixels or percentages, and the cell padding and cell spacing.

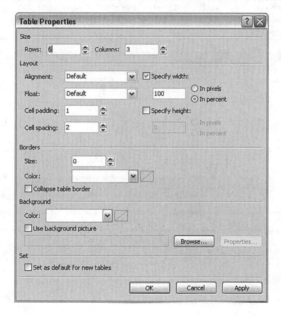

FIGURE 9.5
From the Table Properties dialog you can make changes to the table as a whole.

The alignment and float attributes serve the same purpose: to place the table on the left or right side of the page. The alignment (or align) attribute is deprecated and is being replaced by the CSS float attribute. Therefore, I recommended that you use float to align your table.

Cell padding is the space between the walls of the cell and the content within it (see Figure 9.6). Cell padding of 0 pixels means that the content of the cell is touching the four walls, hereas cell padding of 10 pixels leaves an empty 10-pixel buffer zone between the walls and the content. Cell spacing, as shown in Figure 9.7, is the space between the cells that separate them from each other. Cell spacing of 0 pixels means that the cells touch each other, whereas cell spacing of 10 pixels means there is a 10-pixel gap between each cell. Cell spacing is especially useful if you want to create a table with clearly defined borders between the cells because the cell spacing area is transparent and shows the background color of the table.

FIGURE 9.6
Other than the use of cell padding, these two tables are the same. The cells have a white background color, and the tables have a gray background color.

Table 1: Cell Padding 5 pixels	
Cell 1	Cell 2
Cell 3	Cell 4

Table 2: Cell Padding 0 pixels	
Cell 1	Cell 2
Cell 3	Cell 4

FIGURE 9.7
The cells in these two tables use different values for cell spacing. The cells have a white background color and the tables have a gray background color.

Table 1: Cell Spacing 5 pixels	
Cell 1	Cell 2
Cell 3	Cell 4

Table 2: Cell Spacing 0 pixels	
Cell 1	Cell 2
Cell 3	Cell 4

FIGURE 9.8
Borders in real life: Table 1 as it appears in Figure 9.7 but with the addition of a three-pixel border that wraps around the outside of the table.

Table Border

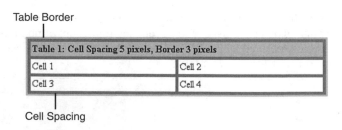

Table 1: Cell Spacing 5 pixels, Border 3 pixels	
Cell 1	Cell 2
Cell 3	Cell 4

Cell Spacing

The Borders setting values define the thickness and color of the border of the table. The border is a box that surrounds the entire table (see Figure 9.8). By default the border is invisible (0 pixels). Depending on the settings, the border can be unique in that it has a 3D look to it: the top and left sides are slightly lighter in color than the bottom and right sides. The Collapse Table Border check box changes the relationship between the table border and the outer cell spacing.

The Background setting sets the background color or background image of the table. By default tables are transparent and the background color or image shines through. If you define the color of a cell or group of cells, they will no longer be transparent. To make a table with white cells and blue lines around each cell, set the table background color to blue and the cell background color to white. The cell spacing remains transparent and lets the blue color shine through and the white cells block the background color.

The Set value lets you define the current table layout as the default layout for future inserted tables.

Using Cell Properties to Change the Appearance of Your Cells

You can also change the appearance of a single cell, or group of cells, in a table by highlighting the cell and selecting Cell Properties from the context menu or choosing Table, Cell Properties on the menu bar. This opens the Cell Properties dialog shown in Figure 9.9.

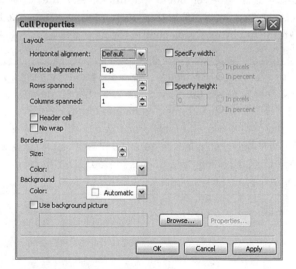

FIGURE 9.9
The Cell Properties dialog.

From here you can change the layout, borders, and background of each cell or a group of cells. The Borders and Background settings work in much the same way as in the Table Properties dialog, but there is some new functionality in Layout:

The Horizontal and Vertical Alignment settings define where the content appears within the cell. Horizontal Alignment works just like alignment in a word processor (left, right, center, justified), and Vertical Alignment defines whether the content within the cell should be positioned on the top, middle, or bottom of the cell.

The Rows and Columns Spanned setting changes the layout of the table by letting the cells span more than one row or column. If you let one cell span two rows, the displaced cells in the row below shift to the right to make room. As a result, the rightmost cell protrudes from the right side of the table. If you let one cell span two columns, the remaining cells in the row shift to the right and the leftmost cell protrudes from the right side of the table. These functions can easily make your table very confusing, so use them with care.

The Specify Width and Height setting gives you the ability to specify the width or height of the selected row or column in pixels or percentages. The effect is the same as when you used the mouse to drag the width and height of the rows and columns, but is more precise because you set the values manually.

The Header Cell setting changes the content of the cells to center-aligned and bold as is normal in table headers. The name *Header Cell* is a bit misleading because you can apply the effect to any cell in a table, not just the header.

The No Wrap attribute tells the cell not to split lines even if they don't fit within the cell. If No Wrap is checked, lines of text that are too long to fit on one line do not continue on the next line but instead hide behind the next cell.

By the Way

When you insert content in a HTML page, the order of the elements applied to that content matters. That is to say the closer an element is to the actual content, the more important it is. In practical terms this means that the *cell properties* are more important and take priority over the *table properties* because they are closer to the cell content. You will meet this principle, referred to as the *cascade*, again when you are introduced to Cascading Style Sheets in Hour 10, "Bringing Style to the Substance with Cascading Style Sheets."

Using AutoFormat to Quickly Change the Look of Your Tables

Making tables more interesting to look at can be an arduous task. To help ease the workload, Expression Web has a long list of prepackaged table layouts at your disposal through the AutoFormat option. To apply one of these layouts, all you have to do is select the table you want to change and click the Table AutoFormat button on the Tables toolbar. Doing so opens the Table AutoFormat dialog shown in Figure 9.10.

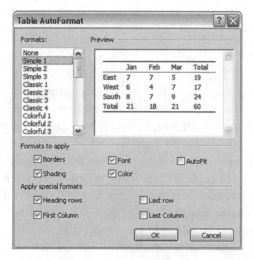

FIGURE 9.10
The Table Auto-Format dialog can be used to make your tables look great with a few mouse clicks.

From here you can preview the various layouts available and make changes to them using the check boxes. All these table layouts are different and the check boxes affect them in different ways depending on the layout, so it's a good idea to experiment to get that perfect look. When you are satisfied with what you see in the preview, click OK and Expression Web applies the AutoFormat. If it is not what you wanted, simply press Ctrl+Z or select Edit, Undo from the menu bar and try again.

If you already know what Table AutoFormat you want, you can select it from the Table AutoFormat Combo drop-down menu on the Tables toolbar. This bypasses the Table AutoFormat dialog and applies the AutoFormat directly.

Table AutoFormat creates a series of different CSS styles and applies them to the table. To change the final look of your table, you need to change these styles. In upcoming hours, you will learn how to modify existing styles and create new ones from scratch.

Using the Table Layout Tool to Make Nonstandard Tables

Draw Layout Table

Draw Layout Cell

Sometimes you might want to make less structured tables or use a table to create a certain layout. This is where the Table Layout Tool comes in. The Table Layout tool gives you the option of resizing individual cells without affecting the other cells on the column or row (as long as you don't try to make them bigger than the row or column or smaller than the content of the individual cell). You can use the Table Layout tool to edit an existing table or you can draw new tables and cells using the Draw Layout Table and Draw Layout Cell functions, all found on the Tables toolbar.

 Table Layout Tool

To activate the Layout tool, place the cursor anywhere inside the table and click the Show Layout Tool button. This changes the appearance of the table in Design view by giving the table a green outline and each of the cells a blue outline (see Figure 9.11). It also tells you the actual pixel size of each of the rows and columns. Hovering the mouse close to the corners or the left and right edges of each cell turns the pointer into an angled symbol to indicate that you can change the size or shape of that cell. If you click and drag the sides or corner of a cell to resize it, the Layout tool creates new cells to accommodate the new layout. You can achieve the same results by splitting cells and changing their widths and heights manually, but the Layout tool makes this process much easier. Be advised that editing an existing table with the Table Layout tool can be difficult because tables are quite inflexible. In many cases it's easier to create a new layout table from scratch than to edit an existing table.

FIGURE 9.11
The table as it appears with Show Layout tool activated.

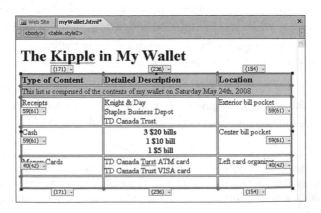

Create a Nonstandard Table Using the Layout Tool

Although you can use the Layout tool to change your existing tables, it is far more useful to create new and nonstandard tables.

1. In Design view, click the Draw Layout Table button on the Tables toolbar. This changes the mouse pointer to a pencil. Draw a new table underneath the old one by clicking and dragging the mouse across the page. Make it slightly smaller than the first table.

2. Click the Draw Layout Cell button on the Tables toolbar and draw a series of cells within the new table. You need to click the Draw Layout Cell button again each time you want to draw a new cell. Make sure the cells are of different sizes and that they don't line up as shown in Figure 9.12.

▲

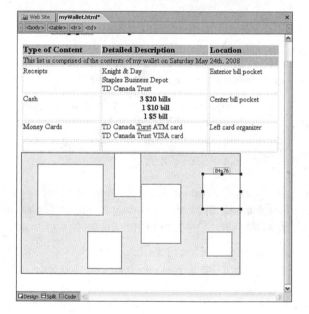

FIGURE 9.12
You can create a nonstandard table by drawing cells using the Draw Layout Cell button.

With this method, you can create tables that bear little resemblance to the normal structured ones. But if you click outside of the new table, you can see that what you created is nothing more than a complicated table with a series of split and merged cells. There are some limitations to drawing new cells in a table by using the Draw Layout Cell function: First, the cells can't overlap. Second, you can draw cells only in the empty areas of the original table. Last, the cells snap to nearby rows, columns, and the outer edges of the table. After you create the new nonstandard table, you can use all the tools and functionalities described earlier to change its appearance.

Summary

Tables are an integral part of web design both as a tool to display data and as a means to create layouts. In recent years, designers and developers have moved away from using tables as a design tool and started using them exclusively for their intended purpose: to display tabular data.

In this hour, you learned how to create tables and how to modify their appearance using the many tools available in Expression Web. You learned how to change the sizes of tables and cells, how to add and remove cells, and how to change the background color of both the table as a whole and individual or groups of cells. Finally, you learned how to create nonstandard tables using the Table Layout tools.

In upcoming hours you will learn how to create page layouts without using tables, and how to use CSS to style your tables to create layouts like the ones you applied with AutoFormat.

Q&A

Q. *It seems cumbersome to first insert a table and then set all the properties. Is there a way to perform both actions at once?*

A. Yes, there is. If you place your cursor where you want the table to appear and select Table, Insert Table from the menu bar, an Insert Table dialog opens with the same options as the Table Properties dialog. Using this function lets you set the table properties before inserting the table.

Q. *You said that the* `align` *attribute is deprecated and that I should use the* `float` *attribute instead. But* `float` *has only an option for left and right and no center. What do I do if I want to center my table on the page?*

A. In the coming hours, you will dive headfirst into the world of Cascading Style Sheets. The idea behind CSS is to move all styling elements out of the main body of the page and into its own section. This applies as much to tables as anything else. In fact, most of the styling you did in this hour was CSS, although you didn't know it. In the next hours, you will learn how to control the styling of your document and an important part of this is to learn how to position and align content on the page. If you are in a hurry and want to get your table centered right away, go to Hour 11, "Boxed In Part 2: Knee Deep in CSS," and read the portion on centering an image using CSS.

Q. *Even though I grabbed the edge of my table and made it smaller, it still appears larger when I preview the page in my browser. What am I doing wrong?*

A. By default the table width setting is 100%. When you change the width by dragging it in Design view, you are not changing it to a pixel width but changing the percentage width. If you want your table to be a set or fixed width, you need to go to the Table Properties dialog and change the width from percent to pixels. Keep in mind that 100 or fewer pixels is a very small size, so you will have to change the pixel size to something larger. After you change the size to pixels in the Table Properties dialog, you can resize the table in Design view and the size stays the same when you preview the page in your browser.

Workshop

The Workshop has quiz questions and exercises to help you put to use what you just learned. If you get stuck, the answers to the quiz questions are in the next section. But try to answer them first. Otherwise you'll only be cheating yourself.

Quiz

1. *There are three different methods for changing the height and width of rows and columns. Name them.*

2. *What is the difference between cell padding and cell spacing?*

Answers

1. To change the height and width of rows and columns, you can use the Distribute Rows and Columns buttons on the Tables toolbar; resize the rows and columns manually by clicking and dragging the dividing lines; or use cell properties to change the height or width of individual cells by entering the desired value in pixels or percentages.

2. Cell padding is the space between the cell walls and the content within the cell. Cell spacing is the space between the cells.

Exercise

Add more rows and columns to the table and insert new content. Change the background color of the table and set the color of the cells to white. Make the table 600 pixels wide and change the column widths so that the first and last columns are smaller than the middle one. Use the Table AutoFormat function to restyle the table so that the rows have alternating colors.

HOUR 10

Bringing Style to the Substance with Cascading Style Sheets

What You'll Learn in This Hour:

- ▶ What Cascading Style Sheets are
- ▶ How to create new styles from scratch
- ▶ How to modify existing styles using the style tools
- ▶ How to use styles to change the appearance of words, sections or even the whole page

Introduction

Although it might be informational, a website with no style is plain boring and probably won't get many visitors. Now that you have a firm grasp on how to create content for your website, it's time to make it look good. Enter CSS, or Cascading Style Sheets, a code language that lets you change the appearance of your pages and sites without messing up the Hypertext Markup Language (HTML) code. This is where Expression Web 2 really excels. With Expression Web 2's built-in CSS capabilities, creating standards-based and cross-browser–compatible styles is easier than ever before, even if you don't understand exactly what's going on.

Expression Web gives you a multitude of ways to create and apply styles, many of which don't require you to write a single line of code. In fact, you can make highly advanced and elaborate styles and layouts using these tools without even glancing at the actual code!

Styles can apply to individual objects, sections of a page, or even an entire site. It all depends on what you, the designer, want to do. Styles can do simple things such as change the font or color of a heading, or advanced things such as position content and set behaviors and multiple styles at the same time. Right now CSS is probably the most powerful tool in a web designer's arsenal and it is the basis of most modern websites and blogs. Designers and developers with strong CSS skills are in high demand, and because Microsoft built Expression Web specifically to handle and generate proper standards-based code and CSS, you already have a leg up just by using the program.

CSS Sans Code

Because of Expression Web's setup, you don't need to know anything about CSS code to create styles in your document. In fact, creating and applying styles to documents can be as easy as a couple of mouse clicks.

Creating Styles with a Click of Your Mouse

In this example, you change the style or look of the subheadings in the `default.html` document. The idea of this exercise is to show you that changing one style can affect multiple sections within the page. If you haven't already done so, open the `default.html` page in Design view.

1. With the `default.html` page open, click the New Style button in the Apply Styles task pane in the lower-right corner (see Figure 10.1). This opens the New Style dialog.

2. In the New Style dialog, open the Selector drop-down menu and scroll down to h2 (see Figure 10.2). Select h2 or, alternatively, type **h2** in the Selector bar. Doing so means the style you are creating applies to all the text that has Heading 2 as its style.

FIGURE 10.1
The Apply Styles task pane.

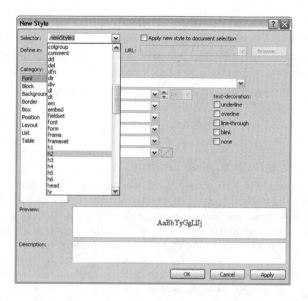

FIGURE 10.2
The New Style dialog showing the Selector drop-down menu with h2 chosen.

3. With the Font category selected, change the `font-family` to Arial, `Helveti-ca`, `sans-serif` with the drop-down menu. Set the `font-size` to 1.2 and change the `units` to em. Set the `font-weight` to bold and `text-transform` to uppercase. Finally change the `color` to gray using the drop-down menu. As you make these changes, you will see the changes in real-time in the Preview box and see the code being generated in the Description box (see Figure 10.3). Click OK to apply the changes.

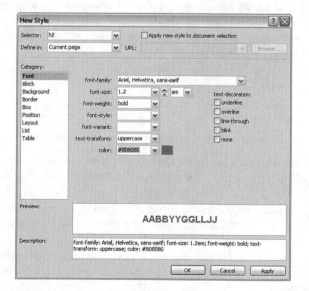

FIGURE 10.3
The New Style dialog with all the new h2 styles set.

By looking through the page in Design view, you can see that the subheadings you styled with Heading 2 have changed. They are now a different font, all uppercase, and gray in color. Now that you've changed the subheadings, you probably want to change the main heading as well. To do so, simply click the New Style button again and follow the same procedure you used to change the subheadings, but change the Selector to h1 instead of h2. Because h1 is the primary heading, it should be slightly larger than h2, so a size of 1.4em is appropriate.

Font Sizes and How to Use Them

When you changed the font size of the styles, you probably noticed that you had many different units from which to choose: px, pt, in, cm, mm, pc, em, ex, and %. You are probably familiar with px (pixel), in (inch), cm (centimeter), mm (millimeter), but pt (point), em (em space; historically the width of the letter m but now the height of the letter m), and ex (x height; the height of the lowercase letter x) are new to most people. You are probably a bit confused also about why there are so many options. When you work in a word processing application you just set the font size, so why do you have to decide what kind of measurement to use when it comes to websites? The answer is both simple and complicated: The content of a website, although most often viewed on a computer monitor, a multitude of different media might display it—from cell phones to text readers and even paper printouts. CSS gives you the ability to define different styles depending on what type of media the viewer is using. So, although it makes sense to size content displayed on a computer monitor using pixels, it might make more sense to size content intended for printouts in centimeters or inches.

There is also the issue of absolute and relative sizes. Inches, centimeters, and millimeters are absolute sizes, meaning that they *should* always be the same size no matter what medium is displaying them. Pixels, em spaces, and ex heights are relative sizes, meaning they will vary in size depending on the medium displaying them and the settings in the program used to display them. (Pixel measurement is a bit different because it is relative based on the pixel size and resolution of the display unit; that is, better resolution means smaller pixels.)

So, how do you decide which unit to use? There is no definite answer to this question, but you are safe if you go by these two rules:

▶ Use px for content that has to have a set size (images, tables, fancy headings, menus, and so on).

▶ Use em for content that the user can resize to facilitate readability.

Many users have browsers that allow them to increase the size of the font on the page. em facilitates this sizing. In contrast, older browsers do not allow resizing of text sized with px.

The downside to using em as the sizing unit is that it is not consistent throughout different fonts, so a size of 1.2em in one font might be small but in another font might be large. On average, 0.8em equals 10 to 12px.

For further reading on the em size and why you should use it I recommend the article The amazing em unit and other best practices found at http://www.w3.org/WAI/GL/css2em.htm.

Creating Inline Styles

The previous example demonstrates how to make styles that affect all the content to which they apply, including new content you add later. If you want to make a style change to just one section of the page and do not use the style elsewhere, you create what is called an *inline style*.

1. In Design view, place the cursor anywhere inside the first paragraph to select it. Click the New Style button in the Apply Styles task pane as before.

2. In the Selector drop-down menu, select (Inline Style). Below the Selector you see that Define In field is `Current tag: <p>`, meaning that this inline style applies to only the content inside this paragraph.

3. In the Font category, set the `font-weight` to `bold`. In the Border category, uncheck the Same for All boxes and set the `border-bottom-style` to `solid`, the `Bottom border-width` to 2px and the `border-bottom-color` to gray (see Figure 10.4). Click OK.

As you can see in Design view the font in the first paragraph is now Bold and there is a 2 pixel thick line separating it from the rest of the text.

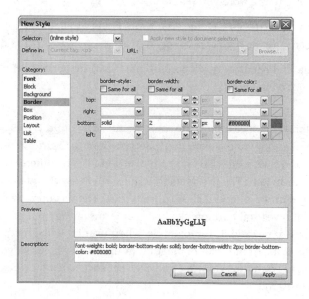

FIGURE 10.4
Under Border in the New Style dialog you can set the style, width and color of each of the four border sides..

Styling Small Selections

In the extreme, you can even set the style of just a small selection of words or even one word or one letter within a word by creating spans within the text and applying styles to them. You can do this in two ways.

Either:

1. In Design view, select the word `kipple` on the second line of the second paragraph.

2. Using the tools available from the Common toolbar, change the `font` to `Courier New`, give the word an outside border using the Outside Borders button, and change the font color to green using the Font Color button.

Or:

1. In Design view, select the word `kipple` on the second line of the second paragraph.

2. Click New Style in the Apply Styles task pane to open the New Style dialog. Check the Apply New Style to Document Selection box to ensure that the style applies only to the word you selected.

3. Under the Font category, change the `font-family` to `Courier New, Courier, monospace`, change the `font-color` to `Green`.

4. Under the Border category, set border-style to `solid`, `border-width` to 1px, and `border-color` to `Green`.

These two methods produce almost the same result: .style1 and .newStyle1, new style classes applies only to the word *kipple,* sets the font to Courier New, changes the color to green, and puts a one-pixel green box around it. The differences between the two methods are obvious: The first method is quick and easy if you are making rudimentary changes and produces a class called .style1. The second method is more cumbersome but gives you far more flexibility in terms of the final product and produces a class called .newStyle1. For example, when using the first method, the color of the box is the same as the color of the font. In the second method, you can set the color of the box to whatever you want and even set each side of the box to a different color (see Figure 10.5).

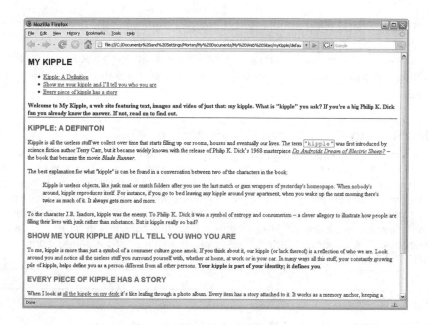

FIGURE 10.5
`default.html`
as it appears in
Firefox with the
inline style and
the span style
applied.

Setting the Font Family for the Entire Document

Now you know how to make changes to preset styles, sections, and individual selections of a document. But what if you want to define certain attributes for the entire page, such as setting all text to one particular font family unless otherwise specified? By default, unstyled HTML text displays in Times New Roman. You can apply styles to *any* tag within the HTML code of the page, even the <body> tag that wraps all the content. By creating a body style, you can affect all the content within the <body> tag (that is, all the content on the page). Here is how to change all the text in the document to Arial, Helvetica using the <body> tag:

1. Click New Style in the Apply Styles task pane to open the New Style dialog. You do not need to select or highlight any portion of the document to create the body style.

2. In the Selector drop-down menu, select body or type **body in the Selector area.**

3. Under the Font category, change the font-family to Arial, Helvetica, sans-serif. Click OK.

By setting the font-family of the <body> tag, you changed to the new font any text that has not had its font-family defined by a custom style. Because you created a special style for the word *kipple*, it retains the Courier font. The same is true for the headings although you can't see it because the body font and the heading fonts are the same.

By the
Way

How Exactly Do Cascading Style Sheets Work?

This last example begs the question "Why does the word *kipple* retain its special font-family even when the font-family for the entire document changes?" The short answer is that this is where Cascading Style Sheets get their name: They work based on a *cascade*, meaning that the last style or rule in the sequence has the highest priority and is the one applied. This is of course a very simplified version of events and it doesn't always apply, but for this book it is sufficient. For an in-depth look at Cascading Style Sheets, pick up a copy of Eric A. Meyer's book CSS: The Definitive Guide.

▼   ## Try it Yourself

Styling Links (AKA Get Rid of the Underline)

You probably noticed that even though you changed the font-family for the entire document, the links retain that garish blue color and underline. The first things new web designers want to know are how to get rid of the underline and change the color of links. As you might have guessed, the answer is by using styles.

In Hour 7, "Get Visual Part 2—Advanced Image Editing, Thumbnails, and Hotspots," you learned that all links are defined using the <a> tag. So, it follows that if you create an a style, you change the links.

1. Click New Style in the Apply Styles task pane to open the New Style dialog. You do not need to select or highlight any portion of the document to change the link style.

2. In the Selector drop-down menu, select a or type **a in the Selector area.**

3. Under the Font category, check the none option under text-decoration (even though it is not checked, the default setting for links is underline, so you have to explicitly tell the browser to not apply this option). Click <$I<body> tag;font family, applying to documents>OK.

Now the underline is gone but the links are still blue. Most designers want their links to be a different color, and to change the color, you have to modify the style you just created. You can do this using the Modify Style function.

1. To access the styles you have already created, click the Manage Styles tab in the Apply Styles task pane. The Manage Styles task pane gives you a list of all the styles relating to the current document and uses visual aids to tell you what styles are active and what styles are applied to the current selection (see Figure 10.6). If you place the cursor on a link, you will see that the a style highlights, telling you that this is the last style in the cascade applied to your selection.

FIGURE 10.6
The Manage Styles task pane gives you information about available styles, active styles, and what style is applied to the current selection.

2. To edit the existing style, right-click the a style and select Modify Style from the context menu. This opens the Modify Style dialog, which is the same as the New Style dialog.

3. Under the Font category, change the font-color to a bright orange using the More Colors option (see Figure 10.7). Click OK.

Now all the links are orange instead of blue. But so are the subheadings!

Using the Cascade to Override Styles

Back in Hour 5, "Get Connected—Building Hyperlinks for Navigation and Further Exploration," you set the subheadings as bookmarks using the <a> tag and now the color of the a style is overriding the color of the h2 style. This is where the cascade shows its true strength: Using CSS you can define multiple attributes to the same content and the browser picks the one that is most relevant based on a set of rules. In this case you want to create a style that applies to only text that is both a subheading and a link.

FIGURE 10.7
The More Colors option is always available whenever you set a color. From here you can pick a color from the expanded palette or use the eyedropper tool to pick a color from anywhere on your screen (even outside Expression Web).

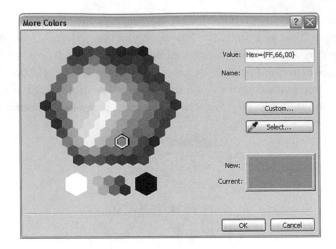

1. Click the New Style button in the Manage Styles task pane to open the New Style dialog.

2. In the Selector bar, type **h2 a**. This literally means *Heading 2 links*. In the Font category, change the **font-color** to gray and click OK.

Now the subheadings return to their gray color because the browser picks the most specific style in the cascade (h2 a is more specific than either h2 or a).

Watch
Out!

Caveat: Not Everyone Has Your Fonts!

You might have noticed when you select a font style that Expression Web offers you font *families* rather than particular fonts. This is because HTML knows that not every computer has every font, so it gives the browser a variety of similar-looking fonts to choose from. There are three main font families based on the most common fonts that almost all computers have installed by default:

Arial, Helvetica, sans-serif

Times New Roman, Times, serif

Courier New, Courier, monospace

All these families work the same way. The browser looks for the first font to see whether the computer has it installed. If not, the browser goes to the second font. If the computer has neither of the two fonts installed, the browser looks for the first font that falls under the category (sans-serif, serif, or monospace).

You can set your text to any font you want but if you go outside the three main font families, you increase the chance that the computers used to view your page don't have the necessary fonts and the page will not display properly. If the browser cannot find the defined font, it picks one of the default fonts—in certain cases that can lead to some strange results.

To be certain your page appears the same across all computers and browsers, I strongly advise you to stick to the three main font families for HTML text.

CSS Tools in Expression Web

Expression Web has a variety of built in tools to help you create CSS correctly and efficiently. You already used some of them in earlier examples, and now it's time to take a closer look and familiarize yourself with each of them individually.

The Quick Tag Tools

Working with HTML documents it can be hard to remember, or even figure out, exactly what is going on because most of the content is in tags within tags within tags. Trying to navigate through this mishmash of code can be a daunting task for even an experienced developer. To fully understand why a certain element or segment of text looks and behaves the way it does, you need to know exactly what tags are applied and in what order. If you had to do this manually, it would be next to impossible. But with the Quick Tag Tools, it is so easy it borders on the absurd. To get a complete ordered list of all the tags applied to an element in Design, Split, or Code view, simply place the cursor on that element and look at the top of the view pane. There the Quick Tag tools list the entire sequence of tags and give you the option to edit each of them individually (see Figure 10.8).

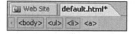

FIGURE 10.8
The Quick Tag tools list all the tags applied to the selected content in order.

The Quick Tag tools also interact with other tools, such as the Tag and CSS Properties task panes and the Apply and Manage Styles task panes, to give you a complete picture of what Expression Web is doing to the content.

The Quick Tag Selector is the bar itself. After you click something in the page, the Quick Tag Selector displays all the applied tags. By hovering over each tags displayed on the bar, you cause a box in Design view to highlight the affected area of that tag. From here you can click any tag in the Selector to display its tag or CSS properties or to show what style is applied. You can open the Quick Tag Tools drop-down menu by clicking the arrow button next to the tag and make changes to the tag without navigating through all the code (see Figure 10.9).

FIGURE 10.9
You trigger the Quick Tag tools drop-down menu by clicking the down arrow next to each tag.

From here you can trigger the Quick Tag Editor that lets you edit the tag by clicking Edit Tag, insert new HTML, and even wrap the existing tag in a new tag (see Figure 10.10).

FIGURE 10.10
You trigger the Quick Tag Editor from the Quick Tag Selector.

You can also remove the tag altogether, change the positioning of the content, or select just the content or the whole tag in Code view.

The Quick Tag tools are an important part of the CSS creation and editing process because all tags have attached styles, and you need to know what tags are at the end of the cascade to see what styles apply to a tag and what if anything needs to be changed.

Did you Know?

Not only are the Quick Tag tools excellent for helping you keep track of your own work, but they also make short process out of dissecting complicated websites designed by others.

The CSS Properties Task Pane

The CSS Properties task pane gives you a more detailed breakdown of what styles are applied to the selected elements and exactly what they do.

Did you Know?

If you can't find the CSS Properties task pane go to Task Panes on the main menu and select CSS Properties. It will appear in the bottom left hand corner.

The top half of the task pane provides a list of all the applied rules or styles (the cascade), and the bottom part lists the attributes applied to the selected rule. You can select individual rules by clicking them in the top half of the task pane or by clicking the tags in the Quick Tag Selector. By default the bottom half of the CSS Properties task pane displays a list of all the available attributes for the selected style. If you want to see only those attributes that have a value, click the Summary button. As you have learned, CSS allows the same attribute to have many different values and the browser picks the one furthest down the cascade. The CSS Properties task pane shows you which attribute values are applied and which are ignored by using a red line to strike out the ones not in use (see Figure 10.11). This way you can easily see how the cascade is flowing and track errors in value attribution.

FIGURE 10.11
The red line shows that the Expression Web is ignoring the **font-family** attribute of the **body** style in favor of the one from **.newStyle1**.

The CSS Properties task pane lets you make direct changes to the selected CSS style by entering new values for all the attributes. This is a quick way to make the same kinds of changes you made in the Modify Style dialog, but it doesn't give you the same kind of trial-and-error environment because all the changes are immediate. The CSS Properties task pane works in direct conjunction with the Apply and Manage Styles task panes.

The Apply Styles Task Pane

The Apply Styles task pane provides a visual representation of the applied and available styles by previewing them in a list (see Figure 10.12). The primary function of this task pane is to provide an easy way to apply styles to the selected content. To do so, simply select the content in Design view and click the desired style.

You can also use the Apply Styles task pane to remove styles from the content and select all the content to which the style is applied on the page.

The Manage Styles Task Pane

The Manage Styles task pane works in much the same way as the Apply Styles task pane, with the one major difference that you can't simply click a style to apply it to a page (you have to right-click it and select Apply Style from the context menu). The

FIGURE 10.12
The Apply Styles task pane displays all the applied and available styles and provides an easy way to apply new styles to the selected content.

Manage Styles task pane provides a complete list of all the styles in the page as well as a preview of the selected style (see Figure 10.13). As the name suggests, the Man-

FIGURE 10.13
The Manage Styles task pane displays a complete list of all styles related to the open page and is an excellent tool for managing these styles.

age Styles task pane is an excellent tool for managing styles both when you want to edit a particular style and also when you start dealing with styles stored in different locations such as multiple style sheets.

The combination of these functionalities makes Expression Web an incredibly powerful tool when it comes to creating, editing, and troubleshooting CSS code. By familiarizing yourself with them you can work not only quicker and more effectively but also learn how to use CSS in a fun and hands-on way.

Color Coding in Apply and Manage Styles Task Panes

A colored dot that sometimes has a gray ring around it prefixes the styles in both the Apply and Manage Styles task panes. The dot's color indicates the category to which each style belongs:

▶ Blue means the style is a selector such as p, h1, a, or blockquote.

▶ Yellow means the style is an inline style.

▶ Red means the style is a CSS ID (prefixed by #).

▶ Green means the style is a CSS class (prefixed by a period [.]).

A gray circle surrounds the colored dot if the style is in use in the current page.

You will learn what CSS IDs and classes are in Hour 11, "Boxed In Part 2: Knee Deep in CSS."

Try it Yourself ▼

Use Various CSS Tools to Apply and Change Styles

Now that you know all the different CSS tools available, it's time to put them to use. In this example, you use the various task panes to apply styles to content and then change the styles without using the Modify Style dialog.

1. In Design view, find and highlight the word *homeopape* in the blockquote.

2. With the Apply Styles tab selected in the task pane, click the .newStyle1 style to apply it to the selected text.

3. Click the <span.newStyle1> tag in the Quick Tag Selector to select the correct style. If Summary is active in the CSS Properties task pane, click the button to deactivate it so that you get a list of all available attributes.

4. Use the CSS Properties task pane to change the font-color to Maroon by clicking the drop-down menu under Font and Color (see Figure 10.14). Scroll down to font-variant and set it to small-caps.

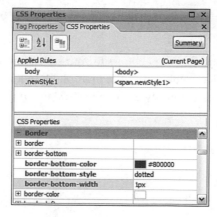

FIGURE 10.14
Changing the values in the CSS Properties task pane makes instant changes to the CSS and the page.

▼

5. To change the border, scroll down until you find the `border` attribute and click the + sign to see all the available attributes. Delete the current attributes by clicking the `border` attribute value and pressing the Delete key or the Backspace key on your keyboard. Scroll down to `border-bottom` (you might have to change the layout of your workspace to see the whole name) and set the `border-bottom-color` to Maroon, the `border-bottom-style` to dotted, and the `border-bottom-width` to 1px.

The changes you just made to the `.newStyle1` style are instant and affect both words that Expression Web applied the style to (see Figure 10.15). This technique is effective

FIGURE 10.15
`default.html`
as it appears in
Firefox with all
the new styles
applied.

for making smaller adjustments or changes to your styles, but be careful: Unlike the Modify Style dialog, you cannot back out of multiple changes with a simple click. If you make many changes to your style, it can be hard to retrace your steps even with the Undo button.

Summary

Using Cascading Style Sheets gives you precise and easy control over how your content appears to the viewer. And with Expression Web's many integrated CSS tools, even a novice can create advanced and standards-based styles without writing a single line of code. In this hour, you learned how to use these tools to edit existing styles and create new ones as well as how to apply styles to the whole page, sections of a page, and individual words. You saw how easy it is to modify existing styles using the Modify Style dialog and the CSS Properties task pane, and how the Quick Tag tools can help you find the relevant tags and styles quickly and decipher complicated code to see how and why elements in the page look the way they do.

Cascading Style Sheets apply to the page in a cascade. In this hour, you got a basic understanding of what this means and how to use this knowledge to style your content and solve problems. But so far you have only scratched the surface of what CSS is capable of. In the next hours, you will learn how to use CSS as a layout tool and unlock its true potential as well as how to move beyond simple point-and-click page styling to full-fledged CSS authoring and the creation of separate style sheets.

Q&A

Q. *I changed my text size from 12 px to 12 em but now the text is incredibly large! What is the correct equivalent to 12 px in ems?*

A. 1 em is the width of the letter 'm' that is defined as standard in the browser the user uses. So 12 em is the width of 12 m's next to one another, thus the huge size. Because em is a relative size measurement there is no correct answer to this question. Depending on what font you are using a 12 px equivalent is usually between 0.8 and 1 em. To get the perfect size you need to do a bit of trial-and-error. Just remember that when dealing with ems you should always use decimals rather than full integers.

Q. *I followed the tutorial and applied a class to some text but nothing happened!*

A. If you created a class and nothing happened one of two things went wrong: Either you didn't actually create the style (by accidentally pressing Cancel perhaps?) or the style wasn't actually applied to the content. First check if the style is listed in the Manage Styles task pane. If it is, click on the element you wanted to style and check the Quick Tag Selector to see if the correct selector or class is applied. If you created a new class and the selector only says <p> or <h1> you need to apply the class manually by selecting the selector and clicking on the class in the Apply Styles task pane.

Q. *When I select the different colors from the drop-down color options they are replaced by a weird code starting with # and followed by six letters and numbers. What is this?*

A. When working with colors in the digital realm every shade has a distinct hexadecimal code preceded by #. That way the color is interpreted the same way by all applications, whether it be an image editor, web browser or word processor. In CSS you set colors by using their hexadecimal codes.

Workshop

The Workshop has quiz questions and exercises to help you put to use what you have just learned. If you get stuck, the answers to the quiz questions as in the next section. But try to answer them first. Otherwise you'll only be cheating yourself.

Quiz

1. *What part of the document does a CSS style apply to?*

2. *What happens if several styles with different values for the same attributes are applied to the content?*

Answers

1. CSS styles are applied to the content within their respective tags; that is to say, a p style will be applied to any content within the <p> tags, an a style will be applied to any content within a <a> tag, and so on. You can also create spans around content and apply styles to them as well.

2. If several different attribute values are applied to the same content from different styles, the browser goes through the cascade and selects the attribute that is furthest down the line or is most specific. In most cases, this means the style that is attached to the closest tag.

Exercise

Two other styles in the `default.html` page were not styled in the earlier examples: the paragraph and the block quote. Use the techniques you learned in this hour to create a p style and a `blockquote` style, and apply some different attributes to them. Remember that because the `font-family` has already been set in the body style, you don't need to change it. Try experimenting with background colors, borders, and text decorations and explore the many different options available under the Font category.

HOUR 11

Get Boxed In, Part 2: Knee Deep in CSS

What You'll Learn in This Hour:

▶ How to create and apply classes to individual tags

▶ How to use divs define sections of content

▶ How to apply classes and IDs to divs to style sections of content

▶ How to use pseudoclasses to give visual cues to the visitor

▶ How the box model works and how to use it to create layouts

Introduction

In the last hour, you learned how to use Cascading Style Sheets (CSS) to style text content. But that's just one small part of what CSS can do. You realize the true strength of the CSS styling language only when you use it not only to style individual elements but also to define different sections within a page that have different styles, and to create and manage layouts and position content.

CSS lets you build a hierarchy of the styles applied to different portions of your page so that a paragraph in one part of the page can have a completely different style from a paragraph in another part of the page. Likewise, CSS can organize content within the page so that certain content appears to the left or right of other content even though it is not in a table.

To understand how CSS operates as a layout tool, you first have to understand the box model. In this hour, you will explore the box model and see how it interacts with your content. Through this knowledge you will get a firm understanding of how putting things in boxes can create advanced and visually stunning layouts without destroying the markup.

CSS Classes—Because Not All Content Should Be Treated Equally

In Hour 10, "Bringing Style to the Substance with Cascading Style Sheets," you learned how to apply styles to a page using the standard selectors such as p, h1, h2, and a. But these styles applied to the entire page, so you had to make an inline style to change the style of just one section of the page. This is an acceptable solution if the change happens only once, but if you plan to use this special style again somewhere else in the page, this approach quickly becomes cumbersome. You need a way of grouping the content into separate classes so that each section can get its own style even though the same selectors define them all—enter CSS classes.

Creating a Class and Applying It to the Content

A CSS class defines a subsection of the content that has its own set of styles. An example illustrates this best: Right now there is no clear separation between the beginning part of the default.html page and the rest of the content. To remedy this, you can make a class to style this portion of the page:

1. With the default.html page open in Design view, place the cursor inside the first paragraph to select it. In the Apply Styles task pane, right-click the inline style you created in Hour 10 and select Remove Inline Style from the context menu. This returns the paragraph to its original appearance.

2. Click the New Style button and change the Selector name to **.header**. The punctuation mark in front of the name defines this style as a class.

3. In the Font category, set font-variant to small-caps. In the Background category, set background-color to a light green using the More Colors palette. In the Block category, set text-align to justify.

4. In the Border category, uncheck all the Same for All Boxes and change the bottom values to solid, 2px, and gray. Click OK to create the new style class.

5. To apply the new class to an existing element within the page, place the selector on the element and click the .header class in the Apply Styles task pane. Apply the .header class to the first paragraph.

When you click the first paragraph after applying the new class, you can see that the p tag in the Quick Tag Selector has changed to include the new class. It now reads <p.header>, as in Figure 11.1.

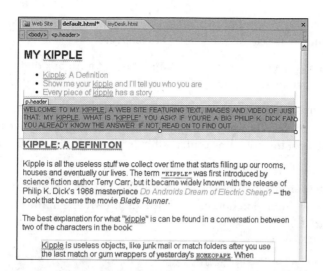

FIGURE 11.1
The `.header`
style applied to
the first para-
graph in
`default.html`
.

Using the method described here to apply a new class results in the class being applied to the last tag in the chain of the selected items. This means that when you have grouped objects such as lists, you have to pick which tags you want to apply the class to. If you click one of the list objects on the top of the page and apply the class, it affects only the selected list item. If you highlight the entire list or select the `<ul>` tag from the Quick Tag Selector, Expression Web applies the class to the list as a whole.

Using CSS Classes to Center an Image

This way of using classes is often preferred when positioning content like images in pages. You might recall from Hours 6, "Get Visual Part 1—Adding Images to Your Page," and 7, "Get Visual Part 2—Advanced Image Editing, Thumbnails, and Hotspots," that the `align` attribute is deprecated. And although you can position elements left and right using the `float` attribute, there is no real option to position items in the center of the page. To properly center nontext content with standards-based code, you need to use CSS. But although you want the *option* to center your images and other content, you don't want to center every image. Making a class to center content is the perfect solution to this problem.

Before you start, replace the current `myDesk.html` file with the fresh one from the project files for this hour. You should do this because when you inserted and changed the properties for the images in Hours 6 and 7, you created a series of styles. This new file has no styles and gives you a fresh start.

1. With the `myDesk.html` page open in Design view, click the New Style button and change the Selector name to **.alignCenter**.

2. In the Box category, uncheck the Margin: Same for All box and set `right` and `left` to `auto` (leave top and bottom empty).

3. In the Layout category, set `display` to `block`. This tells the browser that whatever content this class is applied to is to appear as a separate block or box independent of the rest of the content (that is, on its own line). Click OK to create the new class.

4. Click the Kenny thumbnail and click the new `.alignCenter` class to apply it. The Kenny thumbnail now centers itself on its own line in the page as shown in Figure 11.2.

FIGURE 11.2
The Kenny thumbnail centered using the **.alignCenter** class.

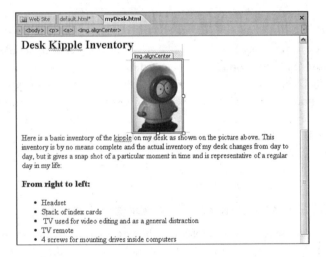

You can create similar classes for `.alignLeft` and `.alignRight` by setting the `display` attribute under the Layout category to `inline` (to keep the image on the same line as the text) and setting the `float` attribute to `left` for `.alignLeft` and `right` for `.alignRight`. That way you don't have to use the Picture Properties dialog to position your images, but you can apply classes to them individually instead.

Using Boxes to Separate Content

Using CSS classes in the ways described in the previous section is an excellent way of applying changes to multiple individual objects throughout a page. But sometimes you want a whole section of a page to have a different look from the rest. You can use classes for this purpose, too, but rather than applying them to selectors such as p, h1, a, and img, you now apply them to a new tag called <div>.

By the Way

I am not entirely sure what <div> actually means. In my research I have found many suggestions, some more vulgar than others, and the one that sounds the most reasonable to me is that *div* is short for *divider*. But it has recently been suggested to me that it stands for *division* so I guess the search for the actual meaning continues.

To understand what the <div> tag does, you need to delve a little deeper into the inner workings of tags and CSS. When Expression Web applies a tag to content, it draws an invisible box around the content. You can see a visual representation of this phenomenon when you hover your mouse pointer over the tags on the Quick Tag Selector bar and the corresponding boxes are outlined in Design view. When you create a style using CSS you are, in reality, applying a set of variables to this box and what's inside it. This is why when you open the New or Modify Style dialog, you always have the option of creating top, bottom, left, and right borders around the content even if it is a single word in a sentence. The <div> and <span> tags are used to create such boxes that wrap around the content and their tags so that attributes such as size, background color, and positioning can be applied to the content as a whole. In short, creating a div and putting content into it is like drawing a box around content on a page.

Creating a Div and Placing It Around Content

To understand when and how you would use divs to wrap content, you are going to apply the .header class to all the content before the first subheading in default.html. As you saw from the previous example, adding the .header class to individual sections of the page causes Expression Web to treat each section as a separate entity (refer to Figure 11.1). Now you want to treat the heading, the list, and the first paragraph as a single entity. Before you go on, remove the .header class from the first paragraph by placing the cursor in the paragraph, right-clicking the .header class in the Apply Styles task pane, and selecting Remove Class. Or you can do so by opening the Tag Editor from the drop-down menu on the <p.header> tag in the Quick Tag Selector bar and removing class="header" from the tag (see Figure 11.3).

1. With the default.html page open in Design view, drag and drop a <div> instance (found under Tags in the Toolbox task pane) into the page. Expression Web can be very finicky about where you can drag and drop a div, so for best results try to drop it slightly below a paragraph. When you properly insert the div, a new empty horizontal box appears (see Figure 11.4).

2. To move the content into the div, simply highlight the main heading, list, and first paragraph with the mouse, and drag and drop it into the div.

FIGURE 11.3
The class is defined within the tag and can be edited using the Tag Editor.

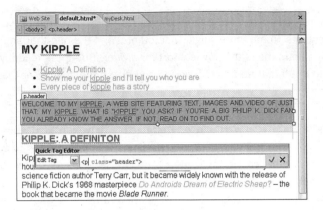

3. With the new content nested inside the div, select the `<div>` tag from the Quick Tag Selector bar and click the `.header` class in the Apply Styles task pane. Expression Web applies the class to the div and, as you can see in Figure 11.5, the tag changes to `<div.header>`.

FIGURE 11.4
Inserting an empty div directly below the first paragraph by dragging and dropping it from the Toolbox task pane.

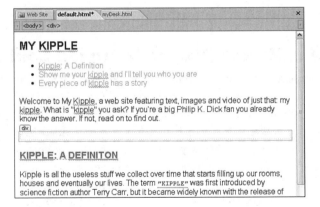

Creating Custom Styles Within Classes

Now that you have created a div with a class, you can create custom styles that affect only the selectors within that class. You do so by making the selector a subelement of the class. To do so, create a new style but give the selector a prefix in the form of the class name. For example if you want to create a custom style for the paragraphs within the div that belongs to the .header class, give it the selector name `.header p`. That way the browser applies this custom style to the paragraphs within the div rather than the standard p style because the `.header p` style is further down the cascade and has preference. You can apply this technique to any standard selector

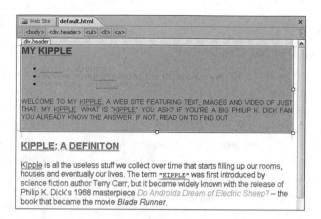

FIGURE 11.5
The `.header`
class is applied
to the div and af-
fects all the con-
tent within it.

whether it is a heading, paragraph, link, block quote, or something else. Many new web designers wonder how you can create several different paragraph styles within one document. Well, now you have the answer!

Introducing ID—Class's Almost Identical Twin

In addition to style classes, you also have style IDs. The ID differs little from the class—so little, in fact, that many wonder why it exists at all.

The ID works in the same way as the class: You can apply attributes to it, apply it to any tag, and create custom styles that appear only within divs that belong to this ID. The only difference between the class and the ID is that whereas you can use the class many times throughout a page, you can use the ID only once. (Or, rather, if you want your page to remain compliant with web standards, you can use an ID only once per page—most browsers allow the repeated usage of the same ID in a page even though it's technically a breach of the standards.)

So, what is the point of using IDs or having them at all? From a designer and devel-oper standpoint, the ID is a great tool for separating content and making the code more readable. As an example, a common practice when designing blogs is to use IDs to define the main sections of the page and classes to define components that re-peat several times within these sections. For example the front page of my blog (http://blog.pinkandyellow.com) has an ID called *content* that holds all the articles and each article is kept in a class called *post*. For someone looking at the code, it is far easier to understand what is going on in large pages if the developer lays out the code this way.

Try it Yourself

Use an ID to Center the Page

Another common question from web designers is how to center the contents of a page using CSS. There is a lot of confusion about how to do this, and most of it results from the fact that people think of web design tools as word processing applications on steroids. But, as you have seen, this couldn't be farther from the truth. In the past, a common way of centering the content on a page was to put it in a one-cell table and center the table using text-align. This is not an ideal solution because it puts all the content inside a table and, as you learned in Hour 9, "Get Boxed in Part 1: Using Tables for Content," tables should be used only for tabular content.

Even so, the table idea is a good one; it's just using the wrong type of box. If you paid close attention to the earlier sections of this hour, you might already have figured out how to do this using only CSS.

1. As before, drag and drop into the page a <div> instance found under Tags in the Toolbox task pane. Place it directly under the div you created earlier.

2. Create a new style and give it the Selector name #wrapper. The # prefix means that this is an ID.

3. In the Box category, uncheck the Margin: Same for All box and set left and right to auto. Leave top and bottom blank (see Figure 11.6).

FIGURE 11.6
Setting the left and right margins of the **#wrapper** ID to **auto**.

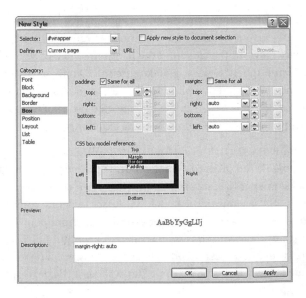

4. In the Position category, set `width` to `600px`. Doing so defines the width of the box. Click OK to create the new ID.

5. In Design view, highlight all the content underneath the new div, and then drag and drop it into the div. Click anywhere inside the first div and use the Quick Tag Selector to select the `<div.header>` tag. Grab the `div.header` block selector on top of the outlined `div.header` box in Design view and drag and drop it into the new div before the other content. When you click the main heading of the page, the Quick Tag Selector displays **`<body><div><div.header><h1>`**. When you click the **`<div>`** tag, a box appears and highlights all the content (see Figure 11.7).

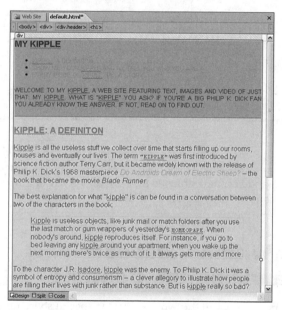

FIGURE 11.7
With the div tag selected in the Quick Tag Selector a highlighted box appears around all the content contained within the new div.

6. Select the div tag from the Quick Tag Selector bar and click the new #wrapper ID in the Apply Styles task pane to apply the ID. The tag changes to `<div#wrapper>`. Save and press F12 to preview the page in your browser. The results should look something like Figure 11.8.

When you apply this ID to your div, Expression Web reduces the width of the div to 600px and tells the browser to place the div within two equally wide margins: one on the left and one on the right. Naturally this results in the div box appearing in the middle of the screen. To position the content to the left or right of the screen, simply remove the two margin attributes and set `float` to `left` or `right` instead.

FIGURE 11.8
The **#wrapper** ID applied to the outermost div reduces the width of the box to 600 pixels and centers the content in Firefox.

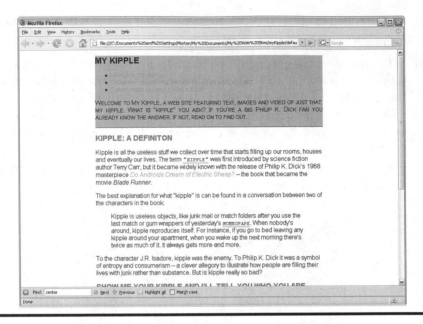

This is the pure CSS method for centering content in the browser. In rare cases it doesn't work properly because some older browsers don't follow or understand proper CSS code and become confused by the margins set to auto. Nevertheless, this is the correct way to perform the task.

Classes Within Classes: Micromanaging the Content

In an earlier example, you saw that you can create special styles for selectors within classes. You can take this technique a step further by applying multiple IDs, classes, and selectors within each other. Take the layout in Figure 11.9 as an example.

In this figure, multiple IDs and classes section different parts of the content. By understanding how to properly name your selectors, you can micromanage the content within these IDs and classes for a highly customized look. You do so by creating selector names that have the relevant IDs, classes, and selectors listed with spaces between them. Here are some examples of different selector names:

▶ p styles all paragraphs on the page, both inside and outside the IDs and classes.

▶ #wrapper p styles all paragraphs within the wrapper ID.

▶ #wrapper #top p and #top p style paragraphs within the top ID only.

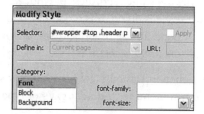

FIGURE 11.9
A layout using multiple IDs and classes to separate the content. IDs are outlined with a solid line and classes are outlined with a dashed line.

▶ `.header  p` styles all paragraphs within the header class regardless of ID.

▶ `#wrapper #top .header p` and `#top .header p` (seen in figure 11.10) style paragraphs within the header class inside the top ID only.

FIGURE 11.10
Setting a highly specific selector name in the New or Manage Style dialog narrows down what content affects by the style.

You can experiment with different selector names by using the `boxExample.html` file found in the lesson files for this hour.

Did you Know?

Pseudoclasses

In addition to selectors, classes, and IDs, HTML supports something called *pseudoclasses*. These specialized versions of selectors come into play when the user interacts with the page; that is, hovers over or clicks content or a link. There are five such pseudoclasses, all of which are normally used in conjunction with the <a> tag:

▶ `:active` refers to an element that is currently active. For example, a link during the time the user is clicking it.

▶ :focus refers to an element that currently has the input focus, meaning that it can receive keyboard or mouse input. To understand focus, think of an input table with the current cell highlighted—that cell has the focus. When you press the Tab button the focus changes to the next cell.

▶ :hover refers to an element being hovered over by the mouse pointer.

▶ :link refers specifically to an element that is an unvisited hyperlink. Unlike the preceding pseudoclasses, :link can apply to the a tag only.

▶ :visited refers to a link that has already been visited. Like the :link pseudoclass, :visited can apply to the a tag only.

▼ **Try it Yourself**

Use Pseudoclasses to Style Links

If you do not define an a style, a hyperlink has :link set to blue, :active set to red, and :visited set to purple. If you define only an a style, it overrides all the default settings and the link appears the same regardless of what the user does. To give the visitor a visual guide to what she is doing, it is a good idea to style the main pseudoclasses for links within your page. To use pseudoclasses, all you have to do is attach them directly after the selectors in the selector name.

1. With default.html open in Design view, create a new style. In the Selector area, use the drop-down menu to find a:active or type **a:active**.

2. In the Font category, set the color to red (**#FF0000**). Click OK to finalize the new style.

3. Create a new style and give it the selector name a:hover. In the Font category, check the underline box under text-decoration. Click OK to finalize the new style.

4. Create a new style and give it the selector name a:visited. In the Font category, set the color to gray (#808080). Click OK to finalize the new style. You can see the result in Figure 11.11.

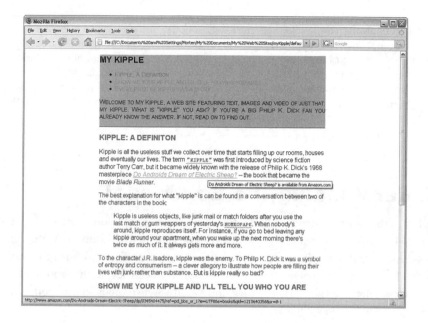

FIGURE 11.11
The different pseudoclasses applied to the **<a>** tags in **default.html** become visible only when you preview the page in a browser.

You will not see any changes in Design view, but when you save and preview the page in your browser, you will see that the links on the page are orange when they have not been visited and are not being hovered over. They have an underline when they are being hovered over, turn red when you press and hold them, and turn gray if they have already been visited. Note that because you attached the pseudoclasses to the general a style, they are applied to all the instances of the <a> tag in the page including the subheadings that work as bookmarks. And because the pseudoclasses are more specific, they override the h2 a link as well. If you want the h2 links to have separate pseudoclasses from the other links on the page, all you have to do is create a new style with a selector name such as h2 a:hover.

For even more advanced control, you can combine several pseudoclasses by stacking them. As an example, right now when you hover over a link, it retains the current color and displays an underline regardless of whether you visited it before. By creating a separate style with the selector name a:visited:hover, you can display hovered-over visited links in a different color. Just as with selectors, classes, and IDs, you can attach any styling attribute to pseudoclasses.

You can apply the pseudoclasses `:active`, `:focus`, and `:hover` to many selectors, not just links. For example, the `:hover` pseudoclass is sometimes used to highlight sections of lists, tables, and paragraphs to help with readability. When doing this, it is important to make the nonlink components visually different from the links to avoid confusing the visitor. The `:hover` style applied to nonlink content commonly changes the background color of the content rather than the font color.

Understanding the Box Model

Earlier in this hour you learned that when you attach tags to your content, Expression Web creates an invisible box around the content. To understand how the content behaves and how you can style it, you need a firm understanding of the box model. Fortunately the people behind Expression Web considered this and built a box model reference right into the New and Modify Style dialogs so that you don't have to remember how it works.

To get a better understanding of what the box model is and how you use it, let's take a closer look at the `.header` class you created in `default.html`. To do so, right-click the `.header` class in the Apply or Manage Styles task pane and select Modify Style to open the Modify Style task pane. The box model reference is located under the Box category, as shown in Figure 11.12.

FIGURE 11.12
The New and Modify Style dialogs include a CSS box model reference guide under the Box category.

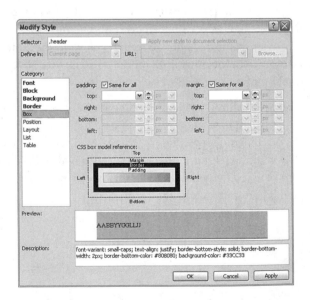

All content wrapped inside tags has four main areas. In the center is the content itself, and surrounding the content is the padding. The padding is the breathing space that separates the content from the next area, the border. The padding retains the same background color or image as the content. The border is the outer edge of the box. It can be given any color, be solid, or have a number of different textures. Outside the border is the margin. The margin works as the buffer area between the outer edges of the box (the border) and the other content on the page. The margin is transparent and you cannot give it a distinct color.

You can set the values of each of the four sides of the padding, border, and margin independently or in groups. To set all four sides of the padding, border, or margin, check the corresponding Same for All box and enter the desired value in the first box. To set the values for each side independently, uncheck the Same for All box and set each value. If you leave any values empty, the default value applies. The default value is usually 0px.

The tricky part about the box model is the calculation of width and height. Generally, the width and height of any boxed element are equal to the distance from side to side or top to bottom of the content area before the padding is applied. The thickness of the padding, borders, and margins add to the total width and height of the box. This means that if you create a div with a width of 600px, as you did earlier, and give it a border of 2px on each side and a padding of 10px on each side, the total width of your div is 624px. As a result, if you want to keep the total width of your div at 600px, you need to subtract both your margin width and your padding width and set the width of your div to 576px. It's not rocket science, but if you forget this little piece of information you could easily end up with content that doesn't fit and not understand why.

Try it Yourself ▼

Use the Box Model to Style Content

Now that you know how the box model works, you can use it to create layout elements that are far more functional than tables. In this example, you change the appearance of the top part of the default.html page by changing the .header class style.

1. With default.html open in Design view, right-click the .header class and select Modify Style to open the Modify Style dialog.

▼

2. Earlier you set the background color of the .header style to green. Go to the Background category and change the background-color to a very light gray by entering the value **#F8F8F9**.

3. In the Border category, set the top border-style to double, the top border-width to 1px, and the top border-color to silver (#C0C0C0). Leave the bottom border-style at solid but change the bottom border-width to 1px and the bottom border-color to the same silver (#C0C0C0). By leaving the left and right borders empty, you are telling the browser the borders should remain at the default 0px and are invisible.

4. If you move the Modify Style dialog to the side you can see that there is no space between the edge of the colored box and the text, so the text appears attached to the left wall. To solve this problem, change the padding of the div: Under the Box category, uncheck the Padding: Same for All box and set padding right and padding left to 10px. This creates a 10-pixel space between the inner edge of the box (the content) and the borders. You can use the Preview box to make sure the space is created correctly. Click OK to apply the changes to the style.

When you save and preview the page in your browser, you can see that the top part of the page now has a much nicer layout with subtle graphic elements, such as a double line at the top and a single line at the bottom (see Figure 11.13). Because the

FIGURE 11.13
By utilizing your knowledge of the box model, you can create visually pleasing layouts without using graphics or tables.

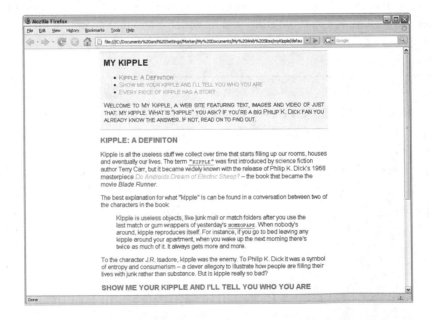

outer #wrapper ID defines the width of the div you were working on and .header has no defined width of its own, you don't have to worry about calculating how thick the padding and borders are. When the width is not set, the browser considers it set to automatic and conforms to the width of whatever outside element has a width defined (or the width of the browser window, if no width is defined). If the div had its own width defined in the Position category, you would have had to subtract 20 pixels from the width to leave space for the left and right padding you inserted.

Summary

As you can see, CSS is a powerful tool that goes far beyond merely changing the color and size of fonts. In this hour, you got a glimpse of how you can use CSS to create highly complex and visually compelling layouts and how easy it is to make dramatic changes to the look of the page without destroying the content in the process. The examples in this hour merely scratch the surface of what is possible when you use CSS as a layout tool, but they give you a good idea of what you can do. Finishing this hour, you have better ideas of why having strong CSS skills gives you a leg up in the web design market and why Expression Web is an excellent tool not only to create but also to learn CSS.

In this hour, you learned how to move beyond simple text styling to create classes that change the appearance of specific elements within a page. You also learned how to group sections of the page using divs and how to assign IDs and classes to these divs to get detailed control of your content. You learned how to set selector names so that certain styles apply to only certain elements within an ID, class, or subclass, and how to apply and modify those styles to change the overall look of your page. In addition, you got an introduction to pseudoclasses and learned how to use them to style active content within a page to give the visitor a more interactive experience. Finally you learned how the box model works and how you can use it to create layouts and style content.

In the next hour, you will look at the CSS code and learn how to manipulate the code to achieve the same results you saw in this hour. You will also learn how to completely separate the style from the content by creating standalone style sheets and how to apply the styles you have already created to other pages you build.

Q&A

Q. *I can't find this Quick Tag Selector bar you keep talking about! Where is it?*

A. By default the Quick Tag Selector is on, but you might have accidentally turned it off. If it is not visible directly under the tabs at the top of the View pane, open the View menu from the menu bar and click Quick Tag Selector to activate it. The Quick Tag Selector has an orange box with a check mark to its left when it is active.

Q. *I changed the name of a style/class/ ID I created and now it isn't applied to the content. Why is that?*

A. If you change the name of a style, class, or ID, you also have to change the name in the tags that the style, class, or ID you applied it to. You can do this by selecting the tag using the Quick Tag Selector and opening the Tag Editor.

Q. *I followed the tutorial and created pseudoclasses for my links, but I still can't see them in Design view. Am I doing something wrong?*

A. Design view displays only the plain link style, not the pseudoclasses. To test the pseudoclasses you created, you have to preview your page in a browser.

Workshop

The Workshop has quiz questions and exercises to help you put to use what you just learned. If you get stuck, the answers to the quiz questions are in the next section. But try to answer them first. Otherwise you'll only be cheating yourself.

Quiz

1. *What is the difference between styles, classes and IDs?*

2. *Can you apply multiple styles, classes or IDs to the same item?*

3. *What is the difference between padding, border and margin in the Box model?*

Answers

1. A style is a set of styling parameters applied to a specific selector such as p, h1, ul, li or td. A class is an independent set of styling parameters that can be applied to any selector as well as divs and spans. An ID is similar to the class except each ID can only be used once per page.

2. Yes, you can apply multiple styles, classes and IDs to an item, but not all at the same time. To do this you need to place the different styles, classes and IDs in concentric circles around the item. For instance if you want a block of text to be affected by an ID, a class and a specific style you need to place the content inside a div with the class applied that is surrounded by a div with the ID applied.

3. The padding is the space between the content and the inner sides of the box. The border is the demarcating line that separates the inside and the outside of the box. The margin is the space between the outer sides of the margin and the surrounding content.

Exercise

Create a new div below the first one to surround the remaining content of the page. Create a new class called .content and apply it to the div. Use your knowledge of the box model to position the text so that it lines up with the text in the first div.

HOUR 12

Styling with Code: Fully Immersed in CSS

What You'll Learn in This Hour:

▶ How to read CSS code

▶ How inline styles differ from other styles

▶ How to apply styles, classes, and IDs to tags in Code view

▶ How to create external style sheets and apply them to multiple pages

Introduction

In Hours 10, "Bringing Style to the Substance with Cascading Style Sheets," and 11, "Boxed In Part 2: Knee Deep in CSS," you learned how to create styles and apply them to content in Design view. But that's just half the story. To fully grasp what CSS (Cascading Style Sheets) is all about, you need to go to the source and learn how to read the code.

Fortunately CSS code is quite simple to learn, especially when you have Expression Web's many CSS tools at your beck and call whenever you get confused. Just as in Design view, you have full access to the CSS task panes when you are working in Code view and all the tools you used in the past two hours are available for use in the same way.

The main purposes of this hour are to go beyond the basics and learn how styling really works and how to create, apply, and modify styles without using the tools every time. Because although the tools Expression Web provides are excellent, they are sometimes cumbersome to use, especially if you are making quick minor changes and already know what to do. Other benefits to using Code view are that you have more control when it comes to the placement and attribution of tags and you can get a better overview of what is happening to your code. On top of that you get a much clearer picture of the meaning of the phrase *separating the style from the content*.

In addition to learning how to read, write, and dissect CSS code, this hour will cover how to create separate style sheets and apply them to multiple files. You will also see how easy it is to move styles from one file to another and apply a style created in one file to other files without having to re-create it. By the end of this hour, you will have the necessary tools and understanding to use CSS not only as a styling tool but also as a platform to create visually stunning websites with clean and concise code that looks the same across most if not all browsers and platforms.

Introducing CSS: The Code Version

In the last two hours, you created a series of styles, classes, and IDs. In this hour, you will inspect and expand on these so if you didn't do all the tasks in earlier hours, you should replace the `default.html` file and the `myDesk.html` file with the final ones from Hour 11.

To work, CSS requires two sets of code: the styles themselves and the tags to which the styles are attached. Let's take a closer look at the styles themselves as they appear in code form. Expression Web 2 gives you multiple ways of viewing the CSS code. By far the easiest way of doing so is simply to hover over the style in question in the Manage Styles task pane. When you do so, a ScreenTip opens to display the entire style code in a pop-up window (see Figure 12.1).

FIGURE 12.1
Hovering the mouse pointer over a style in the Manage Styles task pane brings up a ScreenTip that displays the CSS code for that style.

With the `default.html` file open, hovering over the h1 style gives you the following output:

```
h1 {
    font-family: Arial, Helvetica, sans-serif;
    font-size: 1.4em;
    font-weight: bold;
    text-transform: uppercase;
}
```

This is a typical style. It consists of the style name followed by a set of curly braces. The braces contain all the actual styling code: Each attribute followed by its respective values after a colon. A semicolon separates the attributes.

As you can see, the CSS code Expression Web 2 generates is very easy to read. In fact the only reason why each attribute is on a separate line is for readability. If you wanted to, you could remove all the line breaks and write the entire style on one line, but as you can see it would be much harder to read:

```
h1 {font-family: Arial, Helvetica, sans-serif; font-size: 1.4em;
 font-weight: bold; text-transform: uppercase;}
```

> Because of the limited physical width of this book the entire line doesn't fit on one single line when printed. Normally if you look at the line in Expression Web 2 it would appear on one line. Just like in this book there are times when CSS confined to a single line is arbitrarily divided into multiple lines by the application you are using to look at the code. Even so the style works the exact same way. The information you should walk away with here is that it is the *semi-colons* that define when a line of code ends, not the line breaks.

By the Way

Now that you know what the CSS code looks like, the next logical question is, "Where is it located?" If you paid close attention when you created the styles in the last two hours, you might already have a good idea. Directly under the Selector box in the New and Modify Style dialog was the Define In box, which was set to *Current page*. That means all the styles you created so far are stored in the same page as the content—more specifically at the top of the page inside the <head> tag. The <head> tag contains functional but nonvisual content and information about the current page.

To see where the styles are stored, switch to Code view and scroll to the top of the page. Directly under the <meta> tags is a tag that says <style type="text/css">. You can find all the styles within this tag (see Figure 12.2).

In Hour 8, "Cracking the Code—Working in Code View," you were introduced to the Code View toolbar. Now is a good time to use it. To get an idea of how much code Expression Web 2 created for you when you created the styles, place your cursor on any of the lines with CSS code and click the Select Tag button on the Toolbar. This highlights all the CSS code. But reading this code can still be quite daunting. Currently you have 12 styles defined and many style sheets have several hundred styles or even more.

To find a particular style in Code view, all you have to do is click the style in question in the Manage Styles task pane and Expression Web 2 highlights the style for you. You can even use the arrow keys to navigate between styles for quick and easy access to the particular style, class, or ID you want to work on.

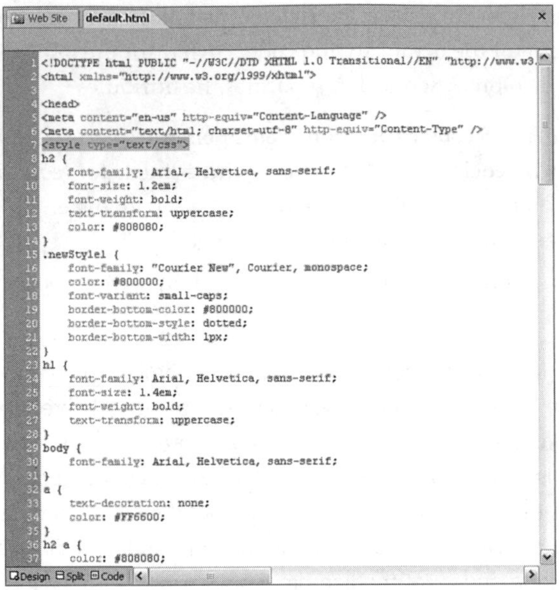

FIGURE 12.2
You can find the
CSS code at the
top of the
`default.html`
page inside the
`<head>` tag in
Code view.

The Value of Separation

Throughout this book there have been several mentions of the styles being *separate from the content*. Now, for the first time, you see what this means in real life: The style code is quite literally separate from the rest of the content in the page. There are several reasons for this. First, keeping the styles separate means that style code does not clutter the content portion of the page. Second, it makes it easier to make changes to both the styles and the content because they are easily distinguishable. Last, it means that you don't have to insert styling code in the page whenever you add new content.

When you add CSS code to the head of an HTML page, the browser reads it and applies it to whatever content it finds below. In practical terms, it works kind of like a coin sorter. If you just dump various coins in a bucket, they have no order. But a coin sorter sorts, separates, and puts each different coin size in its own collector. In HTML, the CSS code becomes the different coin slots and as the content flows through the filter, the different kinds of content fall into their appropriate slots. So rather than sorting each piece of content individually by applying styles directly to it, CSS works as a template from which all the content sorts simultaneously.

Understanding Inline Styles

But what is a rule without an exception? In Hour 10 you created an inline style that applied to just one section of the page. You removed that inline style and replaced it with a class in Hour 11, so you need to make a new one. But this time you will see what goes on in the code and, through that, learn how the inline style gets its name.

1. With the `default.html` page open in Split view, scroll down to the bottom of the page and place the cursor anywhere inside the last paragraph. Click the New Style button to create a new style and use the drop down menu to set the selector name to (`Inline Style`).

2. In the Font category, set the `font-size` to `0.8em` and the `font-variant` to `small-caps`. In the Block category, set `text-align` to `center`. Click OK to apply the new inline style, the result of which you can see in Figure 12.3.

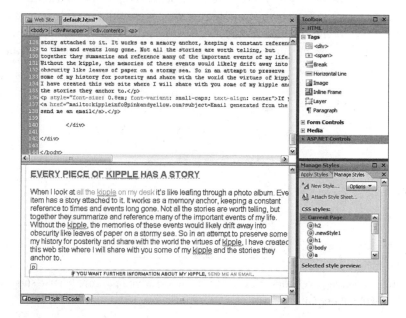

FIGURE 12.3
You can use inline styles to create specialized styles for small segments of content that should appear different than the regular content.

The last paragraph of the page changes appearance after you apply the inline style. But what matters is what happened in Code view. Look at the tag for this particular paragraph:

```
<p style="font-size: 0.8em; font-variant: small-caps; text-align: center">
```

Rather than creating a new style and adding it to the list at the top of the page, Expression Web 2 added this style inside the tag of the affected paragraph. The style is in the same line as the content—hence the name *inline style*. This explains not only why the style you just created affects only this particular paragraph but also serves as a good example of why you should always try to keep your styles separate from your content. Just imagine what your HTML code would look like if every tag had to contain the necessary style attributes! With that said, inline styles are useful if you need to apply a special style featured only once in the entire page or site.

Creating a New Style in Code View Using IntelliSense

In Code view, you can make direct changes to the CSS code or create new styles with the help of IntelliSense. In this example, you create a new `img` style from scratch to give the image the appearance of having a white background with a gray border.

1. With the `myDesk.html` page open in Code view, find the `<style>` tag and place the cursor directly after the end bracket of the tag. Press Enter to create a new line.

2. To create the new style, type **im** and IntelliSense suggests **img**. Press the Enter key to accept `img`, press the spacebar, and type a beginning curly bracket **{**. In response, IntelliSense automatically moves you to the next line, inserts the end curly bracket on the line below, and brings up a list of all available attributes that apply to the **img** tag (see Figure 12.4).

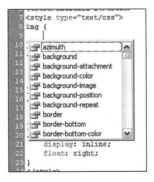

3. To create five-pixel padding around the image, type **pa**. IntelliSense suggests `padding`. Press Enter to complete the word.

4. IntelliSense now opens a ScreenTip to tell you what kind of information the padding attribute requires. Because you want five-pixel padding on all four sides, you can type **5px** and be done with it. If you want different values for each side, follow the ScreenTip and type, for example, **5px 4px 4px 10px**. Complete the line by entering a semicolon and pressing Enter to create a new line.

5. To create a border, you need to set three attributes: `border-style`, `border-width`, and `border-color`. To help you remember this, IntelliSense reminds you and helps you set all three variables on one line: On the new line, type **border:**. This opens the ScreenTip for the **border** attribute. IntelliSense now asks you for the values it needs. First up is `border-width`. Type 1px and press the spacebar. The ScreenTip automatically jumps to the next variable, `border-`

color, and opens a drop-down menu of colors for you. Pick the gray color and press the spacebar. IntelliSense now asks you for the border-style (see Figure 12.5). Select solid from the drop-down menu and finish the line with a semicolon. The two new lines should read padding:5px; and border: 1px gray solid;.

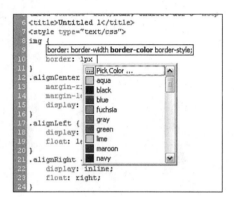

To see the effects of your changes, click anywhere inside Design view to apply the changes and scroll down to see the image. The thumbnail now has a one-pixel solid gray border and five pixels of white padding. This example shows you how easy it is to write and make changes to CSS code in Code view and also how IntelliSense works with you to simplify the code-writing process.

Applying Classes to Tags in Code View

In Hour 11, you learned to apply special styles to certain content with the use of classes. In one example, you used classes to change the position of the Kenny thumbnail in the myDesk.html page. This example provides a good basis for learning how Expression Web 2 applies classes to tags in Code view. If you open myDesk.html in Split view and click the Kenny thumbnail, the relevant code highlights in Code view (see Figure 12.6).

```
<img alt="Kenny figure" height="147" src="Images/KennyOriginal_small.jpg"
width="100" class="alignCenter" />
```

Inspecting the tag code you see that a new attribute at the end: class="alignCenter". This is how Expression Web 2 applies classes to tags, whether they are selectors, spans, or divs. To change the class, all you have to do is edit the class name in Code view. In Hour 11, you learned how to create two more alignment classes, and if you did so you can change the class name to either alignLeft or alignRight and immediately see the changes in Design view. Adding a class to an existing tag is just as easy: Simply type the word **class** before the end bracket of the beginning tag and IntelliSense gives you a drop-down list of all available classes.

FIGURE 12.6
The **img** tag for the thumbnail highlights in Code view when you click the image in Design view.

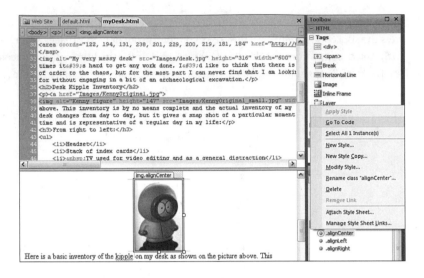

To see the CSS code for the class in Code view, right-click the class in the Manage Styles task pane and select Go to Code. No matter where you are in the program, this function takes you straight to the relevant CSS code in Code view.

Using Divs and Spans to Separate Content

This chapter touched on both the <span> tag and the <div> tag earlier and now it's time to take a closer look at these separators. The main difference between the two is that span is an inline separator, whereas div is a block separator. In other words, span's display attribute is inline by default, whereas div's display attribute is block. You saw the difference between the two when you used the .centerAlign class to center the thumbnail earlier: The inline value means that the content, although separated from the surrounding content, is still on the same line as the rest. In contrast, the block value creates a block or box on its own line that holds only the content inside the tag.

The default.html page contains two instances of the <span> tag that you created to highlight the words *kipple* in the first paragraph and *homeopape* in the block quote. If you find the words in the Design portion of Split View, and click them, you can see the corresponding <span> tags and how they are applied:

```
<span class="newStyle1">&quot;kipple&quot;</span>
```

As you can see, the class application is no different in the span tag than in any other tag. But because you were just starting to learn how to create styles, you didn't give the class a proper name, so it has the nondescript name newStyle1. It's important to give all your styles, classes, and IDs proper descriptive names so that you know what they do. But how do you do so without afterward going into the code and manually changing all the references to the style?

Renaming Styles and Applying the Change to All Tags in a Page

When you work with large pages or sites, you often run into situations in which you need to rename a style, class, or ID. The problem is that Expression Web 2 already applied these elements to many tags within your pages and if you change the name of the style, class or ID, all the references have to change as well. To help simplify this process and save you from the trouble of tracking down every reference to your now changed style, class, or ID, Expression Web 2 can make all the substitutions for you.

1. With the default.html page open in Split view, navigate both the Code and Design view so that you can see both span instances you created earlier (kipple and homeopape).

2. In the Manage Styles task pane, right-click the .newStyle1 class and select Rename Class "newStyle1" from the context menu. This opens the Rename Class dialog.

3. In the Rename Class dialog, give the class the new name **highlight**. Be sure to enable the Rename Class References in This Page box and click OK.

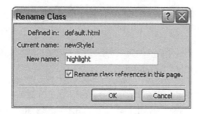

FIGURE 12.7
The Rename Style, Class, and ID dialogs give you the option of renaming all references to the renamed element in the current page or in all pages affected by it.

When you click OK not only does Expression Web 2 rename the class, it also changes the references to the class in the page, as you can see in Code view. Changing all the references to a style, class, or ID to correspond with a name change extends to external style sheets, meaning that when you learn how to create an external style sheet and apply it to multiple pages, Expression Web 2 changes all references to the changed name throughout all these pages for you, even if they are not open!

In Hour 11, you used divs to create blocks that separated and sectioned the contents of the page. default.html now has three divs: one outer box with the ID wrapper and two inner boxes with the header and content classes. To see how Expression Web 2 applies those divs, click the heading in Design view to see all the tags applied to it. By clicking the <div#wrapper> tag in the Quick Tag Selector, all the content affected by the tag highlights both in Code and Design view. To find only the beginning tag, click the Find Matching Tag button on the Code View toolbar. As you can see, the application of an ID is very similar to that of a class: <div id="wrapper">.

Because divs box in larger sections of content, it can be hard to see exactly where they apply and how much content they contain. You already saw how to use the Quick Tag Selector to highlight all the content affected by a tag. Another way is to use the Select Tab button on the Design View toolbar. If you need to see where the end </div> tag is located, click the Find Matching Tag button again and Code view jumps to the end tag.

Creating Divs in Code View

As you experienced in Hour 11, dragging and dropping divs into Design view can be quite tricky. A much easier and more effective way of applying divs is to use Code or Split view because in Code view you can see exactly what content you are wrapping and place the beginning and end tags in the precise location you want them. You already inserted three divs in the default.html page and now you are going to insert the same divs in the myDesk.html page.

1. With the myDesk.html page open in Split view, click the heading to navigate both views to the top of the page.

2. From the Toolbox task pane, drag an instance of the <div> tag into Code view and place it directly over the line that reads <h1>My Kippled Desk</h1>. This creates a beginning and an end div tag: <div></div>.

3. Highlight and cut out the </div> end tag by pressing Ctrl+X. In Code view, navigate to the bottom of the page. There you can see that the </body> tag is now red with a yellow background, indicating that the code is broken. Paste the </div> tag you just cut out into the line directly above the </body> tag. If you click an element on the page, you can see that the <div> tag is now present in the Quick Tag Selector.

4. Now you are going to box in the header content. Find the beginning div tag you just inserted and add a new line directly underneath it. Drag and drop a new `<div>` tag into the new line or enter **`<div>`** manually. IntelliSense creates the end tag for you to keep the code from breaking. Again highlight and cut out the end tag. Because this page doesn't have a descriptive section, the header should contain only the heading, so place your cursor at the end of the line containing the heading and press Enter to create a new line. Paste the **`</div>`** end tag you cut out into this new line or enter **`</div>`**.

5. To wrap the rest of the content in another div, add a new line directly underneath the one with the `</div>` end tag you just inserted and create a new `<div>` tag. Cut out the end tag and place it at the bottom of the screen above the first `</div>` end tag you inserted.

The `myDesk.html` page now has three divs just as the `default.html` page does. But the classes and IDs you used to style the divs are still in the `default.html` file. To apply them to `myDesk.html` as well, you need to create an external style sheet.

Creating External Style Sheets

By far the most powerful feature of CSS is that it gives you the ability to create styles, classes, and IDs stored in one central location and applied to many different pages or entire sites. This is where the *Sheets* part of the name Cascading Style Sheets comes from.

An *external style sheet* is a dedicated file with the extension `.css` that contains only style code. Until now you have inserted all the style code you created into the head of your HTML pages, but doing so limits their application to that particular page. Now you are going to move the styles from the HTML page to a new style sheet so that you can apply the same styles to multiple pages.

To create an external style sheet, you first have to create the `.css` file itself. The easiest way to create a `.css` file is to right-click in the Folder List task pane, and then select New, CSS in the context menu. This creates a new file named `Untitled_1.css`. In most cases the style sheet name is simply `styles.css`, but it is often a good idea to be more specific in naming to ensure that you know which site each sheet belongs to. After creating the new file, give it the name `kippleStyles.css` as shown in Figure 12.8.

FIGURE 12.8
It's usually a good idea to give your **.css** files site-specific names to make sure you know where they belong.

Opening the new CSS file, you can see that it is completely empty. That is because unlike HTML and other markup files, a CSS file doesn't need any code other than the actual styles to function. And because it's a new file, there are no style definitions yet.

The next step is to attach the style sheet to your pages by using the Attach Style Sheet button in the Apply and Manage Styles task pane. With the `default.html` page open, click the Attach Style Sheet button to open the Attach Style Sheet dialog (see Figure 12.9).

FIGURE 12.9
The Attach Style Sheet dialog lets you attach an external style sheet to the current page or all pages in the site using either the link or import method.

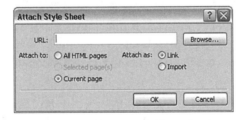

From here you can browse to the style sheet you want to attach and choose whether you want to attach it to all the pages in your site or just the current page. (The Selected pages option becomes available if you highlight a series of pages in the Manage Folders task pane before opening the Attach Style Sheet dialog.) You also have the choice of whether to attach the style sheet using the link method or the import method. They produce nearly the same results, but use the Link option for the most consistent results.

The Difference Between Linking and Importing

There are two methods for attaching a style sheet to an HTML file: linking and importing. The difference between the two is subtle and comes into play only in special cases.

The linking method simply tells the browser that there are styles stored in the linked file for application to the content below. If you want to attach another style sheet to the page, you add a new link and so on. The linking method works across all browsers, no matter how old.

The importing method is somewhat different. First, you can use it within a style sheet to import another style sheet so that instead of calling two style sheets from the HTML file you call one and then the first style sheet calls the second one. But more importantly the importing method does not work with some older browsers and this prevents older browsers from trying to read style code they can't understand. However this applies only to very old browsers and should not be a deciding factor in picking one method over the other. For all intents and purposes, both methods work the same way.

Browse and select the `kippleStyles.css` file you just created, select Attach to All HTML Pages and Attach as Link. This attaches the new style sheet to all the HTML pages within your site by inserting the following line of code in the <head> tag:

```
<link href="kippleStyles.css" rel="stylesheet" type="text/css" />
```

The attached style sheet now appears in the Manage Styles task pane under the styles embedded in the current page (see Figure 12.10).

Moving Styles To and From the External Style Sheet

After attaching the external style sheet to all the pages in your site, the styles set in the `kippleStyles.css` file affect all the pages instead of just one. You have already created many styles in different pages, but they are stored in the head of each page and not in the style sheet. The obvious way to solve this is to cut and paste the code out of the pages and into the style sheet, but this method is both cumbersome and prone to error. Expression Web 2 provides a better solution in the form of the Manage Styles task pane.

For this exercise it is a good idea to close the Toolbar task pane and let the Manage Styles task pane cover the entire height of your screen. You can always reset the task panes later.

Did you Know?

FIGURE 12.10
The newly at-tached style sheet appears in the Manage Styles task pane underneath the locally embed-ded styles.

1. With the `default.html` file open, click and drag the body style from the Current Page area down to the `kippleStyles.css` area. When you let go, the style appears below the `kippleStyles.css` heading.

2. Using the same method, move the rest of the styles, classes, and IDs from the Current Page area to the `kippleStyles.css` area (see Figure 12.11).

FIGURE 12.11
You can move styles, classes, and IDs from the current HTML file to the new **.css** file by dragging and dropping them into the new file area in the Manage Styles task pane.

3. When you finish moving all the styles, classes, and IDs to the `kippleStyles.css` area, scroll to the top of `default.html` in Code view. Note that all the style code is gone. All that is left is the `<style>` tag. In the Manage Styles task pane, right-click any of the styles and select Go to Code. The new `kippleStyles.css` style sheet opens, and you can see that all the code previously housed in the head of the HTML file is now in the style sheet.

4. Open `myDesk.html`. Note that the styles you just moved from `default.html` now appear under `kippleStyles.css` in the Manage Styles task pane for this page. Using the same technique, move the styles from `myDesk.html` to `kippleStyles.css`.

5. Press Ctrl+S to save the changes. This opens the Save Embedded Files dialog, which asks whether you want to save the changes to the `kippleStyles.css` file (see Figure 12.12). Click OK.

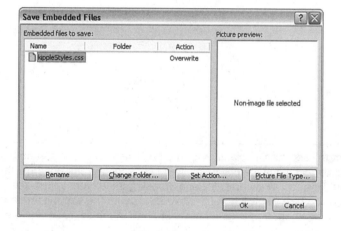

FIGURE 12.12
When saving an HTML file after making changes to styles contained in an external style sheet, Expression Web 2 always opens the Save Embedded File dialog to ask whether you want to save the changes made in the style sheet as well.

The `kippleStyles.css` file now contains all the styles from both `default.html` and `myDesk.html`. Expression Web 2 still applies the styles to the content of those pages, and they appear the same in Design view and in any browser you preview them in.

Inspecting the code in `kippleStyles.css` you can see that the order of the styles corresponds with the list of styles in the Manage Styles task pane. If you change the order of the styles in the task pane, the code reorganizes in the same manner. This is because the order of styles in the style sheet is relevant to the cascade: The lower in the sheet the style is, the more weight it has in deciding what the content should look like.

In some cases a style, class, or ID applies to only one page. In that case, it is a good idea to keep the element in the relevant page rather than in the style sheet. For example, in `default.html` you created a class called `highlight` that applied to two words as an inline style. Now the style sheet contains this class, but because only the `default.html` page uses it, the class should be only in that file. To return this particular class back to its original location, simply open `default.html` and drag and drop the `.highlight` class back to Current Page (see Figure 12.13).

FIGURE 12.13
The final style structure of
default.html
.

Did you Know?

If you want to keep a style, class or ID in both style sheets you can use the same drag-and-drop technique to copy them. To do so, simply press and hold the Ctrl key on your keyboard while dragging and dropping the element. Just keep in mind when you do so that you will now have two styles with the same name and the one in the style sheet that is listed furthest down in the cascade has precedence.

Applying External Styles to a Page

Styles nested in an external style sheet act in the same way as styles nested in the current document. Therefore Expression Web 2 applies them in the same way. Earlier in this hour you created a series of divs to section out the content in the `myDesk.html` page. Now that you have attached the external style sheet, you can apply the same IDs and classes you used to change the layout of `default.html` to change the layout of `myDesk.html`.

1. With the `myDesk.html` file open in Split view, click anywhere inside the page in Design view and click the first `<div>` tag in the Quick Tag Selector to select the

div that wraps all the content. This highlights all the content in both Code view and Design view.

2. In the Manage Styles task pane, right-click the #wrapper ID and select Apply Style from the context menu (see Figure 12.14). The tag in the Quick Tag Selector and in Code view changes to <div#wrapper> and the wrapper ID is applied.

FIGURE 12.14
Applying a style from an external style sheet is no different from applying a style nested within the file itself.

3. In Code view, move the cursor one line down to select the next <div> tag, right-click the .header class in the Manage Styles task pane, and select Apply Style. The tag changes to <div.header> and the .header class is applied.

4. In Design view, click anywhere inside the content contained in the last div and select the <div> with no class or ID in the Quick Tag Selector. In the Manage Styles task pane, right-click the .content class and select Apply Style. The tag changes to <div.content> and the .content class is applied. Save the file and preview it in your browser (see Figure 12.15).

By previewing the page in a browser, you can see the styles you created for default.html applied to myDesk.html. But there is a problem: The large image of the desk seems to be protruding to the right. This is because the image itself is 600 pixels wide and you added both padding and a border to the img property itself and padding to the .heading class. There are two ways to solve this problem: reduce the size of the image or change the width of the wrapper ID. In this case, the second option is the easiest.

FIGURE 12.15
The layout IDs
and classes cre-
ated for
default.html
applied to
myDesk.html.
It looks consis-
tent when pre-
viewed in a
browser.

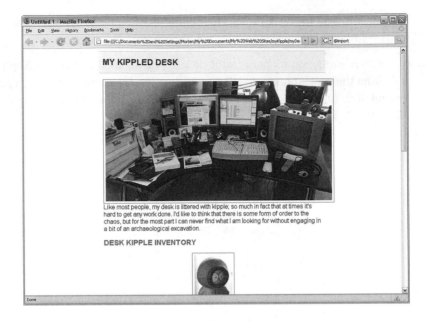

To change the width of the wrapper ID, right-click it in the Manage Styles task pane
(it doesn't matter what file you currently have open in Expression Web 2) and select
Modify Style. Under the Position category change the width value to 650px. Save the
style change and preview the page in the browser. Now the image fits within the text
area but floats to the left. To solve this problem, simply select the image in design
view and apply the .alignCenter class. Finally apply the .alignLeft class to the
Kenny thumbnail and the layout of the myDesk.html page is complete (at least for
now). Because you changed the width of the #wrapper ID now nested in the
kippleStyles.css file, the change also applies to the default.html page when you
open it in a browser (see Figure 12.16). That way you can keep the look of the entire
site consistent when you make changes.

FIGURE 12.16
The subtle changes to the **#wrapper** ID and the application of the **.alignCenter** and **.alignLeft** classes to the images make a big difference in the way the browser displays the page.

Summary

Even though Expression Web 2 creates proper standards-based CSS code out of the box, understanding the CSS code can make your life as a designer a lot easier. In fact, in many cases, it makes more sense to work directly with the code rather than to use the tools in the application. Fortunately you can choose either way and customize your work process depending on the task.

In this hour, you learned how to build a CSS style using code and how to edit it in Code view with the help of IntelliSense. You also learned how to insert spans and divs in your page from Code view, and why doing so is often easier than doing it in Design view. In addition you saw how inline styles differ from other styles and where the name *inline* stems from. You also learned how to rename both inline and other styles without going through all the code and renaming each instance afterward.

Most importantly you learned how to completely separate the styles from the content by creating an external style sheet and how this makes styling groups of pages or an entire website much easier. Understanding this process is fundamental; it dramatically reduces your workload and makes changing and upgrading the look and feel of large websites an easy and straightforward process.

By the end of this hour, you began to realize the true power of standards-based web design and the use of HTML and CSS. In upcoming hours, you will use this knowledge to turn up the "wow" factor of the myKipple site by creating advanced layouts and menus.

Q&A

Q. *When I try to apply an inline style to a single word it is applied to the entire text block instead. What am I doing wrong?*

A. When you create an inline style the new style is applied to the closest tag. That means that unless you have separated the single word from the rest of the block using the <span> tags, the inline style will be applied to the block tag. To apply the inline style to a single word you have to wrap it in <span> tags first and then create the new inline style.

Q. *I followed the tutorial to create divs in code view but everything looks the same as it did before!*

A. When there is a problem with content being wrapped with <div> or <span> tags and nothing looking any different the answer is usually answered by the following three questions: Does the <div> or <span> actually wrap anything? A common mistake when inserting these elements is to forget to place the end tag at the end of the content. This is because both IntelliSense and other tools automatically place the end tag right after the beginning tag before the content. The second question is, do the tags close properly? You may have forgotten to paste the end tag in after cutting it out or you may have placed it in the wrong spot. If so the code will be broken and you should see the little warning sign in the Status bar and find highlighted code further down in the document. Finally did you actually apply the class or ID to the tag? If you click on the content that should be styled by the class or ID and the Quick Tag Selector reads <div> or <span> without the class or style attached you need to apply the style or ID to make everything work properly.

Workshop

The Workshop has quiz questions and exercises to help you put to use what you just learned. If you get stuck, the answers to the quiz questions are in the new section. But try to answer them first. Otherwise you'll only be cheating yourself.

Quiz

1. *What is the difference between a <span> tag and a <div> tag?*

2. *What are the two main methods used to make new styles, classes and IDs you have been introduced to?*

3. *What is the benefit of moving styles to an external style sheet?*

Answers

1. The <span> tag is an inline tag meaning that if applied to content in a line the content stays on the same line. The <div> tag on the other hand is a block tag meaning it creates a new block or line that the content it wraps is placed on. For this reason <span> is used to highlight words or elements while <div> is used to group sections.

2. You now have two methods of creating styles: You can use the New Style button on the Apply and Manage Styles task pane and create a new style through the dialog or you can create a new style from scratch in Code view with the help of IntelliSense.

3. By placing your styles in an external style sheet you can now use the same styles to control the look of several pages. It also means you can make changes to one style and see those changes applied to all the pages it is attached to without ever opening them.

Exercise

Using the techniques you learned, change the layout of the myWallet.html page by adding divs and styling them with IDs and classes to match the default.html and myDesk.html pages.

HOUR 13

Get Visual, Part 3: Images as Design Elements with CSS

What You'll Learn in This Hour:

▶ How to apply images as backgrounds

▶ How to use repeating background images to achieve different looks

▶ How to use background images as style elements

▶ How to replace list bullets with images

▶ How to import and change .psd files directly inside Expression Web

Introduction

In Hours 6, "Get Visual, Part 1—Adding Images to Your Page," and 7, "Get Visual, Part 2—Advanced Image Editing, Thumbnails, and Hotspots," you learned how to insert images as objects in a web page. But if you have spent any length of time on the Web, you know that images are used for so much more and most prominently as design elements. In fact, most of the nontext content you find on a website is an image in some form or another. This is because the basic building blocks of a web page (HTML [Hypertext Markup Language] and CSS [Cascading Style Sheets]) can do only rudimentary tasks such as build boxes with borders. If you want a rounded corner or something more advanced, the only way to make them is to introduce an image. Fortunately HTML and CSS give you a huge variety of ways in which you can introduce images as design elements by adding them as backgrounds, replaced items, or even buttons without thereby displacing the actual content on the page. Understanding how to achieve this means you can take your site from a plain looking boxes-and-borders layout to a graphics-heavy visual masterpiece.

When creating graphics-heavy websites, you move out of the realm of strict web authoring and into that of a designer. This is because, for all their virtues, no web-authoring software yet includes full-fledged design capabilities; they can't make graphics from scratch. Microsoft Expression Studio includes a powerful design application in Expression Design, but most designers are already using Adobe Photoshop as their base of operations. For this reason Expression Web 2 includes a powerful Photoshop import feature that lets you import .psd files and slice them into workable pieces right in the web-authoring application. This feature is a huge time saver as long as you know its capabilities and limitations. The lessons of this hour show you how to use the Photoshop import feature to generate workable graphics and then use these in conjunction with CSS to create visual design elements for your site.

Images as Backgrounds: A Crash Course

In Hours 6 and 7, you learned how to insert images into the content of your page. But as you saw, those images were content elements. What you want now are design elements and that requires a somewhat different approach.

As you have already learned, when you insert an image into a web page, you are actually inserting a replaced item, a link that is replaced with an external file. This same technique can be used to replace items such as CSS backgrounds, meaning that rather than giving your box a flat color (or no color) background, the background is the image of your choice.

Furthermore you can control the way in which this image displays to achieve different effects. As with the content images, any image used as a background must be RGB and of one of the three main formats GIF, JPEG, or PNG.

▼ **Try it Yourself**

Use an Image as a Background with CSS

In the lesson files for this hour is a folder named Graphics that contains a series of image files. Before going any further, you need to create a new folder called Graphics and import these files into it using the technique you learned in Hour 6.

In this first lesson you are going to apply an image as a background to see how you can easily change the look of an entire page even with a very small image file.

1. With the default.html page open in Design view, right-click the body style in the Manage Styles task pane and select Modify Style.

2. In the Background category, use the Browse button next to the background-image attribute to navigate to the Graphics folder you just created. Select the file called tile.gif and click OK. In the Preview box, you see a red-and-black background graphic appear behind the text (see Figure 13.1). Click OK.

▲

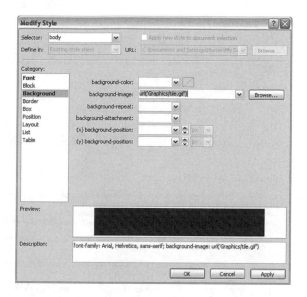

FIGURE 13.1
Using the Modify Styles dialog to select an image file as a background image for the **body** style.

In Design view, you now see that the entire background of the page has been overtaken by a red-and-black diagonal stripe pattern. But if you open the `tile.gif` file you just inserted as a background in your regular file explorer outside of Expression Web 2, you will see that it is in fact just a 20 pixel–by–20 pixel image. So, how is it covering the entire background? By default, if you set an image as a background for any style, the image automatically repeats or tiles both horizontally and vertically from the uppermost left corner down to the end of the page. This gives the designer the ability to use a tiny image to cover a large area. Otherwise the background image would have to be as big as the display on the largest monitor imaginable with the highest resolution available, and that would be a very large image indeed.

The Background Attributes

To see how this tiling works in real life, you can turn it off. To do so, go back to the Background category of the body style and set the `background-repeat` attribute to `no-repeat`. Now only one instance of the background appears in the upper-left corner (see Figure 13.2).

The background-repeat attribute can be set to one of four values that give you a large variety of options in terms of how to display your background image. You've already seen what `no-repeat` does. `repeat` is the default setting by which the image is tiled both horizontally and vertically. `repeat-x` tiles the image only along the x-axis, meaning there will be one line of tiles along the top going from left to right.

FIGURE 13.2
With the **background-repeat** attribute set to **no-repeat**, the background image appears only once in the upper-left corner of the area.

Background image

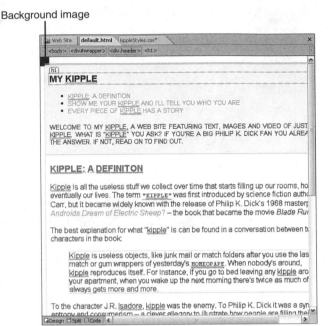

repeat-y tiles the image only along the y-axis, meaning there will be one line of tiles along the left side going from top to bottom.

You can further specify the location of the background image using the (x) background-position and (y) background-position attributes where you can give the background image an absolute position with a numeric value or you can set it to left, center, or right for the x value and top, center, or bottom for the y value. For example, by setting both the (x) background-position and (y) background-position attributes to center, the image will be located in the middle of the area relative to the total width and height of the area within the tags (see Figure 13.3).

The Background category also lets you set the background-attachment attribute for the image. The default value of this attribute is scroll, meaning that the background is affected if you scroll up, down, left, or right in the page just like the rest of the content. If you set this attribute to fixed, the background image is fixed in the same location relative to the browser window, so the image stays even if you scroll through the content.

The background-color attribute comes into play whenever you use a background-repeat value other than default or repeat and when the image does not display for some reason. All the area not covered by the background image has the color defined by the background-color attribute.

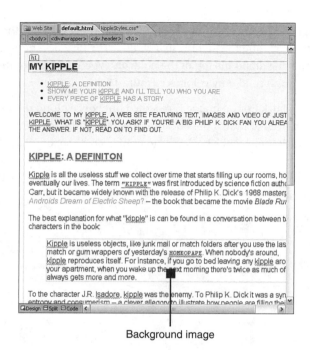

FIGURE 13.3
With the **(x)**
background-
position and
(y) back-
ground-posi-
tion attributes
set to **center**,
the background
image is cen-
tered on the
page relative to
the total width
and height.

Background image

How Backgrounds Relate to the Content and the Page

Background images work exactly the same way that background colors work in styles, meaning they cover the area within the confines of the box that contains the content within the beginning and end tags. In the preceding example, you gave the style that governs the body tag a background image, meaning that the image is applied to the background of the entire page. If you define a background image for any other style you have created, the attributes act in the same way but they will be applied in relation to each individual object they are applied to.

Try it Yourself ▼

Apply a Background Image to the Heading 2 Style

To fully understand how background images in CSS work, you need to see how they relate to the content and to each other. In this example, you apply two background images: one to the body style and one to the h2 style.

1. Open the Modify Style dialog for the body style and change the background image to the file `backgroundTile.gif`.

▼

2. Set background-repeat to repeat-x and click Apply to apply the style to the page without closing the Modify Style dialog. The new background image is tiled in one line along the top of the page and you can see that the bottom of the image has a solid gray color (see Figure 13.4).

3. Because the background image is repeated only once along the top of the screen, you need to match the background color of the rest of the page with the color on the bottom of the background image. To do so, open the More Colors

FIGURE 13.4
Clicking Apply rather than OK in the Modify Style dialog gives you the ability to see the style applied without closing the dialog.

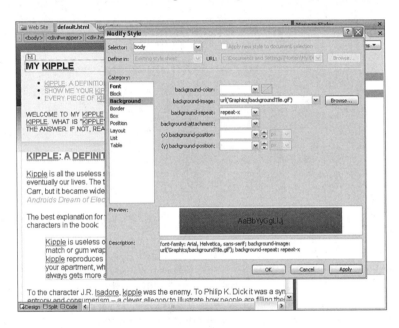

option from the box next to the background-color attribute and click Select to activate the Eyedropper tool (see Figure 13.5). Match the bottom gray color of the background image by clicking the very bottom of it with the eyedropper. This gives you the value Hex={F3,EF,EF}. Click OK and the click Apply to make sure the bottom of the background image merges seamlessly with the new background color you picked. When it does, click OK to finalize the style.

4. With the new background image and color applied to the whole page, it's time to apply a background image to the h2 style. Open the Modify Style dialog for the h2 style in the same way as before and click the Background category.

5. Use the Browse button to set background-image to underline.png. Set the background-repeat attribute to no-repeat to prevent the image from tiling.

6. The name of this file is underline and it is meant to be an underline for the title. But if you look in the Preview box, you can see that the line is in fact hov-

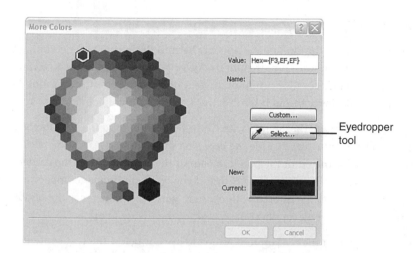

FIGURE 13.5
The Eyedropper tool in the More Colors dialog is a quick way to match colors to images on your page.

Eyedropper tool

ering *over* the text. To solve this, set the (x) background-position to left and the (y) background-position to bottom. Click OK to apply the changes, and then save and preview the page in your browser (see Figure 13.6).

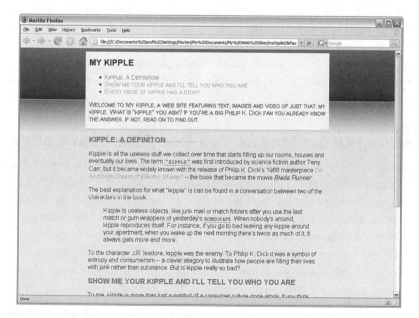

FIGURE 13.6
The new background images are applied to the page: one as a tiled background across the top of the page, the other as a graphic element behind the Heading 2 headings.

As you can see, the backgrounds are relative to the tag to which they are applied; the body background spans along the entire top of the page regardless of how wide the window is, whereas the h2 background hugs the lower-left side of each h2 instance without repeating.

Background Images and the Box Model

Right now the h2 background image appears behind the actual text heading. But, as in this case, you often want a particular image or portion of an image to appear over, under, to the left, or to the right of the text or image content rather than behind it. You can do this easily through some clever use of the box model.

As you learned in Hour 12, "Styling with Code: Fully Immersed in CSS," the background spans the entire area inside the box. The same thing goes for the background image. You also learned that the padding defines the space between the content and the inner edges of the box. This means that if you want an image to appear above, below, to the left, or to the right of your content, you need to increase the padding to leave room for it in whatever direction you want the image to appear.

In this case you want the background image to appear below the text content of the h2 headings. Earlier you set the (y) background-position attribute to bottom, which means the image hugs the bottom of the box. So, if you increase the bottom padding, the image will shift down relative to the text. To do so, open the Modify Style dialog for the h2 style and go to the Box category. The next step is a bit of trial and error: Uncheck the Same for All box for Padding and set bottom-padding to 10px. Click Apply and move the Modify Style dialog to the side to see whether this produced the result you were looking for. In this case the image didn't move far enough down, so use the up and down buttons to increase the bottom-padding value to 12px and click Apply again. If you are satisfied with what you see, click OK to finalize the change.

Stacking Order Means You Can Pile Your Images

Because background images are style elements contained within the box model, they act just like any other feature in the box. The most obvious advantage of this is that it gives you the ability to stack multiple images on top of each other, just like a pile of photos, by setting them as backgrounds for different elements. This method also preserves any transparencies (as long as the browser supports them), meaning you can place one transparent image on top of another one and see one through the other. In fact, using this method, there is no limit to how deep your stack of images can be except the capabilities of the computer that displays them.

As with all other style elements, the cascade decides the stacking order of images used as backgrounds: The tag closest to the content has top position, followed by the second closest, and so on. This way the background of the most relevant object ends up on top.

Try it Yourself ▼

Stack Images Using CSS Backgrounds

CSS allows you to stack multiple images with transparencies on top of one another. To see how this works, you are going to apply different backgrounds to elements in your current page.

1. With the default.html page open in Design view, open the Modify Style dialog for the header class. In the Background category, set the background-image to paperTile.jpg. Click OK to apply the change. This replaces the current gray background with repeated instances of the image.

2. Create a new style for paragraphs inside the header class with the selector name **.header p**. Change Define In to **Existing Style Sheet** and select kippleStyles.css from the URL drop-down menu. This ensures that the new style is saved in the style sheet and not just locally in the default.html file.

3. Set background-image to corner.png. This image is a corner peel from the upper-left corner, so it should appear only once. For this reason, set background-repeat to no-repeat.

4. Because the corner takes up some space in the upper-left corner, you need to set the top and left padding to accommodate the background. Set the top padding to 25px and the left padding to 30px. Click OK to apply the new style, the result of which you can see in Figure 13.7. ▲

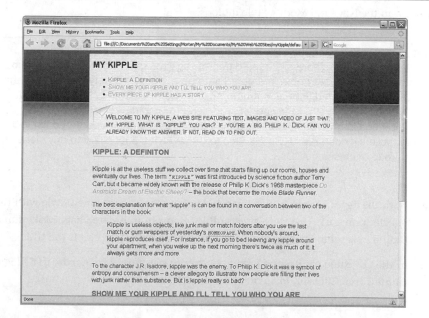

FIGURE 13.7
default.html
now has three background images stacked on top of one another: **backgroundTile.gif**, **paperTile.jpg**, and **corner.png**. Each appears on top of the other because of their order in the page hierarchy.

Using Images as List Bullets

In addition to using images as backgrounds, they have another extremely useful application: replacing list item bullets with image files (see Figure 13.8).

By default a bullet precedes all unordered list items. However, this is but one of many different options. Figure 13.8 shows how the eight main list styles appear in a browser when no additional styling has been applied. But for all their convenience and functionality, these items are very basic and exchanging them for images is a quick and easy way to bring your design to that next level.

FIGURE 13.8
The eight main list styles as they appear in a browser with no additional styling.

Commonly used list styles:

- disk (unordered list default)
- ○ circle
- ■ square
- 4. decimal (ordered list default)
- v. lower-roman
- VI. upper-roman
- g. lower-alpha
- H. upper-alpha

Try it Yourself

Change the List Bullet to an Image

Switching out the bullet for an image is little different from changing the bullet style. Because list items are a special type of content in HTML, there is a separate section for them in the New and Modify Style dialogs.

Did you Know?

> When you are changing the style of lists, keep in mind that depending on what you want to achieve, there are three different tags you can attach styles to. An ol style affects all the list items in ordered lists as a group. A ul style affects all the list items in unordered lists as a group. An li style affects all list items individually regardless of whether they are in an ordered or unordered list. You can target only list items in ordered lists by creating an ol li style and an unordered list with an ul li style. Of course you can also make these styles subsidiary to any class, ID, or group of classes or IDs.

1. With the default.html page open in Design view, create a new style with the selector name ul. This style affects all list items in unordered lists. Make sure Define In is set to Existing Style Sheet and kippleStyles.css is the URL.

2. In the List category, use the Browse button to select the listArrow.gif file (see Figure 13.9). Click OK to create the new style.

FIGURE 13.9
The List category in the New and Modify Style dialogs controls the appearance of both ordered and unordered list items.

The new style you made replaces the bullets in front of the list items with small arrows. As with the backgrounds, any image file can be used as a list bullet (although for obvious reasons I advise you to use small ones). But unlike the backgrounds, the bullet image is not directly related to the box but rather to the first line of text in each item. In practical terms, this means that if you add left padding the distance between the bullet image and the text increases, but if you add bottom padding the bullet stays on the line. This situation can produce some strange results if you use a very large font size because the bullet image stays in its original position in relation to the first line of text rather than grow with the font size. Figure 13.10 demonstrates how both regular bullets and bullet images react to different styling of the li tag. Note that standard HTML bullets size according to the font size.

The height of the image itself decides the vertical positioning of a bullet image, not the font size or any other style element. If you want a bullet image to appear higher in relation to the text, you have to make it physically taller in your image-editing program by adding more space at the bottom of the image.

Watch Out!

FIGURE 13.10
Two identical
lists show how
the standard
HTML bullet and
a **list-style-
image** behave
in relation to the
list item text
when different
style attribute
values are ap-
plied. To show
the bullet in rela-
tion to the box,
each list item
has a one-pixel
gray border on
all four sides.

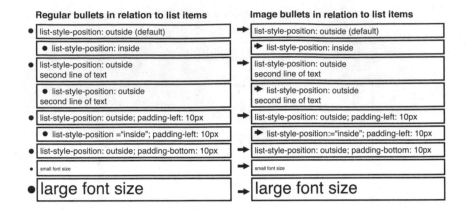

The List category in the New and Modify Style dialogs also includes the list-style-position attribute. It can be set to either inside or outside (outside is default). This attribute describes the position of the bullet in relation to the box. If it is set to outside, the bullet or bullet image appears outside of the box. If it is set to inside, the bullet or bullet image appears inside the box. This value does not change the actual distance between the bullet and the text, however. As you can see in Figure 13.10, the distance remains the same and is changed with the padding-left attribute. The difference between the two becomes apparent when the list item has more than one line of text because if the list-style-position is set to inside, the bullet is treated as if it is part of the text and the second line of text lines up with the edge of the box underneath the bullet.

Because of the somewhat odd behavior of list-style-images, many designers set the list-style-type for the list to none and create an li style using a regular no-repeat background image with the (x) background-position set to left and the (y) background-position set to center instead. Unlike the list-style-image, this background image centers vertically with the box for each line. Keep in mind that if you are doing this, you have to apply the background to the li style. If you apply it to the ul or ol style, the background image is applied to the list as a whole and not the individual list items.

Importing Adobe Photoshop Files

The term *web design* is a somewhat confusing one, especially when it comes to talking about the tools used. One can question whether the actual *design* of a page or site takes place in web-authoring software like Expression Web 2 or whether the designing occurs in other applications, and Expression Web 2 and similar programs merely build the framework to display the design. Regardless of where you stand in this debate, you cannot dismiss one fact: Pure design applications such as Expression Design 2 and Adobe Photoshop play an integral part in creating visually stunning websites.

More than just a tool for photographers to manipulate and clean up their photos, Adobe Photoshop has grown into a design platform from which you can create everything from artwork to broadcast graphics and websites. But creating graphics for a website using Photoshop always involved cropping and exporting images that you imported into the web-authoring application. And because the two applications were not connected, any change required in the image required a new round of exporting and importing the altered image. With Photoshop Import, Expression Web 2 has at least in part done away with this cumbersome process.

Try it Yourself ▼

Import an Image From a Photoshop File

In addition to regular file imports, Expression Web 2 has a dedicated function for importing Adobe Photoshop .psd files. And because .psd files usually contain several layers, you are given the ability to select which layers to include in the import so that you can produce several different images out of one file.

1. With the default.html page open in Design view, click File on the menu bar and select Adobe Photoshop (.psd) under Import. This opens a browser dialog where you select the .psd file you want to import. Select the file named myKipple sticker art.psd from the lesson files and click Open. This opens the Import Adobe Photoshop (.psd) File dialog (see Figure 13.11).

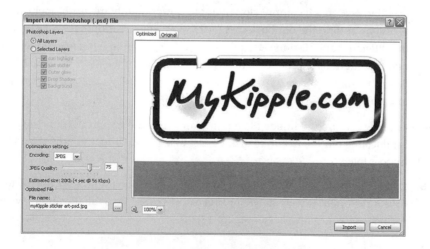

FIGURE 13.11
The Import Adobe Photoshop (.psd) File dialog gives you a series of option for importing and converting Adobe Photoshop files to web-ready images.

2. By default the All Layers option is checked, meaning the output will be the image as it appears with all the layers activated. By checking the Selected Layers option, you can select which layers to include in the final export (see Figure 13.12). The total area covered by the exported image changes with the content you choose to export, so if you uncheck the Background layer, the image size shrinks to contain only the remaining content. You can always click the Original tab to see what you just omitted and how your selections differ from the original image.

FIGURE 13.12
With the Background layer unchecked, the exported area shrinks to contain only the remaining layers.

3. When you are satisfied with your layer selection, you can choose whether to export the image as a GIF, JPEG, or PNG-24 from the Encoding drop-down menu under Compression Settings. If you choose JPEG, you have the further option of deciding how much compression to apply (lower quality means higher compression). Sliding the bar back and forth gives you a real-time preview of what the different compression settings do to the image. Choose the lowest possible quality that doesn't produce artifacts that ruin the image, as is the case in Figure 13.13. For this particular image, you can go as low as 33% without losing much in terms of quality.

4. Give the compressed image file a name and click the Import button. The image is added to your file tree in the Folder List task pane. Drag and drop it into the Images folder.

5. Delete the heading, and drag and drop the new image into the h1 box instead. Give it the alternative text `MyKipple.com sticker`. Save the file and preview the page in your browser (see Figure 13.14).

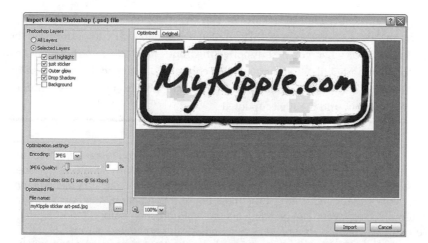

FIGURE 13.13
Setting the JPEG quality too low can lead to unsightly image artifacts. Use the slider to find a good middle ground between compression and quality.

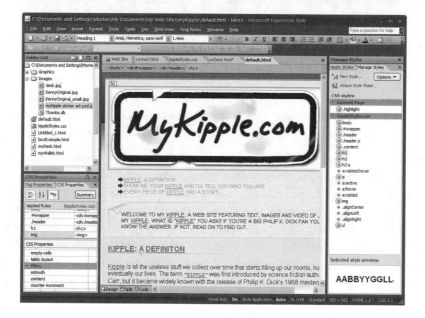

FIGURE 13.14
The imported Photoshop image is inserted in place of the original heading.

After placing the image on your page you might find that it doesn't quite work with the rest of the elements, or maybe you need to omit more layers or even change another element within the image. Because you created the image using the Photoshop import option, Expression Web 2 retains a link to the original .psd file so if you want to make changes to the image, you can do so directly from Design view.

When you right-click an image imported from a .psd file there is a new item called Adobe Photoshop (.psd) in the drop-down menu. From this submenu, you can choose Edit Source to open the original .psd file in whatever software is set as your default

.psd editor (probably Photoshop), or you can choose Update from Source to reopen the Import Adobe Photoshop (.psd) File dialog. From here you can perform all the same functions as when you first imported the image, and those changes will be applied to the imported file. If you have made changes to the .psd file outside of Expression Web 2 and want to update the image in the page to reflect these changes, click Import again and the file is updated.

Watch Out!

Although it is a great tool for easy management of imported images from .psd files, the Photoshop Import function is far from perfect. More specifically, it does not support some of Photoshop's more advanced features, such as blending options and certain effects. To get the most out of this function, it is necessary to flatten blending layers and blending options in Photoshop before importing the file into Expression Web 2 or you might end up with some very strange results. Fortunately the Preview window is accurate; if an effect is not supported, you will see it immediately.

Summary

For your websites to go to the next level, they need to have some visual elements included in the design. That means including images as noncontent elements. You can do this by adding images as backgrounds in your styles, classes, and IDs.

In this hour, you learned how to use images in different ways to make backgrounds work for different purposes. You saw that, through the use of tiling, a small image can be used to cover a large area. Depending on how you choose to repeat these background images, you can achieve many different looks with the same image. In addition, you saw how the background images and background colors can work together to make a consistent visual experience. Using a set of simple background images, you gave the entire page a new look, the heading class a new background, and even added an image-based underline to the h2 style. These diverse applications of background images should give you an idea of how far you can take your designs using more than just colored backgrounds.

Images can also style list items and in this hour you learned how to use the List category in the New and Modify Style dialogs to change the overall appearance of lists to include list-style-images as bullets. Moreover you learned how lists function differently from the other elements of a page and how to use this knowledge to your advantage.

Finally you got an in-depth look at the new Adobe Photoshop import function that lets you import and edit already imported .psd files right inside Expression Web 2 to significantly simplify the process of going from designing to authoring. With a firm understanding of this feature and its limitations, you can make your use of these two very different programs far more effective.

Q&A

Q. *I added one of my own images as a repeating background but I can see where each image ends and the next image begins like if I put tiles on a wall. How do I get that seamless floating feel to my backgrounds?*

A. The tricky part about using tiled images as backgrounds is that the left side has to match the right side and the top has to match the bottom. Otherwise you can see the "seams" between each of them. There is no magical snap-of-the-fingers way of making these images and it requires a lot of trial and error. It is often easier to find free tiling images by searching for "seamless background" on the web and use them.

Q. *I imported a transparent Photoshop file but when it is placed in the page it is no longer transparent. How do I preserve the transparency?*

A. To preserve transparency you have to use either the GIF or PNG file formats. By default imported Photoshop files are saved as JPEG files with no transparency. To make your image transparent, open the Photoshop Importer dialogue again and resave the file as a PNG.

Workshop

The Workshop has quiz questions and exercises to help you put to use what you just learned. If you get stuck, the answers to the quiz questions are in the next section. But try to answer them first. Otherwise you'll only be cheating yourself.

Quiz

1. *Given an image that has a 10 pixel wide solid box on the left, how do you use it as a background for a heading without the text appearing on top of the black box?*

2. *What is the maximum number of images you can pile on top of one another in a web page?*

Answers

1. To avoid having the text appear on top of the box you need to move the text to the right compared to the background image: Set the x-background-position to left and set the left padding to 15px. That way the text will appear 15 pixels to the right of the left edge and 5 pixels to the right of the box.

2. In theory there is no limit to how many images you can pile on top of one another. However in reality you are limited by the connection speed and processing power of the visiting computer: If you start stacking a lot of images the page will be slow to load and the browser may not be able to display the page properly. That doesn't mean you shouldn't do it, just think about how many images are actually necessary. I find that in most cases you can get away with flattening most of the images into one and only using one or two images in the final design.

Exercise

In the lesson files for this hour is the image file named headerBack.png. This image is meant to be the background for the .header style. Replace the current background image with this one. It should repeat only once.

The arrows with which you replaced the bullets in the list are too close to the text. Change the distance between the arrows and the text to give them some more breathing space.

Finally, change the myKipple.com sticker image to a PNG to preserve the background transparency using the Photoshop import functionality.

HOUR 14

Building the Framework

What You'll Learn in This Hour:

▶ How to design the layout of your page using pen and paper

▶ How to separate the of the layout using boxes

▶ How to understand and use CSS positioning

▶ How to create CSS layouts using the prepackaged layouts featured in Expression Web 2

▶ How to apply a separate layout style sheet to existing pages

▶ How to use Eric Meyer's CSS Sculptor to create advanced CSS layouts

Introduction

Designing a web page or website is more than just adding content and applying styles. Layout is also an important consideration. A good layout means better readability and, from that, better communication between the author and the reader. Likewise a bad layout can easily lead to the message getting lost and the reader ending up with a poor understanding of what the author meant to communicate.

So far you have focused mainly on content and learned how to style it. Now that you have a firm grasp on how to do that, it's time to start thinking about how to position the content on the page to make it more accessible, more pleasant, and easier to read. And you want to do this without adding any unnecessary content into your markup. You can do this in several different ways, but in this book the focus is on using groups of divs to contain and separate the content into a cohesive and intuitive layout.

In past hours, you have made some small layout changes to pages using Cascading Style Sheets (CSS). But in this hour, you fully immerse yourself in CSS layouts and learn how to apply them to existing content. You will also be introduced to the CSS Reset and see how it works to make your layouts cross-browser compatible.

The last portion of this hour will introduce you to a third-party application called Eric Meyer's CSS Sculptor. This application greatly simplifies the process of building advanced CSS layouts but is not a part of the standard Expression Web 2 package. It is included in this book because it is an excellent tool for beginners as well as advanced users that want to build CSS layouts without the hassle of having to muck around with the code.

Starting with Pen and Paper

This might come as a bit of a surprise, but it is often a good idea to start designing a website by sketching it out on a piece of paper (see Figure 14.1). Not only is a sketch

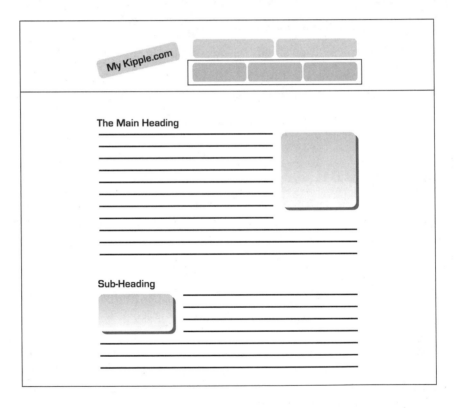

FIGURE 14.1
Drawing a sketch of your site layout on paper is a good starting point that gives you an idea of how to section out the page.

faster and easier to change than any other design method, it also gives you a blueprint of sorts to go by when you start building the framework to display the content of your site.

The benefit of starting with a sketch is that you can see almost right away whether the overall layout works and, if it does, what sections you need to define to make it work. As you learned earlier in this book, creating layouts using CSS means creating boxes within boxes within boxes, and you need to know and understand the relationship between these boxes before you build them.

Figure 14.1 shows a rough sketch of the layout of the main page of myKipple.com. The layout has two main sections: the header and the content. Within the header are several elements: a tiled image background that goes across the screen, an image background that shows a box, an image that shows the page title, and a row of buttons. You can see that the page's content page will be centered. From this information you can draw a set of boxes to indicate how to separate the content (see Figure 14.2).

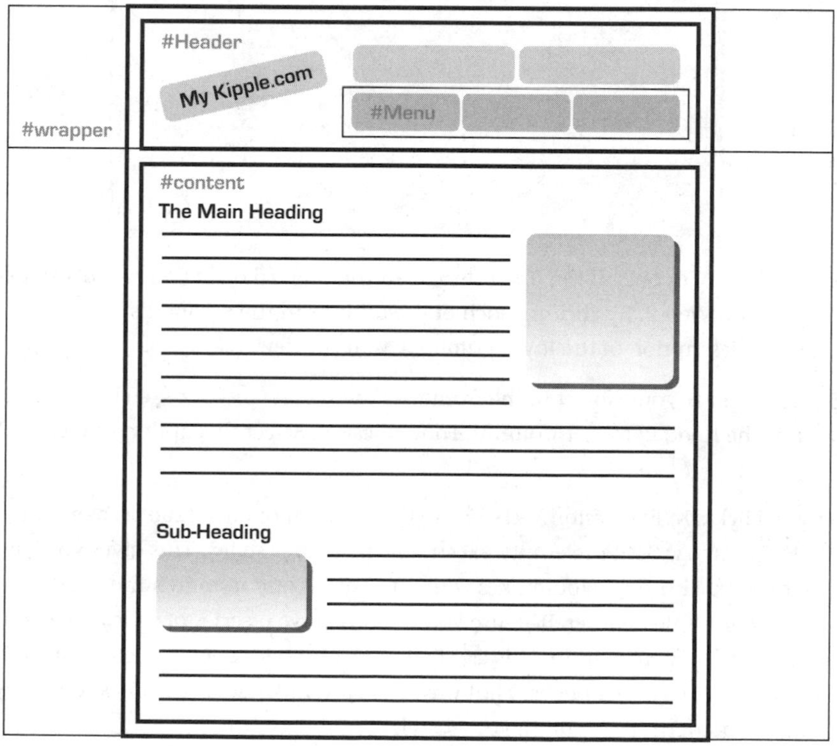

FIGURE 14.2
With the sketch of the page complete it is easy to draw boxes around content and get a clear picture of how the site will come together.

Building the Framework from Boxed Parts

Now that you know how you want to section the page, it's time to build the actual framework. There are many ways of doing this and none of them is wrong. Many designers prefer to build the framework from scratch, but it can be nice to get some help if you are new at design. Expression Web 2 has a series of ready-to-use, prepackaged CSS layouts that give you a bit of a head start.

1. Click New, Page from the File option on the menu bar. This opens the New dialog with the Page tab selected (see Figure 14.3).

FIGURE 14.3
From the New dialog, you can select a series of different prepackaged layouts for different applications including CSS.

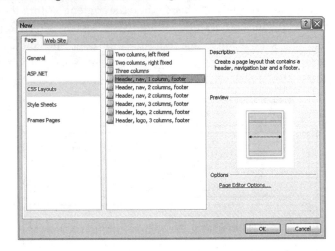

2. Click CSS Layouts in the first list to open the prepackaged CSS layouts in Expression Web 2. By clicking each of the options in the second list, you get a short description of the layout along with a preview.

3. Select the layout closest to the framework you drew in your sketch. In this case, it is the Header, Nav, 1 Column, Footer design. Select this option and click OK.

After you click OK, Expression Web 2 opens two new files: `Untitled_1.css` and `Untitled_1.html`. Both are empty except for the layout styles. This gives you the ability to work with the layout boxes without content and to match the overlay drawings you created earlier. Because you already have a series of styles defined for your pages, what you want to do is create a separate style sheet that contains only the layout portions of the pages. That way you can make quick changes to the layout without bothering with all the other styles.

Employing CSS Reset

Before you do this it is a good idea to insert a CSS reset into your style sheet. A **CSS reset** is a block of CSS code that removes all the preconceived notions that a browser might have about your page by setting everything to zero. Eric A. Meyer created the most comprehensive CSS reset around, and you can find it here: http://meyerweb. com/eric/tools/css/reset./

To apply the CSS reset, simply copy the code in its entirety from the web page and paste it into the top of the Untitled_1.css file you just created. Save the CSS file as layout.css. Because the Untitled_1.html file already links to the CSS file, the link updates automatically. Save the Untitled_1.html file as layoutTest.html.

Updating the ID Names

The next step is to change the ID names to match your drawing. You can do so directly in the CSS file or using the Modify Style option from the Manage Styles task pane. Change the name of #masthead to #header, #top-nav to #menu, and #page-content to #content. Leave #footer as it is. In layoutTest.html, go to Split view and make the same changes to the div IDs.

According to Figure 14.2, the menu ID should reside within the header ID. Go to Code view and move the </div> end tag for the header ID below the one for the menu ID—now the header div wraps the menu div.

Finally wrap all the boxes in an outside box with the #wrapper ID attached. To wrap all the other IDs, create a new <div> on the line before the first div and give it the ID wrapper. With all the changes made, the page's code inside the <body> tags should look like this (comments added to make it easier to read):

```
<body>

<div id="wrapper">
<div id="header">
<div id="menu">
</div> <!— end menu —>
</div> <!— end header —>
<div id="content">
</div> <!— end content —>
<div id="footer">
</div> <!— end footer —>
</div> <!— end wrapper —>

</body>
```

Now that you have inserted a call to the ID wrapper, you need to add another one either directly in the layout.css file or by using the New Style button in the Manage Styles pane.

Styling the Layout Boxes

With the layout boxes created, it is time to style them to make the page match the sketch. This requires the use of all the techniques you learned in earlier hours as well as some new ones. The goal here is to remove all the layout styling from the kippleStyles.css file and store it in the new layout.css file. You can choose to make the following style modifications using the Modify Style dialog, directly in the layout.css file using IntelliSense, or both.

1. The layout drawing calls for a tiled graphic background that goes across the top of the page. Modify the body style by setting background-image to the backgroundTile.gif file found in the Graphics folder, with a background-repeat value of repeat-x and background-color set to #F3EFEF (see Figure 14.4).

FIGURE 14.4
Change the **body** style to add a tiled background that repeats along the top of the page.

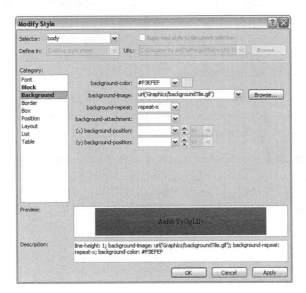

2. The content of the page hovers in the middle of the page with a specific width. Center the content by setting the #wrapper ID margin-left and margin-right attributes to auto. Set the width attribute to 665px (see Figure 14.5).

FIGURE 14.5
It's often just as easy to make quick changes to the styles in a CSS page by editing the code directly. Here the **width** attribute in the **#wrapper** style is set using IntelliSense.

```
44 ins {
45     text-decoration: none;
46 }
47 del {
48     text-decoration:
49 }
50
51 /* tables still need
52 table {
53     border-collapse:
54     border-spacing: 0;
55 }
56 /* ---------------------------------------- */
57 /* END CSS RESET */
58 /* ---------------------------------------- */
59
60 /* CSS layout */
61 #wrapper {
62     margin-right: auto;
63     margin-left: auto;
64     width:
65 }
```

Length
Length value: 665   px
OK   Cancel

3. The #header ID has a background image as well. Set background-image to the headerBack.png file in the Graphics folder and set background-repeat to no-repeat. Because the headerBack.png file is transparent, leave background-color blank to allow the body background to shine through. The #header should have a fixed size no matter what content you add, so set the height value to 130px. That height matches the height of the headerBack.png image. To make the background image for the #header ID line up with the back-ground tiles, set the margin-top value to 7px.

4. On the drawing, the #menu ID is along the bottom and close to the right corner of the #header box. To make this happen you need to make some changes to the position attributes of both #header and #menu. First change the position of the #header ID to relative. Then set the position attribute for the #menu ID to absolute and the bottom and right attributes (under the Position category in the Modify Style dialog) to 0px. Finally set the margin-right attribute to 25px so that the content you put inside the menu div displays on top of the background graphic rather than to its side.

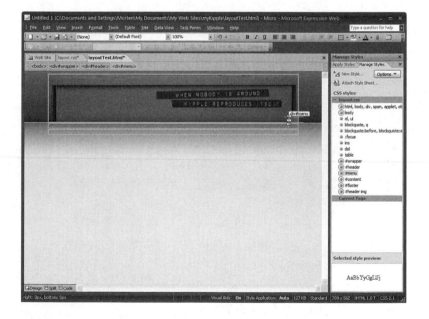

FIGURE 14.6
When everything is set correctly the **#menu** ID should hover to the lower-right side of the **#header** box, independent of the remaining content.

As you can see from figure 14.6 you now have the basic framework for the page as it appears in the drawing. And all this was done using only CSS which means the HTML markup has not changed.

In step 4 you used the position attribute to force the menu div down into the right hand corner of the header. This gives you a first glimpse of the powerful and often misunderstood CSS tool called positioning. Understanding positioning means you have the power to control your content in ways you could never do before.

Understanding Positioning

In the last part of the preceding example you used the position attribute to place a div in the lower-right corner of another div. This is a nice segue into the confusing and often misunderstood issue of positioning in CSS.

If you open the Modify Style dialog for any of the current styles, classes, or IDs, you see that the position attribute (found under the Position category) has five options: absolute, fixed, relative, static, and inherit (see Figure 14.7). The physical po-

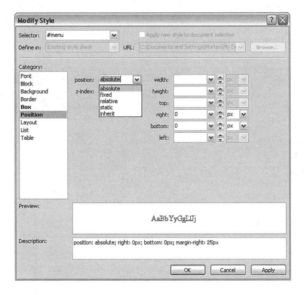

sition of any object in a page depends on what this attribute is set to in the current style and whatever style that wraps it.

position: absolute;

The easiest way to explain an element with an absolute position is to think of it as an image (or any other object) pasted onto a page and largely ignoring the rest of the content. The physical placement of an element with an absolute position is decided by setting the pixel value of its distance from the nearest positioned container with the top, right, bottom, and left attributes. In other words, an object with absolute position that has a top value of 20px and a left value of 30px appears exactly 20 pixels from the top and 30 pixels to the left of the edge of the page or the closest container box that has a `position` value other than `static`. Setting an object's `position` attribute to `absolute` removes it from the flow of the page. That means unless you pay close attention, you might accidentally place objects with absolute positions directly on top of other content.

In the `layoutTest.html` page, the #menu div has an absolute position zero pixels from the bottom and zero pixels from the right side of the #header div because the #header position is set to `relative`. If you change the #header `position` attribute to `static`, the #menu div is positioned absolutely in relation to the nearest parent with a position other than static, in this case the body, which means it aligns itself with the edge of the page and ends up in the lower right of the window.

If you set the `position` attribute of a style, class, or ID to `absolute` without setting values for `top`, `right`, `bottom`, and `left`, the object appears in the default upper-left corner position (see Figure 14.8).

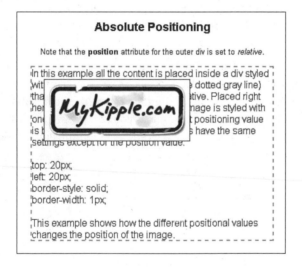

FIGURE 14.8
In this example, the image style has its **position** attribute set to **absolute**. Because the containing div has its **position** set to **relative**, the position of the image is relative to this div rather than to the page as a whole.

position: fixed;

Fixed positioning works similarly to absolute positioning except that where the physical position of an object with an absolute position can relate to other positioned objects, the physical position of a fixed object is always based solely on the outer edges of the page as a whole (see Figure 14.9).

The first version of Microsoft Internet Explorer to support the `fixed` value for the `position` attribute was Internet Explorer 7. Older versions of Internet Explorer do not understand the value and your layout will not work properly in them.

Watch Out!

FIGURE 14.9
In this example
the image style
has the
position at-
tribute set to
fixed. Unlike
Figure 14.8, the
positioning of
the image in this
page is relative
to the page as a
whole.

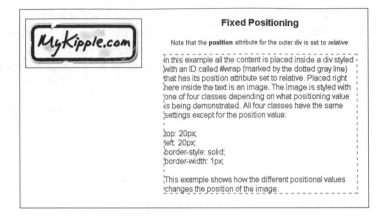

position: relative;

The easiest way to explain relative positioning is to imagine that you cut an image out of a printed page and repositioned it somewhere else on the page. Because you cut out the image from the page, there is a hole where it was and the image covers content wherever you glue it.

Placement of an object with a relative position is in relation to its original location in the flow of the page. As an example, that means an image with its `position` attribute set to `relative` and its `bottom` attribute set to `20px` appears 20 pixels above the location at which it was originally inserted. If you compare Figure 14.10 and Figure 14.11 (in the next section) you can see the differences in the object's placement.

FIGURE 14.10
In this example,
the image style
has its
position at-
tribute set to
relative. The
space the image
would normally
occupy is left
empty but the
image is shifted
to the right and
down because of
the **top** and
left values.

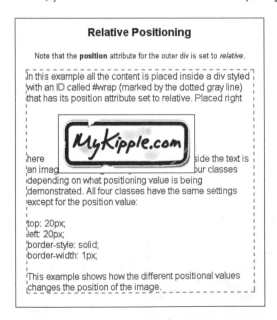

`position: static;`

`static` is the default setting for any style. Setting an object's `position` attribute to `static` places the object in the flow as normal. The object is unaffected by the `top`, `right`, `bottom`, and `left` attributes (see Figure 14.11).

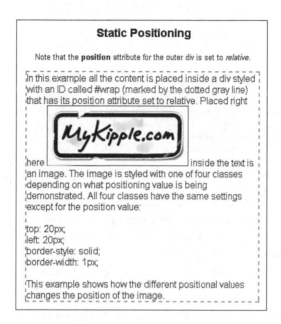

FIGURE 14.11
In this example, the image style has its **position** attribute set to **static**. The image lines up with the rest of the text and is not displaced despite the **top** and **left** attribute values being the same as in Figures 14.8, 14.9, and 14.10.

`position: inherit`

If you look closely you'll see that the value *inherit* appears in almost every drop-down menu when you create CSS. Inherit literally means that the current elements inherits this style from whatever elements is directly above it in the cascade.

Applying the Framework to Existing Pages

Now that you have created the framework for the myKipple site in a different style sheet from the one you were working on before, you need to alter the existing markup files and style sheet. Because `default.html` is the home page, it is a good place to start. Before you go any further, remove the big sticker graphic in the header and move the rest of the content in the header down into the content area.

The first step is to remove the existing IDs and classes from the `<div>` tags within the page. You're doing so because you created a new set of IDs and classes to handle the overall layout of the page. The easiest way to remove the IDs and classes is to do it from Code view, but you can use the Edit Tag function found under the Quick Tag Selector.

Place your cursor anywhere inside the page and click the menu arrow on one of the <div> tags in the Quick Tag Selector. Select Edit Tag from the drop-down menu and remove the class or ID portion of the tag (see Figure 14.12).

FIGURE 14.12
Using the Edit Tag function to change your tags ensures that the change applies only to the tag in question and you won't accidentally delete other code.

After you remove the IDs from the containing tags, you can see that they are no longer in use by looking at the Manage Styles task pane. The dots prefixing *#wrapper*, .header, and .content no longer have a gray ring around them. You can delete these IDs and classes directly from the task pane by highlighting them and pressing the Delete button on your keyboard or by right-clicking and selecting Delete from the context menu.

With the old layouts removed, it is time to apply the new ones. To do this you first have to attach the new layout.css style sheet to the file. As you learned earlier, you do this by clicking the Attach Style Sheet button in the Apply and Manage Styles task panes. Select the layout.css file with the Browse button and be sure to enable the Attach to All HTML Pages option.

With the new style sheet attached, you see a dramatic change in how the page appears in Design view. That is because the new style sheet contains the CSS reset that removes all default styling from the content (see Figure 14.13). Furthermore, when you attach a second style sheet, you insert it below the first one in the HTML code and this means it gets more weight or importance in the style cascade. The CSS reset affects all default selectors, but in the kippleStyles.css file you have already styled several of these so you want your old styles to have more weight. To give kippleStyles.css more weight than layout.css, simply change the order of the two styles as they appear in the HTML code so that layout.css is first and kippleStyles.css is second. After the change, the two lines of code directly before the </head> end tag should read:

```
<link href="layout.css" rel="stylesheet" type="text/css" />
<link href="kippleStyles.css" rel="stylesheet" type="text/css" />
```

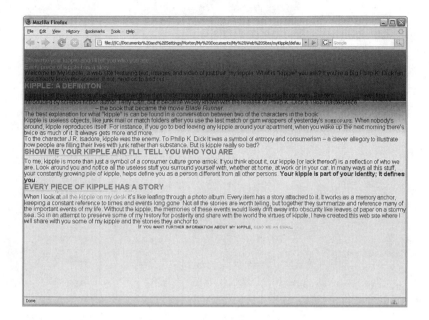

FIGURE 14.13
After applying the CSS reset to your page, all the content that has not been styled will be crammed together. It might look weird but this is actually what you want because it means you now have a clean slate to work with.

If you preview the page in your browser at this point, you will notice two things: First, the text spreads out over the entire width of the page because no you have not applied layout styling. Second, all the text is jammed together; that is, there is no breathing room between the paragraphs, headings, and block quotes except for the h2 headings. This might look like a big problem, but it is exactly what you want: If the different selector boxes are stacked directly on top of one another (meaning there is no breathing room between the paragraphs, headings, and so on), the browser is not making any assumptions about your styles if you do not provide a style. In other words, your page looks the same in all browsers.

Try it Yourself ▼

Apply the New Framework to the Page

Now that you have attached the new style sheet, you can apply the new framework to the page:

1. In Design view, place your cursor anywhere within the content. In the Quick Tag Selector, click the `<div>` tag that immediately follows the `<body>` tag. This is the outermost div that contains all the content, so all the content should highlight.

2. With the first `<div>` tag highlighted, go to the Apply Styles task pane and click the #wrapper ID under the `layout.css` file (see Figure 14.14). This applies the new ID to the tag.

▼

FIGURE 14.14
Using the Quick Tag Selector in conjunction with the Apply Styles task pane ensures that you apply the correct style, class, or ID to the correct tag.

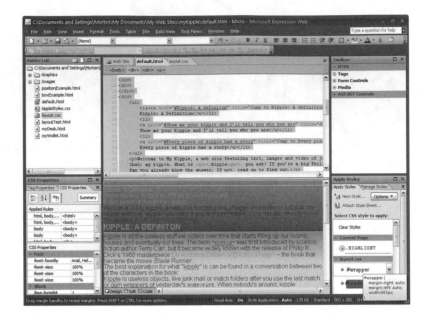

3. In Code View, find the `<div>` tag directly under the one you just changed (which now reads `<div ID="wrapper">`). Place your cursor anywhere inside the new tag and click the `#header` ID in the Apply Styles task pane. When you click Design view to refresh it, the box graphic you earlier set as a background appears.

4. Place the cursor anywhere inside the main content of the page and use the Quick Tag Selector to select the one remaining unstyled `<div>` tag. Apply the `#content` ID to it to wrap the content of the page.

If you save and preview the page in your browser, you see that the page has started to look like the layout drawing from the start of this hour (see Figure 14.15).

Although this page has started to look complete, a few items are still missing: There is no big sticker in the header and there is no menu to the right.

▼ **Try it Yourself**

Add a Header Image and a Menu

In the sketch of the page layout (refer to Figure 14.1), the header features a large MyKipple.com sticker and a menu. These are important elements of any website—the

▼

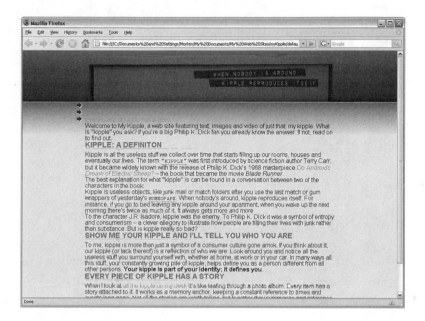

FIGURE 14.15
With the frame-
work applied, the
page has started
to look like the
drawing in Figure
14.1.

header image (or site name) provides as an intuitive link back to the home page and the main menu. In effect, the header functions as a primary navigational tool for the visitor.

1. The Graphics folder contains the image file `kippleSticker.png`. Click and drag the image into the header in Design view and give it the alternative text **MyKipple.com**.

2. When inserted, the image has both padding and a one-pixel gray border (see Figure 14.16). This is because it is being styled by the `img` style you created in an earlier hour. To ensure that the `img` style applies only to images within the `#content` area, use the Manage Styles task pane to change the Selector Name of the `img` style to **#content img**. When you change the style name, the **kippleSticker.png** changes position to hug the upper-left corner of the `#header` box.

3. To line up the `kippleSticker.png` image with the background, you have to create a new style. Click the New Style button in the Manage Styles task pane and set the Selector Name to **#header img**. This style applies only to images within the **#header** ID. Change the Define In field to Existing Style Sheet and select `kippleStyles.css` from the drop-down menu. Under the Box category, set `padding-top` to 30px and `padding-left` to 33px. Click OK to apply the style. The header image now lines up perfectly with the background image (see Figure 14.17).

FIGURE 14.16
When inserted, the **kippleSticker.png** image has both a border and padding applied by the **img** style created in an earlier hour.

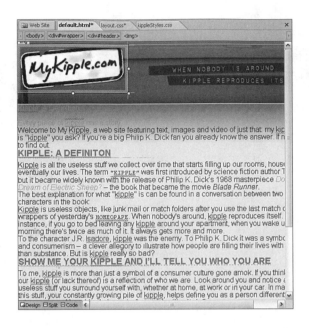

FIGURE 14.17
With the new **#header img** style applied, the image lines up perfectly with the background image.

4. Change to Split view and click the image to find the corresponding code. In Code view, find the end </div> tag, create a new line before it and type **<ul>** (both the image and the unordered list must be contained within the <div>). IntelliSense will create the closing </ul> tag for you. Press Enter to create a new line and type **<li>** to create a list item. Between the <li> and </li> tags, type

Button 1. Repeat the process to create three list items called Button 1, Button 2, and Button 3. In the end, the code looks like this:

```
<div id="header">
    <img alt="MyKipple.com" height="93" src="Graphics/kippleSticker.png"
    width="229" />
    <ul>
    <li>Button 1</li>
    <li>Button 2</li>
    <li>Button 3</li>
    </ul>
</div>
```

5. In Design view, the new list you created appears on top of the other list on the page. To solve this problem, click the list in Design view, select the <ul> tag, and apply the #menu ID using the Apply or Manage Styles task pane. This moves the list to the lower-right corner of the #header box (see Figure 14.18).

FIGURE 14.18
With the **#menu** ID applied to the **<ul>** tag, the list appears at the lower-right corner of the header.

6. To make the list items appear one next to the other rather than in a stack, as they are now, create a new style with the Selector Name **#menu li** to be defined in **kippleStyles.css** and set the display attribute under the Layout category to inline. Click OK to apply the change, and then save and preview the page in your browser. The result should look similar to Figure 14.19.

FIGURE 14.19
Adding the header image and a dummy menu to the page.

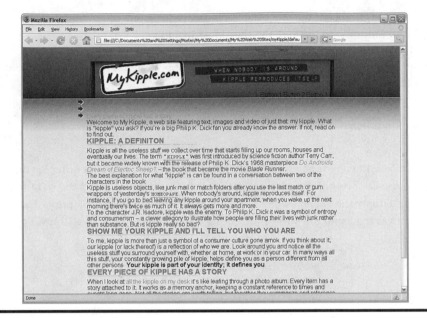

Building the Framework Using Eric Meyer's CSS Sculptor

Not surprisingly, the framework of your page plays an integral role in the design process: Without a solid framework, your page will never look and work the way you intend for it to. Using the prepackaged CSS layouts that come with Expression Web 2 is a good place to start, but as you have seen there are only a few options available. Even after you apply those options, there is still a lot of work to do before they work properly.

In conjunction with the release of Expression Web 2, WebAssist released Eric Meyer's CSS Sculptor—a plug-in that simplifies the CSS-building process. Even though it is a third party application, the extent to which it helps new and experienced designers and developers create solid CSS layouts make it a worthwhile consideration for Expression Web 2 users.

Watch Out!

Eric Meyer's CSS Sculptor from WebAssist is third-party software and is a separate purchase from Expression Web 2. As of this writing, the price is $99.99 from the WebAssist store. I advise you to look through the following tutorials and the examples on the WebAssist website, and carefully consider future projects before you purchase the application. The question you should ask yourself is this: Will I be making a lot of different CSS layouts in the future using the prepackaged layouts in Expression Web 2? If the answer is yes, there is a good chance CSS

Sculptor will be a useful addition to your program package. That said, CSS Sculptor is not an application you *need* to create CSS layouts—it just makes the process a lot easier. In the end, all CSS Sculptor does is build advanced style sheets so that you don't have to do all the styling manually.

To get Eric Meyer's CSS Sculptor, visit the WebAssist website at https://www.webassist.com/professional/expressionweb/ and select the application. After you download and install the application, it automatically shows up in Expression Web 2 under File on the menu bar (see Figure 14.20).

FIGURE 14.20
After installation, CSS Sculptor automatically shows up in the File, New menu in Expression Web 2.

What makes using CSS Sculptor different from using the prepackaged CSS layouts found under CSS Layouts in the New Page option is that CSS Sculptor gives you complete control of all elements of the layout before you actually apply it to a page. The basic premise of the application is that you should have complete control of all aspects of your layout, not just how many boxes it contains. To get a better understanding of what CSS Sculptor does and how it can help you, let's go through the options and see how they work.

The Layout Tab

When you select New CSS Sculptor Page from File on the menu bar, the CSS Sculptor dialog opens to the Layout tab in Expression Web 2 (see Figure 14.21). From this tab, you set the basic layout and design using the drop-down menus. The application provides 30 preset layouts and 11 design schemes. The layouts vary from one to three

FIGURE 14.21
The Layout tab in
CSS Sculptor
lets you set the
basic layout and
color scheme for
your layout.

columns with varying width and position settings and options of headers, footers, and menu bars. The designs are different color schemes that apply to the components.

After you have picked a layout and design scheme, you can change the width and position of the content through the options under Page Structure.

> If you are dissatisfied with your changes or you want to start over you can click the Reset buttons next to either the Layout menu (resets everything except the layout) or the Design menu (resets everything except layout and design) to get back to where you started.

From the Layout Components section, you can turn Header, Top Navigation, Content Area, and Footer on and off with the check boxes and change the number of left and right columns or sidebars to be added to the content area.

The Box Tab

When you are satisfied with the overall layout and design scheme, you move on to the Box tab (see Figure 14.22). This tab is very similar to the Box category found in the New and Modify Styles dialogs in Expression Web 2. From here you see the layout's order in the cascade, and you can control the Box Model aspects of each component.

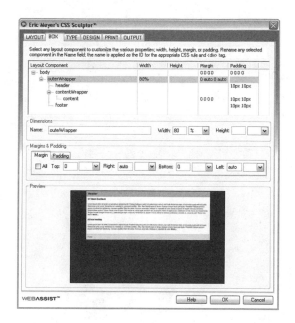

FIGURE 14.22
The Box tab shows you the order of the layout boxes in the cascade, and lets you control the Box Model aspects of each component.

The top window in the Box tab shows you the layout tree and the box values attributed to each layout component. You can select individual components in the tree by clicking them to activate the editing features for each.

After you select a component, you can change its name, width, and height from the Dimensions area. These changes apply throughout the application, so if you change the name, the new name applies to all the relevant components in the page.

Directly underneath you find the tabs for Margin and Padding, where you can set values for each side individually or for all sides at once. These values can be set for each component in the layout tree.

The Type Tab

Next on the list is the Type tab (see Figure 14.23). From here you can set most of the standard type (text) selectors for each layout component you have created.

Just as in the Box tab, the Type tab starts with a layout tree showing all the components and the type styles attached to them. You can select each component individually from the layout component tree to style the content within it further.

In the Type area, you can set all the standard type attributes such as font, size, weight, color, and so on for each main type selector. These styles apply to the currently selected layout component. Using this feature, you can easily set font attributes for the entire page, parts of the page, or elements within a particular box.

FIGURE 14.23
The Type tab
gives you control
of most of the
standard type
selectors for
each layout com-
ponent.

The Design Tab

The Design tab has all the options for the visual aspects of each of the layout components (see Figure 14.24). You can select each component from the layout component
tree to edit its features.

FIGURE 14.24
The Design tab
lets you control
the visual as-
pects, such as
background color
and borders, of
each of your lay-
out boxes.

In the Background section, you can set the background color and background image attributes. The Image Source, Image Repeat and Attachment, and Image Position tabs let you micromanage the background image placement and behavior just like you did in the New and Manage Style dialog earlier in this hour. Likewise, the Border section gives you complete control of every aspect of the border for all the elements in the layout component tree.

The Print Tab

When you style a page using CSS, you have the option of creating a separate style sheet that applies only when the visitor prints out the page on paper. CSS Sculptor automates this process for you through the Print tab (see Figure 14.25). From here

FIGURE 14.25
The Print tab provides separate controls for the style sheet used if a visitor wants to print out the page on paper.

you can turn off styling elements such as width, background colors, and images and create a printer-friendly version of your layout.

You can change the attributes of each individual component on the Print tab by selecting it from the layout component tree, just as with the other tabs, but you can also make global (pagewide) changes using the Global options. As their names suggest, Convert Divs to Page Width sets all the containing boxes to the width of the printable area on the page; Convert Divs to Black and White removes all color information from the divs and their content; and Set Margins and Padding to Zero resets the margins and padding. These options are useful because designers often use div widths, colors, margins, and padding to achieve layouts that work well on a screen but waste ink and space when printed.

The Dimensions option lets you set the width of the components independently. The Display options let you control individual components by hiding them, converting them to black and white, or setting margins and padding to zero just as in the Global options.

The Output Tab

Output is the final tab in CSS Sculptor (see Figure 14.26). From here you can set whether you want the styles embedded in the <head> tag of the current page, placed

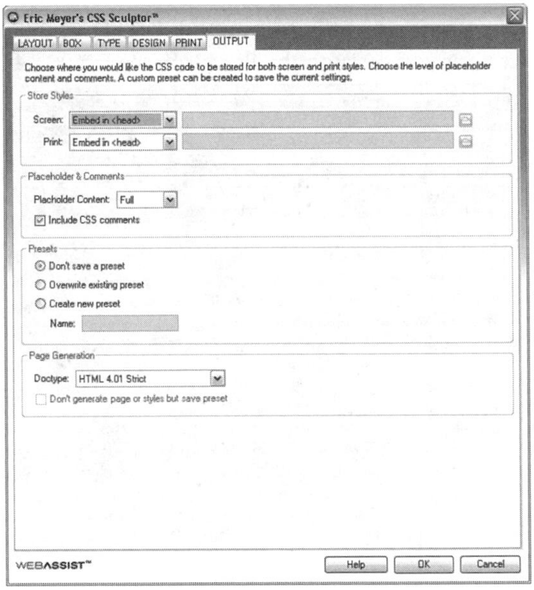

FIGURE 14.26
Among other things, the Output tab lets you decide how you want to save the styles you created using CSS Sculptor.

in a new style sheet, or inserted in an existing style sheet. This is set for the screen and print styles individually.

Under Placeholder & Comments, you control what kind of extra content CSS Sculptor inserts in your pages. The Placeholder Content option lets you choose whether you want CSS Sculptor to include full, minimal, or no dummy content into the layout you create. This feature is useful because, with no content inserted, it can be hard to navigate among different layout components. The Include CSS Comments option inserts nonfunctional content into the CSS code to explain, for future reference, what the different components do.

Presets lets you save and overwrite the existing preset with your current layout or save the layout as a new preset. With this feature, you can create a series of highly customized layouts that you can access from the Layout drop-down menu under the Layout tab.

Finally the Page Generation options let you set the doctype of the pages generated. The doctype tells the browser how to interpret the code in the page. For most purposes, you don't need to change this option. If you chose Overwrite Existing Preset or Create New Preset in the Presets area, you can check the Don't Generate Page or Styles but Save Preset option.

The Final File(s) Generated by CSS Sculptor

When you are satisfied with all the settings and you click OK, CSS Sculptor produces a new HTML file. It also creates any corresponding CSS files if you chose to keep the styles separate. The CSS files contain an abbreviated version of the CSS reset you inserted earlier, and you attach the external style sheets to the HTML page using the @import technique. After CSS Sculptor creates the pages and style sheets with all their dummy content and comments, they work exactly like any other page or style sheet in Expression Web 2.

In the lesson files for this hour is a CSS Sculptor folder that contains an HTML page and two style sheets generated by CSS Sculptor. Look at those files to get an idea of what kind of output this application generates.

Summary

When it comes to communicating a message with visual media, whether printed or on screen, design and layout are paramount. If the content doesn't look inviting, no one will give it a second look. Nowhere is this truer than when it comes to the Web. With the millions upon millions of websites out there, your site has to stand out if it is to generate an audience. To do that it needs to have a solid and easy-to-understand layout and it has to look the same no matter who is viewing it.

In this hour, you learned to use CSS to create layouts. By using CSS, you are separating the layout information from the content information and thereby making it easier for everyone to access the information you are communicating through your site. You learned how to use the prepackaged CSS layouts as a starting point to create a proper framework to house all your content, and you learned how to apply this framework to existing pages using a variety of methods in Code view and Design view.

To ensure that your page looks the same across all browsers, it is necessary to remove all assumptions that a browser might make about the styling of your content. You can achieve this by inserting a CSS reset in your style sheet. This code resets all the styles on the page so that you have a clean slate to start with. And because of the cascade, applying a CSS reset in the top of your CSS file means you can restyle all the content further down in the cascade to get the results you want.

CSS positioning is a topic that can be confusing even to seasoned professionals. This hour presented a thorough walkthrough of what the four different positioning values (absolute, fixed, relative, and static) mean and how they work. Understanding these values, and how to use them, means you can easily create advanced layouts that go outside the norm.

Because creating CSS layouts can be incredibly time-consuming, this hour also covered a third-party application: Eric Meyer's CSS Sculptor. This application gives you far greater flexibility in creating layouts from scratch and is a great help for anyone who works a lot with CSS. With that said, you did the same job yourself in the tutorials in this hour, so CSS Sculptor is not a tool you **must** have in your arsenal. CSS Sculptor is, however, a tool that can help you work more efficiently.

In the next hour, you will learn about buttons and how to use Expression Web 2's built-in functions Expression Web 2to create advanced buttons.

Q&A

Q. *When I create a new CSS layout, all I get is a series of empty boxes. Why is that?*

A. The prepackaged CSS layouts in Expression Web 2 are little more than empty divs with some very basic positioning in them. The intention is to give the user a clean slate to work with, but in reality there is very little difference between using the prepackaged layouts and creating the layouts from scratch. The one advantage of using the layouts is that all the divs have proper names and positions, so you don't have to keep tabs on absolutely everything.

Q. *When I created new menu buttons in the header from Design view, the header image became part of the first line item. What am I doing wrong?*

A. It can be extremely hard to avoid including objects such as images in lists when you create them in Design view. This is why the tutorial specifically asked you to use Code view to create the list. However, there is nothing wrong with using Design view to do this task. The problem of including the image in the list item is easy to fix: All you have to do is go to Code view and move the `<ul>` and `<li>` tags from their current location before the `<img>` tag to a new line directly after the end of the image line (which as you know from an earlier hour is `/>`). Now the image is outside of the list.

Q. *When I added the new* `layout.css` *style sheet, I noticed that there are now many different versions of the styles such as* body *and* p. *Isn't that a problem?*

A. The new style sheet includes the CSS reset, which has all the available selectors listed and set to 0. Further down in the style sheet and in the `kippleStyles.css` style sheet, the same selectors are styled a second and sometimes even a third time. This isn't a problem as much as a deliberate exploitation of the cascade: You reset the styles to 0 at the start and then create new styles that apply fresh styles farther down the line. This piling of styles is a good illustration of how the cascade works and is something you should take note of for future reference: The farther down in the style sheet a style is, the more weight or importance it has.

Workshop

The Workshop has quiz questions and exercises to help you put to use what you have just learned. If you get stuck, the answers to the quiz questions are in the next section. But try to answer them first. Otherwise you'll only be cheating yourself.

Quiz

1. *What is the benefit of using CSS to create page layouts?*

2. *What is a CSS Reset and why should you always use it?*

3. *Given an image placed in the middle of a block of text, briefly describe what happens to the image when its position is set to absolute, fixed, relative and static.*

Answers

1. CSS layouts have many benefits but the most important one is that they give you the ability to completely change the layout of multiple pages without actually changing the pages themselves. You can also create multiple layouts the visitor can choose from to suit her preference without cluttering the markup. Finally you can "port" a good layout to a new page easily by attaching the existing style sheet to the new page and just adding some classes and IDs to the <div>s in the new page.

2. A CSS Reset is a block of CSS code that sets all the different styles and selectors browsers usually make assumptions about to zero. By applying it to your designs you ensure that different browsers don't start changing your designs or layouts on a whim just because the browser designer thinks all paragraphs should have a 15px top padding for instance.

3. With absolute positioning the image is taken out of the flow of the page and will appear in the top left hand corner of the page or whatever containing element has a positioning other than static. With fixed positioning the image is taken out of the flow of the page and will appear in the top left hand corner of the page no matter what. With relative positioning the area the image takes up remains in the flow of the page and the image itself appears in a set position relative to its original location. With no other values attached it will appear where it was placed. Static positioning is the default position and the image will appear in the flow of the text where it was placed.

Exercise

The new `layout.css` style sheet includes a CSS reset that removes all the regular styling from the content within your page. As a result most of, if not all, the text is crammed together. Create and modify styles to space out the text and make it more approachable by using what you learned in this and previous hours. In particular, create or modify the styles for `#content p`, `#content ul`, and `#content blockquote`.

Using what you learned about positioning, try to change the location of different content in the page. For example, see whether you can move the menu in the header to the upper-right corner of the page.

Buttons, Buttons, Buttons

What You'll Learn in this Hour:

▶ How to create buttons using Expression Web 2's Interactive Buttons feature

▶ How to create simple box buttons using CSS

▶ How to make the simple box buttons more advanced by using background images

▶ How to use the sliding doors technique to use one background image for multiple button stages

▶ How to hide the button text from the browser without removing it entirely

Introduction

What makes a website different from all other visual media is the ability to navigate through content with the use of hyperlinks. But plain text hyperlinks are not always the best option. If you want to showcase a particular link or if you are creating a menu, you need to turn those links into buttons.

There are many ways to create buttons, some easy and some more complicated. This hour will explain how to use some button-making techniques and describe their advantages and disadvantages.

As before, accessibility is a primary focus of this chapter. In other words, if you strip away all the styles, graphics, and scripting, there should still be an understandable hyperlink left in the markup. Designers often ignore this aspect that can, in some cases, prevent the visitor from navigating through a site when the images, Flash movies, or other elements don't load properly. But because making buttons accessible is easy, there is no good reason not to do it.

Buttons: A Brief Definition

What is a button in web terms? In the absolute basic form, a *button* is a clearly de-fined and contained visual object on a web page that functions as a hyperlink. This object can be plain text with a background, text with an image background—just a static image or an interactive or animated graphic element that changes with the mouse behaviors. A button differs from a hyperlink in that it is not merely a string of text but is some form of graphic element with a clearly defined active area.

Of course, as with all definitions, experts can question and dispute this one. For this book, however, this definition will suffice.

Creating Interactive Buttons Using Expression Web 2

Expression Web 2 has a built-in feature that lets you build advanced and modern-looking buttons without creating graphics or importing images from a different pro-gram. The Interactive Buttons feature works by creating several different images for the different button states that switch out depending on how the user interacts with the button using JavaScript. As with everything else in Expression Web 2, the code generated for the Interactive Buttons is standards-based and, as a result, the buttons look and work the same in all browsers as long as they support JavaScript. If the user turned off JavaScript or the browser is too old, the viewer sees only the inactive state of the button, but the links within it still work.

Making an Interactive Button

The Interactive Buttons function in Expression Web 2 gives you the ability to create advanced interactive buttons without ever leaving the program or importing graph-ics or images.

1. Create and open a new HTML page called `buttons.html` in Design view. Give it the h1 heading **Button Examples** and create the h2 subheading **Interactive Buttons.** Press Enter to create a new line underneath the sub-heading.

2. To create a new interactive button, open the Insert menu and scroll down to In-teractive Button. Click the option to open the Interactive Buttons dialog.

3. The Interactive Buttons dialog has three main tabs: Button, Font, and Image. The first step in creating a new button is to select the look of the button from the Buttons menu. The different designs are grouped in categories such as Bor-

der, Corporate, Glass, Jewel, and Metal and each category has subcategories. Most of the designs feature text contained inside some form of box, but a few of them are icons with text next to them.

4. After you have selected a design you like, insert the text you want to display on the button in the Text box and set the link you want the button to point to in the Link box. You can link to pages within your site or to any other site on the Web. For this example, give the button the text **Interactive Button** and link it back to the **buttons.html** page (see Figure 15.1).

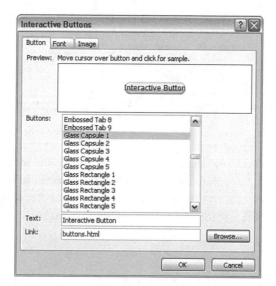

FIGURE 15.1
Under the Button tab in the Interactive Buttons dialog, you can pick the design of your button, set the text to display on the button, and define the link to which it should point.

5. Under the Font tab you can control the font family, style, and size for the text inside the button. Because the button with the font will be converted to an image, you are not restricted by the web-safe fonts and you can pick whatever font you have on your computer. Below the font, style, and size options you can set the font color for each of the three main states of the button: original font color, hovered font color, and pressed font color. Set the original font color to gray, hovered front color to black, and pressed font color to silver. Below these options you can set the horizontal and vertical alignment of the text in relation to the button. The Preview window lets you test the button in real-time to see the changes you have made (see Figure 15.2).

The horizontal and vertical dotted lines in the Preview window are guides to tell you whether your text is properly placed within the button. If the text spills over the lines, the button is too small or the text is too long. You can change the size of the button from the Image tab to make it fit the text.

Did you Know?

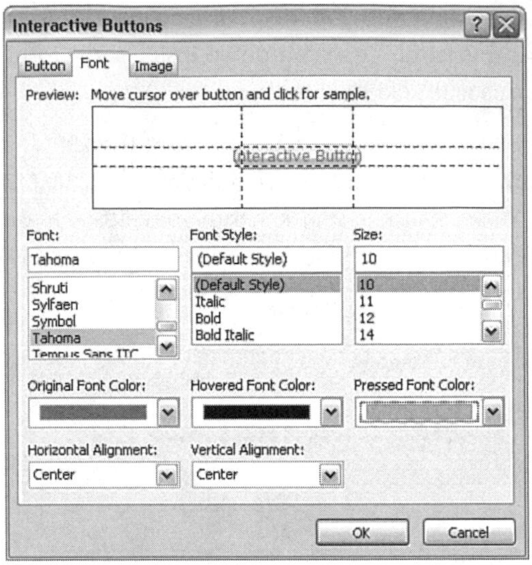

FIGURE 15.2
The Font tab
gives you easy
control of the
text in your but-
ton.

6. The last tab is Image. From here you can change the overall size of the button
    by using the Width and Height attributes. As long as the Maintain Proportions
    box is checked, the button retains its shape. Leave the Maintain Proportions
    box checked and change the width of the Change the Size of the Button to
    125px so that the text fits well within the button area (see Figure 15.3).

FIGURE 15.3
From the Image
tab, you can con-
trol the size,
background
color, and file
type of the im-
ages created by
the function.

7. Below the size settings you can choose whether you want the program to create
    separate images for each of the three button states and whether these images

should be preloaded by the browser when the page loads. By default Expression Web 2 creates three images: one for the button in its resting state, one for when the user hovers over it, and one for when the user clicks it. By unchecking one or more of these boxes, you are reducing the number of images created and one of the remaining images displays in place of the missing image. For example, if you turn off Create Hover Image the regular state image appears when the visitor hovers over the button. If you turn off Create Pressed Image the hover image appears when the button is pressed. Leave the boxes checked.

If you uncheck this box and resize the button, the graphic elements stretch. This makes little difference in the case of square-cornered buttons, but if you are working with circles or oval corners, unchecking this box makes the button look strange

8. The final two options let you decide the background color and file type of the button images after export. If you leave the default option checked, you can pick a background color from the drop-down menu. If you want the button background to be transparent, you have to select the GIF option. When choosing this option, pay close attention to the Preview window to ensure that the outer borders of the button are not too jagged. Leave the background color as it is and click OK. The button is inserted into your page.

The Interactive Buttons function goes through your existing page and finds all the colors you have used so far. These colors display in the color drop-down menus under Document Colors and help you keep the colors throughout your site consistent.

Saving and Editing Interactive Buttons

The interactive button you just created is now in your page, but if you look at your file tree in the Folder List task pane, you can see that no image files have been created. To finalize the process of creating an interactive button, you need to save the page. This opens the Save Embedded Files dialog from which you can define where to save the new button images (see Figure 15.4).

FIGURE 15.4
When you save the page, you also save the images you created using the Interactive Buttons feature.

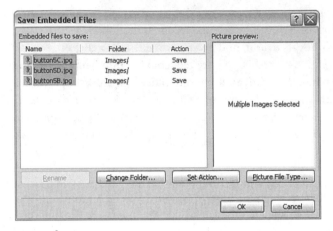

After you save the files, they behave like any other image on the page, which means that even if you delete the button from your page, you do not delete the image files from your file tree.

As with the Photoshop Import feature, Expression Web 2 keeps track of the interactive buttons you create in your pages. This means that if at some point you want to make changes to the interactive buttons, you don't have to make new ones or open each image file individually. To edit an interactive button, all you have to do is right-click it while in Design view and select Button Properties from the context menu. This opens the Interactive Buttons dialog. From this dialog, any changes you make to a button are applied to the page when you click OK. When you save the page again, the new images overwrite the old ones.

Creating Buttons from Scratch Using CSS

Although the interactive buttons that Expression Web 2 creates are great, they don't always work with the design you have envisioned. Designers often have to create their own buttons from scratch to achieve a particular look in their sites. Using the techniques you learned in earlier hours, you can use CSS (Cascading Style Sheets) to make advanced buttons that both rival and sometimes even outdo the interactive buttons you just created.

Creating a Basic Box Button

When designers first started to focus on buttons as a navigational tool they could rely on only basic functionality. The most basic button of all is a string of text with a colored box around it (see Figure 15.5).

FIGURE 15.5
The basic box button was the staple of web design for many years.

Although you could use tables to make this type of button, the "proper" way is to build the button is through the use of CSS like in this next tutorial:

1. In the same page as before, create a subheading and name it **Basic Box Button.** Under that heading, create a new paragraph with the text **Button 1.**

2. Highlight the button text and make it a hyperlink pointing back to the current buttons.html page.

3. Click the New Style button and create a new class called .basicBox. In the Font category, set font-family to Arial, Helvetica, sans-serif, font-size to 0.8em, font-weight to bold, text-transform to uppercase, font-color to black (#000000), and check the None box under text-decoration to get rid of the line under the text.

4. Under Background, set background-color to silver (#C0C0C0). Under Border, set border-style to solid for all, border-width to 2px for all, set the border-top and border-left colors to gray (#808080), and set the border-bottom and border-right colors to black (#000000). This gives the button the appearance of popping out from the screen (see Figure 15.6).

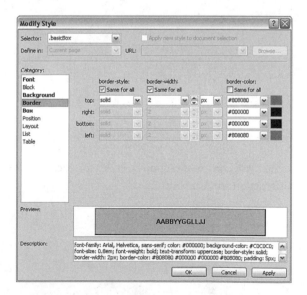

FIGURE 15.6
Setting different colors for the top and left borders and bottom and right borders can create the illusion of the button either hovering over the page (if the top and left borders are lighter) or being pushed into the page (if the top and left borders are darker).

5. In the Box category, set padding to 5px for all four sides. Click OK to create the new class.

6. Select the button text you created and use the Apply Styles task pane to apply the new class.

7. To make the button react when the user hovers the mouse over it, you also have to make a :hover pseudoclass with different styles. Because you want to retain most of the styles, the easiest way to make a new and similar class is to copy and paste the CSS code in Code view and give the new class the selector name .basicBox:hover. After doing this, you can open the new pseudoclass from the Apply Styles task pane using Modify Style and make changes to it.

8. With .basicBox:hover open in the Modify Style dialog, change font-color to white (#FFFFFF) and background-color to a light orange (#FF6600). Click OK to apply the changes, and then save and test in your browser (see Figure 15.7).

FIGURE 15.7
The two button states as they appear next to one another.

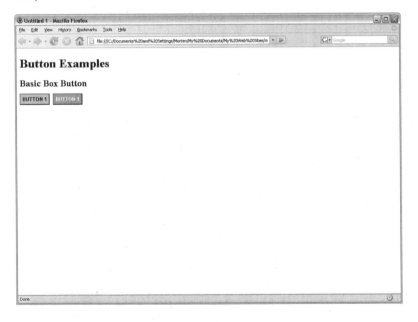

As with all other styles, you can create separate styles for each pseudoclass for more advanced visual interaction with the button.

In this example the actual styling of the button came from applying a class to the <a> tag. But this is not the only way to create box buttons. You could just as easily have grouped one or several buttons within a <div> or <span> class or ID, and created a styles instead. The result would be the same.

Creating an Advanced Box Button with Images

The basic box button might be easy to create, but it is also very dull to look at. Although prevalent in the 1990s, you rarely see this type of button in modern web design. Fortunately you can easily modernize the look of the box button without much

FIGURE 15.8
The Basic Box Button gets a modern look by swapping out the background color for a background image. Button 2 is in the **:hover** state.

extra effort. The key is to replace the background color with a background image, as shown in Figure 15.8.

In this example, you use a different styling technique to apply the same style to multiple buttons:

1. Below the basic box button, create a new headline and name it **Advanced Box Button.** Underneath that, create an unordered list with three buttons: Button 1, Button 2, and Button 3. Make each list item into a hyperlink back to the current page.

FIGURE 15.9
The menu list is
created and the
.advancedBox
style applied.

FIGURE 15.9
The menu list is
created and the
.advancedBox
style applied.

2. Make a new class called .advancedBox by using the New Style dialog. Under
   the List category set the list-style-type to none. Click OK to create the class
   and apply it to the <ul> tag using the Quick Tag Selector (see Figure 15.9).

3. Import the images named blueButtonUp.gif and blueButtonOver.gif from
   the lesson files and save them in a new folder called buttonGraphics.

4. Make a new style and give it the selector name .advancedBox a. In the Font
   category, set font-family to Arial, Helvetica, sans-serif, font-size to
   0.8em, font-weight to bold, text-transform to uppercase, font-color to
   white (#FFFFFF), and check the None box under text-decoration to get rid of
   the line under the text.

FIGURE 15.10
The
.advancedBox
a style is applied
to the new but-
tons, but they
are covering
each other be-
cause the list
item style has
not been modi-
fied yet.

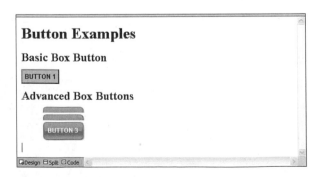

5. In the Background category, set `background-image` to the `blueButtonUp.gif` image you just imported and set `background-repeat` to `no-repeat`. Because the image is larger than the text and you want it to surround the text, go to the Box category and set `padding` to 13px on all sides. Click OK to apply the style (see Figure 15.10).

6. In Design view, you can see that the new button background is applied but the buttons are covering each other. This is because the list items have not yet been styled and the browser is assuming that the list items are the height of the text without the padding. To fix this problem create a new style with the selector name **.advancedBox li** and set the `padding-top` and `padding-bottom` attributes to 13px to match the link style you just created. Click OK to apply the new style and the buttons no longer overlap.

7. To create a hover-over effect, copy and paste the `.advancedBox a` style in Code view and give the new style the selector name **.advancedBox a:hover.** Open the Modify Style dialog for the new style and change `background-image` to `blueButtonOver.gif`. Click OK, and then save and preview in your browser.

Now instead of the background color changing when the mouse hovers over the button, the background image swaps out. And because the background image is part of the a style, the entire image is clickable, not just the text itself.

The problem with this technique is that it requires two images to work. This might not seem like a big deal, but if the user is on a slow connection, the page is on a slow server, or there is something else that slows the system down, the user might experience noticeable lag between hovering over the button and the new background image being loaded. One way around this problem is to preload the images using behaviors, but this requires JavaScript to work properly.

Create Text Free Buttons with Sliding Doors

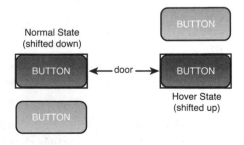

FIGURE 15.11
The name sliding doors refers to the action of sliding the background image so that only half of it is visible depending on how the mouse interacts with the button.

The problem of preloading content has become more prevalent with the emergence of blogs because many blogs have a lot of scripts running at the same time, and it is important to reduce the load on both the network and the computer as much as possible to make things work smoothly. A technique often referred to as *sliding doors* was developed to enable the designer to use one image file as two different backgrounds (see Figure 15.11. This is done by creating a file that has two versions of the background, either on top of or to the side of one another. The name *sliding doors* refers to the action of literally sliding the background from one side to the other to display only half of the image at a time.

You can use a similar technique to hide text content. As you have seen, the regular method of creating buttons requires there to be text superimposed on the background. If you don't want the text to appear, the quick answer is to simply swap out the text for an image and use it as a button. But if you do this, the link is not visible if the image doesn't load or the visitor uses a text-only browser. The way to solve this is to push the text out of the way so that only the background image appears. Another reason to use this technique is that designers often want to use custom fonts or font effects in their buttons. To do this and retain full accessibility, they have to hide the regular HTML text first. In this example, you create a button that uses the sliding doors technique and hides the text at the same time.

1. Import the file named `slidingButtons.gif` into the buttonGraphics folder from the lesson files. Under the three buttons you just created, add a new sub-

FIGURE 15.12
The new button text is wrapped in a **`<span>`** tag and the **`.slider`** class is applied.

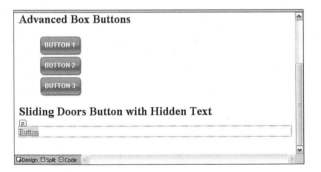

heading and call it **`Sliding Doors Button with Hidden Text`.** Below it, add a paragraph with the text `Button` and make it into a hyperlink pointing back to the current page.

2. Make a new class called *.slider*. Create a span around the new button text using the Toolbox task pane, and apply the `.slider` class to it using the Quick Tag Selector (see Figure 15.12).

3. Make a new style and give it the selector name `.slider a`. Because you are going to hide the text you don't need change any of the Font attributes. In the Background category, set `background-image` to `slidingButtons.gif` and `background-repeat` to `no-repeat`.

4. To create the sliding effect, you need to change the position of the background image as well as define the visible area within the page. The image has two buttons on it: the top one is for the regular state and the bottom one is for the `:hover` state. Set the `(x)` `background-position` to `0px` and the `(y)` `background-position` to `0px`. This locks the image in place.

5. To define the visible area of the button, you need to first set the display attribute under the Layout category to block to create an independent box in which to display the content and then change the size of the box under the Position category. The height of the image is 88px and because you will be displaying half of it at once, the `height` attribute should therefore be 44px. To contain the

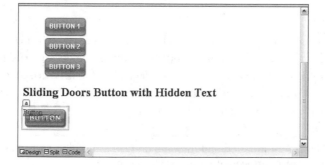

FIGURE 15.13
After styling, the button appears as it should but the text is still visible.

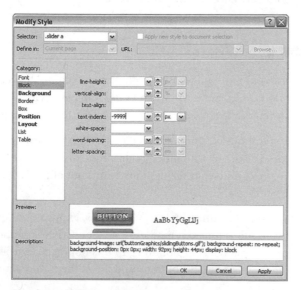

FIGURE 15.14
Setting the **text-indent** attribute to **-9999px** places the text of the button 9999 pixels to the left of the screen, making it invisible to the visitor.

active area of the button to the area of the image, set the `width` attribute to 92px, which is the width of the image. Click OK to apply the style as shown in Figure 15.13.

6. As you can see, the button looks the way it should but the text is still visible. To hide the text, open the Modify Style dialog for the style, go to the Block category, and set the `text-indent` attribute to `-9999px` (see Figure 15.14). Click OK to save the change.

7. Finally create a new style with the selector name `.slider a:hover`. Because of the cascade, any pseudoclass will inherit all the styling from its parent unless the style is changed. Therefore you need to make changes to only the `background-position` attributes and the rest of the attributes will stay the same. Set `(x) background-position` to `0px` and `(y) background-position` to `-44px`. This shifts the background image up 44 pixels and the bottom half is shown in place of the top half. Click OK, and then save and preview in your browser.

Designers frequently use the sliding doors technique to create eye-catching roll-overs without load times getting in the way. In this example, the background image only had two versions, but you could have an image with more instances. Likewise you can place the images next to one another instead of on top of each other and change the `(x) background-position` value instead.

You can find more information and tutorials on how to use the sliding doors technique at the A List Apart website: www.alistapart.com.

Summary

Buttons are an integral part of a website, both as navigational tools and as design elements. Knowing how to make and when to use different styles of buttons will make your life easier as a designer and your sites easier to navigate for the visitors.

Buttons can be anything from simple colored boxes with text inside them to advanced image-based elements with different graphics for each state. The layout and design of the page, and what the designer wants out of it, drive the choice of what kind of button to use.

To simplify the process of creating interactive buttons, Expression Web 2 has a built-in Interactive Buttons function that lets you choose a design and set properties for a wide range of prepackaged buttons. In this hour, you learned how to create and customize these interactive buttons and insert them into your page. The major benefit of the interactive buttons is that even after inserting them in your page, you can always go back to the Interactive Buttons dialog and change the design and font attributes of the button without creating a new one. This high level of flexibility is great when you are designing pages on the fly and you're not sure what the end product will look like. The downside of interactive buttons is that they are limited in the button design.

If you want to move beyond the designs of the prepackaged interactive buttons, the best way to go is to create CSS buttons instead. The advantages of CSS buttons are that they are text based and standards compliant, and a visitor who uses a text-only browser can still see the hyperlinks within the buttons. In this hour, you learned how to create simple box-type buttons with interactive features using CSS. You also learned how to take these buttons to the next level by replacing the solid color backgrounds with images. Finally you learned how to use the sliding doors technique to use one image as the base for multiple different button states by sliding it in the background to show different versions of the same button image.

Q&A

Q. I inserted an interactive button in my page but all I see is a small box with a red X in it. What is wrong?

A. When you make an interactive button, Expression Web 2 creates a series of images to correspond to the different button states. If you are seeing a red X, the link to the image or images is broken, probably because you deleted the images accidentally, didn't save them when you saved the page before closing the application, or moved them to a different folder outside of Expression Web 2. To fix the problem, simply right-click the interactive button in Design view and select Button Properties from the context menu. From here you can make changes to the button or, if you just want to re-establish the images, simply click OK and the button will show up as it is supposed to.

Q. I created a second copy of the sliding doors button but it shows up underneath the first one no matter what I do. Why can't I make these buttons show up next to each other?

A. Although sliding doors buttons can easily be lined up next to one another, the one you made in this example cannot do so without putting each of the buttons in a separate table cell. The reason for this has to do with the hiding of the button text, not the sliding doors function. In the next hour, you will learn how to make a functional horizontal menu using the sliding doors function without using tables.

Workshop

The Workshop has quiz questions and exercises to help you put to use what you just learned. If you get stuck, the answers to the quiz questions are in the next section. But try to answer them first. Otherwise you'll only be cheating yourself.

Quiz

1. *What is the advantage of using Interactive Buttons generated by Expression Web 2?*

2. *When creating the basic and advanced box buttons, do you need to create separate styles for each of the buttons?*

Answers

1. The Interactive Buttons created by Expression Web 2 are accompanied by macros that help the application remember their settings. That means you can completely change the look and functionality of the buttons from the Interactive Button Properties dialog even after they have been inserted.

2. No, not unless you want to. The idea of using CSS to create box buttons is that you can apply the same styling and background (either color or image) to multiple buttons with one set of styles. That way you can make quick changes to multiple buttons throughout your site by changing only a few styles rather than having to change each individual button separately. You can however make individualized buttons with individual backgrounds or styles by wrapping each button instance in a <span> tag.

Exercise

Using the Interactive Buttons feature, create a series of new buttons with different designs and layouts. After inserting them, pick one design you really like and change all the buttons to that look by changing their button properties.

To give the visitor a visual cue that the button has been pressed before, make styles for the :active and :visited pseudoclasses for all the different CSS buttons you created. The :active style usually has a bold appearance (bright colors and dark font), whereas the :visited pseudoclass is usually more muted than the other styles.

HOUR 16

Using Behaviors

What You'll Learn in This Hour:

▶ How to apply behaviors to elements in your site

▶ How to edit existing behaviors

▶ How to change the events that trigger behaviors

▶ What the different behaviors in Expression Web 2 are and how they work

Introduction

HTML (Hypertext Markup Language) and CSS (Cascading Style Sheets) are powerful tools that can take you a long way to making a great website. But for all the virtues of those tools, many tasks are impossible or far too cumbersome to do using them alone. To help simplify some of these tasks, Expression Web 2 comes complete with a set of behaviors to insert into your pages. *Behaviors* are small pieces of JavaScript that, when inserted, perform actions within the page and give the visitor a more powerful interactive experience.

Behaviors: An Introduction

The behaviors in Expression Web 2 can be accessed from the Behaviors task pane which, when selected from the Task Panes menu on the toolbar, opens in the lower-right corner of the workspace next to the Apply and Manage Styles task panes (see Figure 16.1).

When you insert a behavior into your page, you are actually adding a block of JavaScript code to it. *JavaScript* is a basic script language that lets you perform many tasks that are not available or are otherwise hard to achieve using HTML and CSS alone.

Boiled down to its basic components, a behavior consists of two elements: an event and an action. An *event* is an action, usually performed by the user, which tells the

FIGURE 16.1
The Behaviors
task pane.

browser that something happened and asks it to respond by running a script. Events
are standardized code segments that in most cases describe themselves pretty well.
Here are some examples:

▶ **onclick**—When the object is clicked

▶ **ondblclick**—When the object is double-clicked

▶ **onload**—When the object is loaded by the browser

▶ **onmousedown**—When the mouse button is pressed

▶ **onmouseover**—When the mouse pointer is over the object

When triggered, an event sends a set of predefined arguments to the browser that it
passes on to the action. In short, the event describes what needs to happen for the action to trigger.

An *action* is a JavaScript function (tiny program) that executes when the corresponding event occurs. The action receives the arguments from the event and the script
performs the programmed task with these arguments.

▼   **Try it Yourself**

Create a Swap-Image Behavior

The easiest way to understand how a behavior works is to see it in action. So, before
you immerse yourself in all the different behaviors available, you are going to apply
a simple behavior to an image:

1. Create and open a new HTML page called behaviors.html in Design view.

2. From the buttonGraphics folder, drag and drop the blueButtonUp.gif file into
    the page. Give it the alternative text **Behavior button**.

3. Click the image to select it and click the Insert button in the Behaviors task pane to open the Behaviors menu (see Figure 16.2).

FIGURE 16.2
Clicking the Insert button in the Behaviors task pane opens a menu with all the available behaviors.

4. Select the Swap Image behavior from the menu. This opens the Swap Images dialog.

5. In the Swap Images dialog, click the Browse button and select the blueButtonOver.gif image. Click OK and the image location now appears in the Swap Image URL column. Leave Preload Images checked and check Restore on Mouseout Event as well. Click OK to apply the new behavior (see Figure 16.3).

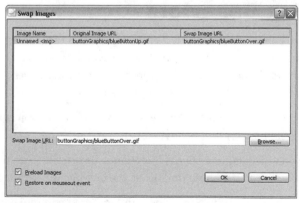

FIGURE 16.3
The Swap Image URL is set and the Preload Images and Restore on Mouseout Event options are checked.

▼

After clicking OK, you see that there are now two behaviors visible in the Behaviors task pane. The first one has the event onmouseout and the action Swap Image Restore, whereas the other has the event onmouseover and the action Swap Images (see Figure 16.4).

FIGURE 16.4
After you add a behavior to an object on the page, it appears in the Behaviors task pane when you select the object.

If you click anywhere else in the page, you see that a different behavior shows up with the event onload and the action Preload Images. To see what the combination of these three behaviors does, save and preload the page in your browser. When you hover your mouse over the image (the onmouseover event), it is swapped for the other image you defined (the Swap Images action). When you move your mouse away from the image (the onmouseout event), the original image is restored (the Swap Image Restore action). The third behavior is triggered when the page loads (the onload event) and preloads the second image into the browser memory so that it is readily available when it is needed (the Preload Images action).

▲

Modifying Behaviors

Each of the three behaviors you inserted into the page has three components: the event, the action, and the variable. To change the event, hover over the event name in the Behaviors task pane and click the drop-down arrow. This opens a full menu of all available events that you can choose from (see Figure 16.5).

To change the variable(s) of a behavior, double-click the behavior in the Behaviors task pane and the dialog for that behavior opens.

The only thing you can't do to a behavior is change its action. To do that, you have to add a new behavior to the object and delete the old one, if necessary.

Experienced designers and people familiar with JavaScript can make modifications of the different behaviors in Code view. Although this book does not cover the modi-

FIGURE 16.5
After applying a behavior, you can change the event by opening the Event sub-menu from the drop-down arrow.

fication of JavaScript in Code view, it is worth your time to look under the hood to understand how exactly behaviors work.

If you click the image you inserted into the page and switch to Split view, you see that the image code is much longer than what you have seen before:

```
<img id="img1" alt="BehaviorButton" height="44" onmouseout="FP_swapImgRestore()"
onmouseover="FP_swapImg(1,1,/*id*/'img1',/*url*/
'buttonGraphics/blueButtonOver.gif')"
src="buttonGraphics/blueButtonUp.gif" width="92" />
```

In addition to familiar components such as id, alt, src, height, and width, the image now has a series of new code elements attached. Those new code elements are the behavior events. Let's take a closer look at the onmouseover event:

```
onmouseover="FP_swapImg(1,1,/*id*/'img1',/*url*/
'buttonGraphics/blueButtonOver.gif')"
```

The first part of this code is the event itself. The next part, FP_swapImg, is the name of the action or function the event is triggering. Every JavaScript function has a name and a set of arguments contained within parentheses and separated by commas. In this case the variables are 1, 1, 'img1', 'buttonGraphics/blueButtonOver.gif', and they tell the script what image to swap out (img1) and what image to put in its place (buttonGraphics/blueButtonOver.gif).

The actual action or function is in the head of the page (see Figure 16.6):

```
function FP_swapImg() {//v1.0
var doc=document,args=arguments,elm,n; doc.$imgSwaps=new Array();
for(n=2; n<args.length;n+=2) { elm=FP_getObjectByID(args[n]); if(elm) {
doc.$imgSwaps[doc.$imgSwaps.length]=elm;
 elm.$src=elm.src; elm.src=args[n+1]; } }
}
```

This is highly technical JavaScript code and you do not need to understand what it means and how it works. What you can do, however, is examine the sequence of

events: When the page loads in the browser, the image on the page loads as normal and the browser loads a second image into memory as per the onload event. When the visitor moves the mouse over the image, the onmouseover event triggers the FP_swapImg action and sends it the arguments img and buttonGraphics/blueButtonOver.gif. The action runs the tiny program with these arguments and replaces the image. When the visitor moves the mouse off the image, the onmouseout event triggers the FP_swapImageRestore action. This action has no arguments because it just restores the old image.

To put this example into context, the interactive button you created in Hour 15, "Buttons, Buttons, Buttons," used the same events and actions along with some additional ones to achieve its hover and click effects.

The Many Behaviors of Expression Web 2

The preceding example introduced you to the Preload Images, Swap Image, and Swap Image Restore behaviors. Those are just three of a series of behaviors you can use to increase interactivity for your visitors. To get the full use out of the program, you should know each behavior and what it does.

Call Script

The Call Script behavior calls a script that is not featured in the prepackaged behaviors in Expression Web 2. To put it simply, Call Script is a behavior where you define the action. When you apply Call Script to an object, a dialog opens asking you for the JavaScript/JScript code (see Figure 16.7). This behavior is for advanced users with previous knowledge of JavaScript.

Change Property

The Change Property behavior lets you change the styling properties of the object to which it is applied. These properties include Font, Position, Borders and Shading, and Visibility.

1. Below the image you inserted earlier, write a couple of lines of text in a new paragraph. With the cursor inside the text, apply the Change Property behavior by clicking the Insert button in the Behaviors task pane and selecting Change Property. This opens the Change Property dialog (see Figure 16.8).

2. In the Change Property dialog, you can choose whether you want to change the properties of the current element or selected element. The Selected Element option lets you pick any of the defined elements within the page. Leave Current Element checked.

3. For this exercise you want to create a box with a gray background around the paragraph when the visitor hovers over it. Click Borders to open the Borders

and Shading dialog. From here you can pick the border style and shading (background color). Under the Borders tab, set the Setting to Box and leave everything else as it is (see Figure 16.9). Under the Shading tab, set the Background Color to Silver (see Figure 16.10). Click OK.

FIGURE 16.9
The Borders tab lets you set the border style and color.

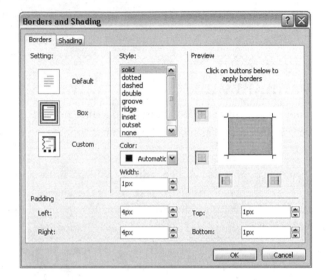

FIGURE 16.10
The Shading tab lets you set the background color or a background image.

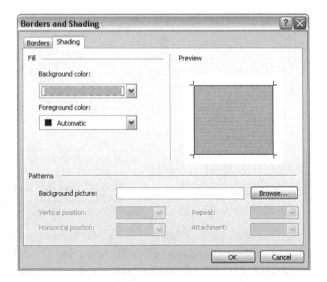

The Borders and Shading options under the Change Property dialog can be confusing because the names and functionality differ greatly from the Add and Modify Style dialogs. (In fact they look more like the Borders and Shading dialogs from Microsoft Word.) Despite this apparent difference, the functions within the two dialogs are the same as the ones in the Add and Modify Style dialogs, and the output is the same as if you were to style the element with CSS.

4. The dialog now lists the style changes you made, as you can see from Figure 16.11, they are CSS code. Make further changes if you like using the other functions. When you are done, check the Restore on Onmouseout Event box and click OK to apply the behavior.

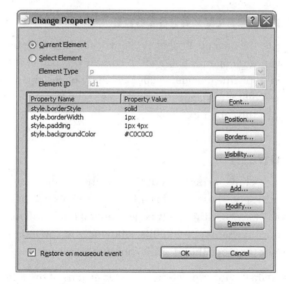

FIGURE 16.11
The Change Property dialog lists the styling changes as CSS code.

When you save and test the page in your browser you see that when you hover over the paragraph, a black border and silver background appear behind it just as if you created a :hover pseudostyle in CSS.

Should I Use CSS or Behaviors?

The preceding examples beg the question: If I can apply both CSS and behaviors to achieve the same result, which one do I use and why? Although CSS and behaviors can perform many of the same tasks, there are different reasons to use (or not use) them. For instance, CSS is a great tool for layout, especially if you have a certain style you are going to use many times throughout your site. But one particular element requires a certain style or behavior, using behaviors can be the better choice because they leave the arguments attached to the element rather than in the style code. For instance if you are creating a series of image-based buttons that all require different images, creating separate styles for every button is cumbersome and creates a lot of style code. One way to circumvent this is by creating an overall style for the buttons and inline styles for each of the backgrounds but that still requires a lot of specialized styling. In contrast, applying behaviors to achieve the same result requires only one function per behavior in the head of the page and the arguments will be attached to each element.

A caveat: Although JavaScript is prevalent throughout the Web, not everyone supports it. In particular, some people and companies block JavaScript in their browsers to prevent malicious scripts from attacking their computers. For those users, and on computers that do not have Java installed, behaviors will not work.

Change Property Restore

As its name suggests, the `Change Property Restore` behavior restores the property changed by the `Change Property` behavior to what it was before the behavior was applied. When you apply the `Change Property` behavior, you have the option to also apply automatically the `Change Property Restore` behavior from within the dialog, as you saw in the earlier example.

Check Browser

The `Check Browser` behavior checks what browser the visitor is using and redirects the visitor to a specific page based on this information. This behavior is useful if you have certain scripts or styles within your page that you know will not show up correctly in a particular browser. Applying this behavior, you can redirect users with this browser to an alternative page that doesn't contain this script.

The `Check Browser` behavior can detect multiple versions of the following browsers:

- ▶ Microsoft Internet Explorer
- ▶ Netscape Navigator
- ▶ Opera
- ▶ AOL
- ▶ WebTV
- ▶ AOLTV
- ▶ HotJava

Did you Know?

Despite the popularity of the Mozilla Firefox browser and the discontinuation of Netscape Navigator, the browser selection lists the latter. Firefox and Navigator are always grouped together due to similar signatures, so if you want to target Firefox, you have to select Netscape Navigator.

In this example, you add the Check Browser behavior to the button you inserted earlier:

1. Select the button you inserted earlier and click Insert in the Behaviors task pane to open the Behaviors menu. Select Check Browser from the menu. This opens the Check Browser dialog (see Figure 16.12).

FIGURE 16.12
The Check Browser dialog.

2. In the If the Current Browser Type Is drop-down menu, select Microsoft Internet Explorer. Leave the Version option set to Any. Check the Go to URL box and set the target page to http://www.getfirefox.com. Check the box under Otherwise, for all other browsers, Go to url and set the target page to http://www.microsoft.com/expression (see Figure 16.13).

FIGURE 16.13
The Check Browser dialog lets you specify a particular browser and set a different target page for that browser.

3. Click OK to apply the new behavior. The Check Browser behavior now shows up in the list in the Behaviors task pane above the two you created earlier. Save the page and test it in your browser. If you click the button while in Internet Explorer, you will be taken to the Mozilla Firefox download page. If you do the same in any other browser, you will be taken to the Microsoft Expression website.

> The tricky part about using this behavior is that because it is JavaScript-based, it loads a bit slower than the rest of the page. This means that, depending on the visitor's computer and connection speed, parts of the page could already be loaded before the behavior redirects the browser. To avoid this problem, designers often build a separate front page that contains only this behavior so that the visitor doesn't get a flash of a broken page before the browser loads the modified one.

Check Plug-In

The Check Plug-In behavior works in much the same way as the Check Browser behavior, except that it checks for installed plug-ins instead of browsers. This behavior is extremely useful if your page features content that requires a particular plug-in to function properly. You have probably encountered this behavior in the past because designers frequently use it to test whether a browser has either the Flash or the Shockwave plug-in.

The Check Plug-in behavior can check whether your browser has the following plug-ins installed:

- ▶ Flash

- ▶ QuickTime

- ▶ RealPlayer

- ▶ Shockwave

- ▶ Windows Media Player

Bizarrely, it does not give you the option of checking whether the browser has the Microsoft Silverlight plug-in installed.

As with the Check Browser behavior, you can select to redirect the browser based on whether it has a particular plug-in installed. In this example, you make a button that points to the popular video-sharing website YouTube. If a user's browser does not have the Flash plug-in installed, she cannot view videos on YouTube, so redirect her to the Flash plug-in download site instead.

1. Select the button you inserted earlier and press Ctrl+C on your keyboard to copy it. Create a new paragraph on the page and press Ctrl+V to paste the button in the new location.

2. With the new button selected, click the Check Browser behavior in the Behaviors task pane to highlight it and delete it by clicking the Delete button (see Figure 16.14). Doing so deletes the behavior from only the selected element and not the other button.

FIGURE 16.14
When you select a behavior in the Behaviors task pane, you can delete it from the element by clicking the Delete button. Doing so affects only the current element.

3. With the new button still selected, click Insert and select Check Plug-In to open the Check Plug-in dialog.

4. In the If the Current Plug-In Is menu, choose Flash. The wording is somewhat strange, but it means *if the current plug-in is installed.* Check the box below and set the target page to http://www.youtube.com. Check the Otherwise, for All Other Plug-Ins box and set the target page to http://www.adobe.com/go/EN_US-H-GET-FLASH (see Figure 16.15).

FIGURE 16.15
The Check Plug-In dialog lets you pick a particular plug-in and set the target of the browser to different pages depending on whether the user's browser has the plug-in installed.

Go to URL

The Go to URL behavior does exactly what it says: If the behavior is applied, the browser goes to the specified URL. In other words, it is a JavaScript method of creating hyperlinks. You can use this behavior in conjunction with other behaviors if you want to make buttons and so forth. When you apply the Go to URL behavior to an element, the Go to URL dialog opens, as shown in Figure 16.16, and you insert the target address.

The Go to URL behavior gives you the ability to make hyperlinks that trigger by events other than the regular clicking of a button. For instance, you can set the event to onmouseover so that the browser navigates to the new address when an element is

touched. Or you can set the event to `onload` to force the browser to navigate to the new address when the element or the page loads.

Jump Menu

The `Jump Menu` behavior adds a drop-down menu with a `Jump Menu` behavior to the page wherever you place the cursor. This behavior is actually a two-birds-with-one-stone approach to making a drop-down menu with some functionality. Technically the jump menu part of the behavior is just the `onchange` event and `Jump Menu` action. Separately the `Jump Menu` behavior inserts a drop-down box to which you attach the behavior. The result is a drop-down menu with a set of choices that link to different pages just like the menu that appears when you hover over the events in the Behaviors task pane.

1. To create a new jump menu, place the cursor where you want the jump menu to appear, click Insert in the Behaviors task pane, and select Jump Menu from the menu. This opens the Jump Menu dialog.

2. The Jump Menu dialog is where you define the different menu options. To add a menu option, click the Add button. This opens the Add Choice dialog. The Choice is the text that appears as an option within the jump menu. The Value is the target URL navigated to when the user selects the choice. This menu lists a series of news sources, so start with CNN as the Choice setting and http://www.cnn.com as the Value setting. Click OK to add the item to the jump menu (see Figure 16.17).

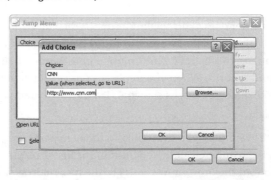

3. Add a series of new links to other news sources to create a list. When the list has several items, you can modify each item, remove them, or move them up and down in the list with the buttons on the side.

4. When you are satisfied with your list, you can decide whether the new pages should open in the current window or a new window using the Open URLs In drop-down menu (see Figure 16.18). Set this option to New Window. You can

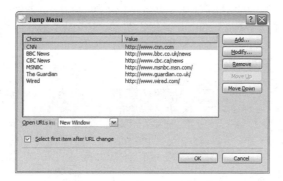

also check the Select First Item After URL Change option. Doing so resets the jump menu to the first item on the list after a URL change. Otherwise the last selected item appears in the jump menu. Click OK to insert the jump menu.

If you save and preview the page in your browser, you can test the new jump menu. Because you set the URL to open in a new window, a new window opens every time you make a selection from the menu. If you had unchecked the Select First Item After URL Change box, the last selection you made would appear in the jump menu when it is not activated.

To change the properties of the menu items, double-click the jump menu in Design view and the Drop-Down Box Properties dialog opens. From here you can add, remove, modify, and reorganize the different list alternatives and even change options such as tab order (for visitors using the Tab key on their keyboard) and whether the visitor can make multiple selections. This is because you are now editing the menu as a drop-down box, not a jump menu. Note that you don't have the Open URLs In and Select First Item After URL Change options in this dialog.

Jump Menu Go

The default setting of the Jump Menu event is onchange. That means whenever the user selects a menu item, the action triggers. But sometimes you want the user to make a selection first and then press a separate button to trigger the action. You can do so with the Jump Menu Go behavior by removing the event and action from the menu itself and giving it to a separate element.

To make this scenario work properly, you have to create a new button with the Jump Menu Go event attached and then change the event of the jump menu.

1. You need to attach the Jump Menu Go behavior to a different element than the jump menu itself. Copy one of the buttons on the page and paste it next to the menu. With the new button selected, delete the onclick event by selecting it and clicking the Delete button in the Behaviors task pane. Click the Insert button and select Jump Menu Go from the menu. This opens the Jump Menu Go dialog (see Figure 16.19).

FIGURE 16.19
The Jump Menu Go dialog lists the available jump menus you can control with the new behavior.

2. Because there is only one jump menu on the page, you have only one option. Had there been several jump menus, you could choose which one the Jump Menu Go behavior would affect. Click OK to apply the new behavior.

3. The jump menu still has the Jump Menu behavior attached. To get the new button to work properly, you have to remove this behavior. Select the jump menu and delete the Jump Menu behavior from the Behaviors task pane by selecting it and clicking the Delete button. This might seem counterintuitive but, as you just learned, the Jump Menu behavior and the drop-down box are two separate entities. Now the button you created in step 1 controls the menu. Save and preview in your browser to test the new behavior.

Open Browser Window

In Hour 5, "Get Connected—Building Hyperlinks for Navigation and Further Exploration," you learned how to make hyperlinks open in a new window. The Open Browser Window behavior takes this to a whole new level by letting you create hyperlinks that open in new windows where you set the parameters for how the window should look and behave. This gives the designer much more control of the experience the visitor has after clicking the link. This behavior is especially useful when you want to open a separate window that displays an image and you want it to be the same size as the image.

1. Drag and drop a new button image into the page and give it the alternative text **Image Pop-Up.**

2. With the new button selected, click the Insert button and select Open Browser Window from the menu. This opens the Open Browser Menu dialog.

3. In the Open Browser Window dialog, set the target URL for the hyperlink. This can be a page within your site or any page or file on the World Wide Web. Use the Browse button to browse to the kennyOriginal.jpg image.

4. In the Window Name box, define a unique name for your window. This name will not be visible, but the browser uses it to identify the window so that you can target it with other behaviors or functions. The window name can contain only numbers and letters, no spaces or symbols. Name the window **image.**

5. The Window Width and Window Height setting define the physical width and height of the new window. The default value is 200px by 200px, which is very small. The kennyOriginal.jpg image is 353px wide and 521px high, so match these values in your window.

6. The window's attributes make up the final set of options in the Open Browser Window dialog. By checking and unchecking these boxes, you turn various features of the window on and off. Leaving all of them unchecked means you get a stripped window with no navigation or other features (see Figure 16.20). Click OK to apply the new behavior.

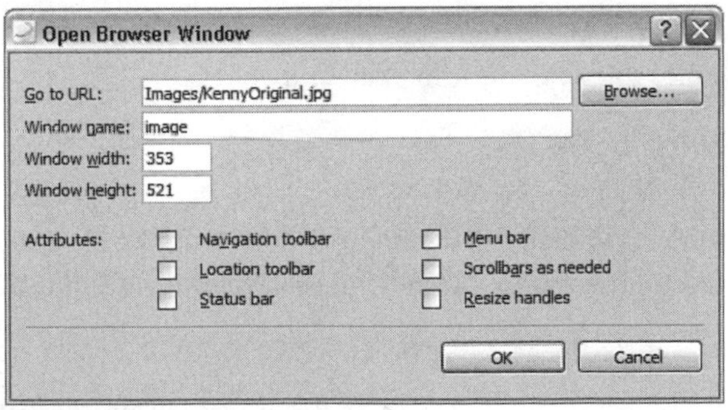

FIGURE 16.20
The Open Browser Window dialog with all the new settings completed.

After saving and previewing the page in your browser, click the New button and a new window opens to the size specified (see Figure 16.21). Note that because you didn't check any attributes, the window has no navigation, scrollbars, or any other features. Furthermore, you can't resize the window.

FIGURE 16.21
The new window's size is according to specifications and stripped of all the extra features a browser window normally has.

Play Sound

The Play Sound behavior plays back a sound file when the desired event triggers. The supported sound file types are

▶ AIFF sound files (files ending with .aif, .aifc, and .aiff)

▶ AU sound files (files ending with .au and .snd)

▶ MIDI sequencer files (files ending with .mid)

▶ RealAudio files (files ending with .ram and .ra)

▶ Wave files (files ending with .wav)

When you apply the Play Sound behavior to an element, the Play Sound dialog opens to allow you to insert the location of the sound file (see Figure 16.22). Keep in

FIGURE 16.22
The Play Sound dialog lets you browse to the sound you want to play when the event triggers.

mind that just like image files, this file has to be available on the World Wide Web either from your own site or an external site. If you insert a link to a file on your local hard drive, only visitors using your computer will be able to hear it.

Popup Message

When an element with the `Popup Message` behavior applied triggers, a warning box with the warning of your choice appears on the screen. Designers often use this behavior to warn visitors about the content about to display, that they are leaving the site, or that they are submitting information to the site. Because you are in complete control of the warning message, you can have it say whatever you want.

To create a popup message, simply add the behavior to an element and the Popup Message dialog opens (see Figure 16.23). There you type out your message and click OK to insert it into the page.

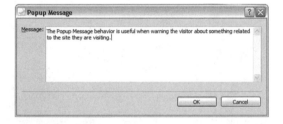

FIGURE 16.23
The Popup Message dialog lets you insert the text you want to display in the warning box.

When triggered, the `Popup Message` behavior creates a warning box with the text you inserted and the visitor has to manually close it to move on (see Figure 16.24).

FIGURE 16.24
The popup message as it appears when triggered in the browser.

Preload Images

The `Preload Images` behavior loads images that are not actually present on the page into the browser memory for future retrieval. This is a useful function if your page contains images that appear when the user performs an action (such as hovering the mouse over a button), and you don't want there to be a lag between the action and the image switching out. You saw the `Preload Images` behavior both when you created the interactive buttons in Hour 15 and when you used the `Swap Image` behavior in this hour.

The `Preload Images` behavior is usually applied to the page as a whole (under the `<body>` tag) with an `onload` event so that it loads with the rest of the page.

1. There is already a `Preload Images` behavior present in your page (you inserted it along with the `Swap Image` behavior). But if you want to insert one, you simply click anywhere within the page and select the `<body>` tag from the Quick Tag Selector before inserting the behavior from the Behaviors task pane. Because you already inserted a `Preload Images` behavior, simply select the `<body>` tag and double-click the behavior from the Behaviors task pane. This opens the Preload Images dialog.

2. When the Preload Images dialog opens, it has one image listed and only the Remove button is active. To add a new image, you first have to use the Browse button to find it. Select any image in your site and click OK. The new image location appears in the Image Source File area and the Add button becomes clickable. Click the Add button to add the new image to the list (see Figure 16.25).

FIGURE 16.25
To add a new image to the Preload Images list, you first have to browse to the image source file location and then click the Add button.

Set Text

`Set Text` is the only behavior with a submenu. This behavior changes the text or HTML content of various fields within the page. To fully understand how this behavior works, you first need an introduction to frames, layers, and text fields. Therefore the `Set Text` behavior will be covered in Hour 17, "Frames and Layers."

Behavior Pitfalls and Expression Web 2 Idiosyncrasies

Like CSS styles, a behavior always applies to the closest tag. That means if you highlight a portion of text and use the Behaviors task pane to apply a new behavior to it, you attach the behavior to all the content within the same tag as the text, not just the highlighted selection. If you want to attach a behavior to a selection of text, you must first wrap it inside a set of <span> tags in Code view and give it a unique ID. However, for some reason, Expression Web 2 treats <span> tags differently from all other tags. So, when you apply a behavior to a <span> tag, Expression Web 2 inserts it without an event! To make the behavior work properly and show up in the Behaviors task pane, you have to manually insert the event ahead of the action in Code view.

Summary

Behaviors are small programs you can attach to elements within your page to create a more interactive experience for your visitors. They can produce many of the same effects you already created using CSS and some that you can't produce using CSS. Therefore behaviors are an important and valuable tool for designers.

In this hour, you learned how to apply behaviors to different elements within a page and how to edit them. More importantly you got a complete walkthrough of all the available behaviors and learned how each one works. Knowing the behaviors in Expression Web 2 is your first step on the path to understanding JavaScript. Looking at JavaScript in more detail is beyond the scope of this book but if you are interested in learning about Java, look at Sams Teach Yourself JavaScript in 24 Hours.

In the coming hours, you will be applying what you learned about behaviors to some of the content in the MyKipple site to create a more interactive experience for the visitor.

Q&A

Q. *When I click the last button with both an Open Browser Window and a Popup Message action, the new browser window opens* behind *the main window while the popup message appears on top. Why is that?*

A. JavaScript is handled in sequence from top to bottom. That means if an object has several actions attached, they will be triggered in the order they appear in the Behaviors task pane. If the Open Browser Window action appears above the Popup Message action, the button will tell the browser to create a popup window on top, then return to the main window and perform the other action. To change the order of the two actions simply click on the Open Browser Window action and click the down button (with an arrow pointing down) in the Behaviors Task Pane. This moves the behavior down in the order. Now when you preview the page in your browser the popup message shows up first and only after you click OK does the new window with the image appear. As you can see, this organization of a popup message and a new window can be used to warn visitors that a new window is about to be opened.

Workshop

The Workshop has quiz questions to help you put to use what you just learned. If you get stuck, the answers to the quiz questions are in the next section. But try to answer the questions first. Otherwise you'll only be cheating yourself.

Quiz

1. *What two components are behaviors comprised of?*

Answers

1. A behavior consists of an event and an action. The event defines the trigger that causes the action to engage. The action contains the small JavaScript program that makes the behavior what it is.

Exercise

Later on in this book you will learn how to use Behaviors to create an interactive menu. Here is a preview:

Create a table with 1 row and 4 colums and place a new button in each of them. Use the different behaviors you learned about in this hour to make the buttons do different things such as changing the properties of a block of text, creating a new window pointing to your favorite web site or simply changing color when you click on it.

HOUR 17

Frames and Layers

What You'll Learn in this Hour:

▶ How to create a frameset to separate the contents of a page

▶ How to edit the frameset and its individual frames

▶ How an inline frame differs from a frameset and how to use it

▶ How to change the content of a frame using the Set Text of Frame behavior

▶ What layers are and how they differ from frames

▶ How to create and edit layers to create an interactive experience

▶ How to use layers and inline frames together to make a preview of a hyperlink

Introduction

So far you have learned how to create page layouts using CSS (Cascading Style Sheets). But there are times when CSS just doesn't cut it, and times when you want some added functionality you just can't get with a style sheet. In this hour, you will learn about frames and layers and see how using these layout tools smartly can improve the functionality of your websites.

Frames and layers are layout tools that have been around for quite some time, and at one time each was the hot new thing in web design. In this hour you will take a closer look at both these techniques and learn when to use (and when *not* to use) them.

Frames: An Introduction

Frames (plural) are a group of web pages displayed together in a web browser. A separate HTML (Hypertext Markup Language) file, commonly referred to as a *frameset*, controls the frames. The frameset creates a group of frames, gives a name to each frame, and tells the browser how to position the different frames in relation to one another. There is also a subset of frames called an *iFrame*. The *i* is short for *inline* and, as its name suggests, this is a box in which a different HTML page displays inside the current page—more on that later.

For the most part, designers use frames to completely separate the navigational tools from the content. That way you can let the user scroll through lists of navigational links or large documents independently of other page elements. The Microsoft Developer Network Library uses frames in this manner to separate the header and sidebar navigation from the document content (see Figure 17.1). That way the visitor has im-

mediate access to the navigational tools in the header and can scroll through the library archive to the left without losing her place in the document she is currently reading. Likewise she can scroll through the document without either the header or the sidebar moving away from its current location.

The MSDN Library page consists of three separate frames that each display different web pages. This layout hints at one of the major problems when using frames: Because the actual page content is separate from the overall layout, the content pages don't contain any navigational tools. As long as they display as intended within the frameset, this is not a problem. But if a user accesses them from outside the frameset, the visitor loses the ability to navigate to the rest of the site. This is especially problematic because search engines usually index individual pages and not framesets, so a visitor that finds a certain page in a search engine is likely to land on just the content page without any of the navigation attached.

Try it Yourself

Create a Web Page with Frames

As it does with CSS layouts, Expression Web 2 comes with a series of preconfigured framesets for you to use. This makes the initial process of building a frames-based web page much easier.

1. In the Folder List task pane, create a new folder called Frames and double-click it to select it. Select File, New, Page from the menu bar to open the New dialog.

2. In the New dialog, select Frames Pages from the menu. This opens the preset frames layouts in the next window and gives you a short description and a preview of each frameset (see Figure 17.2).

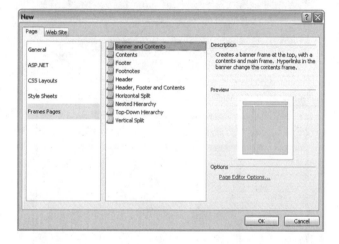

FIGURE 17.2
By selecting Frames Pages in the New dialog, you get a list of preconfigured frames layouts with a short description and a preview.

3. Select Banner and Contents and click OK to build the frameset. This opens the frameset in Design view, and Expression Web 2 asks you to set an initial page or create a new page for each frame (see Figure 17.3).

4. Before you continue, press Ctrl+S to save the frameset. Name the file **frameset.html** and save it in the Frames folder. Click the New Page button in the top banner. This changes the banner to a white page with a cursor in it. Now you are actually looking at two separate HTML pages: the frameset that defines the overall layout, and the new page that is visible only in the banner area. Do the same for the sidebar and the content area as shown in Figure 17.4.

5. Press Ctrl+S again to save the new frame pages. This opens the Save As dialog and highlights the first frame (the banner). Name this page

FIGURE 17.3
After building the frameset, you define the contents of each frame by either inserting the address of an existing page or creating a new page.

FIGURE 17.3
After building the frameset, you define the contents of each frame by either inserting the address of an existing page or creating a new page.

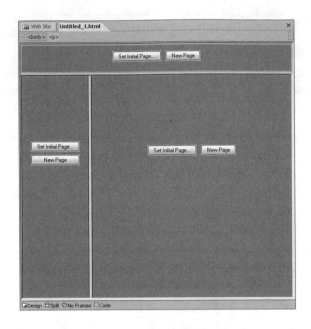

FIGURE 17.4
By clicking the New Page buttons in all three frames, you create three new pages.

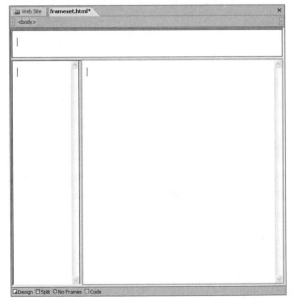

bannerFrame.html and click Save. Expression Web 2 creates the file and the Save As dialog opens again—this time with the sidebar highlighted (see Figure 17.5). Name this page **navigationFrame.html** and click Save. The Save As dialog opens for a third time and Expression Web 2 highlights the main content

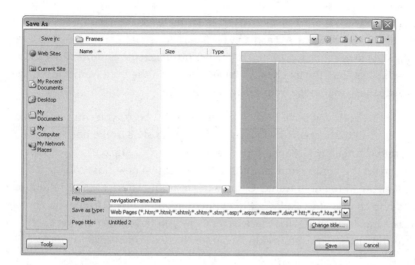

FIGURE 17.5
As you save each page, Expression Web 2 opens the next one and tells you what frame you are saving by highlighting the frame in the preview window on the right. In this image, Expression Web 2 is highlighting the sidebar.

area. Name the final page **kenny.html** and click Save. You saved all the pages and you can now start editing each one individually.

The Frames folder now has four files in it: `frameset.html`, `bannerFrame.html`, `navigationFrame.html`, and `content.html`. The three last pages you created are normal HTML pages that you can open separately. `frameset.html` is an HTML file that contains only information about the spatial relationship between the different frames. Beyond that, it is empty. If you press F12 to preview the page in your browser, you see the three frames but the address bar tells you that you are actually looking at the `frameset.html` file—the other pages are embedded.

Editing Individual Frames

Now that you have created the frames pages, it's time to insert some content into the frames. Because each frame contains a separate HTML page, you can edit it in the same way you have done throughout this book—by inserting text and images and applying styles or style sheets.

> Because you are now working with a frame layout, you have to consider the overall layout of the frameset, not just the individual pages. For instance, applying the `layout.css` style sheet to each frame means they all will have the top background graphic applied to them individually, which will look strange.

Watch Out!

This frameset will be a simple archive with a list on the left and pages for each of the items on the right. Start by placing the cursor in the banner frame and entering

Kipple Archive. Set the font style to H1 and attach the **kippleStyles.css** style sheet to the page using the Attach Style Sheet function. Expression Web 2 applies the new style to only the top frame. In the left frame, create an unordered list and give the first list item the text **Kenny Squeeze Toy.** In the final frame, insert the **KennyOriginal.jpg** image from the Images folder.

Using the CSS skills you have learned throughout this book, you can now make styling changes to the individual pages. Create an li style in the page in the left frame, and change the List-Style-Type setting to None. Create a ul style in the same frame and set the borders and margins to 0px. Create a new class called .alignCenter in the right frame. Change the Margin-Left and Margin-Right settings to Auto and change the Display setting under Layout to Block. Apply the new class to the <img> tag using the Quick Tag Selector. Now you have three different style sets for the three different pages, all working together to create an overall layout (see Figure 17.6).

FIGURE 17.6
The contents of each page within the frameset are styled separately by the styles defined in each page.

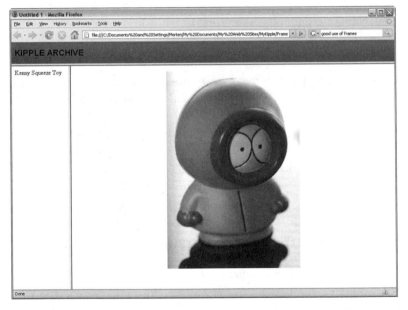

▼   **Try it Yourself**

Edit the Frames Layout

The actual layout and functionality of the frameset as a whole are contained within the frameset.html file, not the individual frames. So, to change the layout and/or relationship between the different frames, you have to edit frameset.html.

▼

There are many ways in which to change the layout of the frames. The simplest one is to grab the frame borders with the mouse and drag them to a different size. But for more detailed control, it is better to use the Frame Properties dialog.

1. To open the Frame Properties dialog, right-click inside the frame you want to change (in this case the left frame) and select Frame Properties from the context menu (see Figure 17.7).

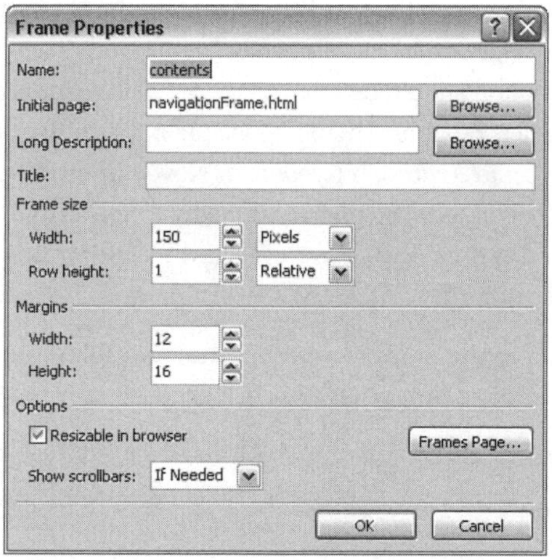

FIGURE 17.7
The Frame Properties dialog lets you configure the properties of the frame in relation to the other frames. These properties have no direct effect on the page within the frame, only how the browser displays it.

2. In the Frame Properties dialog, you can set various different attributes. The Name attribute is the identifying name of the frame. This is the name you use when targeting the frame with links. Change the name to **sidebar.**

3. Initial Page is the first page displayed when a browser opens the frameset.html page. Because this is the navigation frame, leave it the way it is.

4. Long Description and Title are fields used by screen readers to describe the contents of the frame for visitors that cannot see the content. Long Description links to a file with a long description. Title is a short description of the frame. These two attributes work in the same way as the alternative text and long description attached to image files. Leave the Long Description field blank and insert **Kipple Archive list-menu** in the Title field.

5. Frame Size defines the physical size of the frame in relation to the other frames on the page. The Width and Row Height attributes can be set to a numeric value that is relative (in relation to the other frames), percent (of the entire width or height of the page in the browser), or pixels. To give the menu some more room, set the Width attribute to 200 pixels.

6. *Margins* refer to the space between the walls of the frame and the content within it in much the same way that the padding in CSS relates to the box. Changing the margin values in the frame properties creates a smaller or larger buffer zone for the content. Setting the margins to zero can look very strange, but might be exactly what you want if you are styling the individual frame content with CSS. For this example, leave the values as they are.

7. Under Options, if the Resizable in Browser box is checked, the visitor can grab the frame borders and change the size of the frame in the browser (this affects only the page in the browser, not the actual page on the server). In this case, and almost every case, this option should be unchecked. Show Scrollbars gives you the option of deciding whether scrollbars should be visible if the content doesn't fit on the screen. It can be set to Always, If Needed, or Never. In most cases, the If Needed option is the right way to go. The user has no way to see any content that spills outside the frame if this option is set to Never and the visitor has a very small screen or the content is too large to fit. Set Show Scrollbars to If Needed for this frame.

8. The last function in the Frame Properties dialog is the Frames Page button. This button opens the page properties for the frameset page (see Figure 17.8). When

FIGURE 17.8
By clicking the Frames Page button, you can access the page properties for the frameset page. From here you can control the thickness and visibility of the frame borders, among other things.

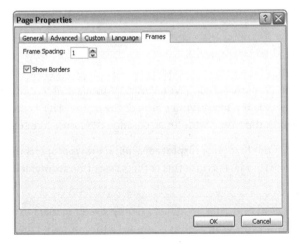

the visitor opens the frameset page, the browser considers this file to be the page and regards the pages within the frames as displayed information. In other words, all the information sent to the browser, such as title, page description, keywords, and so forth, comes from the frameset page. By clicking the Frames Page button, you have access to all these properties. This is also where you control the frame borders. Their width is defined in pixels by the Frame Spacing value and they can be turned on and off with the Show Borders setting. Set the Frame Spacing value to 1px and click OK twice to apply the changes.

You can also split and delete frames just as you would with table cells. To split a frame into two frames, either horizontally or vertically, select the frame by clicking anywhere inside it and choose Format, Frames, Split Frame from the menu bar. This opens the Split Frame dialog where you can choose whether to split the frame in two horizontally or vertically. To delete a frame, select it in the same way and choose Format, Frames, Delete Frame from the menu bar.

Making Framed Navigation

As you learned earlier, the main reason you would use frames is to separate the navigation from the content. After the frameset is set up, this is a simple operation as long as you keep tabs on what you are doing. This is where the frame name comes in. When you create a hyperlink in one frame that you mean to open in a different frame, you target that frame using the frame's name. In the past you had to remember the names of the different frames, but Expression Web 2 has taken away that barrier and made the process much easier:

1. Before you can create a hyperlink to a new page, you need a new page to link to. In the Folder List task pane, open the Frames folder and open the kenny.html file. Click File on the menu bar, select Save As, and change the filename to desk.html. This creates a new HTML file called desk.html (see Figure 17.9). Right-click the image in the new file, select Picture Properties, and change the picture file to the desk.jpg file found in the Images folder. Save the file and close it.

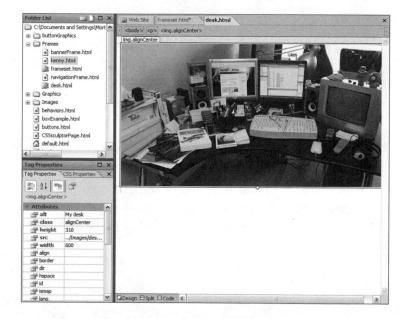

FIGURE 17.9
Creating a new file can be as easy as clicking Save As and changing the name in the Save As dialog. After you create the new file, you can make changes to it without having to worry about the old file.

2. In the `frameset.html` file, add a second list item to the left frame and call it **The Kippled Desk.** Highlight the first line item, right-click, and select Hyperlink from the context menu to open the Insert Hyperlink dialog. Navigate to the **kenny.html** page in the Frames folder. Then click the Target Frame button to open the Target Frame dialog (see Figure 17.10). There you can pick what frame the hyperlink should open the new page in, either by clicking the frame in the Current Frames Page area or selecting one of the Common Targets. Click the left frame in the Current Frames area and the Target setting changes to Main (the name of the right frame). Click OK twice to create the hyperlink.

FIGURE 17.10
The Target Frame dialog lets you pick what frame to target by clicking a visual representation of the current frameset or selecting one of the common targets.

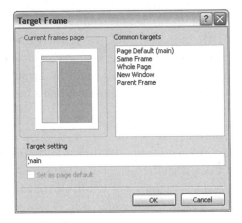

3. Repeat the same process with the second line item and link it to the `desk.html` page you created earlier. Save and preview the page in your browser.

When you click the two hyperlinks in your browser, you see that the right frame changes between the Kenny.html page and the desk.html page whereas the banner and sidebar frames remain unchanged.

Creating and Modifying Inline Frames

Unlike the frameset, which is a series of frames that contain the content, the inline frame (often referred to as the *iFrame*) is a frame inserted into a page to display the contents of a different page. An easy way to understand how an inline frame works is to imagine the frame as a hole cut into the page and filled with the contents from a different page.

Inline frames can be inserted anywhere within an HTML page and, as their name suggests, they work as other inline items. That is, they line up alongside the current line of text. Inline frames are a great way of inserting content from other websites into a page without having to either copy the content over or link to it.

1. Create a new page and call it `inlineFramePage.html`. In the page, insert a headline and two paragraphs of text.

When web designers and developers are working with unfinished pages, they often need some dummy text to work with. The most common dummy text is Lorem Ipsum, and you can find it at http://www.lipsum.com. You define how many paragraphs, words, or bytes you want and the website generates it for you.

2. Place the cursor at the beginning of the second paragraph and press Enter to create a new paragraph. Move the cursor to the new empty paragraph in the middle. Insert an inline frame in one of two ways: select Insert, HTML, Inline Frame from the menu bar, or drag and drop an inline frame from the HTML submenu in the Toolbox task pane (see Figure 17.11).

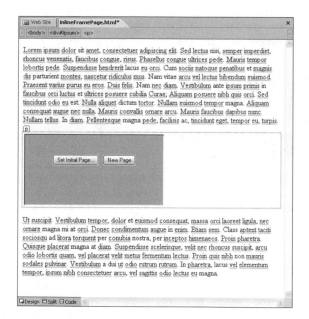

FIGURE 17.11
You can insert an inline frame by dragging and dropping the **Inline Frame** function into Design view from the Toolbox task pane.

3. When you insert the inline frame, Expression Web 2 gives you the same two choices you saw with the frameset: Set Initial Page and New Page. Select Set Initial Page and the Insert Hyperlink dialog opens. The hyperlink you set in this dialog becomes the content of the inline frame. Set the address to http://blog.pinkandyellow.com and click OK. Because this is a live website, Expression Web 2 navigates to the site and inserts the page into Design view if you have an open Internet connection (see Figure 17.12).

FIGURE 17.12
When you set the inline frame hyperlink to an external site, Expression Web 2 loads the external site into Design view.

4. To change the size of the inline frame, select it by clicking close to the outer edge of the inline frame and then drag the handles to the desired size.

Watch Out!

Inline frames can be tricky to handle because if you click anywhere inside the frame after loading the content, you are actually selecting the content within the frame—not the frame itself. To select the inline frame, hover your mouse close to the outer border and click so that you see the Tag Selector iframe appear.

To make more advanced changes to an inline frame, you can change the inline frame properties by right-clicking the inline frame and selecting Inline Frame Properties from the context menu. As you can see from Figure 17.13, the Inline Frame Properties dialog and its functions are similar to the Frames Properties dialog you encountered earlier (refer to Figure 17.7).

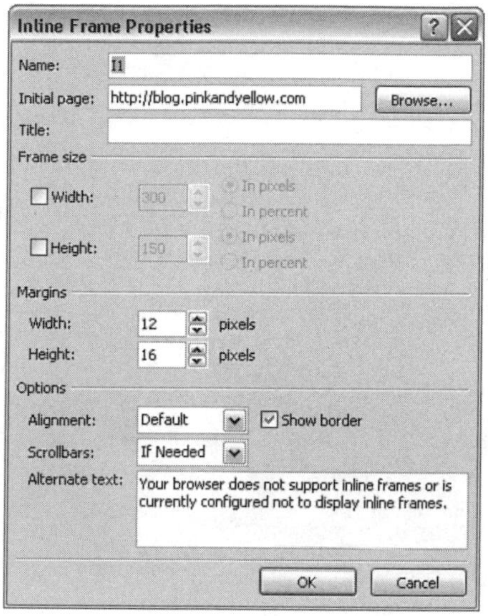

FIGURE 17.13
The Inline Frame Properties dialog gives you detailed control of all aspects of the inline frame.

From here you can change the initial page URL, the size, whether to use scrollbars, the alternative text (if the browser does not support inline frames), and a host of other options. You can also give the inline frame a unique name just like the earlier frames so that hyperlinks and actions can target it.

Set Text of Frame Behavior

You learned about behaviors in Hour 16, "Using Behaviors," but a couple behaviors were not covered: specifically, the Set Text behaviors. Now that you know how to use frames, you can take a closer look at the Set Text of Frame behavior

The Set Text of Frame behavior sends a block of predefined HTML code to the defined frame and replaces the current content of the frame with this code. You can use it to target any frame, whether in a frameset or an inline frame. Because the Set Text of Frame behavior only works on frames displaying pages from the current site, before starting this tutorial you need to change the hyperlink of the inline frame to one of the other pages in the MyKipple site, for example default.html.

1. First you need an element to attach the behavior to. Place the cursor to the right of the inline frame and create a new interactive button by choosing Insert, Interactive Button from the menu bar. Set the button text to **Change Text** and choose one of the layouts available. Make the changes you want to the button, but leave the Link area empty (see Figure 17.14). Click OK to insert the new button.

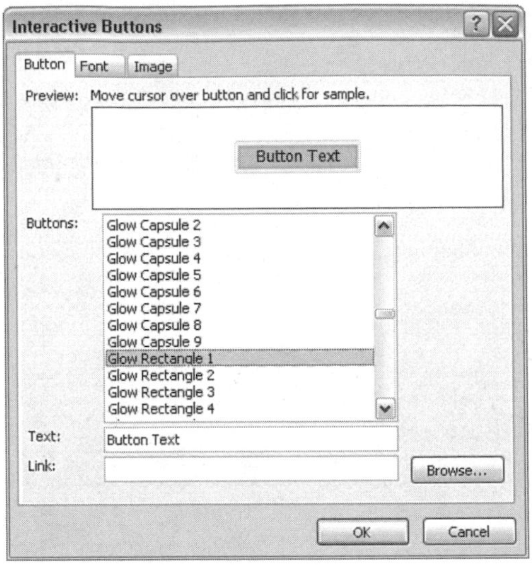

FIGURE 17.14
When you leave the Link area in the Interactive Button dialog empty, Expression Web 2 does not attach an **onclick** event to the button. One has to be inserted later.

FIGURE 17.14
When you leave the Link area in the Interactive Button dialog empty, Expression Web 2 does not attach an **onclick** event to the button. One has to be inserted later.

2. With the new button selected, choose Task Panes, Behaviors from the menu bar. Click Insert and select Set Text of Frame from the Set Text submenu. Doing so opens the Set Text of Frame dialog (see Figure 17.15).

FIGURE 17.15
The Set Text of Frame dialog lets you control what frame to target, what text to insert (in HTML code), and whether you want the frame to retain its background color.

3. In the Set Text of Frame dialog, you can choose what frame to target from a drop-down menu (in this case there is only one frame on the page and therefore only one option). In the Text area, you can insert plain text, HTML code, or a combination of both. The Preserve Background Color check box lets you decide whether you want to keep the background color from the last content visible in the frame. Insert some text with basic HTML coding such as <strong> or <em> and click OK to apply the behavior to the button. A new onclick event appears in the Behaviors task pane with the Set Text of Frame action attached.

4. Save the page (the Save Embedded Files dialog opens to save the image files for the new button) and test it in your browser.

When you click the button you just inserted, the content of the inline frame changes to the text you inserted in the Set Text of Frame dialog (see Figure 17.16).

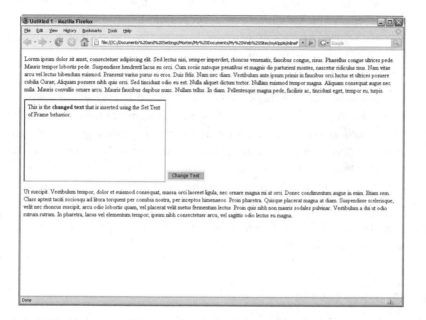

As an example, you could use the `Set Text of Frame` behavior in conjunction with the jump menu to display different messages to the user depending on his selections in the menu.

The Set Text of Frame behavior works by telling the browser to modify the content in the frame. This is why you can retain the background color of the original content when replacing the text. However this also causes a problem: Most browsers will not let you modify the contents of external pages, even if it is just done locally in the browser! As a result, if your frame links to an external page (i.e. a page that doesn't have the same domain name as the current page), browsers including Internet Explorer and Opera will return an Access Denied error and the behavior will not work. As a result the Set Text of Frame behavior can only be used on frames that contain pages from your own domain.

Creating Advanced Functionality Using Layers

Another advanced layout technique is the use of layers. Whereas inline frames are inserted into the content of the page, layers contain boxes that float on top of the content in the page. This can be a very useful tool when you want to create a more interactive experience for the visitor. One of the reasons layers are used is the ability to make them invisible. As a result, you can create highly advanced elements such as pop-up menus or boxes that the user can trigger.

By default, Expression Web 2 places all layers within an absolutely positioned <div> tag so that you have complete control of the position of the layer within the page. Because the layer is absolutely positioned, three attributes control the layer's physical placement. Left controls the distance between the left side of the layer and the left side of the page, Top controls the distance between the top of the layer and the top of the page, and Z-Index controls the imagined position of the layer in three-dimensional space if you stack several layers on top of one another.

When setting the z-index, 0 represents the bottom layer. The element with the highest z-index number is always on top.

Creating a Layer

To help create and edit layers, Expression Web 2 has a specialized task pane just for this layout tool. To open it, select Task Panes, Layers from the menu bar. The Layers task pane opens in the same area as the Behaviors task pane (see Figure 17.17).

FIGURE 17.17
The Layers task pane gives you full access to all the layers and layer functionality on the page.

1. In the `inlineFramePage.html` page, place the cursor at the beginning of the first paragraph. Click the Draw Layer button in the Layers task pane, and draw a small box by clicking and dragging the mouse in Design view (see Figure 17.18).

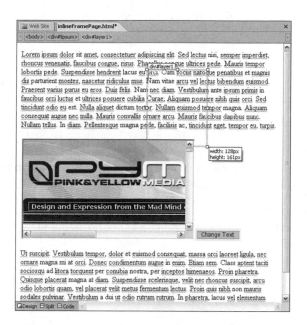

FIGURE 17.18
To draw a layer, simply click the Draw Layer button and then click and drag the layer to the desired size in Design view. You can always resize it later.

2. When the layer is drawn, the cursor should appear within it. If not, click it with your mouse to activate it. Drag and drop the `kennyOriginal_small.jpg` image into the layer. The image should now hover over the rest of the content.

3. In the Layers task pane, right-click the `layer1` instance and select Modify ID from the context menu. Change the ID of the layer to **kennyThumb.**

4. In the Layers task pane, click twice on the layer just underneath the eye to set the Visibility attribute to Hidden (no eye means default, open eye means visible, and closed eye means hidden). The image disappears from the screen (see Figure 17.19). If you look in the CSS Properties task pane, you see that the Visibility attribute has been set to Hidden.

5. Highlight a word in the first paragraph next to the layer you just inserted and create a hyperlink that points to the `kenny.html` file you created in the Frames folder.

FIGURE 17.19
You can use the
eye icon in the
Layers task pane
to toggle a
layer's visibility
among default,
visible, and hid-
den.

6. With the new hyperlink selected, go to the Behaviors task pane and insert a new Change Property behavior.

7. In the Change Property dialog, check the Select Element option, and set the element type to <div> and the element ID to kennyThumb. Doing that means the Change Property behavior will affect the layer you just created.

8. Click the Visibility button and set the visibility style to Visible. Click OK. Check the Restore on Mouseout Event option and click OK to apply the behavior (see Figure 17.20).

FIGURE 17.20
You can use the
**Change Prop-
erty** behavior
to change the
visibility of lay-
ers.

9. The default event for the Change Property behavior you just added is onclick. Change it to onmouseover so that the image becomes visible when a visitor hovers over the hyperlink. Save and test the page in your browser.

When you open your browser and hover over the hyperlink you just created, the layer with the image becomes visible and hovers on top of the text (see Figure 17.21).

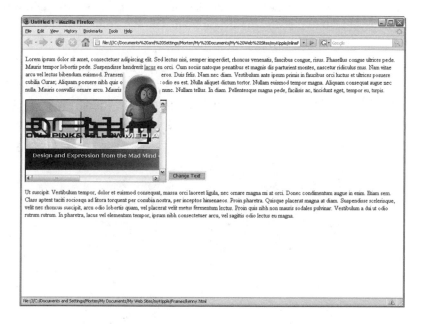

To move the location of the layer, click the layer in the Layers task pane to select it and hover the mouse over the tag selector to turn it into a four-way arrow. By clicking the tag selector, you can move the layer anywhere on the page. As you learned earlier, the layers have absolute positioning, so the distance from the left and top edges of the page or a containing tag with its position defined form the basis for the layers' final position (see Hour 14, "Building the Framework," on positioning).

The reason you need to place the cursor at the beginning of the paragraph you insert the layer into is that Expression Web 2 wraps the layers in a <div> tag. As you learned earlier in this book, <div> tags are block tags that create a new separate line to be on. So, if you place the cursor in the middle of a paragraph, the layer creates a new line that remains empty and breaks up the text. Placing the layer at the beginning of the paragraph doesn't change its position but ensures that the paragraph does not split in two.

Creating a Layer Containing an Inline Frame

You can use layers in conjunction with inline frames to make a fancy pop-up effect in which the user previews the linked page in real-time without going to the actual page

1. Open the default.html page and find the text *Do Androids Dream of Electric Sheep?* that contains a hyperlink to the Amazon.com page for the book. Right-click the text, choose Hyperlink Properties, and copy the hyperlink address by highlighting it and pressing Ctrl+C. Close the Edit Hyperlink dialog without making any changes.

2. Place the cursor at the beginning of the paragraph that contains the hyperlink. Open the Layers task pane and use the Draw Layer function to draw a medium-sized layer directly underneath the hyperlink. From the Toolbox task pane, drag and drop an iFrame into the new layer (see Figure 17.22).

FIGURE 17.22
Layers can contain any kind of HTML element, including inline frames.

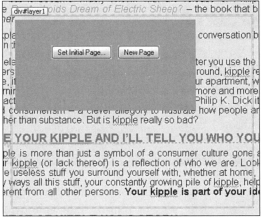

3. Click the Set Initial Page button in the inline frame and paste the Amazon.com link you copied earlier into the address bar. Expression Web 2 might tell you that the content on the page requires extra software to display properly. If it does, just click No. The page might not display properly inside Design view, but it will in a browser. Select the inline frame by clicking close to the outer border and resize it to fit the layer.

4. Change the Layer ID to amazonPreview by double-clicking the layer name in the Layers task pane (see Figure 17.23). Set the Visibility attribute of the layer to Hidden by clicking twice on the area underneath the eye.

5. Select the hyperlink and use the Behaviors task pane to attach a Change Property behavior to it. In the Change Property dialog, select the div element amazonPreview and set the Visibility attribute to Visible. Check the Restore on Onmouseout Event box and click OK to apply the behavior.

6. With the hyperlink still selected, change the event of the Change Property action to *onmouseover*. Save the page and preview in your browser.

FIGURE 17.23
Even after setting the layer's visibility to hidden, the inline frame will still be visible in Design view. But when you preview the page in a browser, you see that the browser hides the frame.

When you hover the mouse over the hyperlink in your browser, the layer opens with the inline frame inside it and shows you what the linked page looks like in real-time (see Figure 17.24).

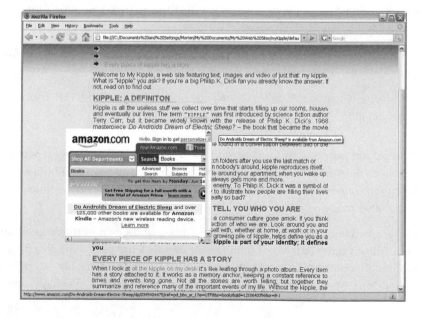

FIGURE 17.24
With the **Change Property** behavior attached to the hyperlink, the layer with the inline frame opens only when the visitor hovers over the hyperlink.

Set Text of Layer Behavior

The Set Text of Layer behavior works the same way as the Set Text of Frame behavior. When applied, it changes the content of the selected layer to the text or HTML content inserted into the Set Text of Layer dialog (see Figure 17.25).

Summary

Frames and layers have been, and still are, important components of advanced web design. In this hour, you got a thorough walkthrough of how you can use these layout elements to add interactivity to your sites.

This hour was packed with a lot of information, so it is not surprising if you feel a little bit overwhelmed by all the new things you learned. To help you make sense of it all, think of it this way:

▶ A frame (and an inline frame) is a *hole cut in the page* and you fill it with the contents of a different page.

▶ A layer is a box placed *on top of* the page and you fill it with HTML content including inline frames.

In this hour, you learned how to set up and use a frameset to completely separate the contents from the navigation. You learned how to define and configure framesets, how to change and resize the individual frames, and how to make hyperlinks that target the other frames.

You also learned how to make and use inline frames, and saw how they can enhance your site. Inline frames differ from framesets in that they are placed inside a page rather than alongside other frames. Designers often use them to display external content, such as other web pages, and interactive content, such as Silverlight applications.

To top off the frames portion of this hour, you learned how to use the Set Text of Frame behavior to change the contents of a frame. You can use this behavior to target both inline frames and framesets.

In the second half of the hour, you learned about layers—more specifically how to create them and edit them. One of the most important features of layers is the ability to hide them and their content and then use behaviors to make them visible again. This technique enables you to make some highly interactive and very impressive features easily.

This hour only scratched the surface of what is possible when using layers. In the next hour, you will create a full fledged drop-down navigation menu using the same techniques you learned here.

Q&A

Q. *I created a new hyperlink in the frameset, but when I clicked it in the browser the contents in the same frame changed rather than the one I wanted to change.*

A. When you click a link and the current frame changes (or a different frame from the intended one changes, for that matter), there is something wrong with your targeting. Most likely you simply forgot to change the target frame or you clicked the wrong target frame in the Target Frame dialog. To fix this problem, open the Hyperlink Properties dialog and ensure that the target frame is correct.

Q. *When I click one of the links, the entire frameset appears in the right frame. Now the entire site is doubled up!*

A. A common problem when using framesets is *nested frames*, which means that the entire frameset opens inside one of the frames. This is because you created a hyperlink to the frameset rather than the actual page you wanted to link to. To avoid this problem, always include the word *frameset* in the filename for your framesets and the word *frame* in the filename of single frame pages.

Q. *I created several different layers, but there is no real system to which one appears on top. What is going on?*

A. If you create multiple layers in one location and you want them to appear in a particular order, you need to change the z-index of each of the layers so that the lowest layer has the lowest number and the highest layer has the highest number.

Workshop

The Workshop has quiz questions and exercises to help you put to use what you just learned. If you get stuck, the answers to the quiz questions are in the next section. But try to answer the questions first. Otherwise you'll only be cheating yourself.

Quiz

1. *What is the difference between a frame and a layer?*

2. *When should you use a frameset rather than a single HTML file to create a page?*

3. *How do you set the position of a layer on your page?*

Answers

1. A frame can be thought of as a hole cut in your page that contains another page. A layer by contrast can be thought of as a box that is placed on top of the content of the page that contains HTML.

2. A frameset should be used if you need to keep the navigation or other elements completely separate from the content so that when the visitor scrolls through the content the other element stays put. A good example would be to use layers to create an index page where the index itself is in one frame and the pages it points to appear in a different frame.

3. By default the layers inserted by Expression Web 2 are placed inside absolutely positioned <div> tags. Therefore they are positioned in relation to the top left corner of the closest element with a position other than static. To position a layer you can either drag it to the desired location using your mouse or set the X and Y values manually using CSS. You can also change the positioning of the <div> tag to any of the other values for a different effect although setting it to static defeats the purpose of a layer.

Exercise

Create a new frameset with four frames and create new files for each frame. Select one of the frames as the navigation frame and create a series of hyperlinks that change the contents of each of the other three frames to different pages on the Web. Use percentages in setting their widths and heights to resize the frames so that they take up the same amount of space.

Create a series of layers slightly offset from one another and insert different images into each layer. Change the z-index for each layer to set the order. Preview the page in your browser to see how the images stack on top of one another. Go back to Expression Web 2 and change the z-index for some of the layers to change the order. Preview the page in your browser again to see what happened.

Create a new button and use the `Set Text of Layer` behavior to change the top layer to predefined text when you click the button.

HOUR 18

Building a Functional Menu

What You'll Learn in This Hour:

▶ How to build a drop-down menu using layers and behaviors

▶ How to build a drop-down menu using unordered lists and CSS

▶ The benefits and drawbacks of each approach

Introduction

In the last few hours you learned about buttons, behaviors, and layers. Now you use that knowledge to create advanced and functional drop-down menus for easy navigation.

Drop-down menus are a great tool for simplifying navigation in a website. They allow you to group several different pages or links together visually and give the user an intuitive and interactive experience when surfing your site.

Creating drop-down menus that work properly is often a challenge for new designers and developers. Much of the confusion probably stems from the myriad of different techniques available and a lack of understanding of the processes behind them as well as the problems created by browser inconsistencies. This is unfortunate because the principles behind creating functional drop-down menus are simple.

This hour shows you how to make proper, functional, and lightweight drop-down menus that you can implement into any site. You will create two menus: one with layers and interactive buttons and one using only CSS (Cascading Style Sheets). Although these two menus function in much the same way, they are completely different when it comes to how they actually work. It is important to know not only how to create these two types of menus, but also the benefits and limitations of each technique.

The Layers Based Menu

Using layers and child layers is a quick-and-dirty way of creating drop-down menus that has been around for some time. This technique allows for great flexibility when it comes to the look and feel of the menu, but the code portion can be very messy. Nevertheless the layers-based drop-down menu is the preferred choice of many designers and developers and you can create it in Expression Web 2 without writing or looking at a single line of code.

Creating the Main Menu

A drop-down menu consists of two groups of elements: the main menu that is always visible and the child menus triggered by the main menu. The main menu buttons can work as buttons or just as triggers for the child menus. In this lesson, you use Expression Web 2's interactive buttons to create the Layers menu.

1. Create a new HTML (Hypertext Markup Language) page and call it `menus.html`. Open the page in Design view.

2. Open the Layers task pane and click the Draw Layer button. Draw a layer the width of the page and about one paragraph in height in Design view. After creating the layer, double-click it in the Layers task pane and change the layer ID to `mainMenu` (see Figure 18.1).

FIGURE 18.1
Naming the layers as you create them is a good habit that prevents confusion when your layouts become more complicated.

3. Click the layer to place the cursor inside it and select Insert, Interactive Button on the menu bar to create a new interactive button.

4. In the Interactive Button dialog, scroll down and select one of the Linked Row buttons. Set the Text option to Home and click OK to insert the button.

5. You now have two choices of how to create more buttons: Either repeat steps 3 and 4 or copy the current button, paste a new one next to it, and double-click the new button to open the Interactive Button dialog and give the button a new name. Either way you choose, create four new buttons and call them News, Gallery, Archive, and Contact (see Figure 18.2).

FIGURE 18.2
The **mainMenu** layer now contains five buttons.

Creating a Submenu

Now that you have designed the main menu, it is time to add the submenus to the page. Each submenu should reside in its own layer, and the layers should be children of the mainMenu layer. This is because when a layer is a child of a different layer, the parent layer defines its position. In practical terms, this means that if the parent layer moves the child layers move with it.

1. To create a child layer, use the Draw Layer button to draw a new layer anywhere on the page (you will position it later). After drawing the layer, click-and-drag the new layer instance on top of the mainMenu layer instance in the Layers task pane so that the mouse pointer changes to include a superimposed box and a + sign. When you let go, the new layer appears slightly indented

under the mainMenu layer in the list. The indentation indicates the new layer is a child of the mainMenu layer (see Figure 18.3).

FIGURE 18.3
The - (minus sign) in front of the **mainMenu** layer and the slight indentation of the new layer indicate that the new layer is a child of the **mainMenu** layer.

2. Change the layer ID of the new layer to newsSub.

3. Place the cursor inside the new layer and select Insert, Interactive Button from the menu bar to create a new interactive button.

4. Choose the Simple Block button and set the button text to **New News.** Under the Font tab, set the Horizontal Alignment to Left. As you can see from the preview, you have to insert a space before the words to separate them from the box graphic. To do so, simply place your cursor at the beginning of the text and press the spacebar once. Click OK to insert the button into the new layer.

5. Press Enter to go to the next line, copy and paste the first button into the second line, and give it the name **Old News**. Repeat the process and make two more buttons called Good News and Bad News.

6. Resize the layer by clicking it and dragging the handles so that the layer borders fit the content (see Figure 18.4).

FIGURE 18.4
After creating all the buttons, you can resize the layer using the handles.

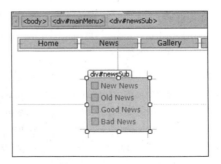

7. Finally, reposition the layer directly under the News button on the main menu where you want it to appear when the visitor triggers it (see Figure 18.5).

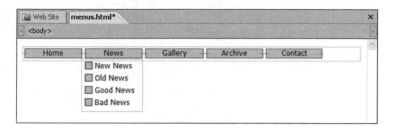

FIGURE 18.5
Because the pop-up layer is likely to overlap parts of the **mainMenu** layer, it is a good idea to wait until you finish the layer before moving it to its final position.

To reposition the layer, hover your mouse over the Tag Selector until the four-direction arrow shows and then drag-and-drop the layer to the location of your choice.

When you save the page, you get a long list of embedded image files that you must save. Click the Change Folder button in the Save Embedded Files dialog and create a new folder called Buttons for all the button images.

After saving the page, preview it in your browser. As you can see, the main menu buttons and the submenu buttons are working properly but the submenu is visible all the time. To create the drop-down effect, you need to apply a series of behaviors to the different elements.

Try it Yourself ▼

Use Behaviors to Make the Drop-Down Menu Drop Down

The whole idea of a drop-down menu is that the submenus are not visible until you trigger them. In Hour 17, "Frames and Layers," you learned how you could use the Visibility property to hide and show layers in the browser. Now you are going to use this technique to trigger the new submenu.

1. The newsSub layer should not be visible unless the user triggers it. Use the eye column in the Layers task pane or right-click the newsSub layer and select Set Visibility: Hidden from the pop-up menu (see Figure 18.6).

The newsSub layer should become visible when the visitor hovers over the News button on the mainMenu layer.

2. Select the News button in the mainMenu layer and apply a Change Property behavior from the Behaviors task pane.

▼

FIGURE 18.6
You can set the visibility of a layer by using the eye icon in the leftmost column in the Layers task pane, or by right-clicking it and setting it from the pop-up menu.

3. In the Change Property dialog, check Select Element and set the element type to Div and the element ID to newsSub. Click the Visibility button and set the visibility to Visible. For this behavior, *do not* check the Restore on Mouseout Event box (see Figure 18.7). If you do, the submenu becomes invisible when

FIGURE 18.7
Use the **Change Property** behavior in the News button to trigger the drop-down menu.

you move your mouse away from the News button and into the menu. Click OK to apply the behavior.

4. In the Behaviors task pane, change the event of the Change Property behavior to onmouseover by clicking it and selecting onmouseover from the drop-down menu.

Now the newsSub menu appears whenever the visitor hovers over the News button. If you test the page in your browser, you see that after submenu triggers, it doesn't disappear again.

5. Select the newsSub layer either by clicking it in Design view or selecting it from the Layers task pane, and go to the Behaviors task pane. Apply a Change Property behavior to the newsSub layer.

6. In the Change Property task pane, leave Current Element checked and set the Visibility to Hidden. Again, *do not* check the Restore on Mouseout Event box. Click OK to apply the behavior.

7. In the Behaviors task pane, change the event of the Change Property behavior to onmouseout. This tells the browser that the menu should be invisible when mouse is no longer hovering over it.

   Save and test the page in your browser and you see that the drop-down menu now stays put when you hover over the first button, but disappears again if you move further down. To fix this you need to tell the browser that as long as the mouse is in the newsSub layer it should remain visible.

8. With the newsSub layer still selected, add a new Change Property behavior and set the Visibility property for the layer to Visible. Click OK to apply the new behavior and change the event to onmouseover (see Figure 18.8).

FIGURE 18.8
The **newsSub** layer needs two **Change Property** behaviors to work properly: one for when the mouse hovers over it and one for when the mouse moves away from it.

Now the drop-down menu works almost the way it should, with one exception: If the visitor moves the mouse to one of the other main menu buttons instead of somewhere else on the page, the submenu stays visible.

9. To hide the submenu when the visitor moves from the News button to one of the other buttons on the main menu, click the mainMenu layer in the Layers task pane layer and apply a Change Property behavior to it. Check Select Element and set the element type to Div and the element ID to newsSub. Click the

Visibility button and set the visibility to Visible. Click OK twice to apply the behavior to the layer and change the event to onmouseout.

Now, finally, the drop-down menu for the News button works properly.

Adding and Managing Several Drop-Down Menus

As you saw in the prior section, to get the drop-down menu to work properly, you have to apply multiple different behaviors to different elements within the page. Unfortunately there is no quick way to automate this process: You have to apply the same set of behaviors to every new submenu.

1. To create a new submenu for the Gallery button, click to select the newsSub layer in the Layers task pane and press Ctrl+C to copy it and Ctrl+V to paste it. The new layer should appear with the name newsSub0 in the Layers task pane as well as on top of the original newsSub layer in Design view.

2. Double-click the layer in the Layers task pane to rename it. Give it the name **gallerySub** (see Figure 18.9).

FIGURE 18.9
You can copy and paste layers from within the Layers task pane. They become independent entities, and it's a good idea to rename them immediately to keep track.

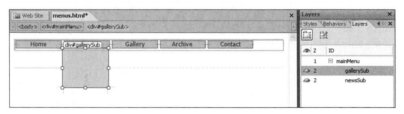

3. Grab the new gallerySub layer in Design view and move it so that it is directly under the Gallery button on the main menu. Toggle the layer visibility to visible by clicking the eye icon in the Layers task pane.

4. Double-click the first button and give it the name **My Kipple**. Rename the three other buttons to **Other Kipple** and **Found Kipple**. Delete the last button (see Figure 18.10).

FIGURE 18.10
The new button titles are longer than the ones in the original layer, so you need to extend the **gallerySub** layer to the right to fit them in.

5. Because the new buttons have longer titles, the layer needs to be wider. There is also one fewer button, so it should be shorter as well. Grab the handle in the lower-right corner and resize the layer so that it wraps the new content.

6. With the gallerySub layer selected, go to the Behaviors task pane. The behaviors from the newsSub layer are still visible, but if you double-click the onmouseout behavior to open the Change Property dialog, you'll be notified that it is no longer working (see Figure 18.11).

FIGURE 18.11
The Previous Target Element Was Not Found warning tells you that although the behavior appears in the Behaviors task pane, it no longer works.

7. Click past the warning box and you see that the behavior is empty. The event is still present but the action is gone. Set the element ID to **gallerySub** and the visibility to Hidden. Open the **onmouseover** behavior and do the same except set the visibility to Visible.

8. To link the new layer to the main menu, select the Gallery button on the main menu and apply a Change Property behavior to it. In the Change Properties dialog, set the element ID to gallerySub and the visibility to Visible. Click OK to apply the new behavior and change the event in the Behaviors task pane to onmouseover.

9. To finalize the process, set the gallerySub layer visibility to Hidden in the Layers task pane by clicking the eye icon twice to get the closed eye. Create a new behavior that sets the visibility of the gallerySub layer to Hidden and attach it to the mainMenu layer. Change the event of this behavior to onmouseout. The mainMenu layer should now have two onmouseout events that both have Change Property actions.

Save and preview the page in your browser, and you see that you now have a menu with two fully working drop-down submenus under the News and Gallery buttons.

Basing Drop-Down Menus on Layers and Behaviors Is a Two-Edged Sword

Although making a drop-down menu using layers and behaviors might seem easy because you can do it all by pointing and clicking different elements, there are some serious drawbacks to this technique. You are required to apply a long list of behaviors to each element just to make the menu work properly, and you have to add even more if you want the buttons to do something. In addition, if you switch the page you have been working with to Split view, you can see that the code generated for this menu is very complicated and hard to read, even for seasoned professionals (see Figure 18.12). As a result, a small error or omission on the part of the designer or de-

FIGURE 18.12
Although the menu looks great in Design view, the code that makes it work is complicated and hard to read.

veloper can have catastrophic consequences for the functionality of the menu as a whole.

On the upside, this technique allows you to use fancy graphic elements as buttons and gives you an easy way to create and control highly interactive menus. Although this book does not cover the topic, for a more customized look, you can create graphic buttons outside Expression Web 2 that work the same way as the interactive buttons.

The drop-down menu tutorial serves as much as a demonstration of what is possible when you use layers and behaviors together as it is an instruction on how to create the perfect menu. When applied properly, this technique produces robust, attractive, and interactive menus that work both as navigation and eye candy. But as you saw, the code is complicated and you have to keep tabs on a lot of buttons and behaviors.

Pure CSS Drop-Down Menus: A Clean Alternative

If you want your page to be as accessible as possible as well as standards compliant and cross-browser compatible, base all your menus on ordered or unordered lists. That way, the menu is still meaningful if the visitor is on an old computer or uses a text-only or text-to-speech browser. Therefore, the ideal solution for making drop-down menus would be to create an unordered list with sublists styled using CSS. In an ideal world, this wouldn't be that much of a problem. Unfortunately the idiosyncratic nature of the most prolific browsers (especially Internet Explorer 6) has made it all but impossible to make a CSS drop-down menu without using some form of custom coding for these browsers or adding JavaScript or behaviors to make everything work properly.

As new versions of the many different browsers come out, these problems with inconsistencies become less and less prevalent. Sometime in the foreseeable future, they will likely disappear completely or at least diminish to the point where they are no longer a concern. In the meantime, designers have to live with one of two options: create pure CSS drop-down menus that might have problems in older browsers, or make menus that have JavaScript built in to fix the browser problems.

This tutorial teaches you how to make a drop-down menu using only CSS and no special browser-specific code (also known as *IE hacks*). As a result, the menu might not work in certain older browsers. This tutorial is to help you understand the principles behind making a CSS-based drop-down menu and is by no means a perfect solution.

Step 1: Make a Menu List

1. In the menus.html page, insert a new div underneath the code for the layers menu in Code view by dragging and dropping a div element from the Toolbox task pane (see Figure 18.13).

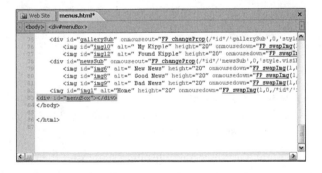

FIGURE 18.13
The Layers menu uses absolute positioning, so to place the new CSS menu below it on the page you have to use absolute positioning with this new menu as well.

2. Create a new ID by clicking the New Style button in the Styles task pane and giving it the name #menuBox. Under the Position category, set the position to

Absolute and the top to 45px. Click OK to create the new ID and apply it to the div you just created by selecting the div and clicking the ID in the Apply Styles task pane. This positions the new div below the Layers menu (see Figure 18.13).

3. Place the cursor inside the new div and create an unordered list with the same five list items you used before: Home, News, Gallery, Archive, and Contact.

4. Now create sublists for the News and Gallery portions. In Split view, select the News list item. In Code view, place the cursor right before the closing </li> tag and press Enter to create a new line. Type **<ul>** to create a new unordered list (IntelliSense closes the tag for you), press Enter again to create a new line, and create a list item by typing **<li>** (see Figure 18.14).

FIGURE 18.14
To create a list within a list, you have to edit the code in Code view. Although doing so is not necessary, splitting up the tags and spacing them as shown in this screenshot helps with readability.

5. Now that you have a sublist, you can go back to Design view and insert four new list items: New News, Old News, Good News, and Bad News. The new list items will appear as a subset of the News list item.

6. Repeat steps 4 and 5 for the Gallery list item and insert the three sublist items My Kipple, Other Kipple, and Found Kipple (see Figure 18.15).

7. To get this menu to work like a menu, you need to turn all the list items (both main items and sublist items) into hyperlinks. Because you don't have anywhere to point them to, make all the list items point back to the current page (menus.html).

FIGURE 18.15
The lists within lists appear as subsets of their parent list items.

Step 2: Styling the Main Menu

Now you have a working set of hyperlinks, but it looks nothing like a menu. The next step is to make the new menu look more like the one above it.

1. To keep the styles separate from the content, create a new CSS file called menuStyles.css. Use the Attach Style Sheet button in the Apply Styles task pane to attach the new style sheet to the current page.

2. Open the menuStyles.css file and paste in the CSS reset found at http://meyerweb.com/eric/thoughts/2007/05/01/reset-reloaded/. Go back to menus.html to see that all the styling has been stripped away from the list items (see Figure 18.16).

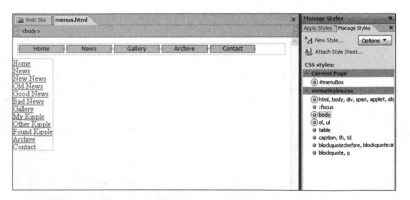

FIGURE 18.16
Applying the CSS reset strips all the styling from the list elements and leaves you a clean slate to work with.

3. In the Manage Styles task pane, click New Style to create a new ID and give it the name **#CSSmenu.** Make sure to define the new ID in the **menuStyles.css** style sheet. Set the Background-Color setting to White, the Margin-Left setting to 10px, the Position setting to Absolute, the Width setting to 700px, and the Float setting to Left. Click OK to create the new style. Apply it to the main menu unordered list by selecting the first <ul> tag from the Quick Tag Selector and applying the ID via the Apply or Modify Styles task pane. The #CSSmenu ID is now the container for all the list items.

4. The next step is to place the list items next to one another rather than on top of one another. To do so, create a new style called #CSSmenu li. This style affects all the list items within the #CSSmenu ID. Change the Font-Family setting to Arial, Helvetica, Sans-Serif; the Font-Size setting to 0.9em; and the Font-Weight setting to Bold. Set the Background-Color setting to White, give all four sides a 1px solid border, and change the Border Color setting to #5D7697. Under the Box category, change the Margin-Right setting to 4px. Leave the rest of the margins and padding empty. Under Position, change the Position setting to relative, the Width setting to 110px, and the Height setting to 20px. Under Layout, change the Display setting to inline and the Float setting to left. Finally, under List, change the List-Style-Type setting to None.

When you click OK to create the new style, the main menu items stack up next to one another from left to right (see Figure 18.17).

FIGURE 18.17
After applying
the **#CSSmenu
li** style, the
main menu list
items stack from
left to right in-
stead of from
top to bottom.

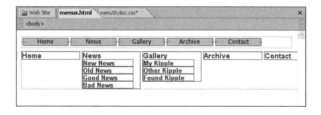

This requires some further explanation. The #CSSmenu li style applies separately to each of the main list items in the #CSSmenu container. By changing the Float setting to Left, you are telling the browser to place each item as much to the left on the line as possible. Therefore the items place themselves next to one another. Another technique that achieves the same result is to change the Display setting to Inline. With the boxes now stacked sideways, the 4px Margin-Right setting creates a space between each item. The Position setting of Relative tells the browser to place each list item (and its subitems) relative to the other items. Right now it has no impact on how the list looks, but it will shortly.

5. To make the list items into buttons, you need to style the hyperlinks. Create a new style called **#CSSmenu li a.** Under Font, set the color to a dark blue

(#000066) and check the None box under the Text-Decoration setting. To center the text vertically, go to Block and change the Line-Height setting to 20px (matching the height of the list item box you set in step 4). Use the eyedropper tool to change the Background-Color setting to the same color as the layer buttons (#99CCFF). Under Box, change the Padding-Left setting to 5px to move the text away from the left edge of the box. Under Position, change the Width setting to 105px (the width of the box [110px] minus the padding [5px]) and the Height setting to 20px. Finally, under Layout, change the Display setting to Block and the Float setting to Left. This makes the area of the hyperlink fill out the box (see Figure 18.18).

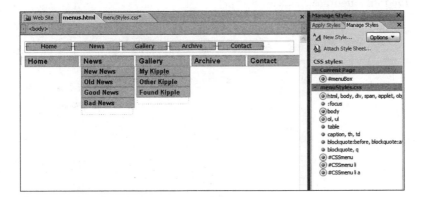

FIGURE 18.18
By adding the **#CSSmenu li a** style, the entire box area of each of the main menu buttons becomes active.

Step 3: Styling the Submenus

At this point the main menu and submenus line up correctly, but there is no visual difference between them. It is always a good idea to give the visitor visual clues that separate different types of content from each other. A simple way of doing this is to give the submenu items a different set of styles than the main menu items.

1. Create a new style with the name **#CSSmenu li ul**. This style affects the box that contains each the submenus. Under Position, change the Position setting to Relative, the Width setting to 110px, the Height setting to Auto, the Top setting to 1px, and the Left setting to 0px. The last two steps ensure that the drop-down box is positioned below the main menu (if the Top setting were Default or 0px, the bottom border would be covered), and that it lines up with the left side of the respective main menu list item.

2. If no other styling is applied, the line items in the submenu inherit the styling from the line items in the main menu. To remove the blue line that boxes in the list items, create a new style called **#CSSmenu li ul li**. In the Border category, change the Border-Style setting to None for all four sides.

3. Finally, style the hyperlinks themselves to make them different from the main menu hyperlinks. Create a new style called **#CSSmenu li ul li a**. Under Font, change the Font-Weight setting to Normal and the Color setting to Dark Gray (#666666). Change the Background-Color setting to White and under Border, change the Border-Left setting to Solid, 3px, and #99CCFF. Under Box, change the Margin-Top setting to 3px. This creates a space between each list item. Under Position, change the Width setting to 102px (105px minus a 3px left border).

With the new styles applied, the submenu now has a distinct look that is different from the main menu (see Figure 18.19).

FIGURE 18.19
The submenu styling produces a visual cue that tells the visitor these buttons are different from the ones on the main menu.

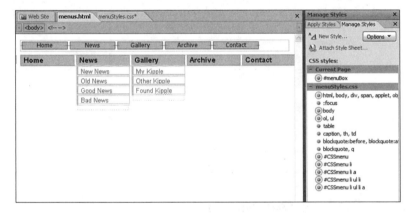

Step 4: Adding Interactivity to the Buttons

To take the menu to the next level, each button should react when the mouse hovers over it. As you learned earlier, this is done by adding the :hover pseudoclass to the a style. In this case you have two separate styles: one for the main menu items and one for the submenu items. When you create a pseudoclass for a style, you only have to include the elements that are different from the main style. All the other styling is inherited automatically.

> It is a good idea to keep the difference between the regular state and the hover state small but noticeable: Dramatic color changes are easily noticeable, but they are the equivalent of shouting at the visitor. A subtle change is more pleasing to the eye and makes the design look cleaner and more professional.

1. Create a new style called **#CSSmenu li a:hover**. Under the Border category, change the Border-Left setting to Solid, 3px, and #5D7697. Doing so creates a 3px blue border on the left side of the button to match the blue border on the

left of the submenu buttons. To prevent the button text from shifting 3px to the right, go to the Box category and change the Padding-Left setting to 2px (#CSSmenu li a has it at 5px). Click OK to save the new style.

By the Way

> If you test the page in your browser, you see that the hover state of the main menu buttons works the way you intended. But the submenu buttons are being styled by the new pseudoclass and the text is shifting to the left.

2. Create a new style called **#CSSmenu li ul li a:hover**. Under the Font category, change the Color setting to #333333. Under the Box category, change the Padding-Left setting to 5px. Click OK to save the new style.

Now all the buttons in the menu are styled properly and have a visual cue when the visitor hovers over them.

Step 5: Making the Drop-Down Menus Drop Down

Now that the menus *look* the way they should it is time to make them *work* the way they should. To do that, you need to hide the submenus first and then make them visible when the visitor hovers over the correct button.

When you made a drop-down menu using layers, you used the Visibility property to hide the drop-down layer and then attached a Change Property behavior to the main menu button to change that visibility. Now you are going to use a similar technique to control the visibility of the submenus. The trick here is that the submenu lists are part of the main menu list items. As such, the submenu list already has the main menu button attached.

1. First hide the submenus so that they are invisible unless the user triggers them. To do so, select the #CSSmenu li ul style from the Manage Styles task pane, right-click, and select Modify Style. Under the Layout category, change the Visibility setting to Hidden—this is the same property you used to hide the layers in the earlier examples. Click OK to apply the modified style. Now the submenus are no longer visible in Design view.

2. Create a new style called **#CSSmenu li:hover ul**. This style is a pseudo-class that triggers when the visitor hovers over a main menu list item, and affects any unordered list contained within that list item. Under the Layout category, change the Visibility setting to Visible. Click OK to apply the new style.

If you save and preview the page in your browser, you see that the drop-down menus now work the way they should (see Figure 18.20). Furthermore the menu is 100%

FIGURE 18.20
The pure CSS
drop-down menu
now works prop-
erly.

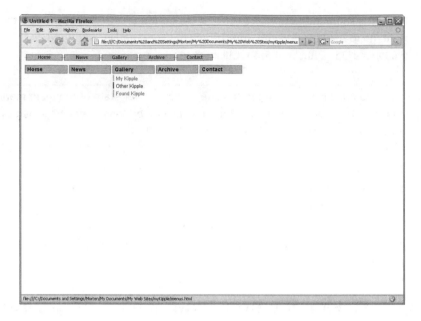

CSS-based, which means it works even if the visitor's computer does not support JavaScript. But most importantly it is fully legible if the visitor uses a text-only or text-to-speech browser.

As you can see in Figure 18.21, with JavaScript and images turned off, the layers-based menu turns into a block of hyperlinks placed closely together and the submenu

FIGURE 18.21
With JavaScript,
images, and
styles turned off,
the layers menu
becomes hard to
use because the
submenu items
are gone, where-
as the CSS
menu turns into
an easy-to-under-
stand bullet list.

items are missing. In contrast, the CSS-based menu reverts to its original form, which is a standard unordered list with sublists. Not only is the menu easier to read, the layout and ordering are intuitive to the visitor even without styles.

> **Not All Browsers Like the Pure CSS Drop-Down Menu**
>
> As mentioned earlier, the pure CSS drop-down menu is not a perfect solution because not all browsers support it. For unknown reasons, Internet Explorer 6 does not support pseudoclasses attached to items other than simple anchors (a style). Because you used the li:hover style to create the drop-down effect, it will not work properly in Internet Explorer 6. To solve this problem you have to either employ a custom JavaScript that simulates the li:hover pseudoclass for IE6 or create a separate menu that replaces the pure CSS drop-down menu for IE6 users. One clever workaround is to place the pure CSS drop-down menu in one layer and a custom IE6 menu in another, and then use the Check Browser behavior to choose what layer to show in the page based on what browser the visitor is using.
>
> The Internet Explorer 6 compatibility issue is a diminishing one because more and more users are upgrading to newer versions of the browser (Internet Explorer 7 has been out for some time and, as of this writing, Internet Explorer 8 is in the final stages of beta testing), and most if not all other browsers support the li:hover property. With that said, you always have to consider the lowest common denominator and whether you should "dumb down" your sites to accommodate it.

Summary

Drop-down menus are important elements for navigation as well as design. A website with functional and well designed drop-down menus gives the visitor a more interactive experience and the website a feeling of professionalism. For this reason and many others, it is important to know how to make drop-down menus that look great and work properly across browsers and platforms.

There are many approaches to creating drop-down menus and in this hour you learned two of them: the layer-based drop-down menu and the pure CSS drop-down menu. Both methods are relatively easy to create and maintain after you understand how they work, and both have good sides and bad sides.

The layer-based drop-down menu gives you complete control of the look of your menu both in terms of buttons and functionality. Because you construct it using images as buttons, you have unlimited options when it comes to what each button should look like. In this hour, you built the menu using the interactive buttons built into Expression Web 2 but there is no reason why you couldn't do the same operation using buttons created in a different design application. You can also open the interactive button images created by Expression Web 2 in a design application and edit them individually. Just keep in mind that if you do, you can't change them in Expression Web 2 without losing the new design.

The downside of the layer-based drop-down menu is that it depends on behaviors and JavaScript to work properly. For most visitors, this is not a problem. But for those who do not have JavaScript activated or are using text-only or text-to-speech browsers, it can cause unwanted results. In addition, the layers-based menu can be hard to handle because you must keep track of a long list of behaviors that work together to make the menu function properly. Forgetting just one of these behaviors can have fatal results for the overall function of the menu.

The pure CSS drop-down menu approaches the task from a completely different angle. Its basis is a simple unordered list with sublists. This is done for several reasons: It makes the contents of the menu accessible regardless of what type of browser the visitor is using; it keeps the styling separate from the content; and it is easy to manage because all you have to do is edit the lists themselves—the design follows automatically.

Whereas the layer-based menu focuses heavily on appearance, the focus of the pure CSS drop-down menu is on function. As a result you cannot get as fancy with the design of the CSS menu, but you can get close. The major downside of the CSS menu is that some older browsers do not support the CSS functionalities properly. That means the menu will not work properly for some visitors using older browsers. You can solve that problem by using JavaScript or browser targeting, but doing so removes some of the simplicity of the process.

There is no right or wrong when it comes to creating drop-down menus. The techniques described in this hour are two of many, and there are thousands of other more or less functional alternatives out there for you to explore. You can find a more advanced version of the pure CSS drop-down menu that incorporates the necessary JavaScript to solve the IE6 problem by going to http://www.alistapart.com and searching for *Suckerfish menu*.

Q&A

Q. *When I tried to insert some text below the menus I created the text ended up behind them instead. Why is that?*

A. Both menus you created in this hour reside in boxes that use absolute positioning. That means they hover on top of the page rather than within it. As a result, when you input content directly into the page, it appears behind the menus rather than below it. To solve this problem, you need to place the menus and content in separate divs and use these divs to create the layout. Look at the menus.html and menuStyles.css files in the lesson files to see how to do this.

Q. *One of the menus is covering the other. How do I change it so that this doesn't happen?*

A. If you have several absolutely positioned elements in the same location on a page the z-index decides which one is "on top". The higher the z-index value, the higher in the stack the content will appear. So for instance if the layers based menu appears underneath the Pure CSS menu, change the z-index of the layers based menu to "lift" it above the other one.

Workshop

The Workshop has quiz questions and exercises to help you put to use what you just learned. If you get stuck, the answers to the quiz questions are in the next section. But try to answer the questions first. Otherwise you'll only be cheating yourself.

Quiz

1. *In this hour you created two different types of drop down menus. Briefly describe the different approaches and how they work.*

2. *What is the main limitation of each of the two menus?*

Answers

1. The first menu is based on layers and behaviors. It works by using behaviors attached to different buttons to change the visibility of the layers that contain the drop-down buttons. The second menu is based on CSS and uses the :hover pseudo-class attached to the list items in an unordered list to change the visibility of the sub-lists within each list item. While the first menu treats each button and drop-down menu as a separate entity, the second one treats the entire menu with main items and drop-down items as one unit.

2. The layers based menu is dependent on JavaScript being supported by the visitor's computer to work. Without JavaScript support the behaviors will not work and the visitor will not be able to trigger the drop-down functions in the menu. The CSS menu uses the :hover pseudo class attached to a list item to trigger the drop-down effect. Some older browsers do not support the :hover pseudo class and as a result the CSS menu will not work properly in these browsers. You can work around this problem by applying JavaScript to the menu to mimic the :hover pseudo-class but then you run into the problem with JavaScript support. As of right now there is no one perfect solution to the issue of drop-down menus.

Exercise

Create a new submenu for the Archive buttons on both menus. Make at least five new menu items for the submenu. Link the buttons in the different menus to random websites to see how they work. Keep in mind that if you want to attach a hyperlink to an interactive button, you have to use the Interactive Button dialog (if you right-click the button and select Hyperlink, text replaces the button). To open the Interactive Button dialog, double-click each button individually. To access the buttons in the hidden layers, you have to make them visible from the Layers task pane first. If you have trouble selecting them, try changing the Visibility setting of the CSS menu to Hidden.

HOUR 19

Dynamic Web Templates

What You'll Learn in This Hour:

▶ How to create a Dynamic Web Template

▶ How to create a new page from a Dynamic Web Template

▶ How to apply a Dynamic Web Template to an existing page

▶ How to edit a Dynamic Web Template and the files created from it

Introduction

Most websites consist of more than a single page. The whole idea behind creating the World Wide Web was the ability to make numerous documents available and then link them together rather than presenting them all at the same time. But this causes a problem: If you have a website with multiple pages and you want to make a design change to all these pages, you have to update each page individually. If your site has only a few pages this is not a problem, but what if it has tens or even hundreds of pages?

In the past, updating large sites was a daunting task because each page contained all the styling information. As a result, webmasters rarely updated designs and sites quickly became outdated. The introduction of CSS (Cascading Style Sheets) solved many of these problems because the designer could now put the styling code in a separate document and modify this file for sitewide changes. This was a huge step forward and paved the way for a whole new generation of site models, including blogs.

But wouldn't it be great if you could take that principle one step further and set your site up so that one file controlled not just the styles but also the common elements of all the pages such as headers, footers, and main menus? This question is already been answered in the form of Dynamic Web Templates (commonly known as *DWTs*).

A Dynamic Web Template is a special type of file built using HTML (Hypertext Markup Language) and CSS to define which areas of a page a developer may edit and which areas are off limits to regular page building. After a DWT exists, you can use it to build new pages in which all you have to do is input new content in the pre-defined areas without having to worry about all the common elements present in every page. More importantly, when you have multiple pages built using a DWT you can change the composition and layout of all the pages by making changes to only the DWT file. In other words, using DWTs makes global alterations to a website a snap.

In this hour, you will learn how to build a DWT and create new pages based on it. You will also learn how to make changes to the DWT and its children, and how to apply a DWT to an existing page. The most important lesson of this hour is that using DWTs wisely can have a huge positive impact on your workload and make updating multipage websites nearly as easy as editing a single page.

Dynamic Web Templates

When you design a website, you should always consider the following question: "How do I make sure it is easy to update the look and functionality of every page within the site?" Depending on the scale of the project and the kind of content you are presenting, the answer to this question can be very different:

- ▶ If you are creating a small-scale site with only a few pages (fewer than 10) and multiple different layouts and designs, you can go with straightforward HTML pages with one or several style sheets attached.

- ▶ If your site is (or could become) larger and you have one or two layouts to implement sitewide, creating pages based on DWTs is an effective solution.

- ▶ If your site has a high number of pages or constantly updated dynamic content (think a news site, forum, or blog), the best solution is to use a Content Management System (CMS) that generates pages dynamically with server-side script and a database—this option is for advanced users only.

For the large majority of sites, the second option is the best choice because it makes for easy page construction and quick sitewide design changes.

Blogs, Forums and Content Management Systems

If you are ready to move beyond the basics you should take some time and familiarize yourself with some of the most common Open Source blogging platforms, forums and Content Management Systems. With these technologies in your tool kit you will be well equipped to provide clients with a wide range of services and options for their web sites.

One of the great things about Open Source software is that since it is being developed by the users themselves the programs are always evolving and there is always someone out there with an answer for you when you run into a difficult problem. For this reason the best place to start learning about these technologies is the home page of the project itself.

If you are new to web design, entering into the world of dynamic web technologies can be a daunting task. But it really isn't as complicated as it seems. If you are looking to learn about Content Management Systems and how database based dynamic web sites work, a good place to start is actually the blogging platform WordPress.

WordPress (www.wordpress.org) was originally a basic blogging platform which over time has grown into more of a simple CMS. I use it for client blogs as well as client web sites that look nothing like blogs. The benefit of using WordPress is the seemingly endless variety of plug-ins that let you expand the platform to do whatever you want. What is great about WordPress is that it is built with the user in mind, so it can be as easy or as complicated as you want it to be. Furthermore it can work as both a blogging platform, a CMS or both – it's totally up to you. Finally the look and feel of WordPress is created using standards based code and CSS, meaning that you can use the techniques learned in this book to completely redesign your WordPress based sites. For more information on how to do this visit my blog at http://blog.pinkandyellow.com where I have created an ongoing series called "WordPress as CMS" where I explore how to rework and redesign WordPress to do whatever you want.

As an added bonus, WordPress has excellent SEO (Search Engine Optimization) built in, meaning that sites built using the platform are easily found on Google and other search engines. That in itself is a huge selling point.

WordPress is not the only option available and it may not be the platform you are looking for. Other popular platforms include PHPBB Forum (www.phpbb.com) on which the large majority of web forums are built and the two full-scale CMSes Joomla! (www.joomla.org) and Drupal (drupal.org) both of which also offer extensive customization and expandability.

How Dynamic Web Templates Work

Now that you have created a DWT, let's take a closer look at how it works. Looking at the page in Code view, you see that it looks pretty much the same as the original file with the exception of a few new lines of commented-out code. The new elements tell Expression Web 2 that a specific Dynamic Web Template controls the page. The elements are commented out because they are not HTML code but rather custom script designed specifically to work with Expression Web 2. As a result, they have no actual function when a browser displays the page and like other commented content the code is ignored completely., But when the application opens the page they link the DWT and its children together.

At the very top of the page, just below the `<html>` tag, is the following line of code:

```
<!-- #BeginTemplate "../mykippleMaster.dwt" -->
```

This code tells Expression Web 2 that a DWT controls the content below and where that DWT is located. If you look at the top of the View pane, you can see that there is a new line directly underneath the Quick Tag Selector that displays the hyperlink to the DWT as well.

Farther down in the document are several code segments that tell Expression Web 2 which areas are locked and which areas are editable. When you create a DWT from scratch, you get a standard HTML page with two editable regions: `doctitle` and `body`. As the names suggest, the `doctitle` region holds the `<title>` tag in the head portion of the page and the `body` region holds the body of the page. The same thing happened when you converted the `default.html` page to a DWT: Expression inserted the `doctitle` region into your page at the end of the `<head>` tag.

Beginning and end codes that are commented out because they are not HTML define the editable regions. For example, the `doctitle` editable region looks like this in Code view:

```
<!-- #BeginEditable "doctitle" -->
<title></title>
<!-- #EndEditable -->
```

Expression Web 2 considers anything within these two code snippets editable. Because code that is invisible to browsers defines the editable regions, you can choose how much you want to micromanage the content within them. The two editable regions you inserted in the `mykippleMaster.dwt` page serve as good examples of this.

If you select the `heading` region in Design view and look at the code, you see that the editable region is contained within the `h1` tags:

```
</h1>
<!-- #BeginEditable "doctitle" -->
        <title></title>
<!-- #EndEditable -->
</h1>
```

That means whatever content you place inside the editable region will be styled with the h1 style. As a result, when building a page based on this DWT, the designer cannot change the style of this content. Expression Web 2 placed the editable region inside the `<h1>` tags because you placed the cursor inside the h1 area before inserting it.

In contrast, Expression Web 2 places the `content` region on the outside of the style tags:

```
<!-- #BeginEditable "content" -->
        <p> </p>
<!-- #EndEditable -->
```

As a result, the content within the region is not yet styled and the designer can apply other tags and styles at will.

Understanding the difference between these two methods of inserting editable regions means that the designer of the DWT has almost unlimited control of the output that comes from pages created with the template.

Creating a Dynamic Web Template

To get a firmer grasp on what a Dynamic Web Template is and how it works, you are going to build a DWT for the MyKipple.com website based on the `default.html` page.

1. With the new `default.html` page open in Design view, click File, Save As on the menu bar. In the Save As dialog, change the file type to Dynamic Web Template (.dwt) and name the new file **mykippleMaster.dwt**. This creates a new DWT.

2. With the `mykippleMaster.dwt` page open in Split view, delete all the text content in the #content div (see Figure 19.1). You can do this by highlighting the text and deleting it in Design view, or by highlighting all the content between the beginning and end `<div id="content">` tags and deleting it in Code view. Make sure you leave the #wrapper, #header, #menu, #content, and #footer divs intact.

3. Place the cursor on the first line inside the #content div and use the Style drop-down menu from the Common toolbar to set the style of the line to Heading 1 (h1). Press Enter to create a new paragraph underneath (see Figure 19.2).

4. Place the cursor inside the first line (h1) and from the menu bar select Format, Dynamic Web Templates, Manage Editable Regions (see Figure 19.3).

5. The Editable Regions dialog lets you add and remove editable regions within your DWT. Under Region Name, enter **heading** and click the Add button (see Figure 19.3). This creates a new editable region called **heading**. Click Close to apply the changes.

FIGURE 19.1
After deleting the content within the **#content** div, you should still see the **#header**, **#menu**, **#content**, and **#footer** divs in Design view.

FIGURE 19.2
Add two empty text lines in the **#content** div— the first one with the h1 style and the second one with the p style.

6. Place your cursor inside the paragraph on the next line and click the <p> tag in the Quick Tag Selector to select the entire line, including the tags. From the menu bar, select Format, Dynamic Web Template, Manage Editable Regions to open the Editable Regions dialog again.

FIGURE 19.3
The Editable Region dialog lets you add and remove editable regions.

7. Create a new editable region called content and click Close to apply the changes. You now have two regions within the page, outlined in orange in Design view (see Figure 19.4).

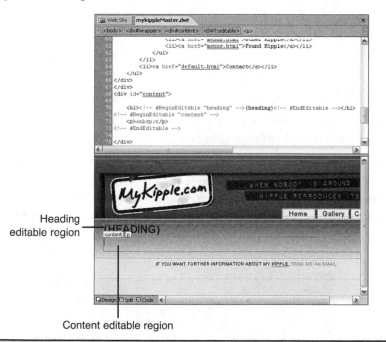

FIGURE 19.4
The Editable Regions heading and content are inserted into the DWT.

Heading editable region

Content editable region

Try it Yourself

Create a New Page from a Dynamic Web Template

When you have a DWT, creating new pages for your project becomes much easier. The DWT contains all the common elements that all pages should feature, and all you have to do is insert the page-specific content. And because HTML is the basis for the DWT, all the CSS styling you attach to the DWT is available in your new page.

1. To create a new page from a DWT, select File, New, Create from Dynamic Web Template from the menu bar.

2. When you create a page from a DWT, the Attach Dynamic Template dialog opens. Select the `mykippleMaster.dwt` file and click Open (see Figure 19.5). An

FIGURE 19.5
Select the DWT you want to base your page on in the Attach Dynamic Template dialog.

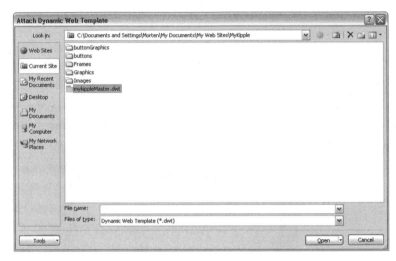

information box opens to report that a number of files updated—his refers to the content of the DWT populating the new file.

3. With the new page open in Design view, you now have only two clickable areas in the page: the `heading` and the `content`. If you move your cursor anywhere else, all you get is a stop sign. Place your cursor in the `heading` area and enter **Kenny Squeeze Toy** (see Figure 19.6). Note that Expression Web 2 auto-

FIGURE 19.6
With the DWT attached to the new page, you can make changes only to the editable regions. The template locks the rest of the page.

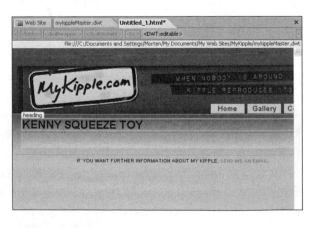

matically applies the h1 style. If you press Enter to create a new line, a warning pops up to tell you that you can't make the change because a Dynamic Web Template is locking the code.

4. Place your cursor in the content region and insert content of your choice. Because this region is not contained within a tag, it is not constrained in the same way the heading region is, so you can add several paragraphs, images, or any other HTML content as you place and style it using the styles and classes in the attached style sheet (see Figure 19.7).

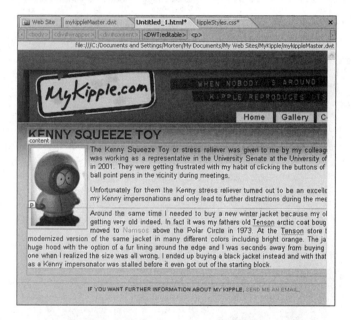

FIGURE 19.7
The content created inside the regions can be styled with any of the styles available in the attached style sheet as well as new styles.

5. When you finish inserting content in the page, press Ctrl+S to save the file. In the Save As dialog, create a new folder called Kipple and save the page in this folder under the name Kenny.html.

By previewing the new page in your browser, you see that although all you did was insert the heading and main content, the page looks and works just like the default.html page. That is because all the common components are the same.

Understanding Dynamic Web Templates

The preceding example should give you a good idea of what happens when you create a new page from a DWT. When you attach a DWT to a new page, what really happens is that Expression Web 2 takes the code content from the DWT and places it in your new page. But unlike a "normal" page, the application knows that only the editable regions within the page should be available for changes, so it looks for the editable regions and blocks all the other content. After inserting content in the editable regions, the result is the same as any other HTML page except that the code contains the commented-out code calls for the editable regions. But because they are commented out, the browser ignores them.

Updating Your Site by Editing the Dynamic Web Template

The reason the editable regions code remains in the page is to give you the ability to change the DWT and by doing so to change all the pages created from it.

1. Open the `mykippleMaster.dwt` page in Split view. Click any of the three menu buttons to highlight the menu code in Code view.

2. Create a new submenu under the Home button by creating a new `<ul>` tag in Code view. Create two subcategories named `News` and `Archive` (see Figure 19.8).

FIGURE 19.8
It is usually easier to edit lists in Code view than Design view because you have more control of how the different elements relate to one another.

3. Save the `mykippleMaster.dwt` page. An information dialog opens to tell you that there is one page attached to `mykippleMaster.dwt` and asking whether you want to update it now (see Figure 19.9). Click Yes. Expression Web 2 now updates all the files built based on the DWT.

FIGURE 19.9
When you make changes to a DWT, Expression Web 2 asks whether you want to update the pages built based on the DWT.

4. When it finishes, another information dialog opens to tell you how many pages Expression Web 2 updated. If you check the Log box, the dialog expands to provide a more detailed log of the update process including a list of what pages the application updated (see Figure 19.10).

FIGURE 19.10
After updating the files connected to the DWT, Expression Web 2 opens an information dialog telling you how many files were updated and if any files were skipped.

If you test the Kenny.html page in your browser, you see that the Home button on the menu bar now has a drop-down submenu even though you didn't make any changes to the page (see Figure 19.11).

This example showcases the true power of DWTs: By making a website where a DWT is the basis for all the pages, you can make consistent changes to the common content in every page by editing just one page.

FIGURE 19.11
By changing the DWT and updating the files it attaches to, you change the contents of all the pages in the site without ever opening them.

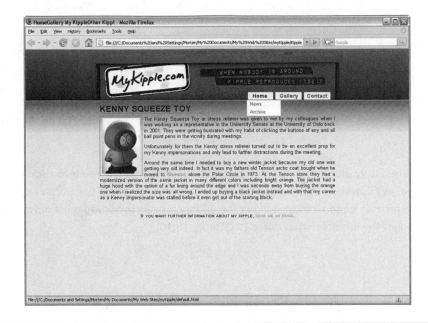

▼   **Try it Yourself**

Attach a Dynamic Web Template to an Existing Page

Sometimes you want to add the new DWT designs to old pages that you already built. Your initial hunch might be to copy-and-paste the contents from this page into a new one, but that is not necessary. Just as you attached a DWT to a new page, you can also attach a DWT to an existing page. In Hour 9, "Get Boxed In Part 1: Using Tables for Content," you created a page called myWallet.html that contained a table listing the contents of my wallet. Now you want this page to match the rest of the pages in the MyKipple site.

1. Open the myWallet.html file in Design view. From the menu bar, select Format, Dynamic Web Template, Attach Dynamic Web Template . In the Attach Dynamic Web Template dialog, select mykippleMaster.dwt.

2. A warning appears telling you that content outside of the <html> tag will be deleted and that if you want to preserve it, you need to move it into an editable region or into the <head> tag. This warning is to alert designers who have attached code, such as a script, outside of the main content of the page. If that is the case, you can click No and move the script. For most situations this is not necessary, so click Yes.

3. Because you did not create the myWallet.html page using the DWT, there are no editable regions defined within the page. Instead of just erasing the content

not already defined in the page, Expression Web 2 makes an educated guess as to what content you want where and lets you correct its choices. When there are no matching editable regions or there is another conflict, the Match Editable Regions dialog opens (see Figure 19.13).

FIGURE 19.13
When the regions in the current page don't match the editable regions, Expression Web 2 lets you match them manually.

From here you can tell Expression Web 2 what content should go in what region. In this example, the <body> tag contains only one block of content and Expression Web 2 is guessing that it should go in the heading region. To change this, select the list item by clicking it and clicking the Modify button.

4. When you click the Modify button, the Choose Editable Region for Content dialog appears. There you can define which new region should receive the content from the old region. Use the New Region drop-down menu to select the content region for the <body> content (see Figure 19.14). Click OK twice to attach the DWT.

FIGURE 19.14
The Choose Editable Region for Content dialog lets you pick which editable region to put different content from the old page in.

As you can see, the conversion to the new look is not flawless. You now have two headings and the in-page styles from the original document have disappeared. But after some tidying up, the page will look the way it should (see Figure 19.15). Now if you make any changes to the DWT, the myWallet.html page changes automatically, too.

FIGURE 19.15
With some tidy-
ing up, the
myWallet.htm
1 page fits in
nicely with the
new design.

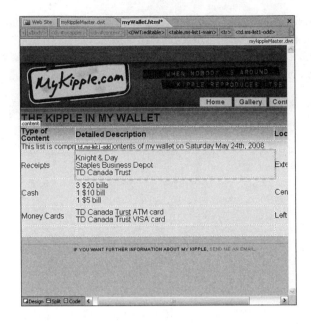

Editable Regions Outside the Body

As mentioned in the beginning of this hour, Expression Web 2 inserts an editable region called doctitle by default in all pages attached to a DWT because the application assumes (as it should) that every page has its own distinctive title. Because the
<title> tag is contained within an editable region by default, you can edit it as you
normally would either through the Page Properties dialog or directly in Code view.

Using the same technique, you can also predefine other head content (editable or
locked) for your pages. Moreover you can use the editable content area in the DWT
to give the page predefined common properties that you or other designers can edit,
add to, or replace when building new pages.

▼   **Try it Yourself**

Create Common Editable Keywords for All Pages

To make a page easier to find for people who search the World Wide Web using
search engines, it should always contain keywords as well as a description that describes the page and its contents.

1. With the mykippleMaster.dwt page open in Split view, right-click in Design
    view and select Page Properties from the drop-down menu. This opens the Page
▼   Properties dialog.

2. In the Title area, enter **MyKipple.com**. In the Page Description area, enter a short description that is common to all the pages. In the Keywords area insert the keywords *kipple, philip k dick, junk, trash, treasure* (see Figure 19.16). Click OK to apply the changes.

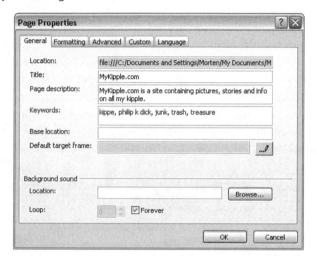

FIGURE 19.16
Inserting content in the Page Properties dialog is an easy way of creating the header code.

3. Toward the top of the page in Code view (most likely line 20) are two new lines of code that start with <meta content="".... These lines define the keywords and description for the page. In this example, you want the keywords to be editable but not the description. To do so, place your cursor at the beginning of the first line in Code view containing the keywords and manually add the following line of code: **<!-- #BeginEditable "keywords" -->** (see Figure 19.17).

FIGURE 19.17
You have to manually add the editable regions outside of the **<body>** tag in Code view.

4. Press the End key or use the mouse to place the cursor at the end of the line. Add the following line of code after the last tag: `<!-- #EndEditable -->`.

5. Save the DWT and click Yes when asked whether you want to update the attached pages.

After applying the changes, open the `Kenny.html` page, right-click, and select Page Properties from the context menu. In the Page Properties dialog, you see that the `Title` and `Keywords` areas are editable but the `Description` and other areas are grayed out (see Figure 19.18). It is also important to note that even though the Keywords section remains editable, Expression Web 2 still inserts the words you added in the DWT. After the application creates the new page, you can edit, add to, or delete those words without the changes affecting the DWT or the other pages.

FIGURE 19.18
The **Description** meta tag was not defined as an editable region in the DWT and is therefore inaccessible in the Page Properties dialog of the pages created with this DWT.

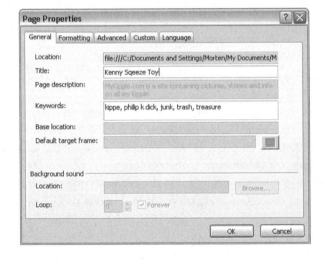

You can insert and edit only the editable regions in the DWT that are outside the <body> tag in Code view. If you highlight code outside of the <body> tag and use the Manage Editable Regions dialog to add a new editable region, Expression Web 2 places the new region inside the <body> tag and wraps all the content. There is also no support for this particular code set in IntelliSense, so you have to write all the code. On the upside, there are only two variations of the editable region code: the begin editable region code (`<!-- #BeginEditable "region-Name" -->`) and the end editable region code (`<!-- #EndEditable -->`). If you can't remember these two code segments, scroll down further in the document, copy the code from a different editable region, paste it where you want the editable region, and change the region name.

Editing Content Outside the Editable Regions in Individual Pages

Although I do not recommend it, you can manually change the content outside of the editable regions in individual pages. While in Design view, the only selectable areas are the editable regions. But if you switch to Code view, you can modify the code manually.

In a page created from a DWT, Expression Web 2 highlights all the code defined by the DWT in yellow in Code view. The highlighting tells you exactly which areas the template controls externally and which areas are open for editing. Nevertheless you can place your cursor anywhere within the code and make all the changes you want. But if you make changes to the highlighted code, Expression Web 2 tells you that you are now changing code defined by the DWT.

When you save the file or switch back to Design view after changing the code outside the editable regions in Code view, Expression Web 2 displays an alert dialog with a warning that the changes you have made are in the code defined by the DWT (see Figure 19.19). The Dynamic Web Template Alert dialog gives you two options: either

FIGURE 19.19
If you change code inserted by the DWT in your page, Expression Web 2 gives you a warning and asks you to explicitly verify that these changes are intentional.

restore the noneditable content (in other words discard any changes made to the code defined by the DWT) or keep the changes. If you choose the latter, you have the additional option of detaching the page from the DWT.

The ability to change the code in individual pages comes with a strong warning because if, later, you choose to make changes to the DWT and update the files attached to it, you permanently erase the changes you made in the individual page code.

If an area within a page will require individualization for each page, it is always advisable to place this area within an editable region and place the default content in the DWT. That way, if you do nothing to the code, it remains the same across every page, but you retain the ability to change the individual pages if you choose to do so. The most obvious example of this would be if you wanted to change menu options in some of but not every page. To do so, simply place the menu list items within an editable region called menu and you now have the ability to change the menu in individual pages if necessary without making those changes sitewide.

Summary

One of the major challenges for web designers and developers is tackling the task of sitewide design updates. If the site's creators do not design it with this in mind, updating it could easily become a large and difficult task.

In this hour, you learned about Dynamic Web Templates and you saw how you can use them to create sites that are easy to expand and update. The Dynamic Web Template is a great tool if all your site's pages have common elements and only certain portions of the page have unique content.

The Dynamic Web Template function inside Expression Web 2 works by linking the DWT to the files it is attached to either because they were built based on the DWT or because the DWT was attached later. These pages contain small segments of code that define editable regions that are accessible to the designer or whoever is creating or editing the page. Likewise all the content outside of the editable regions is off limits and no one can edit it without going directly into the code. This is to ensure that when a developer updates the site by changing the DWT, none of the individual page content gets lost in the process.

After a DWT exists and creators have based a number of pages on it, a change in the DWT spreads through all the other pages, making the new changes sitewide. Rather than having to make changes to all the content in every page, you just change the DWT and Expression Web 2 asks whether you want to update the other pages automatically.

By defining editable (and noneditable) regions within the layout, you can micromanage the contents, both visual and nonvisual, of your pages. In addition, within the editable regions, you can add predefined content for insertion into every page and can edit the individual pages later.

A website designed using DWTs makes life easier for not only the designer but also for the client. In many cases, a client asks to have a site designed where she can add or edit the pages herself. By creating a Dynamic Web Template and building all the pages based on it, the client receives a set of pages where she can edit only the informational content of the site and can't accidentally damage or destroy design elements such as menus and so forth. This makes for a far less intimidating end-user experience because the pages have clearly marked and named regions that the client can edit using principles familiar to anyone who has worked with a word processing application.

Q&A

Q. *I removed one of the editable regions from my Dynamic Web Template, and when I told Expression Web 2 to update the attached pages, the Match Editable Regions dialog popped up. What do I do?*

A. If you remove or rename an editable region, Expression Web 2 asks you where to place the content that used to be in that region. Whether you removed or renamed the region, you have to explicitly tell the program where to place the temporarily orphaned content. If the region has been removed and no new region has been created to take the content, select the item from the list, click Modify and change the New Region setting to None. If you create a new region or rename the old one, change the New Region attribute to the correct region. This situation occurs because all the files that have the DWT attached have code segments calling for the old regions, and you have to redefine the code segments for the page to work properly inside Expression Web 2.

Q. *Can I open and use a DWT created in Expression Web 2 in a different web authoring application?*

A. Yes, as long as they support DWTs you can open your DWT and make changes to both the template itself and its children from other web authoring applications.

Workshop

The Workshop has quiz questions and exercises to help you put to use what you just learned. If you get stuck, the answers to the quiz questions are in the next section. But try to answer the questions first. Otherwise you'll only be cheating yourself.

Quiz

1. *What is the main benefit of using a Dynamic Web Template to design your web site?*

2. *What happens if you manually change the code outside of the editable regions in a page generated using a Dynamic Web Template?*

Answers

1. By using a Dynamic Web Template as the basis for all the pages in your web site you are effectively placing all the controls of the look and functionality of your site in one file so that when you want to make site-wide changes to the layout, design or functionality of your site you can make those changes in one file and see them implemented throughout all the pages.

2. If you change the code outside of the editable regions the page will work with the new code just like any other HTML page. The major concern with doing this is that if you update the page using the DWT, all the changes made outside the editable regions will be deleted and replaced by the original code in the DWT. Therefore if you are planning on having custom code that differs from page to page you should create an editable region to contain this code so that it won't be deleted when the site is updated.

Exercise

In the `mykippleMaster.dwt` file, change the Description meta tag to an editable region so that you can have individual descriptions for each page.

The MyKipple project contains a number of pages that you have already built. Using what you have learned in this hour, attach the `mykippleMaster.dwt` template to all the pages you have created so far and give them all individual titles, keywords, and descriptions.

Get Interactive with Forms

What You'll Learn in This Hour:

▶ How to create a form

▶ How to insert and configure form controls in Design view

▶ How to change the properties of forms and form controls

▶ How to make an email form using the built in features of Expression Web 2

Introduction

The last few years have seen the emergence of the interactive web or "Web 2.0" as people like to call it. The interactive web is an evolution from one-way communication to two- (or three- or four-) way communication where the content becomes a conversation rather than an information session.

At the core of this evolution lies a simple group of tools introduced shortly after the World Wide Web came into existence. These tools are HTML (Hypertext Markup Language) forms, and they give the visitor the ability to input information and communicate with the site rather than just ingest the information on it.

In its most basic form, an *HTML form* is a group of elements that together gather information such as text or choices from the visitor and sends it off to a predetermined location for further processing. A form can be anything from a simple email generator or newsletter subscription signup tool to a fully interactive commenting feature in a blog, a posting feature in a forum, or even a checkout page for an online store. In fact, every time you input information in a web page, whether it be your address when purchasing a book or a status update in your favorite social networking site, you are using forms.

Harnessing the power of HTML forms means that you can create immersive experiences with true interactivity for the visitor and facilitate communication between the owner of the site and those who use the site.

Creating Forms in Expression Web 2

HTML defines all the different form elements and form controls. As a result, when you place these elements inside `<form>` tags in an HTML page, the browser automatically knows what they are and how they are supposed to behave; all you have to do is tell the browser what to do with the information gathered.

To make the creation of forms as easy as possible Expression Web 2 provides all the available form controls in one convenient location: the Toolbox task pane (see Figure

FIGURE 20.1
All the form controls are available under the Form Controls section in the Toolbox task pane.

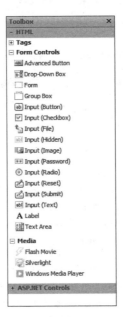

20.1). From here you can drag and drop any of the form controls directly into either Code view or Design view without writing a single line of code.

By hovering the mouse over each form control, Expression Web 2 provides a Screen-Tip with a short explanation of what each control does. These explanations are sometimes a little too short, so here is a more detailed explanation of each of the form controls.

Advanced

▶ Advanced Button creates a button whose actions are defined by the designer by embedding HTML code.

Drop-Down

▶ Drop-Down Box creates a drop-down box where you can define the different options. Hour 16, "Using Behaviors," introduced you to the drop-down box when you used the Jump Menu behavior.

▶ Form is the outer tag that defines the form as a whole. The group of all the elements contained within the <form> tags makes up the form. A page can have multiple independent forms.

Form

▶ Group Box creates a separate subgroup or box within the form. You can use this control to visually separate different sections of a form and still preserve the form's integrity by keeping it together. This is a purely visual tool without any actual function.

Group Box

▶ Input (Button) creates a standard HTML button with an onclick event that can trigger JavaScript (think back to Hour 16). This function is most often used to create Submit, Cancel, and Reset buttons but can be used for any other purpose as well. The Input (Button) function works in much the same way as the interactive button except that you don't control what it looks like—only what the button text is.

Input

▶ Input (Check Box) creates a check box. The check box lets the visitor make yes-or-no choices such as *Send copy of the information to your own email address?*

Input
(Check Box)

▶ Input (File) creates a text box with a Browse button attached that lets the user input a location or browse for a file on her computer to submit along with the rest of the information in the form.

Input (File)

▶ Input (Hidden) creates a hidden text box that is invisible in the browser window but present in the code. This function is often used to insert extra content into a form without giving the visitor a chance to change it.

Input
(Hidden)

▶ Input (Image) makes an image click-sensitive, meaning you can use it as a button. The function also collects the x and y values of where on the image you clicked. This information can be used for added interactivity.

Input
(Image)

▶ Input (Password) creates a text field where you can input a password. When the visitor enters text into the field, each character is replaced by an * symbol.

Input
(Password)

▶ Input (Radio) creates a radio button. These buttons are similar to check boxes, but rather than being standalone yes/no units, they are connected and work as multiple choice.

Input
(Radio)

▶ Input (Reset) creates a reset button that when pressed sets the value of each element in the form to its default setting.

Input
(Reset)

▶ Input (Submit) creates a Submit button that submits the form.

Input
(Submit)

▶ Input (Text) creates a single-line text box that can collect text such as a name or an address.

Input
(Text)

Label

▶ Label associates a label with a form control, meaning that you can create a line of text, image, or other element connected to and working as a description of a specific form control. The Label can also set keyboard shortcuts for specific form controls.

 Text Area

▶ Text Area creates a multiline text box for longer segments of text. You can define how many lines of text the box allows.

Because form controls are a bit cryptic in their description it is easier to understand how they work by seeing them in action. The following exercise uses some of the form controls to make a simple e-mail form.

▼ Try it Yourself

Create an Email Form

One of the most basic and most useful applications of an HTML form is to create an email form for your website. In addition to giving the user the ability to send emails to you directly from your website, an email form can also help reduce the amount of spam you receive every day. If you leave a mailto: hyperlink in your page, spam bots (computers that automatically sift through the Web looking for email addresses and then inundate them with spam) will find the address and use it. If you place an email form on the page instead, the spam bot will have a much harder time finding your address and you will most likely receive less spam.

1. Create a new page from the DWT you created in Hour 19, "Dynamic Web Templates," by selecting New, Create from Dynamic Web Template on the menu bar and save it as contact.html.

2. Change the Heading to **Contact Me** and place the cursor in the **contents** editable region.

3. In Split view, remove the <p> and </p> tags in Code view. Go to the Form Controls in the Toolbox task pane and find the Form control. Anything contained within this control is considered part of the same form. Double-click the Form control to place it in the editable region of the page.

4. Place the cursor inside the new form area in Design view and select Table, Insert Table on the menu bar to open the Insert Table dialog. Set Rows to 5 and Columns to 2. Under Specify Width, check the In Pixels radio button and set the width to 625 (see Figure 20.2). Click OK to insert the table.

5. With the cursor placed in the first cell of the table, enter **Your Name:**. Press the Tab key to move to the next cell.

▼

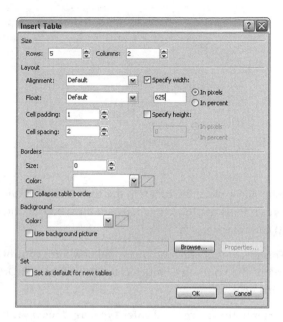

FIGURE 20.2
To keep forms
structured they
are usually
placed inside ta-
bles.

6. Go to the Form Controls on in the Toolbox task pane and find the Input (Text) control. Place it in the cell either by dragging and dropping it or by double-clicking it in the Toolbox (Figure 20.3).

7. In Design view, right-click the new form control and select Form Field Properties from the context menu. This opens the Form Field Properties dialog for this

FIGURE 20.3
The form con-
trols can be in-
serted by
dragging-and-
dropping them
into Design or
Code view or by
placing the cur-
sor where you
want them to be
placed and dou-
ble-clicking them
in the Toolbox
task pane.

form control. Set the Name to fullName, the Width in Characters to 30, and the Tab Order to 1. Click OK to apply the changes (see Figure 20.4).

FIGURE 20.4
By right-clicking a form control and selecting Form Field Properties from the context menu, you get access to the various attributes and features provided for this particular form control.

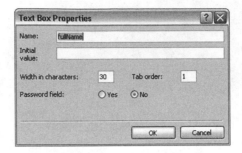

8. Back in Design view, place the cursor in the second left cell and enter **Your E-mail Address:**. Press the Tab key to move to the next cell and insert another Input (Text) control there.

9. Open the Form Field Properties dialog for the new form control and set the Name to email, the Width in Characters to 30, and the Tab Order to 2 to match the first field.

10. Place the cursor in the left cell and enter **Type of Inquiry:**. Press the Tab key to go to the next cell and insert a Drop-Down Box control. Right-click the Drop-Down Box and select Form Field Properties from the context menu to open the Form Field Properties dialog.

11. In the Drop-Down Box Properties dialog, set the Name to options. Click the Add button to create a new choice. In the Add Choice dialog, enter **Question** as the choice and click the Selected radio button under Initial State (see Figure 20.5). Click OK to add the new choice.

FIGURE 20.5
The Drop-Down Box Properties dialog lets you define the default choice and what choices the visitor can select from.

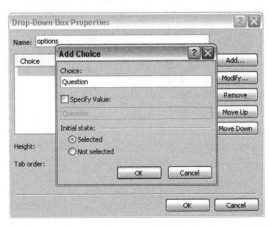

12. Use the Add button to create four more choices: Comment, Suggestion, Kipple Story, and Random Thought. Set the initial state for all of them to Not Selected.

13. When all the choices are created, set the Tab Order to *3* and click OK (see Figure 20.6). The Drop-Down Box automatically resizes itself to fit the longest choice.

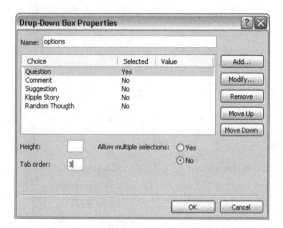

FIGURE 20.6
All the choices are added to the Drop-Down Box.

14. In the fourth left cell, enter **What's On Your Mind?** Press the Tab key to move to the next cell and insert a Text Area form control.

15. Open the Form Field Properties for the Text Area. Set the Name to `comment`, Width in Characters to 55, Number of Lines to 8, and Tab Order to 4 (see Figure 20.7). Click OK to apply the changes.

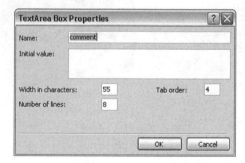

16. Place the cursor in the bottom left cell and enter **Finished?** Press the Tab key to move to the lower-right cell and insert an Input (Submit) and an Input (Reset) form control. This creates two buttons that say Submit and Reset respectively.

17. Open the Form Field Properties for the submit button. In the Push Button Properties, change the Name to `submitButton`, change the Value/Label to `Submit` (with an uppercase S), leave the Button Type set to Submit, and set the Tab Order to 5 (see Figure 20.8). Click OK to apply the changes.

FIGURE 20.8
The Push Button Properties dialog lets you change the text that displays on the button as well as its function.

18. Repeat step 17 for the reset button, but change the Name to resetButton, the Value/Label to Reset, and set the Tab Order to 6.

Now all the basic components for the email form are in place. Save the page and test it in your browser (see Figure 20.9).

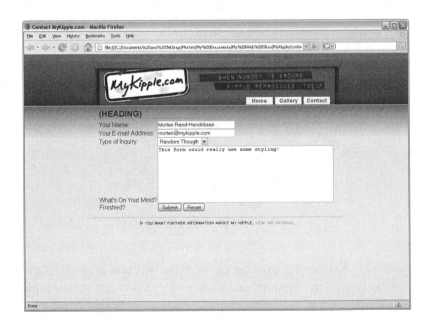

FIGURE 20.9
The **contact.html** page with the email form as it appears in the browser.

As you can see, the form already looks pretty good even though you haven't applied any styling to it yet. And if you test the different elements, you can see that they all work properly: You can insert text into the text boxes, make a selection from the drop-down menu, and all the info resets when you click the Reset button. And because you set the tab order for each element, if you select one and press the Tab button on your keyboard, the next one is automatically selected.

But there is still one major issue yet to be resolved: What happens to the information after you click the Submit button?

Making Use of Form Results

To make an HTML form work, you need two main components: the form itself, which you just created, and the functions that collect the info or results from the form and send them off to be processed. And although building the form is a relatively simple task, getting the form to perform the required actions is a bit more complicated.

After results are submitted from a form, the browser passes on the information to whatever process has been defined by the designer or developer. These processes are called *server-side scripts* and they take the information, make the necessary alterations to it, and send it off to a file, a database, or an email account. And this is where things get complicated:

To process or *parse* the results from the form, the server that hosts the page has to perform some actions. Unfortunately there are several different server languages available and they are for the most part mutually exclusive. As a result, a function that works perfectly on one server might only generate errors on another server. So, before you start applying functionality to your forms you have to find out what language the server the page will be hosted on speaks.

Watch Out!

Most web servers run one of the two main server architectures: Linux Server or Microsoft Windows Server. Both servers support a programming language called PHP, whereas only Windows servers support the application framework called ASP.NET. If you have a Windows server, there is a good chance it has FrontPage Server extensions installed but there is no guarantee. Therefore it is imperative that you find out what architecture the server you plan to put your page on is running and what languages and extensions it supports. If you follow the next tutorial and upload the page to a Linux server or a Microsoft server without the FrontPage Server extensions installed the form will not work properly.

Did you Know?

If you are hosting your page on a Linux server, you need to use PHP to create the email form functionality. Hour 22, "Beyond the Basics: PHP in Expression Web 2," talks about PHP and has a full tutorial on how to make the email form work using this programming language.

▼

Try it Yourself

Send Form Results to an Email

Now that you have a basic form built into your page you need to connect it to the functions that will make it work. Provided your server has FrontPage Server extensions installed, Expression Web 2 has built-in functions that make it easy to create forms to send results directly to a predefined email address, file, or database.

FIGURE 20.10
You can change and configure the different functions of a form from the Form Properties dialog.

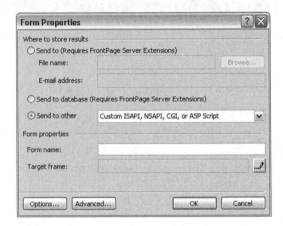

1. Right-click anywhere inside the email form and select Form Properties from the context menu. This opens the Form Properties dialog (see Figure 20.10).

2. Because you want the form to generate an email, select the Send To radio button.

3. In the Send To area, you have two options: You can enter a filename and you can enter an email address. If you enter a filename, the results of the form will be sent to a file stored on the server. The two options can be used separately or together. Saving the results to a file as well as sending them to an email address is an easy way of making sure the message doesn't get lost.

   Click the Browse button next to the File Name area to open the browser and create a new folder called Contact. Click Cancel and enter **Contact/emails.txt** in the File Name area.

Did you Know?

> Step 3 asked you to use the Browse button to create a new folder without actually selecting a file inside this folder. This is a trick you can use to create new folders while inside a dialog without having to close the dialog.

4. In the E-mail Address area, enter your own email address (see Figure 20.11).

5. To further configure the output generated by the form, click the Options button. This opens the Saving Results dialog.

▼

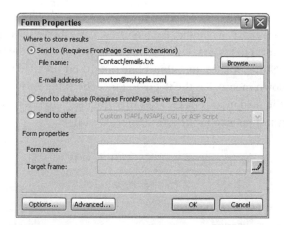

FIGURE 20.11
With the Send To function, you can choose whether to send the results of the form to a file on the server, an email address, or both.

6. The first tab of the Saving Results dialog deals with the file to which the content is saved. From here you can change the location of the file as well as the file format (how the content is displayed within the file). For most purposes, Formatted Text is the best option but there are many alternatives including HTML and XML and text database variants (see Figure 20.12). Below the File Format

FIGURE 20.12
When saving the results to a file, you have a choice of many different file formats.

option, you can check whether you want to include the form field names and whether you want to generate an optional second file. Leave everything as it is in this tab.

7. Under the E-mail Results tab, you can configure what the email sent by the form will look like. The email address bar is self-explanatory and the E-mail Format menu provides the same options as the File Format menu in the prior

tab. Under E-mail Message Header, you can set the Subject line and the Reply-To line for the email generated. Each of these can be set to a standard line of text or to a form field name by checking the Form Field Name box. Check the Form Field Name box for the Subject line and insert the field name **options** (the drop-down menu). For the Reply-to Line, check the Form Field Name box and enter the field name **email**. That way the Reply-To address matches the address the visitor entered in the form (Figure 20.13).

FIGURE 20.13
You can set the Subject line and Reply-To addresses to either a predetermined line of text or get the info from one of the form fields.

8. The Confirmation Page tab provides you with the option of sending the visitor to a specific page in your site after the file has been stored, email has been sent, or both. This can be any page on your site, but it is normal to create a page with a message telling the visitor the process was successful. If you do not insert a link, the server generates a page for you automatically (but this page does not match the rest of your site). Even though the page does not exist yet, set the URL of Confirmation Page to Contact/Confirmed.html (see Figure 20.14). If you have inserted validation scripts in your form (such as scripts to ensure that certain fields are filled out), you can also create a custom page to redirect the visitor to if the form is not properly filled out.

9. The last tab in the Saving Results dialog is Saved Fields. From here you can decide what fields should be saved and submitted from the form. By default Expression Web 2 inserts all the fields including the Input (Submit) button. In almost every case you want to remove this last instance because it is unnecessary (the fact that the file has been saved or the email sent means that the Submit button was pressed). To remove it, simply highlight the submitButton instance in the window and delete it (see Figure 20.15). The Saved Fields tab

FIGURE 20.14
With the Confirmation Page option, you can send the visitor to a specific page after sending the form.

FIGURE 20.15
You can decide what fields are to be saved and submitted from the Saved Fields tab. From here you can also include new fields that contain the date and time as well as information about the user.

also allows you to save the date and time of the form submission in various different formats that you can select from the drop-down menus. Finally you can choose to save additional information about the user including the remote computer name, username and browser type. (Note that the username will be saved only if the user is required to log in before submitting the form.)

10. When you click OK to save the changes, a warning appears and tells you that the file you are trying to link to does not exist and asks you whether you want to save the link anyway (see Figure 20.16). This is because in step 8 you entered a hyperlink to a page you have not created yet. Click **Yes**.

FIGURE 20.16
When you link to a page that does not exist in the local version of the site, Expression Web 2 brings up a warning and asks whether you want to link to this nonexistent file.

11. When you click OK in the Form Properties dialog, another warning will likely appear, telling you that this form cannot be configured to send emails because it is at a disk-based location or on a server that has not been configured to send emails (see Figure 20.17). This is because the email functionality you have con-

FIGURE 20.17
Because your site is stored on your computer and not on a server, you get a warning saying that the email form will not work.

figured requires server-side scripting in the form of FrontPage Server extensions. Your local computer will not have these capabilities installed. The warning asks whether you want to remove the email recipient. Click No to keep the email address in the script. After the page is uploaded to a server with FrontPage Sever extensions, it will work properly.

The email form with all the necessary functionality is now complete.

Other Uses for Form Results

Creating an email form using forms is just the tip of the gigantic iceberg of possibilities that are available. Forms can be used for a wide range of functions that go far beyond simple text communication.

If you open the Form Properties dialog again you'll see that in addition to the Send To option, you can also Send to Database or Send to Other scripts. These functions let you use forms to communicate with and make alterations to databases. The databases can in turn manage content on a website or an online store or even keep track of warehouse stocks for a company. The possibilities are virtually endless.

Setting up a form with a database or script connection requires both a server that supports the chosen script language and a deeper understanding of the use of databases on the Web. For this reason it is outside the scope of this book.

Forms in Code View

As explained in the beginning of this hour, forms and form controls are simple HTML elements. To get an idea of just how simple these elements are (and through that an understanding of why they are so heavily used), let's peek behind the curtain and look at the form in Code view.

To start, click anywhere inside the form while in Split view and look at the Quick Tag Selector. Depending on where you placed the cursor, the last few tags will differ but the main <form> tag should be the first one in the series (see Figure 20.18).

FIGURE 20.18
The **<form>** tag encapsulates all the elements that make up the form.

The <form> tag was the first element you inserted into the page and all the form controls are contained within this tag. By looking at the form code in Code view, you can see that Expression Web 2 has organized it in such a way that it is easy to read.

A closer look at each form control shows you that they are all based on a very basic code formula. Click the first text box as an example. The code highlighted in Code view is simple to read:

```
<input name="fullName" size="30" tabindex="1" type="text" />
```

As you can see, the form function is no different from any other HTML tag and you insert the different attributes in the same way as any other tag. This also means that you can use the Tag Properties task pane to make changes to the form functions (see Figure 20.19).

More than that, it also means you can apply CSS (Cascading Style Sheets) styles to the form controls just as you have done with other tags throughout this book. For example, by making a new style with the selector name form you can set the font family, font size, background color, box, or any number of other style attributes for the forms. Or you can set individual styles for each different form elements separately by applying classes to them.

Put next to one another you can get a clear idea of how exactly the code for each of
the form controls works:

Text box:

```
<input name="fullName" size="30" tabindex="1" type="text" />
```

Drop-Down Box:

```
<select name="options" tabindex="3" >
        <option selected="selected">Question</option>
        <option>Comment</option>
        <option>Suggestion</option>
        <option>Kipple Story</option>
        <option>Random Thougth</option>
</select>
```

Text Area:

```
<textarea cols="55" name="comment" rows="8" tabindex="4"></textarea>
```

Input (Submit):

```
<input name="submitButton" tabindex="5" type="submit" value="Submit" />
```

Input (Reset):

```
<input name="resetButton" tabindex="6" type="reset" value="Reset" />
```

As you can see, each tag starts with the type of function followed by the name you
gave each instance, the tab index, and if necessary the type of control it is.

As you will see in Hour 22 when you will use the same form you just built to create a
PHP-based email form, to unlock the true potential of HTML forms you need to have
a basic understanding of the code behind form controls. This is because the Form

Field Properties dialogs give you access to only a select few of the many attributes and properties available. As a result, they have to be added manually with the help of the Tag Properties task pane or IntelliSense.

Summary

Forms are key components in taking your sites from being one-way monologues to two way dialogues. By including forms in your site, you provide the visitor with a way to interact with the site and make choices or send and receive information based on what she wants. You could go as far as saying that without forms there would be no search engines, social networking sites, or blogs, and the World Wide Web would be little more than a long list of boring archival material.

To get an idea of how prevalent and varied the use of form controls is throughout the Web, think about this: Every time you see a text box, check box, radio button, or any of the other main form elements, you are actually looking at a form. In fact, every time you enter a word into a search engine and click the Search button, you are using a form connected to a massive database!

In this hour, you learned how to build a simple form that lets the visitor input information that is sent to a file on the server as well as to your own email address. You saw that building the form itself is as easy as dragging and dropping the elements into place and using the Form Field Properties dialogs to make them do what you want them to.

You also learned that when dealing with forms you have to take into consideration what kind of server the form will reside on. Because static HTML pages can run on any web server, the transformation of text and selections in a form on a web page to a readable file or email requires server-side scripts, and these scripts have to be written in a language the server understands and allows.

By including forms in your website, you are moving beyond the basics and into more advanced territory. That means there are more things to consider and understand, but the payoffs are also far greater. For an online vendor, the difference between providing an email address and providing the ability to ask questions or communicate with the website owner from inside the website can be the difference between a visitor dropping by and a visitor actually purchasing the services offered. In truth, something as simple as the email form you just created elevates the perceived level of professionalism many times over and makes the visitor feel like you take her seriously.

HTML forms in their most basic form are easy to build and use, and because they are HTML elements, they are not tied to any particular kind of server-side script so they can be used for all sorts of different applications.

Q&A

Q. *I created the e-mail form and tested it in my browser but I am not receiving any e-mails. What am I doing wrong?*

A. For the actual e-mail functionality to work, the pages have to placed on a web server that has FrontPage Server Extensions installed. Since you are testing the pages from your local hard drive through the Expression Development Server, no such extensions are running. In fact you are only testing the form itself, not the server-side scripts. To get the form to work properly and send e-mails it has to be uploaded to a web server with FrontPage Server Extensions installed.

Workshop

The Workshop has quiz questions and exercises to help you put to use what you just learned. If you get stuck, the answers to the quiz questions are in the next section. But try to answer the questions first. Otherwise you'll only be cheating yourself.

Quiz

1. *Give a brief description of what form controls are and what they do.*

2. *What is the number one requirement for being able to use the e-mail form created using the functionalities demonstrated in this hour?*

Answers

1. Form controls are a group of standard HTML components that can be inserted into any web page that give the visitor the ability to interact with the site. Form controls come in many shapes and functionalities; from text boxes to buttons to check boxes and drop down menus. Form controls can be grouped in a web form that when filled out and triggered sends information to the browser memory for further processing. Every time you input information in a web page whether it be a search string in Google, a bid on eBay, a message on Facebook or a blog entry, you are using form controls contained in a web form.

2. For the e-mail form you created in this hour to work, the server it is placed on has to have FrontPage Server Extensions installed. This is a requirement because all the email functionality is based on this technology. Before building and refining this form it is imperative that you contact your web host and ensure that your hosting plan includes FrontPage Server Extensions. If not you have to use a different technology like PHP to create the e-mail form.

Working with Flash and Silverlight

What You'll Learn in This Hour:

► How to place a Flash Movie in your web page

► How to configure the embedding code for Flash movies to ensure cross-browser compatibility

► How a Silverlight application works

► How to place a Silverlight application in your page using the JavaScript and the iFrame methods

Introduction

One of the major turning points in the evolution of web design was the introduction of Flash. By designing interactive components in this new animation platform, designers were no longer restricted by simple roll-overs and straight page changes: All of a sudden there was a way to make incredibly advanced animated buttons, sliding screens, and whatever else the designer could come up with.

Unlike everything else you have been introduced to so far, Flash is not a native web language. And to run Flash content, visitors must have the Flash Player plug-in installed in their computer. On your end it means that any Flash element has to be inserted into a page as a replaced item, much like an image. This puts some restrictions on how you can and should use Flash content in your pages.

For many years Flash has been almost the only option for interactive animation in websites. And with the proliferation of video-sharing sites, such as YouTube, the platform has become as ubiquitous as regular television sets. But Silverlight, Microsoft's newcomer, could challenge that reign of supremacy.

Silverlight is an animation platform, just like Flash, that allows the designer to create highly interactive and animated user experiences. Unlike Flash it is entirely code based, meaning that instead of having a compiled file that contains all the elements,

Silverlight applications consist of a series of files, including a new file type called XAML (short for Extensible Application Markup Language and pronounced "zamel"), that are read and compiled on the spot by the browser and the Silverlight plug-in.

Both Flash and Silverlight applications need special attention when they are included in a website. To make this process easier, Expression Web 2 includes specialized tools to handle these files. In this hour you will learn how to insert and configure both Flash and Silverlight applications into your pages.

Flash: An Introduction

When you encounter Flash content in a web page what you are seeing is actually an external file called a Flash movie. A Flash movie is a file with the suffix .swf and it plays through the Flash Player.

A Flash movie can be anything from a simple button with a hyperlink to a complete web experience with buttons, pages, videos, audio, dynamic content, and links to internal and external pages. All Flash movies are created using the Adobe Flash application and they cannot be altered after they are compiled into an SWF file.

Flash movies were originally created and published using the Flash application from Macromedia. Adobe bought Macromedia in late 2005, so today when you speak of Flash you refer to Adobe Flash.

Because the Flash movie itself is a static file, designers build dynamic fields much like the form fields you created in Hour 20, "Get Interactive with Forms," that obtain data from external files. This allows otherwise static Flash content to become dynamic and interactive for the user as well as the designer and content handler.

Because they are not native web content and require a special plug-in to play, including Flash movies in your web pages requires the use of special code. The Flash movies are inserted by placing them inside elements that work much like inline frames. <tag>There are actually two such tags: <object> and <embed>. In the past the <object> tag worked in Internet Explorer, whereas other browsers used the <embed> tag. Both tags work in newer browsers, but because not every visitor has a newer browser, the norm is to use *both* tags by placing the <embed> tag inside the <object> tag. Expression Web 2 only inserts the <object> tag, so you have to insert the <embed> tag manually if you want to use both.

Try It Yourself ▼

Publishing a Flash Photo Gallery

To give you an idea of how Flash movies can work with external content and to provide you with a component you can use in your design projects, the lesson files for this hour contain a simple Flash-based photo gallery controlled by an external data file and that sources images from external folders. The Flash movie was built using Macromedia Flash MX 2004 Professional and the slideshow was based on an excellent plug-in, SlideShowPro, that you can buy at www.slideshowpro.net. Of course, as with all other Flash content, you need the Flash application to create and modify the movie itself.

1. In the MyKipple project create a new folder called Gallery.

2. Open the Import dialog by selecting File, Import, File on the menu bar.

3. Click on the Add Folder button in the dialog and select the Flash folder found in the lesson files for this hour. When you click on Open, the Import dialog lists all the files with their current and new location (see Figure 21.1). Click on OK and make sure the new Flash folder ends up in the Gallery folder. If not, drag and drop it into the Gallery folder.

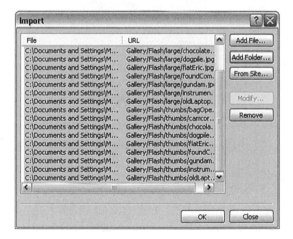

FIGURE 21.1
When you use the Add Folder option, the Import dialog lists all the files with their current and new location.

4. With the Flash folder selected in the Folder List task pane or the Web Site view, create a new HTML page from the myKippleMaster.dwt template by selecting File, New, Create from Dynamic Web Template on the Menu bar. Select File, Save As on the menu bar and give the new page the name **flashGallery.html** (see Figure 21.2).

5. With the new page open in Split view, give it the heading Flash Gallery. Right-click on the page and select Page Properties from the context menu and set the title to Flash Gallery as well.

▼

FIGURE 21.2
With the new HTML page, the Flash folder should now contain three files and two folders.

To insert a Flash movie into the page, you are going to use the built in media functions in Expression Web 2. They can be found in the Media submenu under Insert on the menu bar and in the Toolbox task pane under Media (see Figure 21.3).

FIGURE 21.3
The insert Media options allow you to easily insert Flash movies, Silverlight applications, and Windows media files from the Toolbox task pane and the Insert menu.

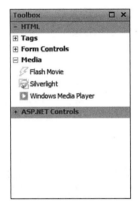

6. Click on the + sign next to Media in the Toolbox task pane to open the media options. Click and drag the Flash Movie option into the content section of the page.

7. The Select Media File dialog opens to ask you to specify what Flash movie you are inserting (see Figure 21.4). Select the flashGallery.swf file in the current folder and click on Insert.

8. A new gray box appears in Design view with a lightning logo and the name of the Flash movie file you just inserted. To play the Flash movie in Design view, right-click on the movie and select Play Movie in Flash Format from the context menu (see Figure 21.5). Now you should see a small image gallery playing inside the box you just inserted.

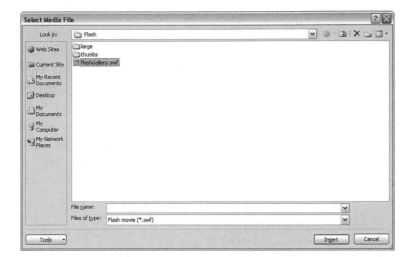

FIGURE 21.4
When inserting a Flash movie, Expression Web 2 asks you to specify what file you want to insert

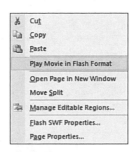

FIGURE 21.5
To play a Flash movie in Design view, you have to select Play Movie in Flash Format from the context menu. Otherwise all you'll see is a gray box.

Now that the Flash movie is inserted into the page, you can start working with it to make it look the way you want. Unless otherwise specified, Flash movies will resize to fit whatever area you insert them into. Note that even though Flash movies contain information about their intended size, Expression Web 2 insists on setting the width and height of all inserted Flash movies to 200 by 200 pixels and scaling the content accordingly.

Try It Yourself

Customizing the Appearance of the Flash Movie

Right now the photo gallery is very small and off to the left side of the page. To make it more appealing, you need to resize it to the intended size and center it on the page. To do this you will use the Flash properties as well as some already familiar CSS (Cascading Style Sheets) styling.

1. When Expression Web 2 inserted the Flash movie for you, it defaulted the width and height to 200 by 200 pixels and the photo gallery scaled itself accordingly. The Flash movie is actually 600 pixels wide and 400 pixels in height. To change this, open the Flash SWF Properties dialog by either right-clicking on the Flash movie and selecting Flash SWF Properties or simply double-clicking on the Flash movie.

2. From the Flash SWF Properties dialog, you can make changes to many different settings. For most purposes, the default settings (sans the sizing) are what you want. Change the width to 600px and the height to 400px. Make sure the Keep Aspect Ratio box is unchecked (see Figure 21.6). Click on OK to apply the changes.

FIGURE 21.6
The Flash SWF Properties dialog gives you control of the playback functionality connected to the Flash movie including size, position, and image quality.

The Flash movie now has the correct size, but if you preview the page in your browser you will see that it is positioned to the left of the page. To make it more visually pleasing, it should be positioned in the center.

3. To position the Flash movie in the center of the page, click anywhere inside the Flash movie in Design view to select the <object> tag and apply the .alignCenter class from the Apply Styles task pane by clicking on it.

Because Flash movies are always contained in an <object> tag, you can apply regular styles, classes, and IDs to this tag to further style the content. When applying styles, it might be easier to imagine the Flash movie as a simple image and apply your styles to it that way. Using CSS to position Flash content is one good example. Another is using CSS to give the Flash movie margins so that it doesn't bump up right next to the other content.

> The contents inside an `<object>` tag can appear either inline or as a block, depending on how you style it. This is important to remember if you insert Flash movies commingled with the text in your page. If no styling is applied, the movie appears alongside the text content just like an image. This can cause your layout to be broken as is often the case when bloggers insert Flash-based ads in their posts without applying styles to them first. As with images, the `.alignLeft`, `.alignCenter`, and `.alignRight` classes are lifesavers for placing Flash movies in your page without ruining the text flow in the process.

Did you Know?

Adding the `<embed>` Tag for Full Cross-Browser Compatibility

As you learned tag, inserting earlier in this hour, there are two tags used to place Flash content in a page, and some older browsers (more specifically Internet Explorer 6 and lower) use only one or the other. Even though most new browsers don't have this problem, it is always a good idea to include both tags to ensure full cross-browser compatibility (that is, that everyone can see your Flash content).

Because Expression Web 2 inserts only the `<object>` tag for Flash movies, you have to insert the `<embed>` tag manually in Code view. For a Flash movie, the `<embed>` tag syntax is extremely simple to remember:

```
<embed src="flashMovie.swf" quality="high" type="application/x-shockwave-flash" width="size in pixels" height="size in pixels" />
```

In the current case the embed code would therefore be

```
<embed src="flashGallery.swf" quality="high" type="application/x-shockwave-flash" width="600" height="400" />
```

To prevent the browser from displaying two copies of the same Flash movie, always place the `<embed>` tag at the very end of the `<object>` tag on the line above the `</object>` end tag, as in Figure 21.7.

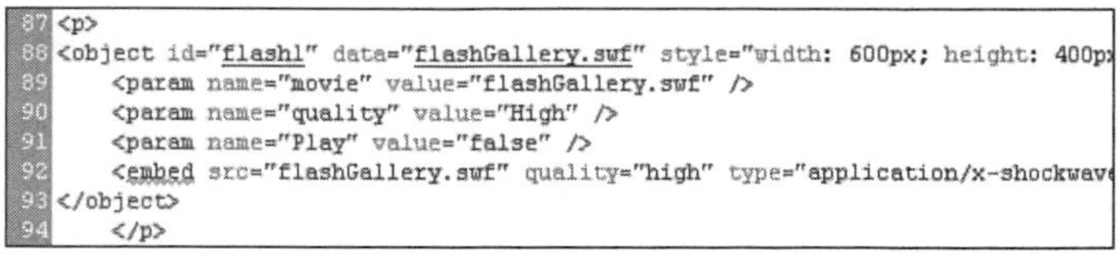

```
87  <p>
88  <object id="flash1" data="flashGallery.swf" style="width: 600px; height: 400px
89      <param name="movie" value="flashGallery.swf" />
90      <param name="quality" value="High" />
91      <param name="Play" value="false" />
92      <embed src="flashGallery.swf" quality="high" type="application/x-shockwave
93  </object>
94      </p>
```

FIGURE 21.7
The **<embed>** tag should always be placed inside the **<object>** tag to avoid having two consecutive Flash movies appear in browsers that support both tags.

The `<embed>` Tag Doesn't Comply with Web Standards!

As explained earlier in this book, Expression Web 2 was created as an application that produces standards-based code out of the box. That means it will not insert nonstandard or deprecated code. The `<embed>` tag was deprecated in favor of the `<object>` tag and as such it is not supported by the W3C (World Wide Web Consortium). For that reason, when you include the `<embed>` tag in your code, a warning about incorrect code appear in the status bar and if you press F9, the `<embed>` tag will be highlighted. Even so, I recommend that you include the `<embed>` tag when you insert Flash movies in your page if you want to keep it accessible for as many visitors as possible.

You Tube and Other External Flash Content

Until a few years ago Flash content was primarily a design element, and you needed to worry about how to include them in your pages only if you designed the site with Flash elements in mind. But then out of nowhere a new video-sharing service called YouTube appeared, and all of a sudden the ability to include Flash content in your site became a must if you wanted to stay current.

Today there are hundreds of different video-sharing sites and almost all of them use Flash as their player platform. These sites build their client base (and revenue) based on getting people to embed the videos into their pages. To make doing so as easy as possible, they all provide the complete embed codes for you to copy and paste into your page. Despite that, many novices still have trouble getting the players to work because they don't understand the difference between Design view and Code view.

If you go to YouTube and find a video you like and want to place on your site, all you have to do is copy the embed code (placed on the right side of the page) and paste it into Code view at the location you want the video to appear. You'll immediately notice that the code looks almost identical to the one Expression Web 2 inserts except that the actual link to the movie itself is different. When the code is in your page, you can change the size and apply styles to it just as you did with the photo gallery.

Silverlight: An Introduction

Silverlight is the newcomer in the world of animation-based web elements. It is based on Microsoft's new code language XAML and is intended to be not only an alternative to Flash but also to introduce new types of functionality to the web as well as offline applications such as presentation software, desktop applications, and so on.

What sets Silverlight apart from Flash is that it is entirely code based and the code is open. That means instead of a precompiled movie as what Flash offers, Silverlight applications are dynamic elements that are created on the spot by the server, browser, and the Silverlight plug-in.

Silverlight applications are built with .NET-based code languages using a combination of Microsoft Visual Studio and a new program called Expression Blend 2, which is included in the Microsoft Expression Suite. One of the driving forces behind Silverlight was to create a work environment where code-based developers and visual designers could work together on the same project at the same time. And because Silverlight applications are 100% code-based, you now have that option: For the code-based developer, the entire application can be written in both the Visual Basic and C# code languages. For the visual designer, the same application can be edited in Expression Blend without ever looking at the code. In short, Silverlight could be the ultimate amalgamation of two technical fields that until now have had a hard time finding a common language.

Placing Silverlight Applications in Your Page

Although Silverlight is a relative unknown in the web market right now, there is little doubt that it will become important enough that you as a designer need to know about it or at least know how to place its contents in your pages.

Because this is an emerging technology, understanding the basics of how Silverlight works gives you a leg up for when the applications become more mainstream. To get a glimpse of how powerful this new technology is and a better understanding of how and why it works, you are going to build a photo gallery application similar to the Flash gallery and place it in your site.

Just like Flash, you need to install the Silverlight plug-in to view Silverlight content. It is a simple one-time browser install, and you can find it at www.silverlight. net.

Did you Know?

Try It Yourself ▼

Create a Photo Gallery Using Slide.Show

As a part of the launch of Silverlight, Microsoft contacted a group of .NET developers and asked them to create custom applications that would be released on an open license so that anyone could download and use them for their purposes. One of these projects, called Slide.Show, was developed by Vertigo (www.vertigo.com) and is published on the Microsoft Codeplex website for public download. This application is a perfect example both of how Silverlight works and how you can use two entirely different methods to place Silverlight content on your page. As a bonus it is an excellent and highly customizable application that lets you build a great-looking photo gallery with very little work.

1. In your browser, go to http://www.codeplex.com/SlideShow to download the source files for the Slide.Show application. To get to the download link, click on the most recent release under Current Release in the upper-right corner (see Figure 21.8). Doing so takes you to a second page where you can download the

FIGURE 21.8
The Codeplex website is a great source for learning materials related to Microsoft products. The link to the Slide.Show download page is in the upper-right corner.

application in a Zip archive as well as Quick Start guides. Download the most recent version (at this writing it is `SlideShowSource-1.1.zip`).

2. Extract the files of the archive to your hard drive.

3. In Expression Web 2, create a new folder under the Gallery folder and call it Silverlight.

You can use several different methods to add a Silverlight application to a web page. In this example you are going to use two: first the JavaScript method and then the iFrame method. The differences and different usage situations will become apparent as you progress.

For a Silverlight application to work, you need several files to be present on the server. Among them are a JavaScript file called `Silverlight.js`, a JavaScript file with the application name, and usually a XAML file (in some cases the XAML is contained in the JavaScript files in which case the XAML file becomes superfluous).

4. Use the Import File option to import the following files from the Slide.Show folder you just exported: Under Slide.Show\scripts\Release, the two files Silverlight.js and SlideShow.js and under Slide.Show\Tests\InlineXaml, the file Default.xaml. Make sure all three files are under the new Silverlight folder in your project, as in Figure 21.9.

FIGURE 21.9
The three files
Silverlight.js,
SlideShow.js,
and
Default.xaml
must be under the Silverlight folder for the application to work.

5. In the Silverlight folder, create a new empty HTML page and give it the name SlideShow.html. Open the page in Split view.

6. For the application to work in the page you first need to tell the browser to open the two JavaScript files. In the <head> of the page, insert the following two lines of code: <script type="text/javascript" src="Silverlight.js"></script> and <script type="text/javascript" src="SlideShow.js"></script>. The first one calls the standard Silverlight control file that is included with all applications. The second calls the JavaScript specific for this particular application.

7. Next you need to call the application in the body of the page. This is done by adding the following script between the <body> tags: <script type="text/javascript"> new SlideShow.Control(new SlideShow.XmlConfig-Provider()); </script>. This inserts an instance of the Slide.Show application into the page and tells the browser that there is an XML (Extensible Markup Language) file with configuration settings in the same folder. In Code view, the page should now look like what you see in Figure 21.10.

FIGURE 21.10
The
**Silverlight.
html** page as
seen in Code
view.

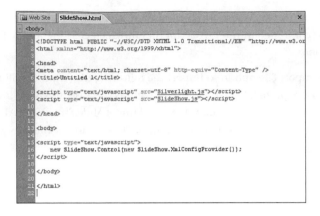

8. Now that you are telling the browser there is a configuration file in the folder,
    you need to add one. Because the configuration file requires a great deal of
    code to work, rather than writing one from scratch, one is supplied in the lesson
    files. Using the Import File option, import the `Configuration.xml` file from the
    lesson files for this hour. If you want an example of more advanced configura-
    tion settings, you can also use the `Configuration.xml` file found under the
    SlideShow\Samples\Vertigo folder.

Previewing Silverlight Applications in Your Browser

To make sure everything is working properly, you should preview the page in your browser. But if you do all you'll see is an empty white page. This is because Silverlight is a
server-side script that must be running on a web server to work properly. In other
words technically you need to upload your files to a web server and test them from
there. Fortunately there is a way around this problem: Because a big part of Expression
Web 2 is the ability to create advanced dynamic websites using Microsoft's server-side
script language ASP.NET, the program comes equipped with a small application called
Expression Development Server. This application creates a virtual server on your computer that behaves like a web server and lets you run server-side scripts in pages even
though they are only stored on your computer. You will be introduced to the Expression
Development Server in more detail in Hours 22, "Beyond the Basics: PHP in Expression Web 2," and 23, "Beyond the Basics Part 2: Building a Site with ASP.NET."

The problem at hand is that the Silverlight script will run only on a web server. So, to be
able to preview the application, you need to make Expression Web 2 think that the
page you are currently working with is actually an ASP.NET page. That way it will be previewed using Expression Development Server and the Silverlight script will run properly.
Doing so is surprisingly simple: Open the HTML file that contains the Silverlight application you want to preview, select File, Save As on the menu bar, and change the file extension to `.aspx`—the extension for ASP.NET pages that can contain regular HTML
code. Now when you open the page it will be previewed in the browser through Expression Development Server and the Silverlight application will run properly.

After renaming the page to SlideShow.aspx, preview the page in your browser. You should see the Slide.Show application without any images in it, as in Figure 21.11. If not, you might be missing the Silverlight plug-in or you are not running the page through Expression Development Server. If you are having problems, look at the Q&A for this hour and see whether you can find the answer there.

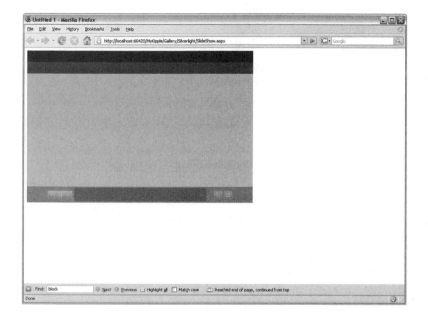

FIGURE 21.11
With the **Configuration.xml** file in place and the page previewed through Expression Development Server, the empty Slide.Show should appear in your browser.

9. The only things missing now are the images themselves. Earlier in the hour you imported a series of images into the Flash folder. Now you can use these same images as the source for your Silverlight application. In the lesson files for this hour is a file called Data.xml. Import this file into the Silverlight folder and test the SlideShow.aspx page in your browser again. If you have set everything up correctly, the images with descriptions should now appear in the Slide.Show application as in Figure 21.12.

FIGURE 21.12
The Slide.Show
application
should now work
properly and dis-
play images with
descriptions.

This was the JavaScript method for inserting Silverlight content into your page. Normally only developers use this method because applications such as Expression Blend
automatically create all the necessary files, including the main HTML file. The reason
you need to know this method is that you need to understand how it works to be able
to troubleshoot the next (and more common) method.

▼ **Try It Yourself**

Inserting Silverlight Applications with Inline Frames

In the previous lesson, you created a page that contained only the Silverlight application. This is done so that it will be easier to embed the application into other pages
later. Now that you have a fully working Silverlight application in your folders, you
can use the iFrame method built into Expression Web 2 to place the application in a
new page.

1. While in the Gallery folder, create a new page from the Dynamic Web Template
   and call it `SilverlightGallery.aspx`.

2. Give the new page the heading Silverlight Gallery and change the page title to
   Silverlight Gallery by opening the Page Properties dialog or changing the text
   between the <title> tags in Code view.

3. Under Media in the Toolbox task pane, drag and drop the Silverlight option
   into the content area of the page.

4. The Insert Silverlight 1.0 dialog (see Figure 21.13) opens to tell you to select the folder that contains the web page, XAML file, and JavaScript file created by the

Insert Silverlight 1.0

To insert a Silverlight-based application into your page, please select the folder that contains the web page, XAML file, and JavaScript file that were generated by your Silverlight authoring program. Click here for more information online.

[Select Folder] [Cancel]

FIGURE 21.13
When you insert a Silverlight element into a page in Expression Web 2, you are asked to point to the folder that contains the application and the web page it is displayed in.

Silverlight-authoring program. This refers to the files and HTML page you just created. Click on Select Folder and the browser window opens. Select the Silverlight folder and click on Open.

5. Another dialog opens to ask you to select the home page of the Silverlight application. This refers to the page that contains only the Silverlight application and nothing else—in this case the file SlideShow.aspx. Select that file and click on Select. An inline frame is now inserted, pointing to the SlideShow.aspx page you created earlier.

6. To ensure that everything looks the way it should, click anywhere outside of the iFrame in Design view and go to Code view. Find the <iframe> tag and ensure that the width and height are set to 600px and 400px, respectively.

7. To center the gallery on the page, select the <iframe> tag using the Quick Tag Selector and apply the .alignCenter class from the Apply Styles task pane.

Save and preview the page in your browser by pressing F12 and you will see that the gallery now works perfectly inside the page. Now you see why the iFrame method is easier: Rather than having to include all the JavaScript and the different external files to make the application work, all you have to do to include the iFrame and everything works. But if something is wrong or you need to customize the application, you have to go in and edit the files in the containing folder.

Normally Silverlight applications come complete with all the necessary elements, but if you need to make adjustments to any of them, either because you want to change the look of the application through the configuration settings or you want to change the contents through the data source, you have to understand how these files work together to deploy the application.

▼   **Try It Yourself**

Make the New Galleries Available

Now you have two galleries and naturally you want people to be able to open and watch them. To do so you need to add links to them in the main menu of the site.

1. Open the `mykippleMaster.dwt` file in Split view.

2. Click on the menu and go to Code view.

3. Under the Gallery menu remove one of the submenu items and change the other two to `<li><a href="Gallery/Flash/flashGallery.html">Flash Gallery</a></li>` and `<li><a href="Gallery/SilverlightGallery.aspx">Silverlight Gallery</a></li>`.

4. Save the DWT file and click on Yes when you are asked to update all the associated pages.

▲

Now when visitors hover over the Gallery button in any of the pages, they are given the option of visiting either the Flash gallery or the Silverlight gallery.

Earlier you saved the `SlideShow.aspx` and `SilverlightGallery.aspx` pages as ASP.NET files to be able to preview them through Expression Development Server. Now that you have finished the pages, you should change their extensions back to `.html`. This is because ASP.NET files run only on Microsoft servers, whereas HTML files run on all servers and the files do not actually contain any ASP.NET content. After it's on a server, the Silverlight application will work regardless of what the file extension is.

Bonus: Making the Galleries Your Own

You can customize both the Flash gallery and the Silverlight gallery introduced in this hour with your own images and descriptions. As you learned earlier, all the images are placed under the Flash folder, thumbnails in the thumbs folder, and the full images in the large folder. Both galleries use XML files to define the image locations, titles, and descriptions. You can change these using Expression Web 2 and make the galleries feature your own images.

The Flash image gallery is controlled by the `images.xml` file found in the Flash folder. The syntax of that file is very simple:

```
<album
        title="Random Kipple"
        description="Some random photos of my kipple"
        lgPath="large/"
```

```
        tnPath="thumbs/"
        tn="thumbs/bagOpennies.jpg">
                <img
                        src="bagOpennies.jpg"
                        title="Bag O' Pennies"
                        caption="A small hemp bag filled with pennies" />
</album>
```

To add another image, all you have to do is add another <img> tag with the src, title, and caption attributes defined. To add another album, just create a new <album> tag and insert the new information. To add more <$I<img> tag><$I<album> tag>images, simply place the large version in the large folder and the thumbnail in the thumbs folder.

One caveat: The images.xml file and image folders need to stay in the same folder as the Flash movie. Otherwise the movie will not work.

The Silverlight image gallery is controlled by the Data.xml file found in the Silverlight folder. The syntax is very similar to that of the Flash gallery:

```
<album
        title="Random Kipple"
        description="Some random photos of my kipple"
        image="../Flash/thumbs/bagOpennies.jpg">
                <slide
                        title="Bag O' Pennies"
                        description="A small hemp bag filled with pennies"
                        image="../Flash/large/bagOpennies.jpg"
                        thumbnail="../Flash/thumbs/bagOpennies.jpg" />
</album>
```

Likewise, to add another image, just add another <slide> tag with the title, description, image, and thumbnail attributes defined. To add another album, just create a new <album> tag and insert the new information. In this example, the URL that points to the images starts with ../ to make the browser go down one folder and then into the correct folders.

In addition to changing the images in the Silverlight gallery, you can also change many of the look and behavior attributes. To get further information, check out the many demos in the application folder you downloaded.

Summary

Both Flash and Silverlight are technologies that can add an unparalleled level of visual impact and interactivity to web pages. These applications are created using dedicated programs (Adobe Flash for Flash files; Microsoft Visual Studio and Microsoft Expression Blend for Silverlight), and inserted into your pages as finished elements.

Because the files are external content, Expression Web 2 is mainly used to position and style the boxes they are inserted into: Flash movies are inserted into the page using either the `<object>` or the `<embed>` tag. In most cases you want to use both, with the `<object>` tag surrounding the `<embed>` tag, even though the `<embed>` tag has been deprecated. This is because many older browsers do not fully comprehend or support the `<object>` tag yet.

Flash movies are placed in boxes on the page and you can apply standard CSS styling to their `<object>` tags to set the placement, borders, backgrounds, and whatever else you feel like. If you ignore the Flash content, an inserted Flash movie acts just like any other replaced item (such as an image). In other words, you have full control of where the movie appears. In this hour, you learned how to embed a Flash movie into your page and use CSS to change its position and styling.

Silverlight is a new technology that has been on the market for only a couple of years. It offers a great alternative to Flash and has many features you can't get with the rival. Most importantly Silverlight is entirely script based, so both developers and designers can work on the application at the same time without having to compile and decompile them repeatedly.

Unlike Flash movies, Silverlight applications require a series of different files to work properly. In this hour you used the Microsoft Codeplex project Slide.Show, created by Vertigo, to get a feel for how exactly this works.

Silverlight applications are housed in folders that contain several JavaScript files along with a web page that contains only the Silverlight project, a XAML file, and any external configuration and data files. In this hour you created such a folder and inserted the necessary files to make the basic web page work. This method used for inserting Silverlight content is called the *JavaScript method*. It is complicated but gives you unlimited control.

After creating the folder with all the necessary files, you used the inline frame method built into Expression Web 2 to insert the Silverlight application into a page.

Silverlight is a server-side script, so it will not run properly on your computer unless you use a virtual server. In this hour, you learned how to trick Expression Web 2 into previewing the pages with Silverlight content through Expression Development Server by changing the file extensions of the pages to `.aspx`.

Q&A

Q. *When I preview the* `FlashGallery.html` *page in Internet Explorer, I get a warning that the program has restricted the website from running ActiveX controls that could access my computer. What do I do?*

A. Embedded content such as a Flash movie uses ActiveX controls to play. For some reason, when you view a local web page, Internet Explorer blocks this type of content and you actively have to tell the browser to accept it by clicking on the warning bar at the top of the page and selecting Allow Blocked Content. This happens only for local files; after the page with the Flash movie is on a web server, you no longer receive this warning.

Q. *I tried previewing the* `SlideShow.html` *file in my browser but all I got was a blank page.*

A. Silverlight is a server-side script, meaning that the server actually performs operations with the script when it is displayed. When you preview HTML pages in your browser through Expression Web 2, no server is used. To preview Silverlight content, you have to run the page through the virtual server called Expression Development Server, which is built into Expression Web 2. To do so, rename your file by changing the extension to `.aspx`. This tricks Expression Web 2 into thinking the file is a dynamic web page that requires server-side scripts to work and Expression Development Server kicks in.

Q. *The Flash image gallery/Silverlight image gallery shows up but there are no images!*

A. Both the Flash and the Silverlight image galleries source their content from outside the application itself. They get their data from the `images.xml` and `Data.xml` files, respectively, and the images are stored in the Flash folder under the large and thumbs folders. For the galleries to work properly, it is imperative that the folder structure described in the hour be retained. The Gallery folder should contain two folders: Flash and Silverlight. All the Flash files should be in the Flash folder and all the Silverlight files should be in the Silverlight folder. If your folder structure is correct and you are still not seeing anything, go to the finalized version found in the lesson files and replace your files with the ones provided.

Workshop

The Workshop has quiz questions and exercises to help you put to use what you have just learned. If you get stuck, the answers to the quiz questions are in the next section. But try to answer the questions first. Otherwise you'll only be cheating yourself.

Quiz

1. **What are the two methods of embedding Flash movies in a HTML page and which one is the correct one?**

2. **Which is better? Flash or Silverlight?**

Answers

1. The two methods are using the <object> tag and using the <embed> tag. Although, technically, the <object> tag is the correct standards based method it is advisable to also place an <embed> tag within the <object> tag to account for the lack of support for the latter in older browsers like Internet Explorer 6. Always remember to nest the <embed> tag *inside* the <object> tag or you will get two instances of the Flash movie in browsers that support both.

2. If you ask Adobe, the answer is Flash. If you ask Microsoft, the answer is Silverlight. In reality they are completely different applications that both have advantages and disadvantages. Flash is well established and has a high penetration rate (meaning most computers can play Flash movies). Silverlight is new on the market but offers a whole new range of functionalities. All things being equal the real question you should ask yourself is what programming language you are most comfortable with. If you already know ActionScript and have worked with Flash in the past, you can always "safe it" and stick with that platform. If you come from or work with a development team that uses .NET architecture you already have a leg up when starting to work with Silverlight. So to answer the question: There is no "better", just different.

Exercise

Use CSS positioning to change the location of the embedded Flash and Silverlight applications. Give them a white background and a thin grey border by setting the padding and border attributes.

Embed a YouTube video into one of your pages, and use the <object> and <embed> tags to resize the video so that it fits half the page. Use CSS to restyle the video and change its positioning so that the text flows around the video.

Open the images.xml and Data.xml files in Expression Web 2 and change the order of the images. Use copy and paste to create new albums for both galleries and test them to see how the applications react to the new content.

Beyond the Basics: PHP in Expression Web 2

What You'll Learn in This Hour:

▶ How to install PHP on your computer

▶ How to configure and use the Expression Development Server to test PHP scripts locally on your computer

▶ How to create a PHP-based email form

▶ How to use PHP to test whether form fields are filled out and that the email was successfully sent

Introduction

If you have surfed the World Wide Web for any length of time you have probably noticed that not all web pages have the .html suffix. When you visit more advanced sites you'll often see that the filenames in the address bar end with .asp, .php, or any number of other suffixes. All these file types hint at the server-side technology used to generate the pages.

Although HTML (Hypertext Markup Language) is a great code language with a wide variety of applications, it is capable of making only *static* pages. A *static* page is one where the designer or developer inserts all the content and it remains the same until someone manually edits the file. In contrast, most large websites including news sources, blogs, social networks, and so on consist of dynamic pages. A *dynamic* page is one where the page itself contains only the framework and content is gathered from other sources such as databases, other sites, or visitor input. The one thing all of these dynamic pages have in common is that they all use some form of server-side scripting language to generate their content.

One of the most prevalent and popular open source server-side script languages is PHP,. PHP is a direct competitor to Microsoft's application framework, ASP.NET, and until recently they have often been mutually exclusive because the Windows Server support for PHP has been unreliable and slow forcing, many web hosts to remove the option altogether. However, with the release of Windows Server 2008, full PHP support is now available on Microsoft servers as well, giving you the choice of using ASP.NET or PHP. Parallel to this, Expression Web 2 was equipped with PHP support giving designers and developers the ability to build sites and applications without looking elsewhere for their PHP scripting.

As you learned in Hour 20, "Get Interactive with Forms," the type of server hosting your site determines what kind of server-side scripts you can use. In Hour 20, you built an email form that utilized FrontPage Server extensions for its functionality. This form would require a Windows Server architecture to work. In this hour, you learn how to use the new PHP features built into Expression Web 2 to create a PHP version of the same form that can be used in sites hosted on a Linux server.

PHP: An Introduction

PHP is a code language used to create *dynamic web pages;* that is, pages whose content is generated by the web server rather than stored in the pages themselves. Advanced PHP pages are little more than a framework with a bunch of design elements and boxes populated with content as the visitor clicks different buttons. You could say it is an extremely advanced version of the Dynamic Web Template where the template is the page itself and the content comes from a database or other external sources.

PHP can also perform other tasks such as processing form results, submitting content to databases, and editing files. To get an idea of just how powerful PHP is, consider that the vast majority of the millions upon millions of blogs floating around the Internet these days run off PHP. Because of this, many new PHP applications customized for blogging are developed every day.

The power of PHP lies in its capability to work alongside standard HTML code. That means you can choose whether you want to place your PHP scripts in a separate file or place them within your HTML pages inside the HTML code. In practical terms, that means you can create an HTML page with dummy content and when you are finished with the layout, you can replace the placeholder content with a PHP script that grabs the real content from an external file, database, other website, RSS (Really Simple Syndication) feed, or a form. To make the file with the PHP script work, it has to have the extension `.php` rather than `.html`, but even so all the HTML code renders normally. In fact, if your site is hosted on a server with PHP installed, you can save all your HTML files as `.php` files without any difference in how the pages display in a browser.

What Does PHP Stand for Anyway?

If you look up the definition of PHP, you get the following explanation: *"PHP" is a recursive acronym for "PHP: Hypertext Processor."* But that really doesn't explain anything because the long version of the acronym contains the acronym itself! This phenomenon is referred to as a *recursive acronym* and is fairly common in the geeky world of programming. More than anything, the use of recursive acronyms in programming is a tongue-in-cheek way of dealing with the fact that for the most part these acronyms really don't mean anything. In PHP's case, however, the acronym originally had a meaning: PHP used to stand for *Personal Home Page tools* (without the "t"), but as the language morphed into a more advanced programming language this description became obsolete and the new recursive acronym was adopted in its place.

For more examples from the geeky world of recursive acronyms take a look at the list found here: http://en.wikipedia.org/wiki/Recursive_acronyms

Installing PHP on Your Computer to Test PHP Scripts

Because PHP is a server-side script, pages with PHP code will not work properly if you test them in your browser as you have with HTML pages. This is because unlike HTML, which renders in the browser, PHP renders in the server and it sends the resulting information to the browser for display. One way to work around this problem is to upload your PHP files for testing on a web server that has PHP installed and test them live, but that is a cumbersome and ineffective method requiring time, a live Internet connection, and available server space. Another way to approach the issue is to run a web server with PHP installed on your local network. This solution is common in larger companies but is not feasible (or economical) for smaller companies and those just starting out with web design.

The ideal solution would be if you could test your PHP scripts locally on your computer in the same way that you have been testing your HTML pages. To answer this call, Expression Web 2 comes equipped with an application called the Expression Development Server. This application within the application is a program that emulates a web server and lets you preview pages with server-side scripting as if it a real web server were hosting it.

The Expression Development Server can preview ASP.NET as well as PHP scripts, but for the PHP scripts to function properly you first have to install PHP on your computer. PHP is free open source software that you can legally download and install on your computer.

1. In your web browser, go to www.php.net/downloads.php to find the latest release of PHP (pt the latest stable PHP release is version 5.2.6) (see Figure 22.1).

FIGURE 22.1
The PHP website found at www. php.net provides new as well as old versions of PHP for download.

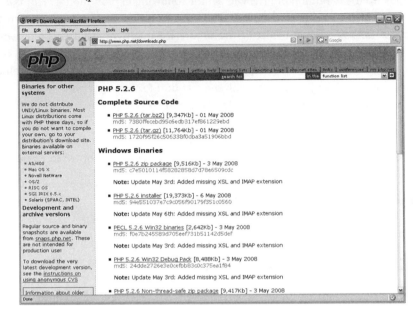

2. Download the zipped package found under Windows Binaries and save it on your computer.

3. When the download of the zip file is complete, extract the archive to a new folder called PHP directly under C:. You can extract the file using any zip-compatible software or by right-clicking the archive, selecting Extract All, and following the Extraction Wizard (see Figure 22.2).

FIGURE 22.2
Extract the contents of the zipped archive you downloaded to C:\PHP.

4. Open the new folder and find the file called `php.ini-recommended`. Select the file and make a copy of it by pressing Ctrl+C and then Ctrl+V. That way you have the original file as a backup if something goes wrong.

5. Right-click the new file and select Rename from the context menu. Change the name of the file to `php.ini`. This file contains all the configuration settings for PHP on your computer.

6. Open Expression Web 2 and select Tools, Application Options on the menu bar (see Figure 22.3).

FIGURE 22.3
Application Options are under Tools on the menu bar.

7. In the PHP section at the bottom of the Application Options dialog, use the Browse button to navigate to the location where you installed PHP (C:\PHP) and select the file named `php-cgi.exe` (see Figure 22.4). Click OK to apply the changes.

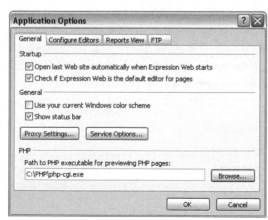

FIGURE 22.4
You need to tell Expression Web 2 where the **php-cgi.exe** file is located for the program to be able to use it to preview pages.

Now PHP is installed on your computer and once you restart Expression Web 2 it will use this installation of the program when testing PHP pages.

> As you learned earlier, you can place PHP script directly inside the code of an HTML page or in a dedicated file. When a browser opens a file containing PHP code, the browser looks for special PHP tags called *delimiters* that define which portion of the code is PHP and which is not. The regular HTML code then processes normally while the code inside the PHP delimiters goes to the server for interpretation.

Using PHP and HTML to Create a Contact Page

PHP is a fairly simple code language when you know how to read it. But for a novice it can be rather intimidating. Therefore let's create some basic examples of how you can use PHP alongside HTML to build a contact page.

1. Create a new page from the `mykippleMaster.dwt` Dynamic Web Template and save it as `contact.php` either by changing the Save As type or simply changing the file extension manually.

   All PHP code has to be contained within PHP delimiters. Unlike the regular HTML tags you have used earlier, all PHP content is included inside the tag itself; that is, between the < and > brackets rather than between two tag sets. The standard syntax for PHP code is <?php ?> where the PHP code goes in the space between.

   Expression Web 2 not only has full IntelliSense support for PHP but also has a series of common PHP scripts built into the Insert menu for easy access and use. Many of these code segments come equipped with the beginning and end delimiters. The most basic command of any code language is the one that prints a line of text on the screen. In PHP, this command is `echo`. So, to insert a heading using PHP, you need to insert the `echo` command.

2. In Code view, erase the (`heading`) text and place the cursor in the heading editable region.

3. Select Insert, PHP submenu on the menu bar and choose Echo (see Figure 22.5). This inserts the PHP delimiters as well as the `echo` command.

   The echo command display any text inserted inside quotation marks as regular HTML text in a browser:

4. With the cursor placed after the `echo` command (in green) in Code view, enter **"Contact Us"** with the quotation marks included (see Figure 22.6).

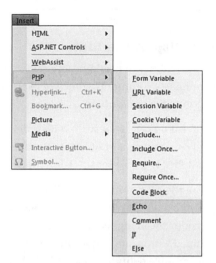

FIGURE 22.5
Expression Web 2 has a set of built in PHP scripts accessible from the PHP submenu under Insert.

FIGURE 22.6
You insert the **echo** command with delimiters and a value in Code view, but they do not show up in Design view.

If you have installed PHP on your computer, you can now save and preview the page in your browser. If PHP installed and configured properly, the page appears with the text Contact Us in the header.

▼   **Try it Yourself**

Use PHP Variables to Display Content

Using PHP you can define variables that display using the echo command. You can define these variables with the PHP command, somewhere else on the page (such as the head), or even in a separate file or database.

To define a variable, you give it a name that starts with a dollar sign ($). The name must start with a letter and can only consist of letters, numbers, and underscores. It is also important to know that PHP is a case-sensitive language.

1. Place the cursor before the echo command in Code view and press Enter to create a new line. Insert the following line of code: **$heading = 'Contact Us'**;. The first part of the code (**$heading**) is the name of the variable. The content of the variable is contained within single quotation marks and the semicolon marks the end of the variable definition just as in CSS.

   To call a variable to display, all that's needed is to insert the variable name after the echo command.

2. Press Enter to move the echo command to a new line and delete the "Contact Us" text. In its place, insert the variable name $heading (see Figure 22.7).

FIGURE 22.7
A variable replaces the echo text.

Save and test the page in your browser, and you see that it looks the same as before.

PHP in Design View

You probably have noticed by now that the results of the PHP code do not appear in Design view. This is because Design view is a web browser emulator and does not have a web server simulator connected to it. As a result, the only way of previewing your PHP code is to test it in your browser locally through the Expression Development Server, on a local web server, or on a live web server on the World Wide Web.

Creating an Email Form Using PHP

In Hour 20, you created an email form using the built-in functionalities of Expression Web 2. This email form generated an email sent to a specified address by way of the FrontPage Server extensions on the web server. But not all web servers have FrontPage Server extensions installed, and on those servers the email form only generates code errors. If your site is hosted on a Linux server, a PHP-based email form is a rock-solid alternative.

Creating the Form

The first step is to create a new email form for the contact page.

1. With the contact.php page in Split view, remove the <p> and </p> tags in the content editable region. Go to the Form Controls on in the Toolbox task pane and insert the Form control.

2. Place the cursor inside the new form area in Design view and select Table, Insert Table on the menu bar to open the Insert Table dialog. Set Rows to 5 and Columns to 2. Under Specify Width, check the In Pixels radio button and set the width to 625.

3. Insert the names for each of the five form boxes in the left columns. From top to bottom they are Your Name:, Your E-mail Address:, Type of Inquiry:, What's On Your Mind?, and Finished?.

4. In the first right cell, insert an Input (Text) control. Click the box to highlight it in Code view. Find the Name value and change it to **YourName**.

   When you click the Submit button on a form, all the form fields are sent to the browser memory. To identify which content comes from which form field, you need to give each form field a unique name. You can do that from the Tag Properties task pane or with the help of IntelliSense in Code view.

5. With the Input (Text) control still selected in Design view, find the Name variable in the Tag Properties task pane. Give the box the name **fullName** (see Figure 22.8).

FIGURE 22.8
You can use the
Tag Properties
task pane to de-
fine all available
variables for any
form control.

6. Use the Tag Properties task pane to set the tab index to 1 and the size to 30.

7. Insert a new Input (Text) control in the next cell below and use the Tag Properties task pane to set its name to **emailAddress**, size to 30, and tab index to 2.

8. In the third right cell, insert a Drop-Down Box control. Right-click the Drop-
   Down Box and select Form Field Properties from the context menu to open the
   Form Field Properties dialog.

9. In the Drop-Down Box Properties dialog, use the Add button to create five
   choices: Question, Comment, Suggestion, Kipple Story, and Random Thought.
   Set the initial state for Question to Selected and the other choices to Not Selected.

10. Use the Tag Properties task pane to set the name to **inquiryOptions** and the
    tab index to 3.

11. In the fourth right cell, insert a Text Area. Use the Tag Properties selector to set
    cols to 55, name to **thoughts**, rows to 8, and tab index to 4.

12. In the bottom right cell, insert an Input (Submit) button and an Input (Reset)
    button. Use the Tag Properties selector to change their values to Submit and
    Reset, respectively. Set their tab index orders to 5 and 6.

You now have an email form that looks the same as the one you created in Hour 20
(see Figure 22.9). But as with the other form, this one does nothing until you attach
some functionality.

Making the Form Work

When the visitor clicks the Submit button in the email form you just created, four
strings of text with the names fullName, emailAddress, inquiryOptions, and

FIGURE 22.9
The email form is built.

thoughts are created and sent to the browser. In the form in Hour 20, code inserted by Expression Web 2 intercepted the strings, and all the necessary actions performed by that code was instead done by the FrontPage Server extensions. Now you want to re-create those same functions using PHP instead.

To perform the actions needed to send the email to the desired address, you are going to make a new PHP file that contains the code that writes and sends the email.

1. Create a new PHP file by selecting File, New on the menu bar and choosing PHP under the General option.

2. Delete all the code in the new file so that it is completely blank and save it as emailProcessor.php in the Contact folder.

   Now you need to send the information from the contact.php file to the new file. By default the Form form control has a built-in action triggered by the onclick event attached to the Submit button. You are going to use this action to send the contents of the form to the new file.

3. With the contact.php file open in Design view, click anywhere inside the form and select the <form> tag from the Quick Tag Selector.

4. In the Tag Properties task pane, click the action tag to activate it and click the ... button. Doing so opens the Select File dialog. Navigate to the Contact folder and select the emailProcessor.php file. Click Open to set the action (see Figure 22.10). Save contact.php.

FIGURE 22.10
By setting the
action attrib-
ute of the form
to a file, you
send the infor-
mation from the
form to that file.

Now you need to set up the PHP functions that generate the email.

5. Open the `emailProcessor.php` file in Code view. Place the cursor at the top of
the page and click Code Block in the PHP submenu options under Insert on the
menu bar. Doing so inserts the PHP delimiters `<?php ?>`.

6. With the cursor between the delimiters, press Enter several times to create some
space.

To get a PHP script to send an email, you use the `mail()` function. The syntax
of this function is as follows:

mail(to,subject,message,headers,parameters)

Of these, the `to`, `subject`, and `message` variables are mandatory whereas the
`headers` and `parameters` variables are optional. For the email form you are
creating, you will be using the `to`, `subject`, `message`, and `headers` variables.

FIGURE 22.11
IntelliSense
helps you keep
track of the
many variables
necessary when
using PHP func-
tions.

To help you remember the order, IntelliSense displays a ScreenTip with the different sections as you insert them.

7. On a new line, type `mail()`. This brings up the IntelliSense ScreenTip for the
`mail()` function (see Figure 22.11).

8. IntelliSense asks for the names of each of the variables, but you haven't created
the variables yet. To keep track of what the different variables are supposed to
contain, enter the function of each variable as its name and end the line with a

parenthesis and a semicolon. When finished the line of code should look like this: `mail($to, $subject, $message, $header, $parameter);`.

The next step is to create new variables that contain either predefined information or information received from the form.

9. First you need to create a `$to` variable to tell the program where to send the email. Create a new line above the `mail()` function and enter the variable name **$to** followed by your email address, like this: `$to = 'you@yourdomain.com';`.

When an HTML form is submitted, all the contents are sent using a method called `POST`. To capture that content, you need to use a form variable. A form variable looks like this:

`$_POST[];`

The original variable name is inserted in single quotation marks between the two brackets.

10. Create a new line. The `$subject` variable should contain the choice the visitor made in the Type of Enquiry field in the form. The name of that field was `inquiryOptions`. To insert that content into a variable, you have to create a form variable: `$subject = $_POST['inquiryOptions'];`.

Skip the `$message` variable for a moment. The `$header` variable can have several different headers, including `From`, `Cc`, and `Reply-to`. In this case, you want the `From` header to match the email address of the sender.

11. Create a new line. Set the `$header` variable to receive the content from the emailAddress form field: `$header = $_POST['emailAddress'];`.

Now all that is missing is the message, or body, of the email. Before you create the `$message` variable you need to learn a few more things about PHP syntax. First, PHP allows you to mix straight text and code as much as you want. Second, to make a line break in PHP, you need to insert the line break code, which is a backslash followed by a lowercase n, like this: `\n`. PHP understands that this is a line break even if it is sandwiched between two lines of text or other code without spaces.

For the emails generated from your website to make as much sense as possible, it is a good idea to space the content properly. Ideally you want your email body to look something like this:

From: Sender Name

Sender e-mail address: sender@senderdomain.com

Regarding: The selection made from the drop-down box.

Message:

Message entered in the box goes here.

12. The $message variable will be somewhat different from the rest of the variables. Start by making the variable: $message = '';.

13. On the first line of the email body, you want the text From: followed by the name of the sender. Place the cursor between the two single-quotes and enter **From: $fullName\n**.

14. On the next line you want the text **Sender e-mail address:** followed by the email address. The sender's email address was stored in the **$header** variable in step 11. Directly after the \n, without any space between, enter **Sender e-mail address: $header\n**.

15. The third line of the email body should read Regarding: and have the selection the visitor made from the drop-down box. This information was stored in the $subject variable in step 10. Directly after the last piece of code you inserted write **Regarding: $subject\n\n**. Note the double line shift to create a space between the sender info and the message.

16. Finally you want the actual message to appear below the rest of the content. The word Message: should also appear on its own line. Directly after the last \n, enter **Message:\n$thoughts\n**.

The entire variable should now read:

$message = "From: $fullName\nSender e-mail address: $header\nRegarding: $subject\n\nMessage:\n$thoughts\n";

17. To make the sender's email address appear in the From field in your email reader, you need to make a small change to the mail() function: Replace $header with **"From: <$header>"**.

18. Because you will not be using the $parameter variable, remove it from the mail() function.

The final code, as shown in Figure 22.12, generates emails laid out exactly as the earlier example from the contents of the email form (see Figure 22.12).

FIGURE 22.12
The finished
**emailProcess
or.php** file as it
appears in Code
view.

> ### I'm Not Receiving Any Emails from the Form!
>
> If you test the page in your browser and try to send an email to yourself, you quickly discover that nothing happens. This is because in addition to having PHP running on your computer, the email() function requires a working email server. To test this functionality, you need to upload the contact.php and emailProcessor.php files to a server with working email functionality.

Added Functionality

There are still a couple of things to add before the email form is complete. For one, the visitor has no way of knowing whether the email was sent. Additionally, the form currently sends an email even if there is no information entered. You can fix both these issues by adding some simple PHP code.

Creating Landing Pages for Success and Failure

As a courtesy to your visitor, you should always tell her whether the email was sent. You can do so by using "landing pages" that the browser navigates to depending on whether or not the email was sent.

In the project files for this hour, you will find three HTML files called success.html, failure.html, and error.html. Import all three files into the Contact folder in your site.

PHP is actually a programming language you can use to create small programs that behave according to your input. One of the many things you can do with PHP is define a set of conditions that have to be met for some specific action to occur and also say what happens if the conditions are not met.

1. If the email is sent successfully, you want the browser to be redirected to the success.html page. To do this, you use the echo function in conjunction with an HTML meta tag called Refresh to redirect the browser. On a new line, enter **echo "<meta http-equiv=\"refresh\" content=\"0;URL=success.html\">";**. The **Refresh** meta tag can be used to delay the redirection to a new page. The delay, measured in seconds, is defined by the content variable. The backslashes in front of the quotation marks tell the PHP interpreter that they are not PHP code but HTML.

2. Likewise if the email is not sent you want the browser to be redirected to the failure.html page. On a new line, type **echo** "<meta http-equiv=\"refresh\" content=\"0;URL=failure.html\">";.

3. To let the server know when to say the email was sent, you first have to define what you consider a success. In the case of the email form, a success would

mean that the `mail()` function executed properly. To define the `mail()` function executing properly as a success, place the cursor at the beginning of the line that has the `mail()` function and enter **$success =**.

Now that you have a way of measuring whether the email was sent and you have the resulting actions for what should happen in either case, you need to make a small program that tells the server when to do what. This is done by using the `if` and `else` statements. Like the names suggest, the `if` statement checks whether a certain condition is met. If it is, the attached action takes place. The `else` statement kicks in whenever the `if` condition is not met. In this case, you want the `if` condition to be the $success variable. If it is met, the `success.html` page should display and if not, the `failure.html` page should display.

4. Create a new line above the `redirect` meta tag that leads to the success.html page and enter **if ($success){**.

5. Create a new line directly below the `redirect` meta tag and close the curly bracket **}**.

6. Create a new line under the last one and enter **else {**. Close this curly bracket on a new line after the **redirect** meta tag that leads to the `failure.html` page.

Figure 22.13 shows the `emailProcessor.php` file as it appears in Code view with the new conditional redirects added. The browser now directs to either the `success.html` or `failure.html` pages depending on whether the email is sent.

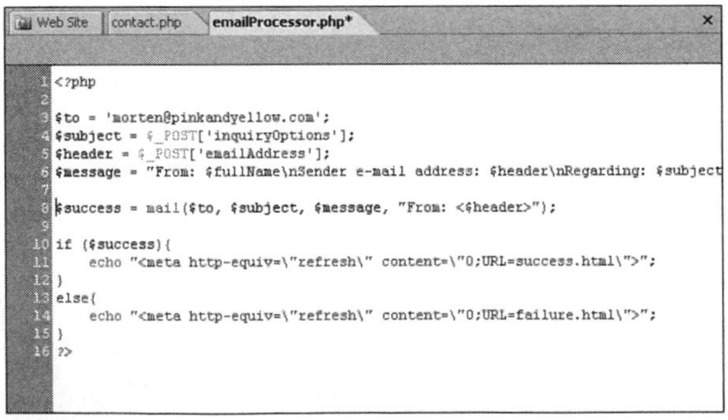

FIGURE 22.13
Add the conditional **redirect** tags to tell the visitor whether the email was sent.

```
<?php

$to = 'morten@pinkandyellow.com';
$subject = $_POST['inquiryOptions'];
$header = $_POST['emailAddress'];
$message = "From: $fullName\nSender e-mail address: $header\nRegarding: $subject

$success = mail($to, $subject, $message, "From: <$header>");

if ($success){
    echo "<meta http-equiv=\"refresh\" content=\"0;URL=success.html\">";
}
else{
    echo "<meta http-equiv=\"refresh\" content=\"0;URL=failure.html\">";
}
?>
```

Creating a Filter to Stop Empty Messages

The easiest way to weed out nonsense emails and accidental clicks is to set up the email form so that if the visitor doesn't enter an email address, the message is not sent. To do this you need to test whether the $header variable (which contains the contents of the emailAddress field from the form) is empty.

1. Create a new line above the $success variable. To see whether the $header variable is empty, enter **if ($header =="")** {. (In programming, a single equal sign means is the same as, whereas two equal signs mean is identical to.)

2. If the $header variable is empty, the browser should be redirected to the error.html page where the visitor is told to enter an email address. Create a new line and enter **echo "<meta http-equiv=\"refresh\" content=\"0;URL=error.html\">";**.

3. Insert one more line and enter **exit;** to stop the script from executing further. Close the curly bracket }.

The final version of the emailProcessor.php file should now look like this:

```php
<?php

$to = 'morten@pinkandyellow.com';
$subject = $_POST['inquiryOptions'];
$header = $_POST['emailAddress'];
$message = "From: $fullName\nSender e-mail address: $header\nRegarding:
$subject\n\nMessage:\n$thoughts\n";

if ($header=="") {
  echo "<meta http-equiv=\"refresh\" content=\"0;URL=error.html\">";
  exit;
}

$success = mail($to, $subject, $message, "From: <$header>");

if ($success){
        echo "<meta http-equiv=\"refresh\"
content=\"0;URL=success.html\">";
}
else{
        echo "<meta http-equiv=\"refresh\"
content=\"0;URL=failure.html\">";
}

?>
```

To sum up, here is what happens step by step: When the visitor enters information into the email form and clicks the Submit button, the different variables are sent to the emailProcessor.php file. From here each value is given a variable name and inserted in various sections of the email body. Then the script tests to see that an email address was entered. If no email address was entered, the browser is redirected to the error.html page. Otherwise the script continues on to send the email. If the email is successfully sent, the browser is redirected to the success.html page. If for some reason the email was not sent, the browser is redirected to the failure.html page.

Summary

If you want to move beyond static pages and add dynamic content and true interactivity to your sites, you have to employ server-side scripting. And when it comes to server-side script languages many argue that PHP reigns supreme. Even though PHP is technically a direct competitor to Microsoft's own application framework, ASP.NET, Expression Web 2 comes equipped with an extensive range of tools to create, write, edit, and deploy PHP-based pages.

To test your PHP scripts locally on your computer, you first need to install PHP. In this hour, you learned how to install this free open-source software and set up Expression Web 2 so that it deploys when you test your scripted pages through the Expression Development Server.

One of the major benefits of PHP is that the scripts can live alongside HTML code, which means you can build your pages as you normally would and substitute your static content for dynamic content without breaking HTML. It also means that even with PHP scripts installed, you still have full control of the layout and functionality of your pages through the use of tags, CSS, and the other techniques you learned by reading this book.

In this hour, you learned about basic PHP scripts and saw how a script can insert content into a page. You built an email form based on PHP that can be uploaded to a Linux server (the form from Hour 20 works only on Microsoft servers). Using PHP scripts, you went beyond simply generating an email and created conditional rules that sent the visitor to different pages depending on whether the email was sent. Finally you created a conditional rule that tested whether the visitor inserted an email address before submitting the form.

PHP is an advanced coding language and in this hour you got only a fleeting glimpse of what can be done with it. By using the PHP tools in Expression Web 2, including the full IntelliSense support, you are well equipped to dive into the world of server-side scripting. If you want further information about PHP including tutorials, visit the official PHP website at www.php.net or the W3C schools at http://www.w3schools.com/PHP/.

Q&A

Q. *When I tested my PHP page in the browser after installing PHP, the address in the address bar changed to http://localhost: and some number. What happened to my original address?*

A. When you run a page through the Expression Development Server, the application creates a temporary simulated server on your computer. The address changes because the page is not merely read from its original location as it is when you test an HTML page but is rendered through the server. Thus the browser is displaying the server output and because the server is hosted on your computer, it is a local host.

Q. *When I tested the email form using the Expression Development Server, all I got was a page displaying the PHP code.*

A. This problem could be caused by two different things. Either you didn't change the suffix of the contact page to .php but left it as .html, in which case the Expression Development Server will not deploy and the page will be rendered as straight HTML, or PHP is not running properly. First check that your contact page is named contact.php. If so, make sure you followed all the steps when installing PHP on your computer.

Workshop

The Workshop has quiz questions and exercises to help you put to use what you just learned. If you get stuck, the answers to the quiz questions are in the next section. But try to answer the questions first. Otherwise you'll only be cheating yourself.

Quiz

1. *What is the difference between the e-mail form you created in this hour and the one you created in hour 20?*

2. *How does the browser know what part of a PHP page is PHP code and what should be considered standard HTML?*

Answers

1. The e-mail forms you created in the two hours are virtually identical. The difference lies in how the data or information generated from the forms is handled once the visitor presses the Submit button. In the form created in this hour the data is sent to a PHP file that parses the information and creates an e-mail message that is sent to the defined address. In the form from hour 20 the data is processed by the FrontPage Server Extensions on the server and the e-mail is generated by them. One of the biggest distinctions between the two is that while the PHP functions are contained in a separate file in this example, the FrontPage Server Extensions code is contained within the form code itself.

2. One of the many benefits of PHP is that it can live along side regular HTML code without any problems. When the browser opens a PHP page it reads all the regular HTML code as it normally would and only sends the PHP code contained within the PHP delimiters <?php ?> to be processed by the server before being displayed. This way the server only helps out when needed and the browser does the rest of the work. In the extreme this means that you can create PHP pages that contain nothing but HTML and the browser will read them as if they were HTML pages.

HOUR 23

Beyond the Basics, Part 2: Building a Site with ASP.NET

What You'll Learn in This Hour:

▶ How to use an existing ASP.NET site as a base to build a new site

▶ How an ASP.NET master page works and how to edit it

▶ How an ASP.NET web form or page works and how it relates to the master page

▶ How dynamic sites use source files to distribute content to different pages

▶ How to use CSS and HTML techniques to modify an existing ASP.NET site

Introduction

In Hour 19, "Dynamic Web Templates," you learned about Dynamic Web Templates (DWTs) and how to use them to create an easily updateable website with a consistent look. Then in Hour 22, "Beyond the Basics: PHP in Expression Web 2," you got a first glimpse of how server-side scripting can be used to create websites with highly advanced dynamic content and interactivity. Now you are going to put the two together to make a website controlled by a master page layout and filled with dynamic content.

Even though Expression Web 2 comes equipped with script support and basic tools for PHP authoring, it is nothing compared to what the application offers when it comes to Microsoft's server-side script language, ASP.NET. Expression Web 2 is built around ASP.NET and offers extensive and unprecedented authoring and deployment tools and support for novice as well as advanced users.

As with PHP, the core concept of ASP.NET is to leave the generation of the content of the page to the server so that the designer or developer needs to do only minimal changes to files for maximum results. Likewise, ASP.NET code can live alongside regular HTML to simplify authoring. As a result, by deploying ASP.NET scripts you can perform the same actions (populating text fields, sending and receiving information from forms, and so on) you did in Hour 21, "Working with Flash and Silverlight," and many others as well.

Because building an ASP.NET-based site from scratch requires a relatively high level of programming know-how and skill, rather than building it from scratch you will use a prebuilt site provided by Microsoft to learn about ASP.NET and how it works.

Watch Out!

> To run an ASP.NET website, you need a server that supports this scripting language. In other words, your site has to be hosted on a Microsoft server. Before you start working with ASP.NET it is vital that you ensure that your server supports this language, otherwise you are wasting your time.

Getting a Jump Start by Using a Starter Kit

Building ASP.NET applications from scratch can be quite intimidating for a novice. To help with the learning process, Microsoft has created a set of Starter Kits that you can download from the Expression website. The kits contain fully working and fully customizable sites that utilize regular as well as advanced scripts to create highly functional and great-looking sites. In this hour, you will use the Design Portfolio Starter Kit to get a better understanding of what ASP.NET is and how Expression Web 2 can help you build sites employing this technology in a fast and efficient manner even without a firm understanding of the code language itself.

▼ **Try It Yourself**

Downloading and Installing the Starter Kit

The Expression website features learning tools such as videos, articles, tutorials, and downloads to help you get started using the different applications in the Expression Suite. For Expression Web 2, the Starter Kits can be a great help when taking your first steps with ASP.NET.

1. In your web browser, go to http://expression.microsoft.com and click on the Learn tab (see Figure 23.1).

2. Click on Starter Kits and you are taken to the Expression Starter Kits page. As of this writing the page has only two starter kits, both for Expression Web. Download the Design Portfolio Starter Kit to your computer.

3. Extract the contents of the zip archive you just downloaded (called ExpressionWebPorfolioStarterKit.zip) to a folder of your choice. The extracted folder will contain a folder called Expression Portfolio Starter Kit and a Microsoft Word document. The folder contains a new folder called Portfolio

▼

FIGURE 23.1
The Expression website found at http://expression.microsoft.com is a great source for learning tools all the programs in the Expression Suite.

Starter Kit and a Microsoft Word document that is identical to the one in the first folder.

4. Move the Expression Portfolio Starter Kit folder to your Web Sites folder (see Figure 23.2).

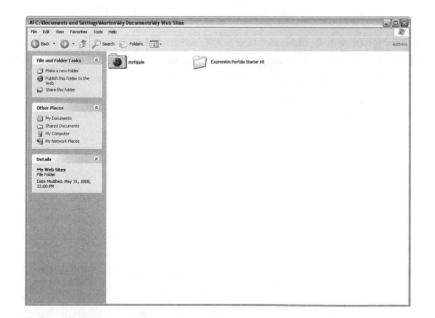

FIGURE 23.2
My Web Sites folder as it appears with the MyKipple project as well as the new Expression Portfolio Starter Kit folder.

5. Open Expression Web 2 and select File, New, New Web Site from the menu bar. In the New dialog, select Empty Web Site under General and use the Browse button to navigate to the Portfolio Starter Kit folder under the Expression Portfolio Starter Kit folder. This is the location of all the necessary files (see Figure 23.3).

FIGURE 23.3
Create a new empty website located in the folder you just installed. This lets Expression Web 2 know that there is a site in the folder.

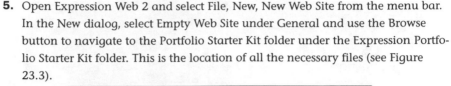

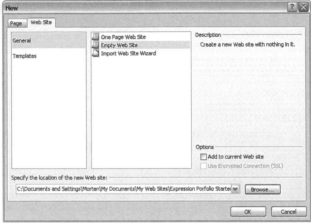

The site link *must* be to the Portfolio Starter Kit folder and *not* the Expression Portfolio Starter Kit folder or the site will not work properly.

As you can see from the Folder List task pane and the Web Site view, the Portfolio Starter Kit has a long list of pages and assets already installed (see Figure 23.4). Now that the site is properly linked from within Expression Web 2, you can open the pages, make changes, and test the site from within the program through Expression Development Server.

The ASP.NET Master Page

Looking at the list of files in the Portfolio Starter Kit, the file that sticks out the most is arguably the most important one: `Default.master`. This file can be compared to a highly evolved version of the Dynamic Web Template, but this comparison hardly does it justice. The ASP.NET master page is the control center for the entire site. And whereas the DWT merely provided its child pages with static and styling content, the master page provides functionality as well as sitewide control.

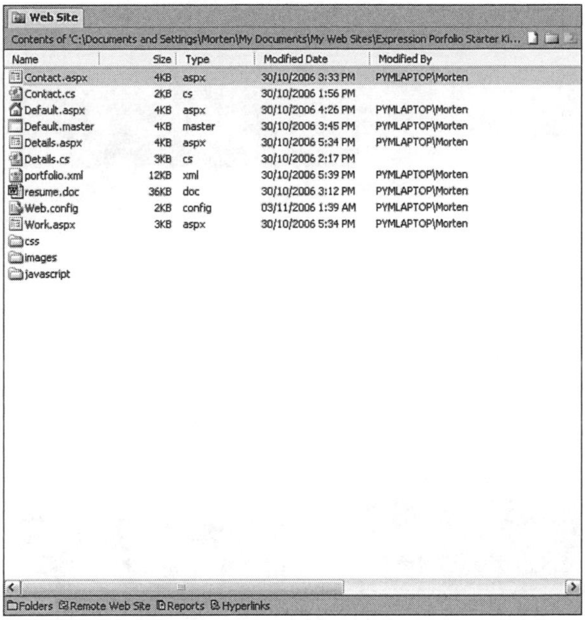

FIGURE 23.4
The Portfolio
Starter Kit con-
tains several
pages along with
assets that to-
gether make up
the functionality
of the resulting
site.

In Hour 19 you learned that when you build a page based on a DWT, the code content of the DWT is copied over to the new page. As a result every time you make a
layout or style change in the DWT, all the associated pages have to be updated and
have their code changed. In contrast, the ASP.NET master page *is* the source of all the
layout and styling code. So, instead of this code being copied over to each individual
child page, the children go back to the master page for layout, styling, and other
common elements and contain only the info for the individual page contents. In
other words, this is a truly dynamic site where all the files are generated from one
central location.

To understand how this works, open the `Default.master` page in Design view. At
first glance it looks like any other HTML page, but if you look closer you will see two
areas highlighted by a faint purple outline. By clicking on them you will see that
they are named `NavContent` and `MainContent`, respectively (see Figure 23.5). Each is
a `ContentPlaceHolder`, the ASP.NET equivalent of the editable regions of the DWT.

The `ContentPlaceHolders` (also called *content regions*) . work in much the same way
the editable regions work in a DWT: When a page is generated from the master page,
only the areas within the content regions can be edited; the master page controls
everything else. But unlike the pages generated by the DWT, you have no way of editing the code outside of the content regions in each individual page because the
code is present only in the master page.

FIGURE 23.5
The `NavContent` and `MainContent`**Content-PlaceHolder**s are highlighted with a purple outline. In this image both are highlighted simultaneously for visual reference.

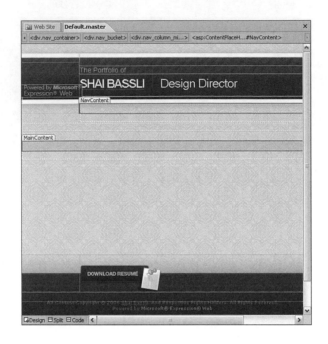

Managing the content regions is done the same way that you managed the editable regions: Under Format on the menu bar is a submenu called Master Page, and within that submenu is the Manage Content Regions option (Figure 23.6).

FIGURE 23.6
You can manage the content regions from the Manage Content Regions option found in the Master Page submenu under Format on the menu bar.

In the Manage Content Regions dialog (see Figure 23.7) you can add, rename, and remove content regions with the click of a button. In addition, you can use the dialog

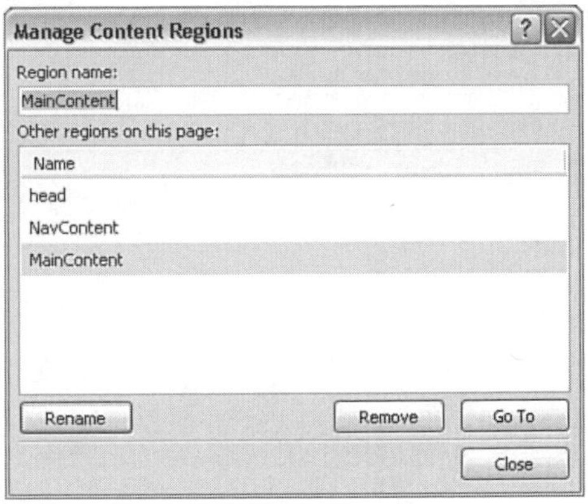

FIGURE 23.7
The Manage Content Regions dialog can also be used to quickly navigate to a particular region in Design view.

to navigate to the different content regions. This option is especially useful when your layout has many regions and you are confused about where a certain region is placed. The Go To option works only in Design view.

The Master Page in Code View

When switching to Split view, the first thing you'll notice is that all the contents of the `.master` page are placed in a form. You can see this because wherever you click inside the page, the two first tags on the Quick Tag Selector are always `<body>` and `<form#form1>`. That's because all ASP.NET sites that use `.master` pages consist of ASP.NET web forms that are populated. This will all make more sense in a few minutes.

Looking at the code, you will see that for the most part it looks like any other HTML page. But if you click on one of the content regions in Design view you will see that the corresponding tags are somewhat different from what you have encountered before (see Figure 23.8).

The `<asp:ContentPlaceHolder ID="NavContent" runat="server" >` tag is the ASP.NET master page equivalent of the `<!-- #BeginEditable "heading" -->` tag of the DWT with a few major differences. Whereas the DWT tag worked solely as a helper for Expression Web 2 to know what regions were to be editable, the ASP.NET tag is an actual functional part of the page just like any other tag. It tells the browser that the tag is an ASP function and that within it there will be ASP.NET-generated content. In addition it gives the area a name in the form of an ID and tells the browser where the script should run (on the server).

FIGURE 23.8
The NavContent
Content Region
in Design view
with the corre-
sponding code.

Try It Yourself

Change a Content Region

The ASP.NET content regions work in much the same way as the DWT editable regions and you can edit them in the same way in the master page. By default the
Portfolio Starter Kit has three content regions: head, NavContent, and MainContent.
But if you look at the head editable region in Code view you will see that it is empty
and the title tag is in a noneditable part of the page. As with the MyKipple project,
you want the title, keywords, and description tags to be inside an editable region so that they can be customized for each individual page.

1. In Code view, find the ContentPlaceHolder tag for the head content (it should
   be on line 9).

2. Create a new line between the beginning and end tags and cut and paste the
   <title>Main</title> tags from line 7 into the new line (see Figure 23.9).

FIGURE 23.9
The **<title>**
tag is moved
into the head
content region.

```
8
9  <asp:ContentPlaceHolder id="head" runat="server">
10 <title>Main</title>
11 </asp:ContentPlaceHolder>
12
13 <style type="text/css" media="screen">
```

3. Press Enter to insert a new line underneath the <title> tags and create a new
   <meta> tag like this: <meta content="" name="keywords" />. This tag will

be filled with the keywords inserted in the Page Properties dialog of each individual page.

4. Insert a third line and create a new <meta> tag for the page description: <meta content="" name="description" /> (see Figure 23.10).

FIGURE 23.10
The head content region now contains the title, keywords, and description of the page.

When you save the master page, you will notice that unlike when you made changes to the Dynamic Web Template in Hour 19, you are not asked whether you want to update the files related to the master page. This is because rather than copying all the code over into each individual page, the pages created from the master page are built dynamically by the browser when they are displayed. Therefore the updates happen instantly when the browser opens the pages.

ASP.NET Content Pages

As with the Dynamic Web Template, the master page only serves as the framework that tells the browser what the pages of the site should look like. To create the actual site, you need content pages. In the Portfolio Starter Kit are four such content pages: Contact.aspx, Default.aspx, Details.aspx, and Work.aspx.

Open the Default.aspx page in Design view. The page looks the same as the Default.master page, but if you click around inside it you will see that you can place your cursor inside only the two editable regions, NavContent and MainContent. The NavContent area contains the navigational buttons for the page, whereas the MainContent area contains all the individualized page content. The NavContent is editable because the site is designed so that the button for the current page looks different from the other buttons. To set up the buttons for each page individually is an easy way of doing this.

Content Pages in Code View

The Default.aspx page looks the same as the Default.master page (except for the content of course) in Design view, but Code view is a different story. If you switch to Split view, you will see that the code for the page contains only the link back to the

`Default.master` file off the top followed by the contents of the content regions. None of the styling, layout, or other code is present in this file. Only when you look at the code of a content page does the concept of web forms truly begins to make sense:

In plain English each `.aspx` page is an advanced web form, just like the email form you created in Hour 20, "Getting Interactive with Web Forms," and Hour 22, "Beyond The Basics: PHP In Expression Web 2." This form, when opened in a browser, submits its contents to the `.master` page, which is then displayed with the contents inserted. In fact the actual page itself exists only when the server puts the content (the `.aspx` file) and the template (the `.master`) file together and then send it to the browser. Just like in *The Matrix* when the little boy bends the spoon with his mind, the answer to the question "Where is the page?" is "There is no page!".

Websites like the Portfolio Starter Kit site are commonly referred to as *dynamic* websites because the pages are created dynamically on demand by the browser and the server when the visitor opens them. In contrast, a *static* site consists of pages that have already been built and visitors simply download them to their browser when the pages are opened.

▼ Try It Yourself

Give the Page a Title, Description, and Keywords

Even though the `Default.aspx` page is in fact just a web form that contains only the individual contents of the page, it is still edited just like the other web pages you have been working with whether it be HTML or PHP.

As you can see in Code view, even though you made alterations to the head content region in the master page, there is no corresponding content region in the web form. To be able to define the content for the head region, you first have to create a new content field in the web form.

1. With the `Default.aspx` page in Split view, navigate the Code view section to the very top and place the cursor on line 2. Press Enter twice to create some space.

2. Place the cursor on line 2 and type **<asp.** IntelliSense will immediately suggest **<asp:Content**, which is what you want. Press Enter to insert the code (see Figure 23.11).

3. Press the spacebar and IntelliSense pops up a new menu suggesting `ContentPlaceHolderID`. Press Enter to insert the code.

4. The cursor is now placed inside the quotation marks. Type **head** and use the right arrow key or End to get to the end of the line.

▼

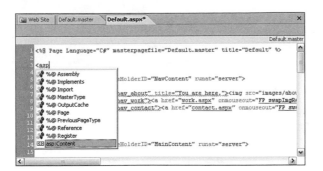

FIGURE 23.11
IntelliSense has full support for ASP.NET and is a great tool when writing and editing **.aspx** pages.

5. Press the spacebar again and IntelliSense provides a new menu of suggested code. Use the arrow keys to select runat and press Enter to insert the code. Now IntelliSense offers only one option, server, which is the correct one. Press Enter again.

6. Finally close the tag with a > and IntelliSense automatically inserts the corresponding closing tag (see Figure 23.12).

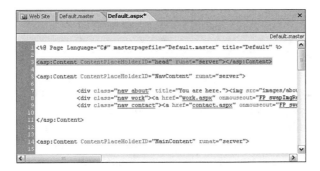

FIGURE 23.12
The **ContentPlace HolderID** tag for the head region is inserted with the help of IntelliSense.

After the content region has been inserted, you can make changes to the head tags using the Page Properties dialog.

7. In Design view, right-click anywhere inside the content regions and select Page Properties from the context menu (if you click anywhere else nothing will happen).

8. In the Page Properties dialog, change the Title to My Portfolio or anything else you want. Create a description for the page as well as some keywords and click OK to apply the changes (see Figure 23.13).

Going back to the top of the page in Code view, you can see that the title has been changed in the first line whereas the keywords and description have been inserted

FIGURE 23.13
With the head
content region
inserted, you are
free to edit the
title, description,
and keywords for
the site using
the Page Proper-
ties dialog.

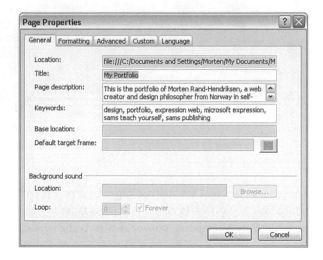

into the content region you just created. Now when a browser opens the page, the title, description, and keywords are inserted into the correct regions in the master page.

Getting Data from External Sources

One of the major benefits of creating dynamic websites is the ability to gather content from external sources and display it in the current page without actually having to place it there. By using an external source for your content you can use one source to populate multiple pages with different layouts at different times. When a change is needed, all you have to do is change the source file and all the dynamic pages that get their content from it will automatically be updated too.

To see this process in action, preview the `Default.aspx` page in your browser. When you press F12 or choose Preview in Browser from the File menu, Expression Development Server is engaged and a virtual server displays the ASP.NET site as if it were hosted on a web server.

On the right side of the About page, under Featured, are three thumbnails representing projects. When you hover the mouse over each of them, a larger version appears with name, description, and a link to further reading about that project. If you click on the Work button you see the same thumbnails again, only this time there are nine of them arranged in three rows and columns (see Figure 23.14). Although the layout of the thumbnails in the two pages is dramatically different, all are gathered from the same source.

Back in Expression Web 2 you will see that the featured thumbnails are replaced by broken image links (a small square with a red x in them). This is because, as with

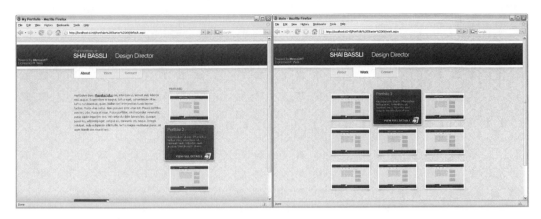

FIGURE 23.14
The About and Work pages both feature external data from the same source displayed in different ways.

PHP, Design view is unable to display the results of server-side ASP.NET scripts. Nevertheless, by clicking on the images, you can see the code that generates them (see Figure 23.15).

FIGURE 23.15
In place of the actual thumbnails that appeared when you previewed the page in a browser, by clicking on the Featured section you get the ASP.NET code that gets the content from the external source.

The code put in place to display the thumbnails and all their functionality is quite complicated, but even with little to no experience with programming you can still figure out what is going on. Take a look at the first line of code in the block:

```
<asp:DataList runat="server" ID="MyDataList" DataSourceID="MyXmlDataSource"
```

```
RepeatLayout="Flow" RepeatDirection="Vertical">
```
In plain English, it reads, "Here follows a data list to be created by the server. The name of the data list is MyDataList and it will contain items provided by a source named MyXmlDataSource. The list items will be repeated in the vertical direction."

The code that follows, wrapped in the <ItemTemplate> tag, describes the look and behavior of each of the list items and the server will cycle through this list for each of the items as they are placed on the page when it is displayed.

But there is still one question left unanswered: Where do the data and images come from? All we know so far is that the source is called MyXmlDataSource. To find the source, use the Find feature: Place the cursor anywhere in Code view and press Ctrl+F. In the Find dialog, type **myxmldatasource** and click Find. Doing so takes you to the next place where **MyXmlDataSource** is mentioned:

```
<asp:XmlDataSource ID="MyXmlDataSource" DataFile="portfolio.xml"
XPath="portfolio/portfolioItem[@featuredItem='true']" runat="server">
```
It is in this line of code you find the source of the list: a file called portfolio.xml.

Go to the Folder List task pane and open the portfolio.xml file. As you can see, this is a pure data file that contains a series of variables defined for each item in a list. The variables include name, summaryDescription, fullDescription, webSiteAddress, fullSizeIimage, and so on. Using this information in conjunction with the different web forms of the site, the browser and the server can build multiple different layouts and pages.

▼   **Try It Yourself**

Modify the External Source for Immediate Sitewide Effects

By modifying the portfolio.xml file and adding a few image files to your project, you can make dramatic changes to the Portfolio Starter Kit site in a snap. In this example you are going to change one of the portfolio items to the MyKipple project.

1. In the project files for this hour are three image files called mykippleFront_lg.jpg, mykippleFront_sm.jpg, and mykipplecontact_lg.jpg. Import them into the images folder in the project.

2. In the portfolio.xml file go to line 5 and change the name value to MyKipple.com.

3. On the next line remove the dummy summaryDescription and insert a short description of the project, something like *This is the end result of the project I made by reading this book.*

4. Go to the next line, remove the dummy content, and insert a new fullDescription. This one should be substantially longer than the summary.

▼

5. Change the `webSiteAddress` to http://www.mykipple.com.

6. Change the `fullSizeImage` to images/mykippleFront_lg.jpg.

7. Change the `thumbnailImage` to images/mykippleFront_sm.jpg.

8. Under `detailImages`, remove two of the entries and change the two other to images/mykippleFront_lg.jpg and images/mykipplecontact_lg.jpg.

9. Save the file (see Figure 23.16).

FIGURE 23.16
The **portfolio.xml** file with the first list item changed to the MyKipple.com project.

Without making any changes to any of the other pages, open `Default.aspx` in your browser. As you can see, the first portfolio item has been changed to the MyKipple.com project. The same is true for the Work page. And if you click on the View Full Details option, a new page appears and displays all the info about the project.

Personalizing and Styling an ASP.NET Site

Now that you have seen how advanced the functionality of the Portfolio Starter Kit is, you might want to use all or part of the site as a basis for your own website. But to do this you need to personalize and customize the site so that it reflects you and your company and doesn't look like the many other sites built from the same files. Doing this might seem like a daunting task but you shouldn't be too surprised to learn that even though this site uses ASP.NET, the look and feel of the site is still firmly based in the same CSS (Cascading Style Sheets) techniques you have learned through reading this book. In fact, if you have a lot of time and patience, you can actually make the Portfolio Starter Kit look exactly like the MyKipple.com site!

Making changes to a dynamic site is a bit trickier than making changes to one with static pages because not all the information is contained in the same file. But by keeping your tongue straight in your mouth (as we say in Norwegian), you can make quick changes for maximum effect: You just need to know where to make them.

Changes that affect all pages across the site should be made in the `.master` file. Changes that should appear only in individual pages should be made in the `.aspx` files using HTML. Finally changes to content provided by external data sources such as `.xml` files or databases should be made in the respective sources. To find out whether a certain item in a page is generated from an external data source, open the page in Design view and see if the content appears. If it does, it is HTML based. If doesn't show up, but is replaced by a tag or block of code, it is generated from an external source.

▼   **Try It Yourself**

Make Sitewide Changes

Not surprisingly, layout and style changes that should affect all the pages on the site are made by modifying the master page.

1. Open the `Default.master` page in Design view.

2. In the header of the page, highlight the name and change it for your name or the name of your company. Also change the title to your title or the tag line for your company.

3. Scroll down to the bottom of the page and find the footer. Change the contents so that the copyright is attributed to you or your company.

4. Highlight your name or the name of your company in the footer, and use the Insert Hyperlink dialog to turn it into a hyperlink pointing to your website.

   Because the design of the site is created using regular CSS, you can make changes to the site by modifying the CSS. Now you can use your CSS skills to change the look of the header.

5. In the lesson files for this hour is an image file called `newTop.jpg`. Import this file into the Images folder.

▼

6. To find out what style controls the header background, place the cursor any-where inside the header and click on each of the tags in the Quick Tag Selector from right to left checking the corresponding style in the Manage Styles task pane. By clicking on each of the styles in the task pane and looking at the pre-views, you will discover that the background is defined by the `.name_container` class. Right-click on this class and select Modify Style from the context menu.

7. In the Modify Style dialog, go to Background and change the `background-image` to the new file you imported in step 5, `newTop.jpg`. Click OK to apply the change.

8. You might have noticed that regardless of what you write, the first letter of the title in the header is capitalized. To change this, click on the title to see what style is affecting it. Click on the `<span.title>` tag in the Quick Tag Selector and go to the CSS Properties task pane. Here you can see that text-transform is set to Capitalize. Using the CSS Properties task pane, change `text-transform` to lowercase (see Figure 23.17).

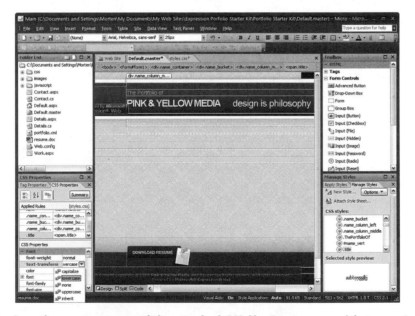

FIGURE 23.17
Because the master page is controlled by CSS you can change the de-sign of the site by using the Modify Styles task pane, the CSS Properties task pane, or even by editing the style sheet directly in Code view.

9. Save the master page and the attached CSS file. Preview any of the pages in your browser and you will see that the changes have been applied to the site as a whole.

Now that you know how to make changes to the look of the site, it's time to look at how you can make changes to the content of the different pages within the site. Making changes to the individual pages contained in the Portfolio Starter Kit allows you to further personalize the site and is also a necessary step to ensure that the people who visit the site get the message you want to convey. This is particularly true for the Contact page.

▼ **Try It Yourself**

Configure the Contact Form

The final page of the Portfolio Starter Kit is a contact form much like the one you created in Hour 20, "Get Interactive with Forms." To personalize the contact page, you need to make changes to two files: `Contact.aspx` and `Contact.cs`.

1. Open the `Contact.aspx` page in Design view.

2. Each of the web forms (pages) in the site has some page-specific content. This content is created and styled using the same techniques you have used throughout this book. At the top of the `MainContent` region is a mailing address and an email address. Change these to your name, mailing, and email address as you would in any other HTML page.

   Below the addresses is the email form. This form was created using the ASP.NET form controls, not the HTML form controls you used in earlier hours. The ASP.NET form controls are in the Toolbox task pane in the Standard submenu under ASP.NET (see Figure 23.18).

FIGURE 23.18
Although they look similar, the forms in the ASP.NET site are made using the ASP.NET form controls found under ASP.NET in the Toolbox task pane.

▼

3. If you look through the code of the Contact.aspx page, you will notice that there is nowhere to input the email address the email should be sent to. This information is stored in the Web.config file. Open the Web.config file and find the EmailTo attribute on line 11. Change the value to your email address. You can also change the default subject line if you want.

4. Save both pages.

Summary

As websites become more advanced and you start looking for added functionality, ASP.NET gives you options that are far outside of the scope of straight HTML. With this server-side script language, you can make highly advanced dynamic websites with increased interactivity and features that are sure to impress any client.

ASP.NET is Microsoft's server-side scripting language and as such it is an integral part of Expression Web 2. But because it is a server-side script language, it requires a whole new set of skills that reach far beyond the scope of this book. For this reason you were introduced to the Portfolio Starter Kit, an ASP.NET-based website designed by Microsoft to give new designers a first look at ASP.NET, and used it to learn the basics of how these sites work.

An ASP.NET site is different from everything you have encountered so far in this book because unlike the regular HTML and PHP pages and even those generated from a Dynamic Web Template, the individual pages of an ASP.NET site exist only when a visitor opens them. In other words, rather than being stored on the server as individual fully programmed pages, the contents of an ASP.NET site are stored in web forms (files with the suffix .aspx) and external data sources such as XML files. When the visitor opens one of these forms, the browser and the server work together to put the contents of the form into the layout of the master page, and look through the form to see whether other content should be sourced from external data sources. It all sounds very complicated, but when you are working with larger websites with hundreds or even thousands of pages, this type of structure combined with a database to hold all the external content is far more feasible than making each page individually.

In this hour, you learned the basics of how an ASP.NET site works and what makes it different from other static sites. You learned how to edit the master page to change the content regions that can be defined for the individual pages. And even though it is based on ASP.NET, the layout of the master page is still nothing but HTML and CSS.

You also learned how to change the contents of individual web forms and how they interact with the master page to create a complete page. In addition you took a closer look at how external data files are used as sources to generate content for multiple pages, and you saw how easy it is to change these external data sources for immediate and sitewide results. Finally you learned how to customize the project to work as a basis for your own web portfolio or another project.

Now you have the basic skill set to customize the Portfolio Starter Kit site and make it your own. Even if you don't want to use it as a basis for your own or a client website, the project is an excellent tool to learn more about how ASP.NET works and how you can employ it to create richer and more interactive web experiences for the visitors.

The Expression website has a second Starter Kit, called Partner Portal Starter Kit, which introduces you to elements such as login control, calendar controls, and style sheet switches. This starter kit is not covered in this book but it is based on the same principles as the Portfolio Starter Kit. You can apply the same techniques learned in this hour to personalize it as well.

Q&A

Q. *The Porfolio Starter Kit doesn't work! I can open it in Expression Web 2 but when I try to preview it all I get is a weird error message. What is going on?*

A. Unlike a web site built using static HTML pages, a dynamic web site like the Portfolio Starter Kit has a specific folder and file structure that must be maintained for everything to work properly. If you are getting an error message when previewing the page in your browser, it is most likely because you didn't set the correct folder as the site folder when you first created the site. As was stated earlier, the site link *must* be to the Portfolio Starter Kit folder and *not* the Expression Portfolio Starter Kit folder, or the site will not work properly.

Workshop

The Workshop has quiz questions and exercises to help you put to use what you have just learned. If you get stuck, the answers to the quiz questions are in the next section. But try to answer the questions first. Otherwise you'll only be cheating yourself.

Quiz

1. *What is the primary difference between a static HTML based site and a dynamic ASP.NET based site?*

Answers

1. As the name suggests, the static HTML site consists of a series of pages that are static, meaning they can only be changed by editing the content manually on the server. The dynamic ASP.NET site on the other hand consists of a series of pages that are populated by the server when they are opened. They get their content from different sources and are updated by changing the sources rather than the pages themselves. This way you can make sweeping changes to many pages by altering their data sources. Dynamic pages can also gather content from sources outside of the current web site.

Exercise

In this hour you learned to insert a new title, description, and keywords in the `Default.aspx` page. Open the three other `.aspx` pages, insert the necessary content regions, and give each of them an individual title, description, and appropriate keywords. Keep in mind that the `Details.aspx` page will display the full information from the `portfolio.xml` data source, so the description and keywords need to be generic enough to describe all the different projects.

Edit the `portfolio.xml` file to create new portfolio items. To do so you also need to add new image files to the Images folder. The easiest way to do this is to open existing image files in your favorite image editor, replace the contents of these files with new content, and save them with new and descriptive names just as was done with the images for the MyKipple project.

HOUR 24

Publishing Your Website

What You'll Learn in This Hour:

▶ What the four different publishing options are and how they differ

▶ How to set up your site for publishing using FTP

▶ How to use the Remote Web Site view to publish and update your site

▶ How to change the publishing and HTML optimization settings

Introduction

The final and arguably most important step in creating a website is publishing it so that it is available to your intended audience, whether it is on a local network, an intranet, or the World Wide Web.

In practical terms, publishing a website means taking the files you have been working with on your computer and putting them on a server so that others can access them. There are many ways of doing this and which method works best for you depends on where the files are going, what software the server is running, and several other considerations.

In the publishing phase of the website building process, Expression Web 2 goes from being a developer and designer tool to a file management tool. When you publish files to an external host, the application keeps track of which files were published and when they were published. That way you can easily see whether a file has already been published or if you have a newer version of the file on your computer that needs to be published in place of an older one.

In this hour you will learn how to use the different publishing methods to manage files on your computer as well as on the final location, and discover how to decide which method will work best for you. You will also learn how to configure Expression Web 2 to automatically update new versions of your files for you and keep tabs on what you have done in the past.

A Word on Domains and Web Hosting

In most cases, a website is intended to be published on the World Wide Web for everyone to see. In that case, you need a web server connected to the World Wide Web on which to place your files as well as a web domain that takes the visitors to your site. The most common way of doing this is to use a web-hosting service that provides both domain name registration and web hosting.

The All-Important Domain Name

Buying a domain name can be a harrowing and frustrating experience because so many names are already taken, and it is important to get an easily spelled and memorable name that reflects your company or service well. In addition, thousands of companies out there prey on designers looking for a specific domain name. If you're not careful, they might snap up your preferred name right before you buy it and ask for a ridiculous fee (in other words, a ransom) to release it to you. A common mistake people make when looking for a new domain name is to search on Google for it. What they don't know is that people monitor Google and other search engines for those searches. When they pop up, those people buy the domain names so that you have to pay them to get the names released. If you are looking to see whether a domain name is taken, you should always use a trusted Whois service such as www.whois.net rather than a search engine. Such services not only tell you whether a domain is taken, but if so who holds the rights to it and when those rights expires.

After you have found a domain name you like, you can buy it from any number of vendors. The price of a domain name depends on the extension you want (.com, .ca, .net, .tv), and some domain extensions (.edu, .gov, and so on) are not available to the public. As of this writing, a .com domain should run between $10 and $20 per year. Pay any more and you are being ripped off!

Most web hosts offer free or discounted domain names with the purchase of a hosting plan, but you don't have to have your domain name registered with your web host unless that is what you want.

After you've decided on a domain name you need to find a place to host your site. Depending on the size of your site, what code language you want to use, and the estimated traffic your site will receive, you have many options to choose from. A small site with limited traffic will do fine with a basic shared hosting plan, whereas a high-traffic site might need a virtual private server or even a dedicated server. In most cases, you can start with a small shared-hosting plan and upgrade when it becomes necessary.

An important thing to consider when buying hosting is what kind of applications you will be running on your site. As you have learned in this book, if you are planning on running ASP.NET applications you need a host that supports ASP.NET. Likewise if you are going to run PHP applications, like the very popular WordPress blogging software, you need a host that supports PHP. Before buying hosting anywhere, always make sure that the hosting plan includes all the features you plan on using.

A bit of research will save you lots of money! There are millions of web hosts and their services and prices differ greatly. By doing some research and asking around, you will quickly find that the same service can be up to 10 times more expensive from one host to another. And the most famous hosts are not always the best ones. I have used five different hosts and they have been progressively cheaper yet offered better service.

Four Different Publishing Options

Expression Web 2 offers four different publishing options to choose from, all with advantages and drawbacks. Which option you should use depends on where you are publishing the site to, what software the server is running, and your own personal preferences.

To select a publishing option, you need to set up your remote website properties. This is done from the Web Site view (see Figure 24.1). On the bottom of the Web Site view are four options: Folders, Remote Web Site, Reports, and Hyperlinks. To access the remote website properties, click on Remote Web Site and click on the Remote Web Site Properties button in the upper-right corner of the view.

In the Remote Web Site Properties dialog (see Figure 24.2), you have four different publishing options:

- ▶ FrontPage Server Extensions
- ▶ Web Distributed Authoring and Versioning (WebDAV)
- ▶ File Transfer Protocol (FTP)
- ▶ File system

These four methods are quite different and serve different purposes. Depending on your server, you might be able to choose from several or be restricted to just one. Knowing the difference between them means you can make the right decision right away and not run into trouble further down the line.

FIGURE 24.1
Remote website properties can be accessed from the Remote Web Site area under the Web Site view.

FIGURE 24.2
The Remote Web Site Properties dialog lets you choose from four different publishing methods.

FrontPage Server Extensions

You were briefly introduced to FrontPage Server Extensions in Hour 21, "Working with Flash and Silverlight," when you used them to create an email form. FrontPage Server Extensions are a set of small programs that run on the web server and give you the ability to add functionality (such as the ability to generate and send emails) to websites. More than that, they keep tabs on your files both locally and on the server to ensure that elements such as hyperlinks are updated if a file is moved from one folder to another, and so on. They follow your web-authoring process to tell you what files have been altered either by yourself or someone else on your team and whether the files on your computer are newer or older than the ones on the server.

As the name suggests, FrontPage Server Extensions were introduced with Microsoft's old web design program, FrontPage, and they have become very common throughout web servers, especially those running Microsoft Windows Server software. The name FrontPage Server Extensions might be a bit confusing because you are actually talking about many different things: the extensions that run at the heart of the server, the extensions that run independently inside your files (such as the email form functions), and the extensions that run in your authoring program keeping tabs on your files and your work.

When you check the FrontPage Server Extensions option in the Remote Web Site Properties dialog, you are telling Expression Web 2 that the server you are publishing the site to has FrontPage Server Extensions installed and that you want to use this technology to communicate the files to and from the server. After set up, the application will use the HTTP (Hypertext Transfer Protocol) or HTTPS (Hypertext Transfer Protocol over Secure Sockets Layer) protocol to send and receive file contents. This is the same protocol you use when you surf the Internet (therefore the http:// prefix in front of all web addresses), which means that even if you are on a computer behind a strong firewall, if you can surf the internet you can use FrontPage Server Extensions to publish content.

To set up FrontPage Server Extensions as your upload option, check the box beside the name and enter your Remote Web Site location in the address box as seen in Figure 24.3. The upload address is usually identical to the address you would enter if you were to visit the site.

You can use FrontPage Server Extensions as your publishing method only if your web server supports this technology. If it does not, you will immediately get a warning message saying the current settings will not work and directing you back to the Remote Web Site Properties dialog where you can make a different choice.

FIGURE 24.3
After selecting
FrontPage Server
Extensions as
your publishing
method, enter
the destination
address in the
address bar.

FIGURE 24.3
After selecting
FrontPage Server
Extensions as
your publishing
method, enter
the destination
address in the
address bar.

**Watch
Out!**

> ### FrontPage Server Extensions Are on the Way Out
>
> Despite their popularity, Microsoft has not supported FrontPage Server Extensions for some time. For this reason there have not been any security updates to the technology for several years and many web hosts are now stepping away and discontinuing their support for these scripts entirely. If you plan on using FrontPage Server Extensions, it is imperative that you contact your web-hosting service to make sure they are supported now and in the future.

WebDAV

WebDAV stands for Web Distributed Authoring and Versioning and is an extension of the HTTP protocol that provides better security in the form of encrypted transmissions (to keep your data secure), file versioning (to prevent files from being overwritten when more than one person is working on them at the same time), and authentication. Unlike FrontPage Server Extensions, which are add-ons, WebDAV is already built into your operating system to handle external links to HTTP addresses.

Setting up WebDAV as the publishing method is done the same way as setting up FrontPage Server Extensions: Simply select the WebDAV option and insert the destination address. Also as with FrontPage Server Extensions, WebDAV has to be supported by your web server for it to work. If it is not supported or not turned on for your specific plan, you will not be able to access the server and Expression Web 2 will generate an error message. Unfortunately this message causes a lot of confusion because the first item on the list of possible reasons why the connection failed is that the server does not have the FrontPage Server Extensions installed (see Figure 24.4). This sugges-

tion is misleading because WebDAV and FrontPage Server Extensions are mutually exclusive. In fact if WebDAV fails, it could very well mean that FrontPage Server Extensions *is* installed on the server and is blocking WebDAV. If you get this message, contact your web-hosting provider and ask whether WebDAV is supported and if so whether FrontPage Server Extensions is interfering with your connection.

FTP

Of all the methods offered, FTP is the most frequently used. FTP or File Transfer Protocol is a very old file transfer method that dates back to 1971. Because of its age, FTP is a very simple protocol that is firmly rooted and supported in networking as well as the World Wide Web. For this reason, FTP can be considered the standard when it comes to file transfer between computers.

In spite of FTP's reliability and ubiquitous support, it has some significant drawbacks, the most important of which is the fact that the protocol is not secure by default. Without using an added layer of security, it is relatively easy for outsiders to monitor an FTP connection and pick up both usernames and passwords. There are methods of adding new layers of security to FTP connections, but none of these are supported in Expression Web 2.

When Expression Web originally came out, the FTP performance was sporadic at best and the many bugs associated with this feature became a major hang-up for early adopters. The release of Expression Web 2 saw significant improvements on this front and the FTP option now works at an acceptable level. Even so, Microsoft is still working to improve this feature for the release of Expression Web 3 and you can expect to see better performance as well as the inclusion of secure FTP in the coming release. Until then, if you want to use a secure FTP connection to transfer your files, you need to use a third party service such as the free and open source FileZilla (www.filezilla-project.org).

Did you Know?

To set up FTP as the publishing method, select FTP from the list and insert the destination address in the address bar as shown in Figure 24.5. Note that the FTP protocol is specified in the prefix of the address, so the address starts with ftp:// instead of http://.

FIGURE 24.5
When selecting
FTP as the pub-
lishing method,
you need to in-
sert the address
with the FTP pro-
tocol in place of
the regular HTTP
protocol.

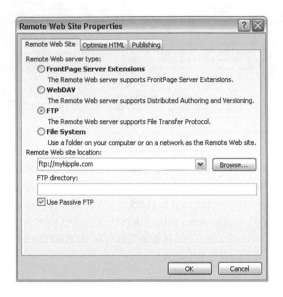

With FTP you also have the option to define a destination folder that the files will be sent to. That folder must already exist on the server. Finally you have the option to turn on passive FTP if active FTP is not working (active FTP is often blocked by firewalls and routers that passive FTP can get through).

When the connection is complete, Expression Web 2 displays a standard password dialog warning you that when using FTP, the username and password are not protected by encryption. Your web host supplies the FTP username and password, and if you are using FTP as your method for transferring files, you should change the password frequently.

File System

The final option is to host your website in a folder on your local computer or in your local network. That option can also be used to place your files on removable devices such as data discs, USB (Universal Serial Bus) keys, PDAs (Personal Data Assistants), MP3 players, or any other storage device that can be connected to the computer. That way you can bring the website with you without having to lug around your entire computer. The file system option is frequently used when publishing to local networks and corporate intranets where the web server is on the same network as the computer being used.

If you are publishing to a local drive, all you have to do is insert the folder name in the address bar. If you are publishing to a local network location or a mapped drive, you need to insert the Universal Naming Code (UNC) path for this location. A UNC path looks like this: \\myServer\sites.

Example: Publishing Content Using FTP

You now have a basic idea of what the four different publishing methods offer and when to use them. After you have selected a preferred method, the actual publishing process is the same. In this example you will see how to use FTP (the most common method) to publish your website to an external web host.

1. In Web Site view, click on Remote Web Site at the bottom of the view, and then click on Remote Web Site Options on the upper right of the view to access the Remote Web Site Properties dialog.

2. In the Remote Web Site Properties dialog, select FTP and enter the destination address provided by your web-hosting service. If you are publishing to a specific folder, enter the folder name in the FTP Directory box. Leave the Passive FTP option unchecked.

3. When you click on OK, a dialog appears asking for your username and password (see Figure 24.6)—your web host provides these.

FIGURE 24.6
When publishing to an external web host, you have to provide a username and password.

After being successfully logged in, you are presented with a view like in Figure 24.7 with the local website on the left and the remote website on the right. The Local Web Site column shows all the files in the folder you defined as your website project in Expression Web 2. The Remote Web Site column shows all the files currently at the remote location you defined in the address bar in step 2.

Expression Web 2 uses icons to tell you about the status of the files in your local and remote locations. In front of every file will be an arrow pointing right (file to be published to the remote location) or left (file to be downloaded from the remote location), a question mark (Expression Web 2 is unsure what to do with this file), or a red balloon with an x in it (don't publish this file). When you log in to your remote location for the first time, all the files in your local view will have an arrow pointing right because none of the files are in the remote location yet.

FIGURE 24.7
When you are
logged into the
web server, you
can see both the
local files and
the remote files
and move them
back and forth.

How you proceed from this point depends on what you want to achieve. If you are publishing your site to the remote location for the first time, checking the Local to Remote option under Publish All Changed Pages and clicking on the Publish Web Site button sends a copy of all your local files and folders to the remote location.

> Depending on how many files you have in your website, publishing the entire website to a remote location can take quite a bit of time. Unfortunately, if you are using FTP and publishing the entire site at once, chances are high that some of the files transferred will be corrupted. This is an ongoing problem with Expression Web 2 and is not normal. For this reason it is not advisable to publish the entire site in one go, but rather to publish one folder at a time. If you want to publish the entire site with one click using FTP, you should use a third-party FTP client.

If you have previously published files to your remote server and you have made changes to only some of your local files, Expression Web 2 inserts the arrow icons on only the files that have been changed and you can use the same option as before to overwrite the old files on the remote location with the new ones.

If files on the server have been changed since you last uploaded them, Expression Web 2 will signify that by attaching an arrow pointing to the left to the files in the remote location. This usually happens if you or a colleague uploads new files from a different computer or if someone made changes to the file directly on the server. If you want to download these newer files and overwrite your local versions, check the

Remote to Local option under Publish All Changed Pages and click on Publish Web Site.

In some cases alterations have been made to both local files and remote files. If that is the case, you can check the Synchronize option under Publish All Changed Pages. This function should be used with caution because sometimes even though the files on the server are newer than the ones in your local folder, they might not be the ones you want to keep and you could inadvertently overwrite important files in your local version of the site.

In addition to using the publishing buttons on the bottom of the Web Site view or between the two columns, you can also drag and drop files and folders between Local and Remote view. This is actually a very effective way of performing targeted updates and gives you very detailed control of which files are located where.

You will often find that your local folder contains many files that should not be put on the remote location for different reasons. For example, there is no reason to upload the Dynamic Web Template file to the server because it is functional only within Expression Web 2. To prevent a file from being included when Expression Web 2 suggests files that should be uploaded or downloaded, right-click on the file and select Don't Publish from the drop-down menu (see Figure 24.8). A red balloon icon is attached to the file and it will be ignored in the publishing process.

FIGURE 24.8
To prevent a file from being uploaded or downloaded, right-click on it and select Don't Publish from the context menu.

Advanced Publishing Settings

You can change the way Expression Web 2 handles local and remote files by default, and configure the application to make changes to the files as they are uploaded. This is all done from the Remote Web Site Properties dialog.

Optimizing HTML

Under the Optimize HTML tab in the Remote Web Site Properties dialog you can instruct Expression Web 2 to remove all or part of the nonfunctional code in your HTML pages (see Figure 24.9). This option is available because both designers and

developers using Expression Web 2 tend to insert a lot of nonessential elements in HTML pages to make them easier to understand. Among these elements are comments explaining the different sections, Dynamic Web Template comments, and whitespace. The rationale behind removing this content is usually to either reduce the file size to improve load times (although this improvement will be negligible at best) or to make the HTML page less readable for people who take a sneak peek at the code.

There are several options for HTML optimization and when they are checked, the selected components are removed as the files are published to the remote location. Here is a quick rundown of each option:

▶ **All HTML Comments**—All HTML comments whether inserted by Expression Web 2 or yourself will be removed. HTML comments are ignored by the web browser and are visible only in the source code. They always start with <! -- and end with - ->.

▶ **Dynamic Web Template Comments**—In Hour 19, you learned that the editable regions in pages based on Dynamic Web Templates are inserted with

HTML comments. These code sections relate only to Expression Web 2 and have no purpose outside the application.

▶ **Layout Tables Comments**—When you use the Layout Tables function to create layouts in Expression Web 2, the application includes comments to these tables.

▶ **Script Comments**—Expression Web 2 includes comments when inserting JavaScript and other script elements in your HTML pages. Likewise it is common to attach comments to scripts to help remember what they do.

▶ **All Other HTML Comments**—This option covers all comments not covered by the other categories and can be used to remove only the comments you inserted without touching the comments Expression Web 2 created.

▶ **HTML Leading Whitespace**—The leading whitespace is the empty space before the first symbol in each line.

▶ **HTML All Whitespace**—In addition to leading whitespace, you can have inline whitespace and empty lines.

▶ **Expression Web Tracing Image and Interactive Button Attributes**—When tracing images and interactive buttons are inserted into a page, Expression Web 2 adds attributes to them for editing purposes (that is, allowing you to open and edit the interactive buttons). These attributes relate only to Expression Web 2 and have no function in a web browser.

▶ **Generator and ProgID Tags**—The Generator and ProgID tags used to be inserted in HTML pages to tell the browser what program was used to create and edit them. This is not done by Expression Web 2 but can apply to pages originally created in other web-authoring applications.

All the changes made by the Optimize HTML options are applied as the files are being published to the remote location. Your local files are not changed. However, if you apply any of these options and then later overwrite your local files with ones from the remote location, all the content that was removed when the files were published will be removed locally as well.

The Publishing Tab

From the Publishing tab (see Figure 24.10), you can define how Expression Web 2 publishes files by setting how the application determines which files to publish as well as set which files are to be published to the remote server by default. In addition, you can tell Expression Web 2 to generate a log file each time it publishes content.

By default, only pages that have been changed in the local website are published to the remote location. You can change this by checking the All Pages, Overwriting Pages Already on the Destination option. That option means every time you publish your site, the entire list of files will be transferred to the remote location. There is generally no reason ever to use this option because it will likely just overwrite existing files with new identical ones.

When you open the Remote Web Site view, Expression Web 2 makes an educated guess as to what files it thinks you will want to replace in your local and remote locations. By default it does this by comparing the files in both locations. However if you are working on the remote files as a team, from several different computers, or on the server itself it can be almost impossible for Expression Web 2 to know which file is the correct one. If that is the case, you can change the setting to Use Source File Timestamps to Determine Changes Since Last Publish. However, if you do that, Expression Web 2 makes the assumption that the newest file has a precedent. That's not always the case, so use this function carefully or you'll accidentally overwrite files you want to keep.

Finally you can choose whether to let Expression Web 2 create a log file during publishing. If this box is checked, an HTML page is created and stored in your Temporary Internet Files folder so that you can check to see that the publishing process went according to plan.

To view the log file after publishing a site, click on the View Your Publish Log File option under Status in the Remote Web Site view (see Figure 24.11). This opens the log

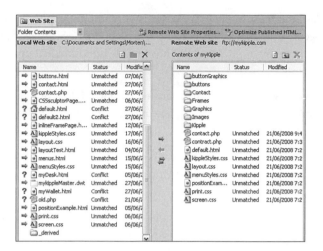

FIGURE 24.11
After publishing
a site using the
Publish Web Site
button, you can
view the log file
by clicking on
the View Your
Publish Log File
option in the Re-
mote Web Site
view.

in your web browser for you to inspect. If you want to save the log file, select Save As
under File in your browser.

Summary

By following the tutorials in this book, you have created a basic website with a lot of
functionality. The last step of any web design process is to publish the site so that
others can access it and enjoy the results of your hard work. That is when Expression
Web 2 goes from being a web design and authoring tool to becoming a file and website management tool.

When your site is completed and ready for the world to see, Expression Web 2 offers
you four different methods for publishing your content, all with benefits and set-
backs. Those methods are FrontPage Server Extensions, WebDAV, FTP, and file system. In this hour, you learned what each of these options mean and when they are
used. Nevertheless, this information is important enough to justify a quick recap.

FrontPage Server Extensions is a method based on the HTTP protocol and is used
when the server supports this technology and *must* be used if your site includes Front-
Page Server Extension functionalities. FrontPage Server Extensions is an old and no
longer supported technology that might die out in not too long. For this reason, contact your web hosting provider and ensure that the technology is and will continue to
be supported before choosing this option.

WebDAV runs on the same protocol as FrontPage Server Extensions, but the two
methods are mutually exclusive. This technology will likely take over for FrontPage
Server Extensions, and requires support from your web hosting provider to work.

FTP is the oldest and most used of the file transfer methods. Although stable, it is also relatively unsecure and Expression Web 2 offers no added security features for this option. Furthermore the application still has trouble handling FTP uploads and downloads properly.

The File System allows you to publish your site to a local folder on your computer, external device, or local network. This option cannot be used for remote servers outside of your local network.

There is no correct answer to the question "Which method should I use?" And, after setup, the actual publishing and file-copying processes are the same regardless of what method you choose.

Expression Web 2 keeps tabs on what you do with your files in the program and makes educated guesses about what files you want to publish to your site. Even so you can change these options either by selecting or deselecting files for upload or changing the publishing settings. You can also use the program to strip your HTML files of nonfunctional content such as comments and whitespace. All this is done from the Remote Web Site Properties dialog.

In this hour, you learned how to set up your site in Expression Web 2 for publishing to the desired location. And with that you have reached the end of the road of the initial design and deployment process. But this is just the beginning. When your website goes live and you start getting visitors, you probably want to make additions and changes to the site or build a subsite. Now that you know how to use Expression Web 2, you can apply the techniques you have acquired to build your knowledge of HTML, CSS, ASP.NET, PHP, and all the other technologies available to you and make informative and entertaining web experiences for the world to see.

Q&A

Q. *I tried uploading my site to my web host using FrontPage Server Extensions / WebDAV but, when I do, I get a warning saying that FrontPage Server Extensions are not installed on the server. What do I do?*

A. To be able to use FrontPage Server Extensions or WebDAV as your publishing method they have to be installed on and supported by your server. Furthermore, they are mutually exclusive, so if you can use one you cannot use the other. The warning message Expression Web 2 generates is a bit confusing because it tells you there are no FrontPage Server Extensions installed even if you are trying to use WebDAV to upload your files. If you get this message using either of these methods, contact your hosting provider and find out if either technology is supported with your plan. Most likely it is not and you will be forced to use FTP as your method for uploading content.

Q. *When I upload several files at a time to my web server using FTP, Expresson Web 2 crashes / the upload takes forever to finish / files are missing or corrupt on the server. What is that all about?*

A. The FTP component built into Expression Web 2 does not work properly. As a result you will experience the program crashing, the upload stalling or files being corrupted if you try to upload many files at a time. For this reason I highly recommend using a dedicated 3rd party FTP program like FileZilla when you upload entire sites or large numbers of files. Not only do these programs work properly, but you can monitor the progress as the files are being uploaded and see if anything goes wrong. Personally I only use Expression Web 2's FTP functionality when I upload less than 10 files at a time and usually only when I am making changes to one file and want to see what happens to it when it goes live on the web. Microsoft is well aware of the FTP issue and is working to resolve it so hopefully we will see a fully working and un-buggy version of this component in the 3rd installment of the application. Until then you are better off looking elsewhere for this service.

Workshop

The Workshop has exercises to help you put to use what you have just learned.

Exercise

Since this is the final hour and you are probably tired of answering questions and doing exercises, I am giving you a challenge instead:

Take all the things you have learned from reading this book and use it to create your own fantastic web site. When you are done, submit it to the book website at http://expression.pinkandyellow.com and I will post it for the world to see.

And last but not least, have fun!

Index

Drop-Down Box form control, 359

drop-down menus, 32

   basing on layers and behaviors, 323-324

   managing, 322-323

DWTs, 338-339

   attaching to existing web pages, 348-349

   changing content outside editable regions, 353

   creating, 341-343

   editable keywords, creating, 350-352

   editing, 346-347

   web pages, creating, 343-345

dynamic web pages, 395-396

dynamic websites, 424

E

E-mail Address links, creating, 78-79

editable keywords, creating with DWTs, 350-352

editing

   content outside editable regions, 353

   DWTs, 346-347

   files in Code view, 53-57

   frames, 293-296

   images, 89, 100

   Interactive Buttons, 255-256

email forms, 32-33

   creating with PHP, 403-404

   empty messages, filtering with PHP, 410-411

   functionality, adding with PHP, 405-408

   landing pages, creating with PHP, 409-410

embedding classes within classes, 172

Empty Web Site template, 42

enabling cross-browser compatibility using embed, 382

errors, viewing in Code view, 56

events, 267

   modifying, 270

   onmouseover, 271-272

Expression Blend 2, 383

Expression Development Server, 386

   PHP scripts, testing, 397-400

Expression web site, installing Design Portfolio Starter Kit, 416-418

external links, 68

   creating, 73-75

   linked pages, opening in new window, 75-76

external sources, modifying in Portfolio Starter Kit, 428-429

external style sheets

   applying to web pages, 198-200

   moving styles to/from, 195-198

external style sheets, creating, 193-194

F

files, CSS, storing, 37

filtering empty email messages with PHP, 410-411

Find and Replace tool, 62

Find Matching Tag button (Code view toolbar), 120

Firefox, 48

fixed option (position attribute), 251

fixing broken hyperlinks, 36

Flash, 33, 375-376

   embed, 381-382

   photo galleries

      customizing, 390-391

      publishing, 377-379

Flash SWF Properties dialog, 380

Folder List pane, 12, 101

folders, creating, 86

Follow Hyperlink button (Code view toolbar), 119

font family, applying to documents, 149-152

font sizes, 146

form controls, 358

forms

   email

      adding functionality with PHP, 405-408

      creating with PHP, 403-404

      filtering with PHP, 410-411

      landing pages, creating with PHP, 409-410

   FPSE, 32-33

   HTML, 357

      creating, 358-364

      in Code view, 371-373

      sending results to email, 366-370

      server-side scripts, 365

   PHP, 32-33

   results, uses, 370

FPSE (FrontPage Server Extensions) forms, 32-33

framed navigation, 297-298

frames, 289, 297, 304

How can we make this index more useful? Email us at indexes@samspublishing.com

Sams Teach Yourself

When you only have time
for the answers™

Whatever your need and whatever your time frame, there's a Sams **Teach Yourself** book for you. With a Sams **Teach Yourself** book as your guide, you can quickly get up to speed on just about any new product or technology—in the absolute shortest period of time possible. Guaranteed.

Learning how to do new things with your computer shouldn't be tedious or time-consuming. Sams **Teach Yourself** makes learning anything quick, easy, and even a little bit fun.

Windows Vista All in One

Greg Perry

ISBN-13: 978-0-672-32889-3

Windows Server 2008 in 24 Hours

Joe Habraken

ISBN-13: 978-0-672-33012-4

Mac OS X Leopard All in One

Robyn Ness
John Ray

ISBN-13: 978-0-672-32958-6

Adobe Photoshop Elements 6 in 24 Hours

Kate Binder

ISBN-13: 978-0-672-33017-9

Microsoft Office 2007 All in One

Greg Perry

ISBN-13: 978-0-672-32901-2

FREE Online Edition

Your purchase of **Sams Teach Yourself Microsoft® Expression Web 2 in 24 Hours** includes access to a free online edition for 45 days through the Safari Books Online subscription service. Nearly every Sams book is available online through Safari Books Online, along with over 5,000 other technical books and videos from publishers such as Addison-Wesley Professional, Cisco Press, IBM Press, O'Reilly, Prentice Hall, Que, and Exam Cram.

SAFARI BOOKS ONLINE allows you to search for a specific answer, cut and paste code, download chapters, and stay current with emerging technologies.

Activate your FREE Online Edition at www.informit.com/safarifree

> **STEP 1:** Enter the coupon code: R6IG-LW3G-VGFH-7KGQ-YF3R.

> **STEP 2:** New Safari users, complete the brief registration form.
> Safari subscribers, just login.

If you have difficulty registering on Safari or accessing the online edition, please e-mail customer-service@safaribooksonline.com